AF772348

# Taxing Income and Consumption

# Taxing Income and Consumption

## The Development of International Tax Law and Policy

*Edited by*

Kerrie Sadiq

*Professor, Faculty of Business and Law, Queensland University of Technology, Australia*

Chris Evans

*Emeritus Professor, School of Accounting, Auditing and Taxation, UNSW Sydney, Australia and Extraordinary Professor, Department of Taxation, University of Pretoria, South Africa*

Na Li

*Faculty of Business and Law, Queensland University of Technology, Australia*

Edward Elgar PUBLISHING

Cheltenham, UK • Northampton, MA, USA

© The Editors and Contributors Severally 2025

Cover image: Pawel Nolbert on Unsplash.

All rights reserved. No part of this publication may be reproduced, stored in a retrieval system or transmitted in any form or by any means, electronic, mechanical or photocopying, recording, or otherwise without the prior permission of the publisher.

Published by

Edward Elgar Publishing Limited
The Lypiatts
15 Lansdown Road
Cheltenham
Glos GL50 2JA
UK

Edward Elgar Publishing, Inc.
William Pratt House
9 Dewey Court
Northampton
Massachusetts 01060
USA

Authorised representative in the EU for GPSR queries only: Easy Access System Europe – Mustamäe tee 50, 10621 Tallinn, Estonia, gpsr.requests@easproject.com

A catalogue record for this book is available from the British Library

Library of Congress Control Number: 2025933278

This book is available electronically in the **Elgar**online
Law subject collection
https://doi.org/10.4337/9781035344598

MIX
Paper | Supporting responsible forestry
FSC® C013604

ISBN 978 1 0353 4458 1 (cased)
ISBN 978 1 0353 4459 8 (eBook)

Printed and bound by CPI Group (UK) Ltd, Croydon, CR0 4YY

# Contents

## PART III INTERNATIONAL TAX: BEPS AND BEYOND



## PART IV TAX SPECIFICS



## PART V TAX REFORM: LESSONS FOR THE FUTURE

# Contributors

**Mahmoud Abdellatif** is Associate Professor of Economics at Qatar University's College of Business and Economics. He served as the Founding Director of the Center for Entrepreneurship (renamed the Center for Entrepreneurship and Organizational Excellence) within the College of Business and Economics, Qatar University, from September 2013 to August 2022. He oversaw the Center's core activities encompassing research, training, entrepreneurship programmes, and startup incubation. Associate Professor Abdellatif has secured research funding from national entities such as the Qatar Foundation and the Qatar Financial Centre. He has collaborated with regional and international institutions such as the United Nations Development Programme and International Bureau of Fiscal Documentation.

**Catherine Brown** is a Professor at the Faculty of Law, University of Calgary, Canada, where she has taught in the areas of tax, trade and business planning. In 2016 she was appointed to the Canada Revenue Agency Offshore Advisory Compliance Committee (OCAC) and to the Public Policy Committee by STEP Canada. In 2018 she was appointed to the NAFTA Chapter 19 (Trade Remedies) roster, part of the NAFTA Secretariat. Her research interests focus on the intersection of international tax, trade and investment agreements.

**Craig Elliffe** is a Professor of Taxation and Law at the University of Auckland, Faculty of Law, New Zealand. He was a tax partner at KPMG and Chapman Tripp for 23 years. Professor Elliffe is the deputy chair of the Tax Advisory Group of Chartered Accountants in Australia and New Zealand and was a member of the Permanent Scientific Committee of the International Fiscal Association and the New Zealand Government's Tax Working Group (2018–2019). He has authored numerous journal articles and books, including the JF Northey prize-winning book *International and Cross-Border Taxation in New Zealand* and *Taxing the Digital Economy: Theory, Policy and Practice*.

**Chris Evans** is an Emeritus Professor of Taxation and former Head of the Australian School of Taxation (Atax), UNSW Sydney, Australia. Professor Evans specialises in comparative taxation, capital and wealth taxation, tax law and administration, and tax policy and reform. He is an International

Research Fellow at Oxford University, an International Fellow of the Exeter University–Institute for Fiscal Studies Tax Administration Research Centre, and an Extraordinary Professor at the University of Pretoria. He has been a Visiting Professor at the University of Canterbury, New Zealand, and the Vienna University of Business and Economics, Austria. He has researched and published extensively. He has served on a number of governmental and professional body committees and working parties in Australia and overseas, including the UK's Mirrlees Committee and the HMRC international panel on tax administration.

**J. Clifton Fleming Jr** is the Ernest L. Wilkinson Chair and Professor of Law at the J. Reuben Clark Law School, Brigham Young University, USA. He has served as Professor-in-Residence in the US Internal Revenue Service Chief Counsel's Office. Professor Fleming's academic and teaching career has spanned the globe. He has been a Fulbright Visiting Professor of Law at the University of Nairobi, a Visiting Professor at the University of Queensland, at the Central European University in Budapest, and at the Murdoch University School of Law in Perth, and a holder of a Visiting Scholar Chair at the University of Florida's Law School. In 2011, he held the Fulbright Distinguished Chair at the Vienna University of Economics and Business, Vienna, Austria.

**Carlo Garbarino** is a Full Professor of Tax Law in the Department of Legal Studies at Università Bocconi, Italy. He is the Director of the Tax and Accounting Observatory at SDA Bocconi and a member of the International Fiscal Association and the European Association of Tax Law Professors. He has held numerous visiting positions, including Hauser Global Visiting Faculty at NYU Law School in 2013, Senior Emily Noel Fellow in 2016, Grotius Research Scholar and Visiting Professor at the University of Michigan (2009–2014), University of Florida (2011), Universidade de São Paulo (2012), and Senior Fellow at Melbourne Law School (2018).

**Marco Greggi** is a Full Professor of Tax Law and International Tax Law at the University of Ferrara, Italy, where he is also a member of the doctoral board. He is also a Visiting Professor at Eötvös Loránd University, Budapest. He is the author of three monographs and over 150 scientific contributions and has permanent teaching positions at the University of Budapest and Beijing (Political Science and Law). He regularly teaches master's and higher education courses in Italy, France and Liechtenstein, and has been a Visiting Professor at numerous universities around the world, where he focused on tax treaties and the application of VAT in relations with foreign countries.

**Michael Lang** is Professor and Head of the Institute for Austrian and International Tax Law at the Vienna University of Economics and Business

(WU), Austria, Academic Director of the LLM programme in International Tax Law, and speaker of the Doctoral Programme in International Business Taxation (DIBT) at WU. Professor Lang is a member of the Editorial Board of the World Tax Journal and one of the Editors-in-Chief of the *Bulletin for International Taxation*. In his research, he focuses on ECJ case law and tax treaty law, and he is President of the Austrian Branch of the International Fiscal Association.

**Jinyan Li** is Professor and Co-director of LLM Tax Programs, Osgoode Hall Law School, York University, Canada. Professor Li has authored, co-authored and co-edited numerous books. Her work has been cited by Canadian courts, including the Supreme Court of Canada. She has also been a consultant to the Asian Development Bank, the International Monetary Fund (IMF), the Organisation for Economic Co-operation and Development (OECD), the Auditor General of Canada, and the Department of Justice of Canada. Professor Li has received numerous awards from external organizations.

**Na Li** is a postdoctoral research fellow at the Faculty of Business and Law, Queensland University of Technology, Australia. Dr Li's's research interests are in the areas of international tax and Chinese taxation. She obtained an LLB from Fudan University in China, an LLM in tax law from Boston University in the United States, and a PhD from Vienna University of Economics and Business in Austria.

**António Martins** is an economist and holds a PhD in Management from the University of Coimbra, Portugal. He is an Assistant Professor at Coimbra School of Economics (FEUC) teaching taxation at undergraduate, MBA, and master's levels. He was the Director of the MSc in Accounting and Finance at FEUC and has been a tax arbitrator since 2012. He is a member of the Centre for Business and Economics Research. His research has appeared in, among others, the following journals: *Accounting, Economics, and Law*; *Intertax*; the *EC Tax Review*; the *Journal of Applied Accounting Research*; the *International Journal of Law and Management*; and the *Bulletin for International Taxation*.

**Irma Mosquera Valderrama** is Full Professor of Tax Governance at Leiden Law School, Leiden University, the Netherlands. She is also the EU Jean Monnet Chair Holder on the topic of EU Tax Governance (EUTAXGOV), and the lead researcher of the European Research Council (ERC) funded project that investigates Global Tax Governance (GLOBTAXGOV). She received her PhD (*cum laude*) in 2007 in the Netherlands. Her areas of expertise are international tax law and comparative tax law in developed and developing countries, exchange of information, global tax governance, and BEPS-related issues in developed and developing countries.

**Ann O'Connell** is an Honorary Professor at the Law School, University of Melbourne, Australia. She has previously been a member of the Australian Treasury's Not-for-Profit Tax Concessions Working Group and an advisor on tax and philanthropy to the Organisation for Economic Co-operation and Development (OECD) in 2015 and 2020. She is the author of *Taxation of Charities and Not-for-Profits* and numerous publications dealing with tax and the not-for-profit sector.

**Robert J. Peroni** is the Fondren Foundation Centennial Chair for Faculty Excellence and Professor of Law at the University of Texas School of Law, USA. He has served as Professor-in-Residence in the US Internal Revenue Service Chief Counsel's Office. His primary areas of teaching and scholarship are federal income taxation, international taxation, natural resource taxation, and professional responsibility/legal ethics. He is one of the top US scholars in international taxation and energy taxation.

**Kerrie Sadiq** is a Professor at the Faculty of Business and Law, Queensland University of Technology, Australia. She is a Chartered Tax Adviser as designated by the Taxation Institute of Australia, a Certified Public Accountant (CPA), and a Chartered Accountant (CA). Professor Sadiq's primary areas of research are international tax, tax expenditures, and capital gains tax. She is the co-editor of the *Australian Tax Review*, an internationally recognised leading academic tax journal. She is an author of contributions to leading Australian and international journals and books and is an author and co-author of leading taxation textbooks. Professor Sadiq is currently undertaking a four-year research-focused Future Fellowship awarded by the Australian Research Council.

**Adrian Sawyer** is Professor of Taxation at UC Business School at the University of Canterbury, Christchurch, New Zealand, and Extraordinary Professor in the Department of Taxation, School of Accountancy, University of South Africa, Pretoria (SA). His research interests include tax compliance literature (including behavioural issues, compliance costs, the role of tax professionals, complexity, ethics, etc.), tax administration issues, developing an international tax organisation, international tax issues, the readability and understandability of the Income Tax Act, the role of taxation in e-commerce, environmental taxes and individual insolvency.

**Stephen E. Shay** is Paulus Endowment Senior Tax Fellow, Boston College Law School, USA, and he has served as a US Treasury tax policy official in both the Reagan and Obama Administrations. Professor Shay consults for international organisations and private parties, and has testified as an expert before judicial and arbitral tribunals on behalf of governments and private litigants.

He has served as an expert consultant to the International Monetary Fund on tax policy missions to Dominica, Kenya, Switzerland, Tanzania and Uganda.

**Victor Thuronyi** received his undergraduate degree in economics from Cambridge University and his law degree from Harvard Law School. He has practised tax law, served in the Office of Tax Policy of the US Treasury Department in 1983–1986, and was thereafter Associate Professor of Law at SUNY-Buffalo Law School until joining the Legal Department of the IMF in 1991. Mr Thuronyi, who served as Senior Counsel (Taxation) of the Fund, has participated in many staff missions involving legislative drafting and advice on taxation laws of member countries of the Fund. He is the author of a number of books and articles on taxation.

**Binh Tran-Nam** is a Professor in the UNSW Business School, Australia, where he obtained his PhD in economics. His research interests embrace taxation and economics. He has published over 100 articles in international journals, including the *Australian Tax Forum*, the *British Tax Review*, the *Canadian Tax Journal*, the *National Tax Journal* and the *New Zealand Journal of Taxation Law and Policy*. Professor Tran-Nam's research has been supported by six Australian Research Council grants. He was awarded the ATTA's 2015 Hill Medal in recognition of his contributions to tax teaching and tax policy in Australasia.

# Foreword

As the authors of the first chapter in this volume note, the pace of change in the global tax system in the recent past has been unprecedented – over the course of a few short years, norms that have been in place for a century have been pushed aside by new regimes and new rules. The underlying issues prompting change and the challenges faced by policymakers remain the same, however. And while it is often difficult to separate the wheat from the chaff when confronted by an onslaught of new information and the documentation it generates, the important works that help establish and reinforce fundamental bedrock principles are quickly recognisable. In the midst of the surfeit of sources, this book emerges as an invaluable survey of the crucial elements of current, likely, and possible changes to the world's tax systems.

The volume's conception began in a multi-year research project undertaken by Kerrie Sadiq, one of Australia's leading tax scholars and a frequent contributor to international tax scholarship. Kerrie enlisted the aid of two other internationally recognised scholars, Na Li and Chris Evans, to help assemble a timely volume with contributions by some of the world's prominent tax experts. The result is this collection of 15 studies that cover the field for scholars seeking a quality critical survey of contemporary tax issues and responses.

Not surprisingly, given the focus of governments worldwide on the significant adjustments to the global tax system overseen in recent years by the OECD, many of the chapters address international tax issues, bypassing the technical minutiae of base-broadening rules or minimum taxes to investigate longer-term impact conceptual issues: what taxes are covered by tax treaties, is there such a thing as tax morale for corporations, what sources do domestic courts draw on when interpreting international tax treaties, and how do we value intangible assets when there are no comparable market transactions to use as reference points? Parallel chapters look more closely at the reform agenda promoted by the OECD, including questions of the legitimacy and inclusiveness of the initiative. Another chapter considers what alternative sustainable responses to profit shifting might be adopted, such as an effective residence-based tax system that includes income derived indirectly through offshore holdings. A further issue studied is the dilemma that the OECD's agenda poses to developing countries which have entered into trade and investment treaties that are incompatible with new taxes proposed by the OECD, and options for addressing the problem are considered.

Separately from the international tax field, chapters on income tax and consumption tax shed new light on perennial issues, starting with a fresh and informative look at the choice of expenditure tax or income tax and the possible use of an expenditure tax to supplement and add progressivity to the income tax. Also examined, drawing on a case study, are the criteria by which policymakers should judge whether the adoption of a new broad-based consumption tax has been successful. Chapters focusing on income tax issues look at the role of a general anti-avoidance provision, whether concessional treatment for charities and not-for-profit entities is wise, and the changing role of the corporate tax as an interim levy on shareholders deferring personal tax on gains derived through an interposed entity. A further chapter looks at a pressing contemporary issue, the use of tax to combat climate change, specifically the role of an emissions trading scheme substituted for the direct taxation of outputs causing climate change. Finally, again using a case study, a chapter considers the never-solved challenge of moving desirable tax reform past inevitable political roadblocks.

In an age of instant access to new information and unlimited sources of commentary and responses to proposals and developments, can a book on contemporary tax issues add genuine value for researchers and policymakers? This volume suggests that the answer is an unambiguous yes. Today's technical changes to tax laws quickly become yesterday's news. In contrast, the fundamental principles that establish tax benchmarks do not date. The benchmarks are the crucial instruments needed to evaluate current, proposed and possible changes to the law and international agreements, providing the insights needed by practitioners and policymakers on future directions of the tax system. The chapters in this volume can be used to acquire and refine readers' understanding of these foundational tax policy tools.

Richard Krever AM
University of Western Australia

# Acknowledgements

We would like to formally express our thanks to all the chapter contributors and anonymous reviewers of each chapter in this book, who have committed to our deadlines and delivered this final product. We thank Dr Peter Mellor, who undertook a multitude of tasks, including proofreading, editing, and writing. Every author has expressed their gratitude to Peter for the research work he carried out and the suggestions he offered for their work. We also thank Miss Stephanie Tytherleigh, editor at Edward Elgar Publishing, for her commitment to this book and for seeing it to publication. Finally, we appreciate the support from the Australian Research Council through the Future Fellowship awarded to Kerrie Sadiq, which allowed this book to come to fruition.

# 1. Introduction: setting the scene

**Kerrie Sadiq, Chris Evans and Na Li**

## 1.1 INTRODUCTION

The question of how best to tax income and consumption is a perennial one, as old as taxation itself. The early twentieth century saw the rise of national income taxes, while the latter part saw a rise in the popularity of consumption taxes. Throughout the same period, international tax issues also became prominent. What is unique to the current century, however, is the speed and magnitude of changes to the tax system at a global level. The past decade has seen unprecedented developments, and taxation reform worldwide shows no signs of slowing down. The development of international tax law and policy is at a crossroads, and predicting the future is challenging.

This book, featuring contributions from 19 pre-eminent international tax experts, investigates recent advances in taxation and, in doing so, provides a well-rounded exploration of the future of tax in a changing world. The diverse team of contributors ensures that there is a comprehensive view of the field, including perspectives from both developed and developing countries. These voices offer unique insights and contributions to a fundamental rethink of current taxation issues. The book builds on seminal work that has shaped past and present tax policy and reform globally, generates new knowledge, extends theoretical perspectives, and informs the development of international tax policies for the future.

The book consists of 15 chapters divided into five parts, providing comprehensive coverage of the field. It covers fundamental issues in tax law and policy, international tax abuse arrangements, and corporate behaviours as significant challenges to international tax lawmakers in the digitalized economy. It also discusses developments and possible approaches to improving international tax laws through a multilateral approach, as well as specific impending tax issues. This comprehensive coverage ensures that the reader gains a deep understanding of the complex and evolving field of taxation and its future challenges.

## 1.2 FUNDAMENTAL ISSUES IN TAX LAW AND POLICY

Part I of this book contains four chapters that consider fundamental issues underlying the current tax regime and ask whether alternative approaches to our current thinking should be considered. Traditionally, fundamental issues of tax law and policy focus on the various elements of a tax system, and such questions as equity and fairness, efficiency, social and economic impact, international considerations, and legal and ethical issues are discussed. Adopting a contemporary approach, this book is no exception as each of these areas is explored in the context of a rapidly changing world.

When we think of tax, our first thoughts generally turn to income taxes, the mainstay of progressive taxation for individuals for over 200 years. Increasingly, however, a tax on personal expenditure (consumption) is seen as an alternative to income tax. In Chapter 2, Victor Thuronyi discusses the suggestions in the literature that such a tax could also be levied at progressive rates and, in doing so, questions which tax base is fairer, whether there are efficiency advantages to an expenditure tax over an income tax, and which tax is easier to implement. To aid the reader in their understanding of this topic, Thuronyi reviews the law and economics literature and provides a roadmap that underpins the chapter. No doubt, and as noted, while the debate about whether an ideal income tax is better than an ideal consumption tax may be theoretically interesting, it lacks practical relevance. The practical question is whether to add a progressive expenditure tax to the tax mix. While Thuronyi describes these long-debated questions, he ultimately proposes a supplemental expenditure tax as a way of taxing the wealthy, concluding that if it is imposed with a large exemption, high rates, and no transition relief, it operates effectively as a wealth tax.

Chapter 3 considers the fundamental question of what constitutes a tax. However, this is done in a contemporary setting by considering what it means for the purposes of double tax treaties, especially where the Organisation for Economic Co-operation and Development (OECD) Model Tax Convention is adopted. While major changes and developments have occurred in international tax law in recent years, Article 2 of the OECD Model Tax Convention, a provision containing the taxes covered by the double taxation agreement, has often been overlooked. With many new types of taxes arising, Michael Lang highlights that it is once again necessary to pay attention to fundamental questions arising in the context of the concept of a tax and the subsequent scope of tax treaties.

In this chapter, Lang analyses and critically assesses the current legal understanding of what constitutes a tax under treaty provisions, which factors are to be considered, and what uncertainties arise with the existing provision. Additionally, he scrutinizes the demarcation of the broad concept of taxes in the treaties from inheritance and gift taxes, which are subject to their own Model Double Convention and have a narrower scope of application. Finally, he provides an outlook on recent proposals and possible adaptations of the OECD Model Tax Convention.

A book that discusses fundamental issues in tax law and policy would be incomplete without a chapter on corporate income tax. Jinyan Li, in Chapter 4, starts by noting that a corporation is nothing but a piece of paper and goes on to consider the role that the legal fiction that a corporation is a person plays in income tax law. Using Canada as a case study, she takes the reader through the technical design features of the corporate tax regime, which are common to many jurisdictions. She articulates the tremendous value of the fiction of saving taxes through deferral of shareholder-level taxation, shifting income, and taking advantage of corporate tax subsidies. Li's exploration of the future of the corporate form in the face of recent tax reforms, such as the Global Minimum Tax and anti-base erosion and profit-shifting rules, highlights the challenges faced by legislators that are created from the ongoing use of the legal fiction that is the corporation.

To conclude Part I of this book, Chapter 5 undertakes an assessment of a well-established consumption tax regime, the Australian Goods and Services Tax (GST), which has existed for more than 20 years. Binh Tran-Nam and Mahmoud Abdellatif adopt a unique approach to their assessment of the GST, going beyond normal tax policy design principles to also analyse it in the context of reducing the reliance on direct taxes and in the context of other OECD countries. In doing so, they discuss the political and administrative dimensions of the GST. Ultimately, Tran-Nam and Abdellatif argue that the GST can be considered a success in terms of public policy and implementation. However, regarding specific policy objectives, the GST reform has scored poorly. In particular, they argue that the GST is not revenue-sustainable in the long run, making future GST reforms such as base broadening or a rate increase both desirable and inevitable.

## 1.3 CORPORATE BEHAVIOURS IN A DIGITAL WORLD

Part I, which ponders the nuances associated with tax law and policy in the modern world and the different methodologies for assessing tax regimes, sets the scene for many remaining chapters. Undoubtedly, globalization and digitalization of the economy are driving international reform. Adding to this is an increased public awareness of the practices of large international taxpayers and an expectation that corporations behave in a certain way. The two chapters in Part II directly address unique issues international tax lawmakers face in a digitalized economy where we have moved from a world of physical goods and services to one where intangible assets are the mainstay of successful multinational entities. In Chapter 6, Kerrie Sadiq questions the role of corporate tax morality in international tax minimization and asks whether multinational entities merely need to pay taxes based on a strict legal interpretation of their obligations under the law or whether a morality lens should be adopted that rejects aggressive tax minimization strategies. A particular focus is placed on corporate responses to calls for greater ethical considerations, along with the role that the social contract, corporate social responsibility and voluntary tax transparency play within the corporate tax regime. Like Li's earlier chapter, which recognizes the benefits associated with the fiction of the corporation, Sadiq's chapter recognizes the benefits associated with the fiction of the multinational entity, allowing morally unacceptable behaviour by multinational enterprises to continue.

While Sadiq's chapter highlights broad ethical issues for multinational entities, in Chapter 7, António Martins presents an issue unique to entities operating in the European Union. Martins focuses on the difficult questions surrounding financial valuation and accounting recognition of transferred assets for the purposes of the exit tax, explaining the complexity introduced by such a tax and using Portugal as a case study. As he highlights, most assets are not traded on the open market or in active markets, and consequently, determining their arm's length value based on comparable transactions is fraught with difficulties. This is especially the case with intangible assets, where valuation methods such as discounted cash flows, comparable sales, or expert appraisals are used but often involve significant judgment and estimation. He concludes that while the use of estimates, value judgments, probabilistic reasoning and similar approaches is crucial to determining the value of an intangible asset, they introduce a degree of subjectivism. The variations that can then arise induce significant changes in the exit tax base.

## 1.4 INTERNATIONAL TAX: BEPS AND BEYOND

A great deal has already been written about the base erosion and profit shifting (BEPS) initiative, led by the OECD, to address strategies used by multinational companies to shift profits from high-tax jurisdictions to low-tax jurisdictions, thereby eroding the tax base of higher-tax countries. Since the BEPS project began in 2013, significant developments in international tax reform have occurred beyond BEPS. A few of these issues are touched on in earlier parts of the book, but Part III specifically addresses issues beyond a traditional discussion of the BEPS initiative, which laid the groundwork for a more transparent and equitable international tax system, to recognize that the landscape is continually evolving. Critical scholarship on the global minimum tax and ongoing international coordination are key elements of the future success of current reform initiatives. Part III of this book challenges the global minimum tax from different perspectives.

Chapter 8, written by Cliff Fleming, Robert Peroni and Stephen Shay, three distinguished tax scholars from the United States of America, discusses the problem that prompted the global minimum tax contained in what is known as Pillar Two of the OECD proposal to address the challenges of the economy's digitalization and whether there is a better solution. They quite correctly note that sovereignty allows nations to set their own tax rates, even when this power is used to adopt low or zero rates to lure business activity and investments away from other countries. The tax competition generated from the adoption of low or no tax rates has led to the global minimum tax. While recognizing that the global minimum tax proposal contained in the OECD Pillar Two approach partially mitigates the evil of tax competition and is a significant step in the right direction, Fleming, Peroni and Shay argue that it leaves substantial room for continuing tax competition and imposes significant transition and complexity costs. Rather than supporting the adoption of the global minimum tax, Fleming, Peroni and Shay argue for the adoption of expanded worldwide taxation without deferral at countries' respective regular corporate rates. Were multinational entity host countries to adopt such an approach, the authors argue that a better result would be achieved.

Fleming, Peroni and Shay briefly comment on the effects of the global minimum tax on developing countries. In Chapter 9, Catherine Brown builds on these effects, were the global minimum tax to be adopted by developing countries, and suggests that the implementation may violate commitments made by host governments to investors under investment treaties or other agreements. Brown highlights the dilemmas faced by developing countries when considering whether to adopt the OECD's proposed tax, particularly as it is these countries that tend to offer tax incentives such as tax holidays, preferential tax rates, tax credits, investment allowances and income exemptions, all of which are likely to be affected and potentially rendered ineffective under the reforms. While some of the incentives are offered unilaterally, Brown explores those subject to tax rulings, fiscal stabilization provisions, or other protections under long-established investment agreements and treaties. Developing countries are, in particular, subject to legal limitations under international agreements, national laws, or private contracts that will prevent them from unwinding tax incentives promised to investors. Many developing countries also face significant legal limitations that prevent them from collecting additional taxes under the new rules. However, failing to implement the global minimum tax still puts developing countries in a vulnerable position as additional tax will then be collected by another jurisdiction. Brown labels this the perfect storm but, in doing so, offers hope for developing countries by suggesting both short- and long-term solutions.

Continuing with the theme of the effects of the OECD reform proposals on developing countries, Irma Mosquera Valderrama, in Chapter 10, explores the legitimacy and inclusiveness of global tax governance in international tax law-making. Mosquera Valderrama addresses the current discussion of the BEPS project within the framework of global tax governance and the conditions under which international tax law-making by the OECD and the G20 is regarded as legitimate and feasible for developing countries. Building on this, she takes a forward-looking approach to address the question of whether the BEPS Inclusive Framework is inclusive enough, and if not, what needs to be done so that all countries (developed and developing) and their interests are represented. Consistent with prior chapters, Mosquera Valderrama also recognizes that international tax is no longer just about technical issues and that political elements must be taken into account.

The work of the OECD and its reform agenda are the topic of discussion throughout much of this book. The foundations of the OECD's views on international tax are contained in its Model Tax Convention and have already been discussed in several chapters up to this point. Of particular note is Chapter 3, which examines the meaning of taxes in that Convention. Chapter 11, authored by Carlo Garbarino, builds on the earlier discussions to consider the convergence or divergence of the OECD approach, not only through the adoption of the Model Tax Convention between individual countries but also through domestic judicial transplants. Garbarino concludes that convergence or divergence can be achieved through law in action, specifically through judicial decisions or administrative guidelines that may be inspired by or refer to the OECD Commentary. Adding to this complexity are interpretive solutions or principles advanced by the OECD Commentary, which can be considered by national judges in the application and interpretation of specific treaties. Garbarino focuses on how this occurs, proposing a model in which OECD interpretive solutions or principles circulate through judicial transplants activated by domestic courts.

## 1.5 CHALLENGES TO SPECIFIC REGIMES

While this book focuses largely on how tax law and policy have evolved recently with ongoing tax reform globally, particularly due to the digitalization of the economy, the evolution reflects broader changes in society. No matter how global coordination and reform progress, the aim is always to ensure that a tax system is one that is fair and efficient. To that end, Part IV challenges two specific aspects of many tax regimes. The first is taxation, or more specifically, exemption from taxation, for charities and the not-for-profit sector. The second is the intersection of energy and taxation with a discussion of the European emission trading scheme.

In Chapter 12, Ann O'Connell critically reviews the Australian tax regime for charities and not-for-profit entities. She notes that tax concessions for charities and other entities are available in almost all countries, and while the concessions in Australia can be traced back to English law, they are now among some of the most generous in the world. Her analysis of the history of concessions discloses that several were granted at a particular time and in circumstances that are no longer relevant. O'Connell considers concessions for membership-based entities, such as agricultural trading companies (co-operatives), included in the 1920s, professional sporting bodies, included in the 1950s, and the gift deduction for school building funds, included in the 1960s. She asks whether the concessions can still be justified. Consistent with the future of tax, O'Connell argues that anomalies within the regime need to be addressed to ensure it is fit for purpose in the twenty-first century.

Just as tax and corporate social responsibility are increasingly intertwined, energy and taxation are linked with environmental policies steered through mechanisms such as carbon pricing schemes. Marco Greggi, in Chapter 13, addresses the latest policies implemented in Europe to reduce greenhouse gas emissions and explores their implications for tax purposes. He argues that the introduction of the Emissions Trading System (ETS) can be considered a success story, as it has proved to be capable of striking a balance between the need for environmental protection and financial sustainability for businesses. However, he notes that while the ETS mechanism is clear, the taxation of ETS certificates is complicated, as it possibly impacts direct taxes and value added tax. Greggi argues that the certificates should be considered services under European value added tax law and be taxed accordingly. The production of certificates by private companies is also considered. This possibility, which is a reality in several states, raises issues concerning the likelihood of tax proceedings originating from the sale of such certificates. Greggi argues that in the future this scenario should be explored, as the possibility of producing certificates (and taxing them properly) would facilitate the green transition, ultimately reducing costs and the adverse impact on businesses.

## 1.6 TAX REFORM: LESSONS FOR THE FUTURE

Parts I to IV recognize that tax reform is an ongoing process that attempts to address evolving economic, social and environmental challenges. However, valuable insights can be gleaned from existing regimes and past reforms. In the final part of this book, two chapters provide insights into what can be learnt from the past. First, in Chapter 14, Craig Elliffe examines New Zealand's general anti-avoidance rule. He starts from the understanding that one of the central themes of this book is the development of tax law. As he notes, this development can take different forms, namely new legislation, case jurisprudence, administrative guidance, or a combination of any or all of these things. New Zealand's experience using a general anti-avoidance rule (GAAR) to combat tax avoidance extends over 140 years. Over this lengthy period, the original and persistent inadequacies in the statute have enabled judge-made changes in the law and provided a significant opportunity to reflect on the structure, role and application of general anti-avoidance laws. Despite the legislative deficiencies in the New Zealand GAAR, the New Zealand anti-avoidance rule is a provision that has been remarkably successful and effective from the perspective of tax system administration. He notes that there are three primary reasons why the New Zealand law effectively prevents tax avoidance. First, the New Zealand tax avoidance experience is mainly a judge-made law, and the New Zealand GAAR might be described more as a signpost pointing out the general direction of travel rather than a detailed map. Second, the New Zealand courts have solved the statutory interpretation question of reconciling the relationship between the specific provisions providing definitive taxpayer outcomes (such as a deduction) and the GAAR, and the 'tandem approach' to the interpretation proposed by the New Zealand Supreme Court recognizes the importance of both the specific provisions and the GAAR. Third, the formulation of the parliamentary contemplation test in the New Zealand Supreme Court provides a framework for determining the features of tax avoidance. Most importantly, it highlights the interaction between a legal and factual analysis. The legal analysis considers the purpose of the provisions, and the objective factual review examines how the taxpayer has used those provisions. This examination of the facts goes beyond the legal form of structures and documentation and considers the commercial and economic reality of what has occurred.

In the final chapter of the book, Chapter 15, Adrian Sawyer reviews the tax policy and legislation with respect to taxing capital gains in New Zealand. As he notes, 'it has … been said that in trying to predict the future it can be helpful to look at the past and assess how today's trends and events reflect history'. To most observers, change is ever-present, especially in tax policy and legislation. For example, attempts to improve tax policy and legislation through reducing complexity and changing drafting styles have usually proved to be futile. Thus, the more things change, it would seem, the more they stay the same. In a New Zealand context, efforts to expand the tax base with a specific tax on capital gains continue to fail, leaving New Zealand as a significant outlier in the OECD for the absence of specific taxation of capital gains. Sawyer addresses such questions as to why this might be, what can we learn, and more importantly, will we learn, or will history repeat itself.

## 1.7 CONCLUSION

This book contains a collection of works authored by renowned scholars, practitioners and policy advisors from around the world on highly debated issues and the most current topics in the international tax field. It covers key jurisdictions such as Australia, Canada, New Zealand, the US and Europe with regard to a broad range of topics on tax regimes, tax abuse, international taxation, tax specifics, and tax reforms and administration. It explores the worldwide view concerning the most recent developments and provides updates on the key tax issues in major economies in a clear and efficient approach to comparative study. The book builds on seminal academic work that has shaped past and present tax policy and reform globally to enable readers to gain in-depth knowledge about the historical, theoretical and practical perspectives of international tax issues and their predictions about the future.

Key issues include taxing income or consumption, improving tax policies and legislation, international tax reform, tax treaties and tax avoidance, corporate tax behaviour, and tax administration and dispute resolution. By providing unique insights and valuable contributions, the book aims to foster a fundamental rethink of these issues in a changing world, with a particular emphasis on the future of tax.

# PART I

# Fundamental issues in tax law and policy

# 2. Should we tax income or consumption?

**Victor Thuronyi**

## 2.1 INTRODUCTION

For the last 200 years or so, income tax has been the mainstay of progressive taxation of individuals. Its main justification is fairness; by exempting a minimum amount from tax and employing a progressive rate schedule, income tax can ensure that wealthier taxpayers pay their fair share of tax, while those with lower incomes pay either low rates of tax or zero tax, in the case of those near the poverty level.

An alternative to income tax would be a tax on personal expenditure (or consumption, which is synonymous). Such a tax could also be levied at progressive rates. Which tax base is fairer – income or expenditure? Would an expenditure tax have efficiency advantages over income tax? Which tax is easier to implement? Questions like these have long been debated in the tax law and economics literature (for at least 100 years in the United States).[1] This chapter provides

[1] Bank reviews three occasions on which a progressive expenditure tax was considered in Congress, namely 1921, 1942 and the late 1990s: see Steven A Bank, 'The Progressive Consumption Tax Revisited' (Book Review: *Fair Not Flat: How to Make the Tax System Better and Simpler*, by Edward J McCaffery) (2003) 101(6) Michigan Law Review 2238. An early pamphlet advocating a progressive personal expenditure tax was Chester A Jordan, *The Spendings Tax* (Southworth Printing Co 1921), cited here mostly to show how old the debate is. Thomas S Adams, 'Fundamental Problems of Federal Income Taxation' (1921) 35(4) The Quarterly Journal of Economics 527 proposed an expenditure tax as a replacement for the surtax (i.e., a supplemental expenditure tax). While Jordan did not get all the details right, and the pamphlet is brief, he did identify that personal expenditure could be determined by including borrowing and cash proceeds, and subtracting cash expended for investments, which is the basic model for a cash flow personal expenditure tax that has been fleshed out by subsequent writers. During World War II, the US Treasury considered a progressive personal consumption tax as

a brief overview of the literature, which has become so voluminous that many readers might appreciate a roadmap.

A specific lens to the literature is applied here: namely, what does it tell us about desirable reforms, with a particular focus on what is practical. There are other aspects to the literature, oriented to developing a better understanding of the tax system. The focus here is on the practicalities of tax reform.

The literature on income vs consumption taxation has a varied focus. Most of it is based on economic theory, while some of it deals with the practicalities of tax reform. Concerning theory, Shaviro finds: 'Reality is simply too messy for overly definite real-world conclusions about the relative merits of these two systems to hold outside the contours of … simplified models.'[2] Scepticism about economic models is justified.[3] Recall that we have just witnessed an important natural experiment about how rationally people behave in regard to their own health, namely the response of the population to the Covid pandemic and in particular getting a vaccine (especially in 2021 when these vaccines were available free of charge, proven to be relatively safe, and very effective in preventing both infection and severe disease). We saw irrational behaviour in the form of vaccine hesitancy by a significant part of the population. This is fairly conclusive evidence that a large part of the population does not behave in rational ways. Any model that assumes rational behaviour is of limited use in describing the world in which we live. Conclusions based on economic models must be taken with a grain of salt.

The literature suggests the following:

1. It is not clear whether an ideal income tax or an ideal consumption tax is a better tax base; there are arguments in favour of either, but depending on what assumptions and value judgments one makes, it could go either way.
2. The choice of income vs consumption as a tax base depends primarily on details of implementation and tax administration. Instead of comparing an ideal income tax with an ideal consumption tax, it makes more sense to compare an income tax as it can be implemented in practice with a consumption tax on the same basis.

---

a means of curbing wartime consumer spending, but it was never enacted: see Milton Friedman, 'The Spendings Tax as a Wartime Fiscal Measure' (1943) 33(1) American Economic Review 50.

[2] Daniel Shaviro, 'Beyond the Pro-Consumption Tax Consensus' (2007) 60(3) Stanford Law Review 745, 750.

[3] For a deeper discussion of the usefulness and limitations of economic models, see Daniel Shaviro, 'The Mapmaker's Dilemma in Evaluating High-End Inequality' (2016) 71(1) University of Miami Law Review 83.

3. Transition rules are important and can dominate the decision whether to switch from an income tax to a consumption tax, or institute a new consumption tax.
4. Tax policy tends to be conservative (or path dependent). The likelihood that the income tax will be repealed and replaced by a consumption tax is very low.[4] Much more likely is that a consumption tax would be added to the tax mix.

Overall summaries on income vs consumption taxation are provided by Shaviro[5] as well as Auerbach.[6] Another overview article by Brooks considers the broader context of the tax mix and includes a historical discussion of thinking about tax.[7]

Zodrow analyses the pros and cons of expenditure tax reforms and concludes that the case for fundamental tax reform involving expenditure taxation is not open-and-shut.[8] He considers transition issues, administrative and compliance costs, distributional effects, and efficiency effects of various consumption tax proposals. Fried concludes that the fairness case for the consumption tax over an income tax has not been made.[9]

Surrey complains about '[t]he energy wasted on academic thinking about a consumption tax' partly on the basis of the deficiencies of a real-life consumption tax as it is likely to be enacted by legislators.[10]

---

[4] But see Edward J McCaffery, *Fair Not Flat: How to Make the Tax System Better and Simpler* (University of Chicago Press 2002) (*Fair Not Flat*) (proposing replacement of the income tax with a progressive spending tax).

[5] Daniel N Shaviro, 'Replacing the Income Tax with a Progressive Consumption Tax' (2004) 103 Tax Notes 91 ('Replacing the Income Tax').

[6] Alan J Auerbach, 'The Choice between Income and Consumption Taxes: A Primer' (2006) National Bureau of Economic Research Working Paper 12307.

[7] Neil Brooks, 'An Overview of the Role of the VAT, Fundamental Tax Reform, and a Defence of the Income Tax' in Richard Krever and David White (eds), *GST in Retrospect and Prospect* (Thomson Brookers 2007).

[8] George R Zodrow, 'Prospects for Consumption-Based Tax Reform in the United States' (2002–2003) 59(2) FinanzArchiv/Public Finance Analysis 264.

[9] Barbara H Fried, 'Fairness and the Consumption Tax' (1992) 44(5) Stanford Law Review 961.

[10] Stanley S Surrey, 'Our Troubled Tax Policy – False Routes and Proper Paths to Change' (1980) 73 Proceedings of the Annual Conference on Taxation Held under the Auspices of the National Tax Association-Tax Institute of America 1, 2.

## 2.2 IDEAL INCOME TAX VERSUS IDEAL CONSUMPTION TAX

The argument between proponents of income and consumption taxes has involved identifying the difference between ideal versions of the two taxes, namely that the income tax reaches income from capital while the consumption tax does not. However, as summarized by Brooks:

> [T]here is not as great a difference between income and consumption taxes as sometimes implied. … [I]ncome from capital can be broken down into the following four components: (1) the real risk-free return to waiting, (2) an inflation premium, (3) a return to risk, and (4) super-normal returns, including returns to entrepreneurial activity and luck. The only difference between a pure income tax and a pure consumption tax is that an income tax is imposed on the real risk-free return to waiting and a consumption tax is not. Further … the real risk-free return to waiting has historically been very small, often less than one percent per year … Those who support an income tax … suggest that, therefore, the equity and efficiency gains of switching to a consumption tax cannot be as great as often alleged. Those supporting a consumption tax … suggest that, therefore, since there is so little difference between an income and a consumption tax, a consumption tax might as well replace the income tax in order to realize huge simplicity gains.[11]

Much of the literature compares an ideal income tax with an ideal consumption tax. While something can be said for this approach, as argued by Bankman and Weisbach,[12] its relevance to policy decisions is limited. To compare policy alternatives by focusing on ideal versions of the alternatives is a flawed approach. It makes more sense to evaluate policy alternatives by considering how they would actually work in practice. As put by Andrews:

---

[11] Brooks (n 7). Similar statements can be found in Shaviro, 'Replacing the Income Tax' (n 5) and Auerbach (n 6). R Glenn Hubbard, 'How Different Are Income and Consumption Taxes?' (1997) 87(2) American Economic Review 138, 138 argues that with respect to efficiency gains 'the distinction between reform toward a broad-based income tax and reform toward a broad-based consumption tax is relatively minor'. See also Joseph Bankman and Thomas Griffith, 'Is the Debate between an Income Tax and a Consumption Tax a Debate about Risk? Does It Matter?' (1992) 47(2) Tax Law Review 377.

[12] Joseph Bankman and David A Weisbach, 'The Superiority of an Ideal Consumption Tax over an Ideal Income Tax' (2006) 58(5) Stanford Law Review 1413. Warren (Alvin Warren, 'Would a Consumption Tax Be Fairer than an Income Tax?' (1980) 89(6) Yale Law Journal 1081) also takes the approach of comparing an ideal Haig-Simons income tax with an ideal consumption tax, as does Fried (n 9).

> [T]he ultimate policy choice to be made is between achievable ends, not abstract ideals. … [T]he most intractable difficulties in the existing income tax arise from the virtual impossibility of achieving a satisfactory reflection of real accumulation in a practical income tax base … [T]hese difficulties could be readily avoided by pursuing the goal of consumption instead of accretion. A consumption-type personal income tax is therefore a better model to follow, in my view, even if a true accretion-type tax would be ideally preferable.[13]

This orientation suggests a way to read Andrews' study, published the previous year.[14] Andrews' main approach is to compare a consumption-type tax with an accretion-type tax, as both can be implemented in practice. The main thrust of that article is that it is impossible to implement an accretion-type personal income tax, largely because of the difficulty in determining fair market values, while, on the other hand, a consumption-type tax can be implemented in a way that is fairly close to the ideal.[15] Similarly, Carlson and McLure conclude that '[p]robably more important than these economic arguments for a consumed income tax are its administrative advantages'.[16]

Bradford similarly identifies

> three broad problem areas in the present US income tax system: first, the extremely varied taxation of the yields from ordinary investment, depending on the industrial sector, the form of business organization, the type of financing, and the purpose of savings; second, the inconsistent taxation of the yield from owner-occupied housing and other consumer durables; and third, the sensitivity of the measurement of the real tax base to the rate of inflation. Correcting these defects … is universally conceded to be impractical.[17]

---

13 William D Andrews, 'Fairness and the Personal Income Tax: A Reply to Professor Warren' (1975) 88(5) Harvard Law Review 947, 947 ('Fairness and the Personal Income Tax').

14 William D Andrews, 'A Consumption-Type or Cash Flow Personal Income Tax' (1974) 87(6) Harvard Law Review 1113 ('A Consumption-Type or Cash Flow Personal Income Tax').

15 There are important exceptions, but these present the same problems as under the income tax. An example is work-related fringe benefits.

16 George N Carlson and Charles E McLure, Jr, 'Pros and Cons of Alternative Approaches to the Taxation of Consumption' (1984) 77 Proceedings of the Annual Conference on Taxation Held under the Auspices of the National Tax Association-Tax Institute of America 147, 151.

17 David Bradford, 'The Case for a Personal Consumption Tax' in Joseph A Pechman (ed), *What Should Be Taxed: Income or Expenditure?* (Brookings Institution Press 1980) 96.

An ideal income tax may therefore be unattainable, and the existing tax, as McCaffery has shown,[18] has become largely a tax on wages.

## 2.3 CONSUMPTION TAX AS EQUIVALENT TO WAGE TAX

Under some restrictive assumptions, a consumption tax is equivalent to a wage tax. These assumptions include a flat rate of tax and an ability to separate earnings that are attributable to work input, as opposed to pure capital investment.[19] These assumptions are not satisfied in practice. Nevertheless, some policy analysts treat a cash flow (or post-paid) consumption tax as equivalent to a yield-exemption tax, i.e., a tax whereby the return on capital investments is exempt from tax.

The yield-exemption and cash flow personal expenditure taxes are not in fact equivalent. This has been pointed out numerous times.[20] Andrews, McCaffery and Viswanathan are among those who have argued that there is a normative basis for taxing actual consumption (i.e., a post-paid tax), not for limiting taxation to wages.[21]

Yield-exemption treatment under a personal consumption tax might be appropriate on a limited basis as a matter of administrative convenience, for example, in respect of consumer durables. Extending yield-exemption treatment any further not only violates the normative basis for the personal expenditure tax but can also lead to tax abuse possibilities.[22]

---

[18] Edward J McCaffery, 'The Death of the Income Tax (or, The Rise of America's Universal Wage Tax)' (2020) 95(4) Indiana Law Journal 1233.

[19] See Andrews, 'Fairness and the Personal Income Tax' (n 13) 953–4.

[20] See ibid; Michael J Graetz, 'Implementing a Progressive Consumption Tax' (1979) 92(8) Harvard Law Review 1575; Edith Brashares and Laura TJ Kalambokidis, 'Assessing the Equivalence of Different Forms of a Consumption Tax' (1995) 88 Proceedings of the Annual Conference on Taxation Held under the Auspices of the National Tax Association-Tax Institute of America 248; Edward J McCaffery, 'A New Understanding of Tax' (2005) 103(5) Michigan Law Review 807 ('A New Understanding of Tax').

[21] Andrews, 'Fairness and the Personal Income Tax' (n 13); McCaffery, 'A New Understanding of Tax' (n 20); Manoj Viswanathan, 'Implementing a (Modern) Progressive Consumption Tax' (2022) 41(2) Virginia Tax Review 241.

[22] See Committee on Simplification, Section of Taxation, American Bar Association, 'Complexity and the Personal Consumption Tax' (1982) 35(2) Tax Lawyer 415; Martin D Ginsburg, 'Life under a Personal Consumption Tax: Some Thoughts on Working, Saving, and Consuming in Nunn-Domenici's Tax World' (1995) 48(4) National Tax Journal 585.

## 2.4 FORMS OF PROGRESSIVE EXPENDITURE TAX

### 2.4.1 Cash Flow Personal Expenditure Tax

A progressive expenditure tax could be implemented in a number of different ways. The approach suggested by Kaldor, Andrews and Graetz involves a cash flow tax at the individual level.[23] Such a tax would be administered very similarly to the income tax. Individuals would receive information returns for wages and from brokerages, banks and other payors. The main difference is that instead of reporting the amount of income or gain, the payor would report the amount of cash flow, i.e., the net amount that the individual withdraws or invests over the year. It is a simpler report because it is just one number. Details would be needed only in some instances, such as for the foreign tax credit limitation. From a compliance and administration point of view, the process would be very similar to what it is today: brokers would send the information return to the tax authorities and to taxpayers, and the numbers would be entered on the tax return.

### 2.4.2 X-Tax

An alternative way of implementing a progressive consumption tax is the so-called X-tax, discussed by Shaviro and Weisbach.[24] As Weisbach explains, the X-tax is basically a standard value-added tax (VAT) of the kind seen in most countries throughout the world, the main difference being that employees are in effect taxable persons. This means that employers would obtain an input credit for the amount of wages paid multiplied by the standard VAT rate (there could be more than one rate, but a single rate is better). Under the X-tax, employees would pay tax not at the standard rate, but under a progressive rate schedule. As a result, the credit obtained by the employer would generally exceed the tax paid by the employees. The X-tax can also be seen as a VAT coupled with a wage subsidy.

An important practical difference between an individual cash flow expenditure tax and an X-tax is that it is much easier to make the former steeply progressive at the top. Making the X-tax steeply progressive would require a high standard VAT rate. The compliance problems of such a high rate are unknown,

---

[23] Nicholas Kaldor, *An Expenditure Tax* (Allen and Unwin 1955) (*An Expenditure Tax*); Andrews, 'A Consumption-Type or Cash Flow Personal Income Tax' (n 14); Graetz (n 20).

[24] Shaviro, 'Replacing the Income Tax' (n 5); David A Weisbach, 'Does the X-Tax Mark the Spot?' (2003) 56(1) SMU Law Review 201.

because no country has implemented VAT at a high rate. (In virtually all countries, the VAT rate is 20% or less.[25]) By contrast, applying a top marginal rate of 50% or more to the taxable consumption of wealthy individuals under a cash flow personal expenditure tax would not raise the same compliance concerns since this rate would be restricted to a small group of individuals, rather than being applicable to all as it would be under the X-tax.

Experience with VAT shows that, although VAT is easier to define and administer than income tax, VAT cannot be said to be a simple tax, either conceptually or practically. The policy and administrative issues would be felt particularly acutely with an X-tax that involved a high rate. It would be much more difficult to introduce progressivity, especially a high degree of progressivity, into the X-tax than into a personal cash flow tax.

For these reasons, it seems doubtful that the X-tax could replace the income tax as suggested by Shaviro.[26]

### 2.4.3 Supplemental Taxes vs Eliminating the Income Tax

Kaldor did not advocate replacing the income tax with an expenditure tax:

> However inadequate the system of income taxation may be in relation to the objectives which it seeks to attain, it is inconceivable that, within any foreseeable period, it should be wholly abandoned in favour of an alternative system based on personal expenditure. … Any attempt to replace it suddenly by an untried system … would be … idealistic and unpractical … [B]ecause of its administrative complexities it would never be a suitable tax for 15 million taxpayers. The most that can be hoped for therefore is to introduce a spendings tax that can be operated side by side with the income tax, and that would take some of the weight off the income tax without imposing an excessive administrative burden. These considerations suggest that the only practicable method of advancing towards the spendings tax principle is to introduce a tax on spending with a sufficiently high exemption limit to confine the liability to a limited range of taxpayers. … [T]he worst features of the present system … relate to the taxation of the upper income groups. … [T]he maintenance of living standards by continued spending out of capital itself is a far more important feature amongst persons with large fortunes than amongst those with moderate resources.[27]

---

[25] Bankman and Schler note that 'a higher flat-tax/X-tax rate than the rates in Europe would be required. As a result, US taxpayers would have more incentive to exploit inconsistent or discontinuous treatment for parties and transactions': Joseph Bankman and Michael L Schler, 'Tax Planning under the Flat Tax' in Henry J Aaron, Leonard E Burman and C Eugene Steuerle (eds), *Taxing Capital Income* (Urban Institute Press 2007) 248.

[26] Shaviro, 'Replacing the Income Tax' (n 5).

[27] Kaldor, *An Expenditure Tax* (n 23) 224–5.

Given what Kaldor said, it is somewhat surprising that so many have been talking about getting rid of income tax and replacing it with a consumption tax.[28] As Kaldor told us, this is not going to happen and it probably would not be a great idea. The focus should therefore be on whether a supplemental expenditure tax – imposed as Kaldor suggested on wealthier taxpayers through the mechanism of a large exemption – makes sense.

A progressive supplemental expenditure tax could take the form of an X-tax or a personal cash flow tax. Both would work, and would have roughly equivalent economic effects, but the personal cash flow tax would be easier to administer. An X-tax would involve increased compliance costs at the business level. An X-tax as a supplemental tax would not need to be imposed at as high a rate as a standalone X-tax, since the bulk of revenue could continue to be collected from income tax.

Of course, if an expenditure tax were enacted as a supplemental tax, the simplification benefits would be reduced or eliminated, because the existing income tax would continue to apply. The issue then becomes whether the benefits from a less distortionary tax system are worth the added administrative and compliance costs.

While the prospect of adding a new tax to the system is not thrilling from the point of view of reducing complexity, there does not seem to be a realistic alternative, at least for countries like the US, which need to raise revenue. The alternative of raising the rates of the income tax is not attractive because high rates would exacerbate the distortions of the current system.

One reason for a supplemental expenditure tax is that no tax instrument perfectly measures the desired tax base in practice, and every tax is subject to both avoidance and evasion. Using more than one tax instrument makes it more likely that at least some revenue will be raised from taxpayers seeking to avoid or evade tax. As Gamage argues, 'any plausible real-world implementation of a progressive consumption tax would contain holes that taxpayers could

---

28 For example, Zodrow and Mieszkowski state the fundamental question as being, 'Should the United States adopt a "fundamental tax reform" in the form of replacing its current personal and corporate income tax system with some form of consumption-based taxation?': George R Zodrow and Peter Mieszkowski, 'Introduction: The Fundamental Question in Fundamental Tax Reform' in George R Zodrow and Peter Mieszkowski (eds), *United States Tax Reform in the 21st Century* (Cambridge University Press 2002) 1. Kaldor, *An Expenditure Tax* (n 23) has also been mischaracterized. For example, Mieszkowski refers to Kaldor as 'advocating the adoption of an expenditure tax in place of the income tax': Peter Mieszkowski, 'The Advisability and Feasibility of an Expenditure Tax System' in Henry J Aaron and Michael J Boskin (eds), *The Economics of Taxation* (Brookings Institution Press 1980) 179.

exploit so as to fund consumption purchases with the returns from their labor while still substantially circumventing the progressive consumption tax.'[29]

Therefore, exclusive reliance on a consumption tax is likely to allow some taxpayers to escape the tax, at least in part, just as exclusive reliance on income tax permits such escapes.

A supplemental personal expenditure tax (SET) has been advocated by Adams, Kaldor and Andrews.[30] McNulty also concludes that 'the add-on rather than the replacement approach seems the much sounder policy path to follow'.[31] Andrews pointed out that an SET would allow reduction of the top income tax rates, thereby reducing the distortions caused by such high rates.[32] Reducing income tax rates would enable simplification of income tax by treating capital gains and ordinary income the same, as was done in the US in 1986 with a top rate of 28%. The distinction between ordinary income and capital gains could be eliminated if the top income tax rate were slightly higher than 28%, but not much higher. Also relevant is whether capital gains are realized at death; if they are, then it makes it easier to eliminate the distinction between capital gains and ordinary income.

### 2.4.4 Viswanathan's Proposal

Viswanathan proposes a variant of a post-paid consumption tax that, instead of being based on individual cash flow, is based on consumption expenditure transactions.[33] This proposal envisages implementing progressive rates based on a database, maintained by the tax service, that would aggregate expenditures made by each individual. This idea seems impractical. The possibility for error in maintaining a database that would determine the appropriate marginal tax rate for each individual is simply too high. While the proposal purports to be applicable even to a consumption tax that would not completely replace income tax, it seems to be geared towards a tax that applies broadly, as

---

[29] David Gamage, 'The Case for Taxing (All of) Labor Income, Consumption, Capital Income, and Wealth' (2015) 68(2) Tax Law Review 355, 370.

[30] Adams (n 1); Kaldor, *An Expenditure Tax* (n 23); Andrews, 'Fairness and the Personal Income Tax' (n 13); William D Andrews, 'A Supplemental Personal Expenditure Tax' in Joseph A Pechman (ed), *What Should Be Taxed: Income or Expenditure?* (The Brookings Institution 1980) ('A Supplemental Personal Expenditure Tax').

[31] John K McNulty, 'Flat Tax, Consumption Tax, Consumption-Type Income Tax Proposals in the United States: A Tax Policy Discussion of Fundamental Tax Reform' (2000) 88(6) California Law Review 2095, 2182.

[32] Andrews, 'A Supplemental Personal Expenditure Tax' (n 30).

[33] Viswanathan (n 21).

opposed to a supplemental tax that applies only at the top. Very wealthy individuals would likely avoid or evade such a tax by arranging their consumption overseas, or through proxy accounts. Like an X-tax, which would have issues at high rates, a proposal to implement the tax via withholding by sellers would stumble in the face of high marginal rates, and therefore would make sense only if consumption tax rates at the top were fairly low. This would negate one of the key features of a supplemental tax that would apply only at the top of the income/consumption/wealth distribution, namely the possibility of applying rather high rates.

### 2.4.5 Mirrlees Review

The Mirrlees Review proposed a rate of return allowance, which would have the effect of exempting the risk-free return from savings.[34] This would be an alternative approach to cash flow taxation and would not capture borrowing to finance consumption. Neither would it impose a tax on existing wealth. For these reasons, the approach seems inferior.

## 2.5 HOW TO IMPLEMENT A CASH FLOW PERSONAL EXPENDITURE TAX

Implementation has been discussed by a number of authors, as well as the American Bar Association Tax Section's Committee on Simplification.[35] The Committee on Simplification included some of the top US tax lawyers of the time, including its chair Martin Ginsburg (husband of former US Supreme Court Justice Ruth Bader Ginsburg, and a very creative corporate tax lawyer[36]).

---

[34] James Mirrlees, Stuart Adam, Tim Besley, Richard Blundell, Stephen Bond, Robert Chote, Malcolm Gammie, Paul Johnson, Gareth Myles, James M Poterba and the Institute for Fiscal Studies, *Tax by Design: The Mirrlees Review* (Oxford University Press 2011).

[35] Andrews, 'A Consumption-Type or Cash Flow Personal Income Tax' (n 14); Graetz (n 20); Victor Thuronyi, 'All of the Above: How to Tax the Wealthy' (2021) 102 Tax Notes International 315 ('All of the Above'); Victor Thuronyi, 'A Supplemental Expenditure Tax' in Geerten MM Michielse and Victor Thuronyi (eds), *Tax Design Issues Worldwide* (Wolters Kluwer 2015); Committee on Simplification (n 22).

[36] Ginsburg once explained to me how he had done some tax planning that turned what Congress had intended as a large tax increase directed at a client into a large tax subsidy. No doubt he managed to work this kind of magic in many other cases as well. This may be part of the reason why Ginsburg insisted that tax was the funniest subject in law school.

The report of the Office of Tax Policy of the US Treasury Department in 1977, *Blueprints for Basic Tax Reform*, presented two model tax systems: (1) an income tax with a broadened base, involving integration of corporate and individual taxes and taxation of capital gains at full rates after allowing an adjustment for inflation, and (2) a progressive cash flow consumption tax.[37] Its main author was David Bradford. The consumption tax used a concept of 'qualified accounts' and would allow taxpayers to purchase financial assets outside of qualified accounts, granting yield-exemption treatment for such assets. This flexibility was later seen as a weakness of the proposal both from a practical standpoint (since it facilitates avoidance) and from a theoretical point of view since, as noted above, yield exemption violates the normative basis for a progressive expenditure tax.

Graetz identifies the following as the most difficult implementation problems:

1. Transition.
2. Coordinating the tax with other countries.
3. Finding a replacement for the corporate income tax.
4. Treatment of gifts and bequests.[38]

For a supplemental tax, as explained in the next section below, transition is not a problem, international coordination is not much of an issue and corporate taxation is not relevant.

*Tax-inclusive vs tax-exclusive basis*: Graetz recommends imposing the personal expenditure tax on a tax-exclusive basis, to avoid anomalies where withholding does not match tax liability.[39] This problem could, however, be avoided by imposing the expenditure tax on a tax-inclusive basis (just as income tax is imposed), but making an adjustment for amounts over- or under-withheld.[40]

37 US Department of the Treasury, *Blueprints for Basic Tax Reform* (1977).

38 Graetz (n 20).

39 Ibid.

40 In the case of under-withholding, the difference between the tax liability and the amount paid by way of withholding or estimated tax payments should be added as an adjustment to taxable expenditure. For example, if the taxpayer receives 100 in salary, the tax rate is 50%, and the taxpayer consumes 50, but the amount of withholding is only 40, the taxpayer will have taken a deduction of 10 for the addition to savings of the amount of salary that should have been withheld as tax but was not. In this case, an adjustment to the tax base should be made in the amount under-withheld, namely 10. The adjustment of 10 serves to cancel out that deduction and gets to the correct tax base of 100. Correspondingly, in the case of over-withholding, a deduction should be allowed by way of an adjustment. This

A tax-inclusive basis would place the expenditure tax on the same basis as income tax in terms of its stated rates, and as explained previously,[41] this can work in practice with appropriate adjustments.

*Fringe benefits*: Graetz notes that the taxation of fringe benefits involves much the same issues as under an income tax.[42]

*Yield-exemption election*: the Committee on Simplification discusses the potential for manipulation if qualified account and prepayment treatment were available on an elective basis.[43] For this reason, the committee recommended that prepayment treatment be only narrowly available, for example, only for consumer durables such as housing, and loan proceeds used to purchase such durables, and concluded that 'the resulting system might be substantially simpler than even that which could be attained under a comprehensive income tax'.[44]

*Life insurance*: Graetz recommends cash flow treatment for life insurance, while saying that yield-exemption treatment could be considered for political reasons.[45] To preclude tax planning that takes advantage of yield exemption, it

---

is an alternative way of solving the problem discussed in Graetz (n 20) 1583–4. One way of looking at this adjustment is to consider under-withholding as a form of borrowing (which is generally included in the tax base) and over-withholding as an investment (since it creates a corresponding asset, namely the right to a refund), for which a deduction should be allowed. In the case of a supplemental personal expenditure tax, income tax could be treated the same way as expenditure tax, i.e., the supplemental tax could be imposed on a basis inclusive of both income tax and supplemental expenditure tax, with the above-described adjustments.

[41] See n 40 above.

[42] Graetz (n 20). In the case of interest-free loans, the expenditure tax treatment is simpler than under the income tax. The standard way to deal with loans under the expenditure tax is to include the loan proceeds in taxable receipts and to allow a deduction when the loan is repaid. If this treatment is followed in the case of interest-free loans obtained from an employer, there will be no need under an expenditure tax to calculate the value of the interest forgone, as there might be under an income tax, since cash flow treatment will reflect the benefit of the loan to the employee. If an interest-free loan to an employee is forgiven, there is no particular issue under an expenditure tax, since the loan proceeds will already have been taxed to the employee when the loan was extended.

[43] Committee on Simplification (n 22). An elective system of this kind was included in the US Department of the Treasury (n 37) and in the Institute for Fiscal Studies, *The Structure and Reform of Direct Taxation: Report of a Committee chaired by Professor JE Meade* (Allen and Unwin 1978) (Meade Report).

[44] Committee on Simplification (n 22) 426.

[45] Graetz (n 20).

would be better and simpler to apply cash flow treatment to life insurance, as is done for investments generally.

*Consumer durables*: Graetz recommends that

> cash purchases of ordinary consumer durables should not be deductible, the asset's yield (imputed rental value) should be ignored, and subsequent sales price generally should be excluded from receipts. In order to avoid problems of taxpayer manipulation, this Yield-Exemption treatment of consumer durables should be mandatory. ... For durables the sale price of which is greater than historical cost, it does not seem unreasonable simply to include the excess in receipts.[46]

Graetz's recommended approach is also simple, since it does not require fashioning special rules for consumer durables; their purchase would be treated the same as that of any other consumption item.

*Consumer loans*: Graetz recommends excluding consumer loans from receipts, as long as they do not exceed a dollar limit.[47] This is motivated by a desire to reduce compliance burdens for lenders and keep things simple for ordinary taxpayers. Given the relatively low cost of producing information in a computerized age, it may be simpler to follow the general rule and include borrowing in receipts. In practice, only the net increase in borrowing for the year as a whole would have to be reported.[48]

*Housing*: Graetz recommends allowing no deduction for cash down payments, but leaving home mortgages out of account.[49]

*Gifts and bequests*: Graetz advocates taxing gifts and bequests to the donee because it is the donee who engages in consumption.[50] He argues that this approach suggests a family unit of taxation, since otherwise 'transfers from parents to children would shift tax to lower brackets'.[51] In other words, under this approach, a transfer of assets from parents to a minor child would not affect tax liability.[52]

---

[46] Ibid 1615, 1618 (footnote omitted).

[47] Ibid.

[48] McCaffery, in *Fair Not Flat* (n 4) 58–61, 133, criticizes the legislative proposal for a 'USA Tax' for its failure to include the proceeds of borrowing as income. He notes that all that is needed is a statement of the net change in debt over the course of the year.

[49] Graetz (n 20).

[50] Ibid.

[51] Ibid 1625.

[52] This problem is noted by Vann: Richard Vann, 'In Defence of the Income Tax' (2019) 34(4) Australian Tax Forum 831. Poole also suggests a family filing unit (reflecting the US Treasury proposal): Kenyon E Poole, 'Problems

*Campaign expenditures*: special rules for campaign expenditures are not needed. As long as they do not qualify for a deduction for charitable contributions, campaign expenditures will fall within the base for a personal expenditure tax. For wealthy individuals who self-fund their political campaigns, the tax could be quite significant, as McCaffery explains,[53] especially if it involves high rates at the top, such as a 90% rate on expenditure over USD 50 million per year.

The Committee on Simplification considers the complexity involved in administering a personal expenditure tax.[54] The key problem areas identified are:

1. Drawing a line between personal consumption expenditures (non-deductible) and business or investment expenditures (deductible), e.g., artwork, antique furniture, coins and stamps.
2. The need for information returns from providers of loans, including consumer credit.[55]

## 2.6 TRANSITION

Graetz questions generally whether transition relief is needed, but if it is granted, he suggests a simple rule allowing 'an immediate deduction of the basis of assets held on the date of enactment (perhaps limited to a maximum dollar amount with a carryover or required spread over a period of years)'.[56]

Graetz notes the problem of pre-enactment cash hoarding.[57] He suggests a declaration of asset and cash balances as of the effective date, which would be subject to penalty of perjury, as well as audits that could focus on large cash withdrawals. The problem is likely to be less severe under an SET, since the rates would be lower than in a situation where income tax was being totally

---

of Administration and Equity under a Spendings Tax' (1943) 33(1) American Economic Review 63.

[53] Edward J McCaffery, 'A Better Hope for Campaign Finance Reform' (2020) 52(2) Arizona State Law Journal 445 ('A Better Hope for Campaign Finance Reform').

[54] Committee on Simplification (n 22).

[55] Kelley suggests that an expenditure tax would require submission of a return showing the taxpayer's assets: Patrick L Kelley, 'Is an Expenditure Tax Feasible?' (1970) 23(3) National Tax Journal 237. While this would no doubt be helpful, it does not seem necessary, particularly if there is a good system of information returns from brokers showing net cash flow.

[56] Graetz (n 20) 1655.

[57] Graetz (n 20).

replaced by an expenditure tax.[58] Poole discusses the problem of anticipatory spending and concludes that this probably would have to be ignored, since it would be administratively difficult to make the tax retroactive.[59] Kaldor suggests in respect of anticipating cash hoarding that 'the Government might find it necessary to announce … that, if introduced, it would have retrospective effect from the date of the first announcement'.[60]

Gamage and Brooks favour current-assessment reforms, since reforms that yield revenue only in future years might tend to be undermined by the affected wealthy taxpayers before the liability arises.[61] They characterize cash flow personal consumption taxes as future-assessment proposals, but acknowledge that such proposals could be combined with acceleration of tax liability if desired. In addition, the path of revenue from a progressive consumption tax would depend on the transition rules adopted. If transition relief for existing wealth were not granted, then a progressive expenditure tax could yield substantial revenue up front. Their argument is therefore best viewed not as a case against a progressive expenditure tax but as a warning to implement such a tax in a way that generates substantial revenue up front.

Schaffa supports a one-time wealth tax, based on intergenerational equity, which could be done via a consumption tax.[62] The lack of transition relief would be a feature of the tax, not a detriment.[63] Similarly, Bankman concludes: 'Economic projections show a significant percentage of the welfare gains from adopting a cash flow tax are attributable to the taxation of preexisting capital. Transition relief, of course, forfeits these gains.'[64]

---

[58] Poole (n 52) also discusses the cash hoarding problem and concludes that it would probably have to be ignored, although the result would be inequity.

[59] Ibid.

[60] Kaldor, *An Expenditure Tax* (n 23) 221. Retroactive application might encounter difficulties in countries with prohibitions against retroactive tax legislation. See generally Victor Thuronyi, Kim Brooks and Borbála Kolozs, *Comparative Tax Law* (2nd edn, Kluwer Law International 2016) 64–9.

[61] David Gamage and John R Brooks, 'Tax Now or Tax Never: Political Optionality and the Case for Current-Assessment Tax Reform' (2022) 100(2) North Carolina Law Review 487.

[62] Daniel Schaffa, 'The Intergenerational Equity Case for a Wealth Tax' (2022) 90(3) University of Cincinnati Law Review 735.

[63] For further discussion of the transition from income to consumption taxation, see Daniel Shaviro, *When Rules Change: An Economic and Political Analysis of Transition Relief and Retroactivity* (University of Chicago Press 2000).

[64] Joseph Bankman, 'The Engler-Knoll Consumption Tax Proposal: What Transition Rule Does Fairness (or Politics) Require?' (2003) 56(1) SMU Law Review 83, 92 (footnote omitted).

## 2.7 CONSERVATISM: SUPPLEMENTAL EXPENDITURE TAX

A supplemental expenditure tax (SET) is a mixed blessing in terms of complexity. On the one hand, the transition to such a tax is fairly easy because it does not involve repealing any aspect of the current system. Income tax would remain in place. None of the problems of what to do with corporate tax and how to coordinate the expenditure tax with other countries arises, because the SET would be in addition to income tax, and the existing income tax provisions concerning international transactions and corporate taxation would remain. On the other hand, the enactment of an SET would offer only limited opportunities to simplify the existing income tax rules (as discussed above, one of the most important of these would be eliminating the distinction between ordinary income and capital gains).

A key benefit of the SET is the reduced economic pressure that would arise from high income tax rates, which would be an alternative to enacting an SET. This is particularly true for capital gains. Capital gains are one area where income tax simplification might be facilitated. The SET would enable a relatively low top income tax rate of perhaps 30%. Such a low rate would facilitate eliminating the distinction between capital gains and ordinary income, which would allow the simplification of many provisions of the tax code.

## 2.8 POLITICS: LIBERAL OR CONSERVATIVE?

Conservatives like low tax rates. Liberals generally favour higher taxes to fund social spending and for redistribution. Liberals have tended to favour a progressive income tax, and conservatives have tended to favour consumption taxation, since it involves a lower burden on capital income. But it is not that simple.

Tax reform proposals can easily metamorphose in the political process (this happens frequently in the US, not so often in countries with a parliamentary system). Bank explains how consumption tax proposals considered in Congress were substituted for each other on several occasions.[65] Proposals can change in terms of rates, exemptions, any number of design features, and transition rules. What comes out of the process as an enacted law may be quite different from the initial proposals.[66]

---

65 Bank (n 1).

66 See, for example, Nicholas Kaldor, 'Comments' in Joseph A Pechman (ed), *What Should Be Taxed: Income or Expenditure?* (Brookings Institution Press 1980) 155–6, discussing the enactment of his expenditure tax proposals in India.

If one thinks about how a proposal might be changed, it becomes difficult to characterize a specific proposal as liberal or conservative.

The argument that a personal expenditure tax is a conservative proposal comes from seeing it as a reduction of the burden on capital income. On the other hand, if it is viewed as a way to more effectively tax the wealthy, it becomes a liberal idea. Liberals would like the fact that a progressive personal expenditure tax could impose a high rate of tax on political campaign expenses.[67] As Auerbach and Hassett point out, a personal expenditure tax is a perfectly feasible alternative to a wealth tax in terms of curbing wealth.[68] Which tax is better depends a lot on the ease of administration and the politics of getting a particular tax enacted.

While Avi-Yonah concludes that a personal expenditure tax is no longer relevant in a time where the focus is on taxing the wealthy,[69] a supplemental expenditure tax is relevant precisely for the same reason – that it is an excellent way of taxing the wealthy. It can be part of a package of measures which includes income tax reform.[70] Less ideally, it could be adopted as a standalone measure, i.e., added to income tax as a supplemental tax without other changes to income tax.

## 2.9 CONCLUSION

While the debate about whether an ideal income tax is better than an ideal consumption tax is theoretically interesting, it lacks practical relevance. Even the debate about whether to replace the existing income tax with a consumption tax is more theoretical than practical. The practical question is whether to add a progressive expenditure tax to the tax mix. A supplemental expenditure tax is particularly relevant today as a way of taxing the wealthy. If imposed with a large exemption, high rates and no transition relief, a supplemental personal expenditure tax is comparable to a wealth tax. It is best combined with other measures for taxing the wealthy, such as taxing capital gains at death, and could facilitate simplification of income tax by eliminating the distinction between capital gains and ordinary income.

---

In his view, the law was doomed from the beginning because it was enacted with loopholes that facilitated its avoidance.

[67] See McCaffery, 'A Better Hope for Campaign Finance Reform' (n 53).

[68] Alan J Auerbach and Kevin Hassett, 'Capital Taxation in the Twenty-First Century' (2015) 105(5) American Economic Review 38.

[69] Reuven S Avi-Yonah, 'The Rise and Fall of the Consumption Tax: A Historical Perspective' (2015) 146 Tax Notes 247.

[70] Thuronyi, 'All of the Above' (n 35).

# 3. Taxes covered: recent developments on Article 2 of the OECD Model Tax Convention

**Michael Lang**

## 3.1 THE RELEVANCE OF ARTICLE 2 OF THE OECD MODEL TAX CONVENTION

Article 2 of the OECD Model Tax Convention on Income and on Capital (Art 2 OECD MC) has been dormant for many years. It has always been taught in every course on international tax law and in every relevant textbook that, in addition to the personal requirements set out in Art 1 OECD MC, the substantive requirements set out in more detail in Art 2 OECD MC must also be met for the application of double taxation agreements in order to be able to apply the distributive rules and the method Article. In practice, however, this point could usually be quickly checked off, since it was usually clear which taxes were covered by a double tax agreement (DTA) and which were not. However, this has changed in recent years. Wei Cui rightly pointed out that Art 2 OECD MC had acquired a significance in the post-base erosion and profit shifting (BEPS) world that it had never had before:[1] many states were considering the introduction of digital taxes or had already actually introduced such taxes. Other states introduced a 'diverted profit tax'[2] or an 'equalization levy on online advertisements',[3] or are currently considering an 'equalization tax on

[1] Wei Cui, 'Article 2 – Taxes Covered' IBFD Global Tax Treaty Commentaries, Global Topics, Policy and History (1 August 2021) [1.1.1.1.2].

[2] Roland Ismer and Alexander Blank, in Ekkehart Reimer and Alexander Rust (eds), *Klaus Vogel on Double Taxation* Conventions (5th edn, Kluwer Law International 2022) Art 2, m no 52 et seq.

[3] Amar Mehta, '"Equalization Levy" Proposal in Indian Finance Bill 2016: Is It Legitimate Tax Policy or an Attempt of Treaty Dodging?' (2016) 22(2) Asia-Pacific Tax Bulletin.

digital services',[4] like the European Union (EU). In all these cases, difficult and often controversial questions arise as to whether the DTAs modelled on the OECD MC are also applicable to these taxes.

The recently much more intense discussion of if and under which conditions such taxes are covered under Art 2 OECD MC suffers from the fact that fundamental questions of interpretation and structure of Art 2 OECD MC and its relationship to other provisions of the OECD MC, as well as other international treaties, are still disputed. Clear and unambiguous criteria on the basis of which new taxes are to be assessed as to whether they fall within the substantive scope of a DTA have still not been worked out. This shortcoming is also reflected in the fact that the question of whether the 'diverted profit tax' is covered by the scope of United Kingdom (UK) DTAs is even being examined by the UK Law Society under abuse aspects.[5] Whether circumvention has been attempted by the legislature should be as irrelevant as attempts at circumvention by taxpayers in other constellations.[6] The only decisive factor is whether the circumvention succeeds or fails. This can only be decided based on the criteria derived from Art 2 OECD MC.

Therefore, this chapter addresses these fundamental questions and builds on the author's own analyses of Art 2 OECD MC, which the author conducted almost 20 years ago,[7] and reviews and, if necessary, further develops them in light of the discussions that have taken place in the academic literature since

---

4 Roland Ismer and Christoph Jescheck, 'Taxes on Digital Services and the Substantive Scope of Application of Tax Treaties: Pushing the Boundaries of Article 2 of the OECD Model?' (2018) 46(6/7) Intertax 573 ('Taxes on Digital Services'); Fred van Horzen and Andy van Esdonk, 'European Union – Proposed 3% Digital Services Tax' (2018) 25(4) International Transfer Pricing Journal 267; Georg Kofler and Julia Sinnig, 'Equalization Taxes and the EU's "Digital Services Tax"' (2019) 47(2) Intertax 176.

5 Law Society Response, 'The New Diverted Profits Tax: Draft Legislation and Guidance' (February 2015) at m no 87 et seq, cited in Georg Kofler, Gunter Mayr and Christoph Schlager, 'Digitalisierung und Betriebsstättenkonzept' (2017) 5b RdW 369, 376.

6 See in more detail Michael Lang, 'Rechtsmissbrauch und subjektives Element' (2019) 5 TPI 227, 231 et seq.

7 Michael Lang, '"Taxes Covered" – What is a "Tax" according to Article 2 of the OECD Model?' (2005) 59(6) Bulletin for International Taxation 216 ('"Taxes Covered"'); see also Michael Lang, 'Tax Treaties and Municipal Tax' (2005) 15 SWI 16 ('Tax Treaties and Municipal Tax'); Michael Lang, 'Der sachliche Anwendungsbereich der Doppelbesteuerungsabkommen auf dem Gebiet der Steuern vom Einkommen und vom Vermögen' in Michael Lang and Heinz Jirousek (eds), *Praxis des Internationalen Steuerrechts: Festschrift für Helmut Loukota zum 65. Geburtstag* (Linde Verlag 2005) 265 et seq ('Der sachliche').

then. The question of which taxes actually fall within the scope of the DTAs will be left aside. Instead, more fundamental considerations on Art 2 OECD MC will be made, which should make it easier in the further academic discussion to measure concrete taxes on the basis of the criteria worked out in more detail.

## 3.2 THE CONCEPT OF TAX

The term 'tax' is – not surprisingly – a central expression in the OECD MC: Art 2 OECD MC speaks of 'taxes on income and on capital', and Art 2 OECD MC is a prerequisite for the application of the distributive rules and the method Article of the OECD MC. However, the term 'tax' is also important as a prerequisite for the application of the provisions on 'non-discrimination', 'exchange of information' and 'assistance in the collection of taxes': all these provisions have in common that their scope is not limited to 'taxes on income and on capital', but that they must be 'taxes' in order to be applicable, although the legal technique leading to that result differs in the provisions of Art 24(6), Art 26(1) and Art 27 OECD MC.

The question of whether a 'tax' exists can also be the subject of a mutual agreement procedure and subsequently, if necessary, of arbitration proceedings:[8] if a taxpayer is refused the application of a distributive rule or the method Article by the tax administration, because in its opinion it is not a question of the levying of a 'tax' and therefore also not of 'taxes on income and on capital', the taxpayer can take this as a reason to initiate a mutual agreement procedure. The same applies if the tax administration of one of the two Contracting States does not wish to apply the prohibitions on discrimination provided for in Art 24 OECD MC because it assumes that the amount of money to be paid is not a 'tax'. Conversely, a mutual agreement procedure can also be initiated if the competent authorities exchange information according to Art 26 OECD MC or support each other in the collection of revenue claims, and the taxpayer is of the opinion that no 'tax' is involved. In all these cases, it is, of course, also possible that the competent authorities try to clarify on their own initiative within the framework of a mutual agreement procedure whether 'taxes' are involved and thus whether these DTA provisions are correctly applied.

The term 'tax' is not defined in the OECD MC. However, Art 2(2) OECD MC contains a definition of 'taxes on income and on capital'. There again, the term 'tax' is used in a somewhat tautological manner.[9] However, 'tax' is still

---

[8] Ismer and Blank (n 2) Art 2 at m no 9.

[9] Sabine Zirngast and Sabine Kanduth-Kristen, 'Der Begriff der "Steuer" und die Vermeidung internationaler Doppel-(Nicht-)Besteuerung' (2016) 26 SWI 547, 549.

part of a definition: with the provision of Art 2(2) OECD MC, the drafters of the OECD MC clearly express that the terms 'taxes on income and on capital' are defined at the level of the DTA and are thus excluded from regulation by the domestic law of the Contracting States. For all definitions under treaty law, the following applies: for each definition, the treaty makes use of expressions that necessarily cannot be defined. If recourse were then made to the domestic law of the Contracting States to determine the content of these expressions, the objective of an independent definition, which is to determine the defined expression without recourse to national law, would be torpedoed.[10] Therefore, the term 'tax' is also to be interpreted exclusively from the context under treaty law.[11] Regardless of what significance one attaches to the domestic law of the Contracting States otherwise under Art 3(2) OECD MC, in this case, this provision cannot also provide a basis to resort to domestic law,[12] for this would undoubtedly run counter to the objective and purpose clearly expressed in this provision, namely not to interpret expressions defined in the Convention according to domestic law. Moreover, as Marjaana Helminen has convincingly argued, an interpretation of Art 3(2) OECD MC that would require the use of domestic law to define the term 'tax' would lead to a circular argument.[13]

---

[10] Further on this argument, see Michael Lang, 'Tax Treaty Interpretation – A Response to John Avery Jones' (2020) 74(11) Bulletin for International Taxation 660, 661; Michael Lang, 'What Is a "Tax Paid in that Other State" under Article 23 of the OECD Model?' (2021) 75(11/12) Bulletin for International Taxation 656, 657.

[11] So apparently Zirngast and Kanduth-Kristen (n 9) 549; Michael Tumpel and Marina Luketina, in Dietmar Aigner, Georg Kofler and Michael Tumpel (eds), *DBA-Kommentar* (2nd edn, Linde Verlag 2019) Art 2, m no 5; possibly differently Kees van Raad, 'The Concept of Tax in the OECD Model' in Bruno Peeters (ed), *The Concept of Tax, 2005 EATLP Congress, Naples* (European Association of Tax Law Professors 2005) 259, 262 et seq; Mario Tenore, '"Taxes Covered": The OECD Model (2010) versus EU Directives' (2012) 66(6) Bulletin for International Taxation; Ismer and Blank (n 2) Art 2, m no 26.

[12] Mario Riedl, 'The Notion of "Tax" According to Article 2 OECD Model Convention 1982 and 2017' in Georg Kofler and others (eds), *Taxes Covered under Article 2 of the OECD Model: The Scope of Tax Treaties in a Dynamic Global Environment of Newly Created Taxes* (IBFD Publications 2021) 3 et seq; Klaus-Dieter Drüen, Christian Kaeser and Michael Schwenke, in Franz Wassermeyer and others (eds), *Kommentar OECD-Musterabkommen 2017* (CH Beck 2022) Art 2, m no 26.

[13] Marjaana Helminen, 'General Report' in International Fiscal Association (ed), *Cahiers de Droit Fiscal International, Vol 101b: The Notion of Tax and the Elimination of Double Taxation or Double Non-Taxation* (2016) 28.

Adolfo Jiménez has suggested that when interpreting the term 'tax' within the context of the tax treaty, provisions of European Union (EU) law and other international treaties in the field of social security should also be taken into account.[14] However, no convincing argument can be found for this: there is no evidence that the drafters of the OECD MC had other international treaties outside tax law in mind when they drafted Art 2 OECD MC. Moreover, most of the rules mentioned by Jiménez were created much later and are merely regional in character – as in the case of the EU – or regulate specific bilateral situations. Many of these regulations can be applied alongside the OECD MC without causing a conflict between the different regulations. If such a conflict should nevertheless arise in an individual case, the rules of interpretation of international law now laid down in the Vienna Convention on the Law of Treaties (VCLT) dictate which rules take precedence, or in the case of the EU, rules of EU law take precedence over the rules of the DTAs concluded between the member states of the EU. A necessity to resolve such conflicts by way of interpretation of the term 'tax' in Art 2 OECD MC or to prevent them from arising in the first place is not apparent. They would above all lead to regionally or even bilaterally different understandings of the term 'tax', which were certainly not intended by the drafters of the OECD MC.

In any case, it follows from Art 2 OECD MC that a 'tax' must meet the requirement of being 'imposed on behalf of a Contracting State or its political subdivisions or local authorities'. The wording would in itself also allow the term 'tax' to be understood even more broadly, and the quoted phrase as a restriction to this. However, the OECD Commentary makes it clear that the term 'tax' is generally – thus obviously beyond Art 2 OECD MC – subject to this proviso.[15] The OECD MC followed up on this terminology later – in 1995 – when Art 4(1) OECD MC expressly declared 'that State and any political subdivision or local authority thereof' to be a 'resident of a Contracting State'.[16] The OECD Commentary on Art 2 OECD MC does not seem to distinguish between 'political subdivisions' and 'local authorities' and mentions as examples 'constituent states, regions, provinces, départements, cantons, districts, arrondissements, Kreise, municipalities or groups of municipalities, etc'.[17] The wording of Art 2(1) OECD MC and of the Commentary seems

---

[14] Adolfo J Martín Jiménez, 'Defining the Objective Scope of Income Tax Treaties: The Impact of Other Treaties and EC Law on the Concept of Tax in the OECD Model' (2005) 59(10) Bulletin for International Taxation 432, 434 et seq.

[15] OECD, *Model Tax Convention on Income and on Capital 2017* (OECD Publishing 2019), Commentary on Article 2, para 1 (OECD Commentary Art 2 OECD MC).

[16] Lang, '"Taxes Covered"' (n 7) 216.

[17] Ibid 217.

to suggest that only 'authorities' at certain geographical levels are covered.[18] Thus, other legal entities, although created by law, do not fall under this provision.[19] Not only federal taxes, however, but also provincial and local taxes levied by provinces and municipalities are covered by the OECD MC.[20] Taxes levied by the EU, however, do not fall under Art 2 OECD MC.[21]

This criterion can be difficult to interpret if the 'Contracting State or its political subdivisions or local authorities' pass on the amounts of the taxes levied to other entities that do not themselves meet the requirements of Art 2 OECD MC.[22] In Germany, therefore, individual authors are of the opinion that the church tax levied together with the income tax, which benefits churches, is not a tax within the meaning of the DTAs.[23] In Austria, the opinion is found that the chamber levy (*Kammerumlage*) levied by the tax offices and benefiting the chamber of commerce is also not a tax according to Art 2 OECD MC.[24] However, there are also levies that are collected by a public entity falling under Art 2(1) OECD MC, from which the public entity retains 4% of the proceeds and passes on 96%.[25] The 4% can be used by this public entity as it wishes, but the idea behind it is probably to compensate the collection effort of this public entity in a standardized way. In such a case, it is unclear what criteria should be used to decide whether this levy is a tax in its entirety, because the public entity still retains 4%, or whether it is only considered a tax on a pro rata basis, or whether it is not considered a tax at all, because the tax amount, with the exception of the 4% retained 'fee' for the collection, in fact benefits another public body in its entirety in any event. In any case, it should also be borne in mind that any entity that levies taxes is also free to decide, in accordance with the rules applicable to it, how to use those taxes. Taxes may be 'earmarked' and committed for specific purposes. This can be done by the public entity itself using these amounts for said purposes, or by using them to subsidize companies or other private entities, or even by transferring the amount of money to other public entities for said purposes. Drawing a line

---

18 Ibid.

19 Ibid.

20 Ibid.

21 So correctly Ismer and Jescheck, 'Taxes on Digital Services' (n 4) 577.

22 Sabine Heidenbauer, 'International Aspects of the Taxation of Savings Income' (2006) 16 SWI 459, 464.

23 Ibid.

24 Rejecting Tumpel and Luketina (n 11) Art 2, m no 7.

25 Cf, e.g., the Austrian real estate transfer tax, only 4% of the revenue of which goes to the federal government, which is responsible for its collection. The remaining 96% goes to the municipalities, which, however, are also 'local authorities' in the sense of Art 2 OECD MC.

between these scenarios is difficult and would be almost arbitrary.[26] Therefore, for the purposes of DTAs, one can assume that a levy is a 'tax' whenever it is levied by public bodies acting 'on behalf of a Contracting State or its political subdivisions or local authorities'. Whether these taxes are then passed on to other entities subsequently is irrelevant to the assessment according to Art 2 OECD MC.

Questions of interpretation also arise regarding other payments imposed by law or other regulations, with which concrete consideration is associated. The OECD Commentary excludes social security charges or any other charges paid where there is a direct connection between the levy and the individual benefits from being regarded as 'taxes on the total amounts of wages',[27] so it can be assumed that the drafters of the OECD Commentary were concerned with the demarcation with regard to taxes in general.[28] This is also reflected in the report of Working Party 30 of the OECD of 12 June 1969.[29] The OECD Commentary and the report of Working Party 30 speak of 'social security charges' and 'social security fees' without specifying what kind of social security system they have in mind. These systems can be designed very differently, if one only considers the differentiation between 'funded' and 'unfunded' social security systems.[30] The insurance concept can also be heavily diluted, on the one hand by substantial funding from other taxes, and on the other by reductions or even exemptions from the obligation to pay contributions, although the individuals concerned are nevertheless entitled to benefits from the system.[31] If one assumes that, in the case of social security, the connection between contributions to the system and benefits from the system can also be very loose, one will then have to apply this standard to the assessment of other charges where there is a 'direct connection between the levy and the individual benefits to be received'.[32] In such cases of a 'direct connection' there is no 'tax'.

Another criterion for a tax is the lack of voluntariness of the payment. This requirement is already made clear by the term 'imposed' in Art 2 OECD

---

26 On the difficult demarcations required in some legal systems for constitutional reasons, cf Michael Lang, 'Die Geldleistung an eine Gebietskörperschaft als Kriterium des finanzverfassungsrechtlichen Abgabenbegriffs' in Metin Akyürek and others (eds), *Staat und Recht in europäischer Perspektive: Festschrift Heinz Schäffer* (Manz 2006) 412.

27 OECD Commentary Art 2 OECD MC (n 15) para 3.

28 Lang, '"Taxes Covered"' (n 7) 218.

29 Working Party No 30 of the OECD Fiscal Committee (Austria–Switzerland), received on 12 June 1969, FC/WP 30(69), m no 27.

30 Jiménez (n 14) 433.

31 More closely, Riedl (n 12) 9.

32 Also Tenore (n 11); Tumpel and Luketina (n 11) Art 2, m no 5.

MC.[33] However, this also gives rise to further implications, as the following example shows:[34] the German Supreme Tax Court (BFH) once had to decide on the case of a taxpayer resident in Germany who had not claimed in the source state the reduction of withholding tax to which he was entitled under Germany's DTA with the source state. After the refund claim in the source state had then become time barred, he requested the entire withholding tax paid in the source state to be credited in Germany. The German Court – rightly – refused to give him credit for the entire tax because the tax had not been levied 'in accordance with the provisions of this Convention'. Ultimately, the taxpayer 'voluntarily' paid a higher amount to the foreign tax authority than he would have been required to under the DTA. Similar arguments can be used to deny the character of a payment as a tax insofar as the taxpayer does not appeal against a payment that was erroneously overcharged according to the tax law of the other state.[35] The same applies insofar as the taxpayer does not exercise a tax option that would lead to a reduction of the foreign tax.[36]

Art 2 OECD MC does not mention 'ordinary taxes' or 'extraordinary taxes', according to para 5 of the OECD Commentary on Art 2 OECD MC, because 'experience has shown that such taxes are generally imposed in very special circumstances. In addition, it would be difficult to define them. They may be extraordinary for various reasons; their imposition, the manner in which they are levied, their rates, their objects, etc'.[37] However, the OECD Commentary also points out the following: 'as it is not intended to exclude extraordinary taxes from all conventions, ordinary taxes have not been mentioned either. The Contracting States are thus free to restrict the convention's field of application to ordinary taxes, to extend it to extraordinary taxes, or even to establish special provisions'.[38]

These formulations leave the reader perplexed:[39] the Commentary leaves it to the Contracting States either to 'restrict the convention's field of application to ordinary taxes' or 'to extend it to extraordinary taxes'.[40] The first suggestion

---

33 Helminen (n 13) 29 et seq.

34 BFH 15 March 1995, I R 98/94.

35 On this point also Cristóbal Pérez Jarpa, 'Industry-Specific Taxes and Article 2 OECD Model Convention 1982 and 2017' in Georg Kofler and others (eds), *Taxes Covered under Article 2 of the OECD Model: The Scope of Tax Treaties in a Dynamic Global Environment of Newly Created Taxes* (IBFD Publications 2021) 215.

36 For more detail see ibid.

37 OECD Commentary Art 2 OECD MC (n 15) para 5.

38 Ibid.

39 To this effect cf. Lang, '"Taxes Covered"' (n 7) 217.

40 OECD Commentary Art 2 OECD MC (n 15) para 5.

seems to imply that extraordinary taxes are covered by a particular treaty unless the Contracting States agree on an explicit exclusion; on the other hand, one could deduce from the second suggestion that, in the absence of a specific provision, extraordinary taxes do not fall under the treaty.[41] These confusing statements in the Commentary are due to the differing views of the members of the Fiscal Committee of the OEEC (Organisation for European Economic Co-operation) at the time the provision was drafted.[42] The decisive discussions took place on 24 January 1957.[43] The representatives of Italy, Denmark and Belgium supported the idea of excluding extraordinary taxes from the scope of the OECD MC. Their preference was to deal with these issues in separate bilateral treaties. The German delegate took the position that if it was not possible to explicitly include all extraordinary taxes within the scope of the OECD MC, they should at least not be excluded. The UK delegate preferred neither to include nor to formally exclude extraordinary taxes. As a result of this discussion, the Committee decided not to mention extraordinary taxes in the OECD Model and asked a working party to explain the reason for this decision in the Commentary. Since the reason was not at all clear, the Commentary is as contradictory as the discussion among the delegates.[44] The history of this provision does not help to answer the question of how extraordinary taxes should be dealt with. Thus, more emphasis should be placed on the wording of Art 2 OECD MC. From the wording of Art 2 OECD MC, one does not get the impression that whether a tax is levied regularly or only under specific circumstances should be decisive. Therefore, there is no need to distinguish between 'ordinary' and 'extraordinary taxes'.[45] All types of taxes on income and on capital are covered.

It is clear, however, that according to Art 2(1) OECD MC, 'the manner in which they are levied' is not relevant for taxes covered by the OECD MC. The OECD Commentary states: 'The method of levying the taxes is equally immaterial: by direct assessment or by deduction at the source, in the form of surtaxes or surcharges, or as additional taxes (*centimes additionnels*), etc.'[46]

The OECD Commentary on Art 2 OECD MC contains extensive information on the treatment of 'penalties' and 'interest'. However, parts of it refer to Art 25 OECD MC: the authors of the OECD Commentary point out that in the

41 Lang, '"Taxes Covered"' (n 7) 217.

42 Ibid.

43 OEEC, Fiscal Committee, Minutes of the 3rd Session held at the Château de la Muette, Paris, 23–25 January 1957, FC/M (57), 4 et seq.

44 Lang, '"Taxes Covered"' (n 7) 217.

45 Ibid; Patricia Brandstetter, *'Taxes Covered' – A Study of Article 2 of the OECD Model Tax Conventions* (IBFD Publications 2011) 64.

46 OECD Commentary Art 2 OECD MC (n 15) para 2.

case of an abolition or reduction of taxation due to a mutual agreement, the penalties and interest related to this taxation should not be levied, and that the same should also apply to transfer pricing adjustments.[47] On the other hand, the OECD Commentary refers to Art 2 OECD MC: 'Clearly a State possessing the right to tax an item of income or capital under the Convention may levy the taxes imposed by its legislation together with any duties or charges accessory to them: increases, costs, interest, penalties etc.'[48] All the more surprisingly, however, the OECD Commentary makes a complete about-face in the following sentence:

> Most States, however, do not consider that interest and penalties accessory to taxes covered by Article 2 are themselves included within the scope of Article 2 and, accordingly, would generally not treat such interest and penalties as payments to which all the provisions concerning the rights to tax of the State of source (or situs) or of the State of residence are applicable, including the limitations of the taxation by the State of source and the obligation for the State of residence to eliminate double taxation.[49]

Why 'interest' and 'penalties' should not fall under Art 2 OECD MC is not explained. It is interesting to note that the quoted sentence only refers to the views of the states, without the authors of the OECD Commentary seeming to identify with them. Thus, in the case of interest and penalties closely related to the tax itself, it can be argued that these are also covered by the scope of the treaty.[50] However, this does not apply if penalties are not directly related to a specific tax liability,[51] or because of formal violations of tax law.[52]

## 3.3 THE STRUCTURE OF ARTICLE 2 OF THE OECD MODEL TAX CONVENTION IN THE FIELD OF TAXES ON INCOME AND ON CAPITAL

In Art 2 OECD MC, the term 'tax' is of utmost importance. Art 2 OECD MC consists of four paragraphs: the first paragraph states that the OECD MC applies to 'taxes on income and on capital imposed on behalf of a Contracting State or of its political subdivisions or local authorities, irrespective of the manner in which they are levied'. The second paragraph defines these taxes:

---

47 Ibid para 4.

48 Ibid.

49 ibid.

50 See also Tenore (n 11); Helminen (n 13) 33.

51 Helminen (n 13) 33.

52 Tenore (n 11).

> There shall be regarded as taxes on income and on capital all taxes imposed on total income, on total capital, or on elements of income or of capital, including taxes on gains from the alienation of movable or immovable property, taxes on the total amounts of wages or salaries paid by enterprises, as well as taxes on capital appreciation.

The third paragraph lists the existing taxes in the two Contracting States to which the Convention applies 'in particular'. Finally, the fourth paragraph deals with the question of under what conditions taxes imposed after the date of signature of the Convention are covered by the Convention.

The definition of Art 2(2) OECD MC is rightly criticized as partially tautological.[53] However, with the chosen technique of definition, the drafters of the OECD MC express that there is no room for the applicability of domestic law. 'Taxes on income and on capital' is a term that is 'not defined' in the tax treaty according to Art 3(2) OECD MC. However, the definition of Art 2(2) OECD MC is not sufficient to determine the content of this phrase. Even so, the context of the OECD MC gives valuable clues: thus, Art 2(1) OECD MC speaks of taxes 'imposed on behalf of a Contracting State or of its political subdivisions or local authorities', 'irrespective of the manner in which they are levied'. Further insights into what is to be understood by 'taxes on income' can be derived from the distributive rules of Art 6 OECD MC and the following Articles, and what is to be understood by 'taxes on capital' from Art 22 OECD MC. These provisions regulate the distribution of taxing rights for these taxes in more detail and are therefore closely related to them.[54] However, Art 2(2) OECD MC also explicitly addresses 'taxes on gains from the alienation of movable or immovable property, taxes on the total amounts of wages or salaries paid by enterprises, as well as taxes on capital appreciation' and includes them in the definition. Especially with the phrase 'taxes on the total amounts of wages or salaries paid by enterprises', Art 2(2) OECD MC mentions taxes that are often not associated with 'taxes on income'. This explicit reference could be seen as an indication that the definition of Art 2(2) OECD MC is very broad. However, it is not easy to say for which other taxes falling under Art 2(2) OECD MC the 'taxes on the total amounts of wages or salaries paid by enterprises' could serve as an example. Therefore, there is much to be said for understanding the examples mentioned as selective, non-expandable extensions of the definition of 'taxes on income and on capital'.[55]

---

[53] Zirngast and Kanduth-Kristen (n 9) 549.

[54] Gerd Erhard, '*Art 2 Unter das Abkommen fallende Steuern*' in Hans Flick, Franz Wassermeyer and Michael Kempermann (eds), *Doppelbesteuerungsabkommen Deutschland-Schweiz* (Otto Schmidt 2023) m no 72.

[55] Thus Ismer and Jescheck, 'Taxes on Digital Services' (n 4) 505.

In addition to the definition of Art 2(2) OECD MC, Art 2(3) OECD MC gives the Contracting States the possibility to explicitly name the taxes to which the tax treaty is to apply. This list serves to illustrate which taxes the two Contracting States want to be covered by the scope of the DTA as 'taxes on income and on capital'. Insofar as taxes are mentioned that would not fall under the definition of Art 2(2) OECD MC, Art 2(3) OECD MC extends the scope of the agreement.[56]

This also applies if contributions are mentioned in Art 3 OECD MC, which not only do not fall under the definition of Art 2(2) OECD MC, but would otherwise not qualify as 'taxes' in the sense of the OECD MC at all. By their inclusion in Art 2(3) OECD MC, they become 'taxes' for the purposes of the DTA. This means that not only can the distributive rules and the method Article be applied to them, but also Arts 24, 26 and 27 OECD MC. In case of doubt, a mutual agreement procedure according to Art 25 OECD MC can be conducted.

Conversely, taxes levied at the time of signing the DTA and belonging to 'taxes on income and on capital' may be missing from the list of Art 2(3) OECD MC. This could be for different reasons: treaty negotiations might have dragged on for so long until the signing of the DTA that new taxes have been introduced in the meantime, which were not included in the list of Art 2(3) OECD MC by the negotiating team of the respective Contracting State, either by mistake, or on purpose – because they wanted to avoid discussions with the other side, which would have meant further delays.[57] It is also conceivable that the treaty negotiators overlooked taxes on income or on capital with low fiscal revenues. This danger exists especially in the case of taxes levied by the 'political subdivisions or local authorities' mentioned in Art 2(1) OECD MC.[58] These may also be taxes the revenue of which is important for the subdivision in question. Especially in countries in which there are a large number of 'political subdivisions or local authorities' and where these are also entitled to levy taxes, it may also be a conscious decision not to mention such taxes in the list of Art 2(3) OECD MC, but to assume that those taxes, which are 'taxes on income and capital', fall under the DTA in any event due to the general provisions of Arts 2(1) and (2) OECD MC.[59] In all these cases, the treaty provisions modelled on Arts 2(1) and (2) OECD MC will ensure the actual applicability of the treaty.

---

56 Lang, 'Der sachliche' (n 7) 265 et seq; agreeing Tenore (n 11); Drüen and others (n 12) Art 2, m no 56.

57 Lang, 'Tax Treaties and Municipal Tax' (n 7) 5; Lang, '"Taxes Covered"' (n 7) 220.

58 Cui (n 1) [5.1.2.1].

59 See also Erhard (n 54) at no 13.

It is more difficult if a fiscally or otherwise significant tax on income or on capital, which is levied by the Contracting State itself, is missing from the list of Art 2(3) OECD MC, so that it would be surprising if the treaty negotiators had simply forgotten about that tax. Therefore, it seems reasonable to conclude that such a tax should not be included in the scope of the DTA at all.[60] However, the 1969 report of OECD Working Party No 30 argues that it is not sufficient to simply not mention a tax that qualifies as a tax on income or on capital in Art 2(3) OECD MC in order to exclude it from the scope of the agreement. It would require an explicit provision in the DTA that this tax, despite its character as a tax on income or on capital, is not covered by the agreement.[61] This OECD report is part of the *travaux préparatoires* of all DTAs modelled after the OECD MC 1977 and subsequent OECD MCs and must be taken into account in the interpretation.[62] Clearly, however, the *travaux préparatoires* of the specific DTA have even greater significance for the interpretation of this DTA, in particular in the case of provisions such as Art 2(3) OECD MC, which is not conclusive. If these *travaux préparatoires* prove the intention of the Contracting States that a tax not mentioned in Art 2(3) OECD MC is not to be included in the scope of the agreement, this will probably have to be taken into account in the interpretation of the DTA. This also applies to situations when the tax is not explicitly described in the DTA itself as not falling under Arts 2(1) and (2) OECD MC.[63]

It is even more difficult when it comes to taxes that do not belong to the classic 'taxes on income and on capital', but for which it could be questioned whether they fall under the definition of Art 2(2) OECD MC at all. In these borderline cases, it cannot be ruled out that these taxes were not included in the list of Art 2(3) OECD MC because it was assumed during the negotiations that they would not fall under this definition anyway. If this motive is reflected in the *travaux préparatoires*, this will in any case also have to be taken into account when interpreting the DTA. If there is no indication of this in the

---

[60] Lang, 'Der sachliche' (n 7) 265 et seq; agreeing Drüen and others (n 12) Art 2, m no 56; differently Tenore (n 11); Helminen (n 13) 28; Stefan Bendlinger and Georg Kofler, 'Geltungsbereich von Doppelbesteuerungsabkommen' in Stefan Bendlinger and others (eds), *Internationales Steuerrecht* (2nd edn, LexisNexis 2019) 536; Tumpel and Luketina (n 11) Art 2, m no 9.

[61] Working Party No 30 of the OECD Fiscal Committee (n 29) m no 27.

[62] Lang, '"Taxes Covered"' (n 7) 221.

[63] For weighing considerations, ibid 221; Martin Klokar, 'The List of Taxes According to Article 2(3) OECD Model Convention 1982 and 2017' in Georg Kofler and others (eds), *Taxes Covered under Article 2 of the OECD Model: The Scope of Tax Treaties in a Dynamic Global Environment of Newly Created Taxes* (IBFD Publications 2021) 104.

*travaux préparatoires*, the interpreting court cannot be reproached if, in light of the view described in the OECD Report of Working Party No 30, it makes the application of the DTA to this tax dependent solely on whether it comes to the conclusion that the tax is covered by the definition of Art 2(2) OECD MC. The fact that Art 2(3) OECD MC contains the phrase 'in particular' facilitates such an interpretation of the DTA.

Art 2(4) OECD MC again extends the material scope of application of the DTA also to 'any identical or substantially similar taxes that are imposed after the date of signature of the Convention in addition to, or in place of, the existing taxes'. Only taxes imposed after the signing of the Convention can be covered by this provision.[64] The provision ensures that changes in the tax system do not necessarily require an amendment of the Convention, but the application of the DTA to new taxes is guaranteed at least under certain conditions.

Art 2(4) OECD MC is only applicable if the newly introduced tax is 'identical or substantially similar'. Thus, a comparability test is required.[65] The subject matter of the tax is important. The tax subject also plays a role. In addition, the basis of assessment may also be of importance. The design of the tax rate plays – if at all – a completely subordinate role.[66] The designation of the tax is just as irrelevant as the purpose for which it is levied.[67] Neither does it matter whether the new tax covers the entire tax object of the previous or still levied tax.[68] In any case, the characteristics of the previous taxes at the time of signing the DTA are decisive.[69] If said characteristics have changed thereafter, these changes may no longer be taken into account in the comparability test.[70]

The newly introduced tax must be 'identical or substantially similar' to at least one of the taxes listed in the provision of the DTA reproduced in Art 2(3) OECD MC. The definition of Art 2(2) OECD MC, however, does not play a role in the comparability test according to Art 2(4) OECD MC:[71] on the one hand, some of the taxes listed in Art 2(3) OECD MC may not fall under the definition of Art 2(2) OECD MC at all and only qualify as 'taxes on income

---

64 Helminen (n 13) 25.

65 Zirngast and Kanduth-Kristen (n 9) 551.

66 Roland Ismer and Christoph Jescheck, 'Der sachliche Anwendungsbereich von DBA in einer Welt nach BEPS: Art 2 OECD-MA (Unter das Abkommen fallende Steuern) und die Einführung neuer Steuern' (2017) IStR 501, 506 ('Der sachliche Anwendungsbereich'); Drüen and others (n 12) Art 2, m no 17.

67 Differently, Ismer and Jescheck, 'Taxes on Digital Services' (n 4) 576.

68 Differently, apparently Erhard (n 54) m no 54 on church tax, because it is based only on church membership and does not cover all income taxpayers.

69 Lang, '"Taxes Covered"' (n 7) 222; Helminen (n 13) 26.

70 Ismer and Jescheck, 'Der sachliche Anwendungsbereich' (n 66) 506.

71 Differently, Tenore (n 11); Drüen and others (n 12), Art 2, m no 69.

and on capital' due to their mention in Art 2(3) OECD MC.[72] Above all, however, Art 2(2) OECD MC is in any case applicable to newly introduced taxes in addition to Art 2(4) OECD MC:[73] a new tax may fall under the DTA either because this results from the comparability test required under Art 2(4) OECD MC, or because it is a tax on income or on capital under Art 2(2) OECD MC. Art 2(2) and Art 2(4) OECD MC are independent of each other. It is sufficient that the new tax falls under one of the two provisions for the DTA to apply to it.

Art 2(4) OECD MC uses the plural in connection with the term 'tax': the DTA is to be applied to 'identical or substantially similar taxes' which are levied 'in addition to, or in place of, the existing taxes'. From this, it is deduced by some authors that 'a tax is similar not to a single tax, but to a combination of several taxes'.[74] This view is also called the 'macro-approach', which 'requires an overall assessment of the place of the respective tax in the tax system as a whole. The question of whether a tax is similar then has to be decided against the background of the entire tax system.'[75] However, it is unclear how such a comparison of a tax with the entire tax system should be made. The use of the plural of the term 'tax' does not force such a 'macro-approach': if Art 2(4) OECD MC speaks of 'taxes' which have to be compared with other 'taxes', this does not at all exclude a single one of these 'taxes' being in turn compared with another single 'tax'. A newly introduced tax may, of course, also be comparable with two or more taxes existing at the time of signing the DTA, but the comparability with a single tax is already sufficient for the DTA to be applicable according to Art 2(4) OECD MC. Other taxes can only be taken into account if the DTA is generally applicable to 'taxes on income and on capital' according to its provision modelled on Art 2(2) OECD MC. However, either by an explicit provision or in another way, a certain tax, which would in itself belong to the 'taxes on income and on capital', has been excluded from the scope of the DTA. In this constellation, a new tax will have to be 'identical or substantially similar' to one of the taxes levied at the time of signing the DTA, but at the same time must not be 'identical or substantially similar' to the tax excluded from the scope of the DTA, in order to comply with the requirements of Art 2(4) OECD MC.[76]

---

[72] On this point, Niels Bammens and Filip Debelva, 'What Is Tax on Capital for the Purposes of a Tax Treaty? An Analysis of Two Recent Belgian Supreme Court Decisions on the Belgian Net Asset Tax' (2022) 76(8) Bulletin for International Taxation 379, 392 et seq.

[73] Cf ibid.

[74] Ismer and Blank (n 2) Art 2, m no 70.

[75] Ismer and Blank (n 2) Art 2, m no 70; cf Ismer and Jescheck, 'Der sachliche Anwendungsbereich' (n 66) 505.

[76] Similarly, Tenore (n 11).

Another question is whether only the taxes of the same Contracting State or also those of the other Contracting State can be used to assess whether a newly introduced tax is 'identical or substantially similar' to a tax existing at the time the DTA was signed. In the present author's opinion – as already explained in more detail elsewhere – the better reasons speak in favour of using the taxes of both Contracting States for these purposes:[77] Art 2(4) OECD MC uses the phrase 'identical or substantially similar taxes' and seems to refer to the list of taxes in the bilateral equivalent to Art 2(3) of the OECD Model. The taxes levied at the time the treaty was signed serve as a benchmark. Art 2(4) OECD MC neither distinguishes between the two Contracting States nor requires that a newly introduced tax be identical or similar to taxes in *both* Contracting States. Thus, even a tax levied only in the *other* Contracting State may serve as a benchmark.[78]

The same view was expressed a little later by the Irish High Court in the *Kinsella* case.[79] Although the Court also concludes that the Italian Capital Gains Tax (CGT) is a substantially similar tax to the Irish taxes specifically mentioned in the Convention, it makes clear its position:

> The issue here is whether CGT is an identical or a substantially similar tax to the existing taxes as defined in article 2.3. In the case of Ireland they are income tax and corporation profits tax (article 2.3(a)). In the case of Italy they are the taxes which are set forth in article 2.3(b). Thus, if Ireland, subsequent to the Convention, introduced a tax substantially similar to one of the enumerated taxes, such new tax would be captured by the Convention. The new tax has to be identical or substantially similar to an existing tax whether that existing tax is Irish or Italian. Such an approach is consistent with the reciprocal nature of the Convention. It is also supported by the obligation of annual notification of tax changes by the contracting states. CGT is, in my view, a substantially similar tax to the Italian taxes listed in article 2.3 and of course is specifically covered in article 12.[80]

Subsequently, the Australian Federal Court took the same view in the *Undershaft* decision:

> The inclusion of both the UK capital gains tax and the UK corporations tax as taxes covered by [the tax treaty] suggests that the parties would have regarded an Australian tax imposed on capital gains, whether through the existing income tax

[77] Cf Brandstetter (n 45) 39; Tenore (n 11).

[78] Lang, '"Taxes Covered"' (n 7) 221; agreeing Tenore (n 11); see further the discussion in Helminen (n 13) 48; Cui (n 1) [5.3.2]; Bammens and Debelva (n 72) 391.

[79] *Kinsella v The Revenue Commissioners* [2007] IEHC 250; [2011] 2 IR 417 (31 July 2007).

[80] Ibid [2011] 2 IR 417 [62]–[63].

> or by means of a new tax, on either individuals or corporations, or both, subsequent to the signing of the UK Agreement ... as 'substantially similar' to either of the UK taxes referred to or to both of them viewed in combination.[81]

Richard Vann has opposed the view taken by the present author and subsequently by the Irish High Court and the Australian Federal Court:

> While it is true that tax treaties are generally symmetrical, the taxes covered list is one case where each country specifies what it wants to be covered on its side. In making up its list presumably the country considers what it does not want to cover as well as what it wants to cover ... Consider the implication of this line of argument for the United States of America (US). The US wishes to cover only its federal income tax in its tax treaties, that is, it wants to exclude state income taxes from coverage. Suppose a treaty [partner's] list in its treaty with the US covers such taxes on its side ... On this line of reasoning, a US state income tax that did not exist at the time of the treaty but was introduced subsequently would be covered by the treaty, a result which would cause significant ructions in the US and is completely contrary to the well-known US treaty position.[82]

The present author shares the view that the provisions of double taxation treaties are designed symmetrically. Unlike Vann, however, the present author sees no reason to see an exception to this principle of symmetry in the listing of taxes in the treaty provision modelled on Art 2(3) OECD MC. States that subject their own taxes to the scope of a Convention and thus ultimately forgo tax revenues naturally have an interest in ensuring that the essential taxes of the other state are also covered by the DTA and that the other state, therefore, also makes its contribution to avoiding double taxation and accepts corresponding losses in its tax revenues. Therefore, in practice, it is by no means a sole decision of each of the two states as to which of its taxes should be covered by the scope of the treaty. In addition, the problem described by Vann would exist in the US even if new taxes were measured only against those levied at the time the DTA was signed, which are explicitly mentioned as taxes of one's own state: if a 'state income tax' levied later is comparable to 'federal income taxes imposed by the Internal Revenue Code', that tax would then also run the risk of falling within the scope of the treaty. The problem correctly identified by Vann with regard to DTAs concluded with the US has, however, been addressed and solved in numerous of these DTAs. For example, the provision corresponding to Art 2(4) OECD MC in the Australia–US DTA – as in several other

---

[81] *Undershaft (No 1) Ltd v Commissioner of Taxation* (2009) 175 FCR 150 [134].

[82] Richard Vann, 'Commentary on Undershaft (No 1) Ltd v Commissioner of Taxation, Undershaft (No 2) BV v Commissioner of Taxation' (2009) 11 International Tax Law Reports 662.

DTAs[83] – reads as follows:[84] 'This Convention shall also apply to any identical or substantially similar taxes which are imposed by either Contracting State after the date of signature of this Convention in addition to, or in place of, the existing taxes.' The provision deviates from Art 2(4) OECD MC insofar as the phrase 'by either Contracting State' was inserted. The wording thus differs significantly from Art 2(1) OECD MC, where the phrase 'imposed on behalf of a Contracting State or of its political subdivisions or local authorities' is used. Apparently, 'its political subdivisions or local authorities' is deliberately not mentioned in the adjustment clause of this DTA. In this way, it is ensured in these DTAs that – contrary to Vann's fear – a 'state income tax' subsequently introduced in a US state does not fall under the scope of the DTA. The 2006 and 2016 US model treaties (US MC) also address and solve the problem, albeit in a different way: these model treaties place at the head of Art 2 the following first paragraph:[85] 'This Convention shall apply to taxes on income imposed on behalf of a Contracting State irrespective of the manner in which they are levied.' In this provision, too, there is apparently a deliberate reference only to 'a Contracting State' and not – unlike in the OECD MC – to 'its political subdivisions or local authorities'. This provision ensures that all taxes covered by Art 2 US MC – and thus also those covered by the scope of application of the Convention on the basis of Art 2(4) US MC – are taxes 'imposed on behalf of a Contracting State'. Therefore, newly introduced state income taxes cannot be subject to the DTAs concluded by the US under these provisions.

[83] See also the Convention between the Federal Republic of Germany and the French Republic for the Avoidance of Double Taxation and the Establishment of Rules for Reciprocal Administrative and Legal Assistance with Respect to Taxes on Income and on Capital, Business Tax and Land Tax, signed 21 July 1959, 770 UNTS 325 (entered into force 4 November 1961) Art 1(3) (now Art 1(4)); Convention between the Government of the United Kingdom of Great Britain and Northern Ireland and the Government of the Republic of Finland for the Avoidance of Double Taxation and the Prevention of Fiscal Evasion with respect to Taxes on Income and Capital, signed 17 July 1969, 718 UNTS 297 (entered into force 5 February 1970) Art 2(2).

[84] Convention between the Government of Australia and the Government of the United States of America for the Avoidance of Double Taxation and the Prevention of Fiscal Evasion with respect to Taxes on Income, signed 6 August 1982, 1424 UNTS 37 (entered into force 31 October 1983) Art 2(2).

[85] United States Model Income Tax Convention (2016) Art 2(1).

## 3.4 THE DEMARCATION FROM INHERITANCE AND GIFT TAX

In addition to the Model Tax Convention on Income and on Capital, the OECD has also developed its own Model Double Taxation Convention on Estates and Inheritances and on Gifts. The first version dates from 1966 and was revised in 1982.[86] The structure of the two Model Conventions is similar,[87] whereby it can be assumed, if only for reasons of chronology, that the 'Model Tax Convention on Income and on Capital' was used for the 'Model Double Taxation Convention on Estates and Inheritances and on Gifts' and that many previously obtained results can therefore be adopted for the 'Model Double Taxation Convention on Estates and Inheritances and on Gifts'.[88] This applies, for example, to the term 'tax', which is relevant not only for Art 2 OECD Estate, Inheritance and Gift MC (1982), but also for the distribution standards and the method Article, as well as the prohibitions on discrimination and the regulations on the exchange of information. The regulations on the prohibitions of discrimination are – just as according to Art 24 OECD MC (2017) – applicable to 'taxes of every kind and description'. Their areas of application therefore overlap. However, a conflict of rules does not exist.[89] 'Taxes' of the Contracting States – if both OECD Model Tax Conventions have been implemented – have to comply with the prohibitions on discrimination contained in both DTAs.[90]

These parallels can also be seen in the fact that both Model Conventions have rules on the substantive scope of application in Art 2(1) OECD MC (2017)

---

[86] In the following, any reference to the OECD Model Double Taxation Convention on Estates and Inheritances and on Gifts concerns the OECD Model Convention in the version as of 1982 (OECD Estate, Inheritance and Gift MC). In all other cases, the OECD MC from 2017 (n 15) is used.

[87] Jan Karol Szczepanski, 'The Dual System of OECD Model Tax Conventions from the Evolutionary Perspective' (2018) 46(10) Intertax 766, 792.

[88] OECD Estate, Inheritance and Gift MC (n 86).

[89] Markus Mittendorfer, 'Double Protection under Art 2 OECD Model Convention 1982 and 2017?' in Georg Kofler and others (eds), *Taxes Covered under Article 2 of the OECD Model: The Scope of Tax Treaties in a Dynamic Global Environment of Newly Created Taxes* (IBFD Publications 2021) 252.

[90] Cf however, Alexander Rust, Gabriela Capristano and Xiangdan Luo, 'Tax Treaty Application Beyond the Scope of Article 2 OECD Model Convention 1982 and 2017 (Mutual Agreement, Non-Discrimination, Mutual Assistance)' in Georg Kofler and others (eds), *Taxes Covered under Article 2 of the OECD Model: The Scope of Tax Treaties in a Dynamic Global Environment of Newly Created Taxes* (IBFD Publications 2021) 286, who apparently assume that only the regulation of one of the DTAs comes into consideration.

and Art 2(2) OECD Estate, Inheritance and Gift MC (1982). The two regulations are similar to each other.[91] Like Art 2(3) OECD MC (2017), Art 2(3) OECD Estate, Inheritance and Gift MC (1982) also contains a provision that lists the taxes which are imposed at the time the treaty was signed. Further, Art 2(4) OECD Estate, Inheritance and Gift MC (1982) has its equivalent in Art 2(4) OECD MC (2017).

A difference to Art 2(3) OECD MC (2017) is that before the list of taxes levied at the time of signing the DTA, the word 'in particular' from Art 2(3) OECD Estate, Inheritance and Gift MC (1982) is missing. Therefore, the list is exhaustive. This is attributed to the fact that the 'taxes on estates and inheritances and on gifts' levied in most states are manageable and the treaty negotiators can therefore be expected to provide a complete list.[92] However, this has the consequence that the list of taxes levied at the time of signing the DTA is conclusive in this case. The definition of Art 2(2) OECD Estate, Inheritance and Gift MC (1982) is therefore meaningless for the taxes levied at the time of signing the DTA and is only relevant for taxes levied later. Taxes levied later can also be covered by the treaty because they fall under the adjustment clause of Art 2(4) OECD Estate, Inheritance and Gift MC (1982), even if they are not covered by the definition of Art 2(2) OECD MC (1982). The absence of the word 'in particular' in Art 2(3) OECD Estate, Inheritance and Gift MC (1982) does not exclude those taxes levied later in this way, which are not included in the list of Art 2(3) OECD Estate, Inheritance and Gift MC (1982), from potentially falling under the DTA. Otherwise, Art 2(4) OECD Estate, Inheritance and Gift MC (1982) would have no scope of application.

More exciting is the question of how the scope of the two Model Conventions can be distinguished from one another:[93] at first glance, there appears to be no overlap in the scope of the two OECD Models. The borderline seems easy to draw: individual and corporate income taxes usually cover what can be generated in the market, while estate, inheritance and gift taxes cover transfers of money or property without consideration.[94] What inheritance and gift taxes and capital taxes have in common is that they apply to property.[95] While

---

91 Lang, '"Taxes Covered"' (n 7) 222.

92 Brandstetter (n 45) 30; Klokar (n 63) 98; Josef Schuch and Shimeng Lan, 'Identical or Substantially Similar Taxes According to Article 2(4) OECD Model Convention 1982 and 2017' in Georg Kofler and others (eds), *Taxes Covered under Article 2 of the OECD Model: The Scope of Tax Treaties in a Dynamic Global Environment of Newly Created Taxes* (IBFD Publications 2021) 140.

93 Lang, '"Taxes Covered"' (n 7) 222.

94 Ibid; Tumpel and Luketina (n 11) Art 2, m no 13.

95 On this point, Lang, '"Taxes Covered"' (n 7) 222.

capital taxes are usually levied on a regular basis, inheritance and gift taxes are levied only when a specific transfer takes place.[96]

However, a closer look shows that overlaps are possible: taxes on income and on capital typically differ from taxes on estates and inheritances and on gifts in that the former occur regularly and the latter irregularly. But there are exceptions in both directions: the analysis of the OECD Commentary on Art 2 OECD MC (2017) – albeit somewhat contradictory – has shown that 'extraordinary taxes' can also be included in 'taxes on income and on capital', and conversely, recurring gifts can also be covered by Art 2 OECD MC (2017).[97] The concept of market income is also vague and seems more borrowed from some national jurisdictions than actually traceable to the treaty.[98] The Schanz/Haig/Simons model would even include inheritance tax.[99] Art 2(2) OECD Estate, Inheritance and Gift MC, conversely, mentions as a criterion for the classification of 'transfers *inter vivos*' that 'such transfers are made for no, or less than full, consideration'. However, this delimitation also remains vague,[100] and methodologically it would be questionable to conclude from these provisions of the 'OECD Model Double Taxation Convention on Estates and Inheritances and on Gifts', first published in 1966, that the 'Model Tax Convention on Income and on Capital', which has older roots, is based on the concept of full consideration.

The demarcation between the two model agreements is facilitated by the provisions modelled on Art 2(3) OECD MC (2017) and (1982), which provide that the Contracting States should list in the DTA itself the taxes that exist at the time of signing the DTAs and are to be covered by one of the two DTAs. In this way, there is clarity with respect to these taxes, although, at least in the OECD MC (2017), it is not entirely excluded that taxes not listed there may nevertheless be covered by the DTA. For taxes introduced later, however, the delimitation is much more difficult, not only because the delimitation of the definitions of Art 2(2) of both DTAs may pose problems, but additionally, according to Art 2(4) of both DTAs, the comparability to the taxes listed in Art

---

96 Ibid.

97 Mittendorfer (n 89) 246.

98 Brandstetter (n 45) 88 et seq.

99 See Daniela Hohenwarter, Georg Kofler, Gunter Mayr and Julia Sinnig, 'Qualification of the Digital Services under Tax Treaties' (Guest Editorial) (2019) 47(2) Intertax 140, 144.

100 Stefanie Gombotz, 'Taxes on Estates and Inheritances and on Gifts According to Article 2(1) and (2) OECD Model Convention 1982' in Georg Kofler and others (eds), *Taxes Covered under Article 2 of the OECD Model: The Scope of Tax Treaties in a Dynamic Global Environment of Newly Created Taxes* (IBFD Publications 2021) 84.

2(3) of both DTAs has to be examined, and this list may also include taxes that are not covered by the respective definition. Therefore, newly introduced taxes that are covered by the definition of Art 2(2) OECD MC of one treaty may also be covered by this treaty due to the comparability test of Art 2(4) OECD MC of the other treaty. Difficulties may also arise if taxes existing at the time of signing the DTAs are amended and tax obligations for certain transactions change from one tax to another.[101]

If a situation is ultimately covered by both treaties, and double non-taxation is the result due to the different distribution standards of each DTA, this is probably not in line with the object and purpose of the regulations.[102] Double non-taxation can indeed be the legitimate result of the application of a DTA if only one state has the right of taxation under the DTA and this state does not make use of its right of taxation under domestic law. However, if the double non-taxation is the result of the application of two treaties between the same states, then this is arguably different.[103] If the double non-taxation resulting from the application of both states is not in accordance with the object and purpose of these treaties, it should be remedied by way of interpretation, if possible.[104] It must also be respected that many states have not concluded a DTA in the area of taxes on estates and inheritances and on gifts, and in these cases, the scope of application of the other DTA cannot be extended indefinitely,[105] and the limits of the scope of application of the 'Model Tax Convention on Income and on Capital' resulting in this way must also be taken into account if a DTA for taxes on estates and inheritances and on gifts also exists between the two states. Whether the scope of application of both treaties can be delimited with the help of these interpretative goals in such a way that they do not overlap is a different question.

## 3.5 OUTLOOK

The difficulties described in the application of the provisions on the substantive scope of application of the DTAs have prompted Roland Ismer and Christoph Jescheck to propose the inclusion of a provision in Art 2(4) OECD MC (2017). This proposal could probably also be applied to Art 2(4) OECD Estate, Inheritance and Gift MC (1982), according to which the competent authorities of the two contracting states should clarify by means of a mutual

---

101 On this subject, see in detail Lang, '"Taxes Covered"' (n 7) 222 et seq.

102 Ibid 223.

103 Ibid.

104 Ibid; Mittendorfer (n 89) 258 et seq.

105 Lang, '"Taxes Covered"' (n 7) 222 et seq; concurring Helminen (n 13) 41 et seq.

agreement procedure whether the new tax is covered by the scope of application of the agreement.[106] One possibility raised by Ismer and Jescheck would be to make the application of the DTA to new taxes conditional on the competent authorities reaching an understanding on the matter.[107] However, Ismer and Jescheck themselves admit that this would limit the rights of taxpayers.[108] The conclusion of such a mutual agreement procedure would be at the undetermined discretion of the tax authorities. Taxpayers would then not be able to enforce the conclusion of such a mutual agreement either in a bilateral procedure or through legal remedies under domestic law.

Alternatively, Ismer and Jescheck suggest that Art 2(4) OECD MC should provide for an obligation of the competent authorities to concur by mutual agreement whether a new tax is covered by the DTA.[109] However, it would be questionable how this obligation could be enforced. There is no obligation to reach an agreement between the authorities, unless in these cases arbitration would then automatically become competent in the absence of an agreement. Merely speaking verbally of an obligation on the part of the competent authorities, without providing for their own mechanisms of enforcement, is of no use. This is shown by the experience with the provision in Art 4(2) subpara (d) OECD MC, according to which 'the competent authorities of the Contracting State shall settle the question by mutual agreement': this provision has proven to be toothless. The 'obligation' cannot be enforced.[110]

Therefore, an addition to Art 2(4) OECD MC, which calls on the competent authorities to conclude a mutual agreement, does not add any value. Art 25(3) sentence 1 OECD MC (2017) already provides a legal basis for this. Even if such a provision is formulated as an obligation, this does not change anything if enforcement mechanisms are lacking. In any case, taxpayers have the possibility, on their own initiative, to request the initiation of a mutual agreement procedure according to Art 25(1) OECD MC (2017) if the authority does not apply the Convention to the new tax on its own initiative and the taxpayer has doubts whether this view is correct. The taxpayer has the possibility to request arbitration then as well only if the competent authorities of both states disagree on the application of DTA to the new tax. Whether the taxpayer also has the possibility, in the case of such a mutual agreement that is unfavourable to that taxpayer, to have this opinion of the two competent authorities reviewed by the courts depends on the respective domestic law and the legal significance of mutual agreements under this law. In legal systems based on the rule of law,

106 Ismer and Jescheck, 'Der sachliche Anwendungsbereich' (n 66) 508 et seq.
107 Ibid.
108 Ibid.
109 Ibid.
110 Ismer and Blank (n 2) Art 4, m no 221.

decisions by administrative authorities, even if jointly taken by authorities of both states, should in any case be subject to judicial review.

## ACKNOWLEDGEMENTS

The author would like to thank Eric Coenen, Bence Péter Komár and Severin Schragl for their support. The manuscript was completed on 29 March 2023.

# 4. The future of the corporate form in income tax: a case study of Canada

**Jinyan Li**

## 4.1 INTRODUCTION

A corporation is nothing but a piece of paper.[1] And yet, this piece of paper enjoys the status of a person and has an independent identity as a taxpayer (the 'separate entity principle'). It can generate tremendous value for its shareholders through tax savings resulting from tax deferral, tax shifting and tax subsidies. Why does tax law allow such value to exist? Meanwhile, to protect the integrity of the income tax system, especially the progressivity of the system by taxing individual income at progressive rates, the tax system contains numerous anti-avoidance rules, which, in effect, 'neutralize' the fiscal effects of the corporate form. So, fictions beget more fictions. What is the future of the corporate form in income taxation? To what extent can the two Pillars (Pillar One and Pillar Two)[2] or the anti-avoidance rules crush the corporate form? This chapter seeks to answer these questions by examining the Canadian income tax system.

Following this introduction, section 4.2 provides an overview of the corporate tax system in terms of its rationale, objectives and technical design. Sections 4.3 to 4.5 discuss the role of the corporate form in achieving tax savings through tax deferral, tax shifting and tax subsidies. Section 4.6 briefly assesses the impact of the anti-avoidance rules and the two Pillars on the

---

[1] H David Rosenbloom, 'Banes of an Income Tax: Legal Fictions, Elections, Hypothetical Determinations, and Related-Party Debt' (2003) 32 Tax Notes International 989.

[2] Organisation for Economic Co-operation and Development (OECD), 'Statement on a Two-Pillar Solution to Address the Tax Challenges Arising from the Digitalisation of the Economy' (OECD Publishing, October 2021) <https://www.oecd.org/tax/beps/statement-on-a-two-pillar-solution-to-address-the-tax-challenges-arising-from-the-digitalisation-of-the-economy-october-2021.pdf>.

future of the separate entity principle. Section 4.7 concludes by predicting that the corporate form will remain, albeit with a declining fiscal effect.

## 4.2 THE CANADIAN CORPORATE TAX SYSTEM

### 4.2.1 Taxing Corporations

The current Income Tax Act (ITA)[3] can be traced to the Income War Tax Act 1917 (IWTA).[4] The IWTA imposed taxes on the income of every person resident in Canada and defined person to include a corporation.[5] The tax personality of corporations was influenced by the US Internal Revenue Code, 1913.[6]

The main reasons for Canada to take this approach were political and pragmatic. Politically speaking, the income tax was introduced to accompany the Military Service Act (the Conscription Crisis) to share the burden and sacrifice of the Great War.[7] Not taxing corporations owned by wealthy individuals would not have been politically acceptable. Practically speaking, the emerging corporate economy meant that there was money to be taxed and corporations were easier to tax than their individual shareholders. In fact, Ontario had already levied a corporate profits tax at that time. Today, making corporations, especially the large ones, 'pay their fair share' remains a political or popular justification for introducing anti-avoidance rules or the two Pillars. Corporations function as deputy tax collectors through withholding of taxes or as information providers to enable effective tax administration.

The corporate tax system in Canada has evolved in technical detail and policy orientation, but the principle of taxing each corporation as a tax unit has remained unchanged.

---

3 Income Tax Act (Can) RSC 1985, c 1 (5th Supp) (ITA).

4 Income War Tax Act 1917 (Can) SC 1917, c 28 (IWTA). For an overview of the importance of the IWTA, see Jinyan Li and J Scott Wilkie, 'Celebrating the Centennial of the Income War Tax Act 1917: The Future by the Light of 100 Candles' in Jinyan Li, J Scott Wilkie and Larry Chapman (eds), *Income Tax at 100 Years: Essays and Reflections on the Income War Tax Act* (Canadian Tax Foundation 2017).

5 ITA (n 3) s 248(1) and IWTA (n 4) s 2.

6 Colin Campbell and Robert Raizenne, 'The First 100 Years: Evolution of the Law, Policy, and Principles' in Jinyan Li, J Scott Wilkie and Larry Chapman (eds), *Income Tax at 100 Years: Essays and Reflections on the Income War Tax Act* (Canadian Tax Foundation 2017) 34–35.

7 Colin Campbell and Robert Raizenne, *A History of Canadian Income Tax, Vol 1: The Income War Tax Act 1917–1948* (Canadian Tax Foundation and Osgoode Society for Legal History 2022) 26–33.

### 4.2.2 Technical Design Features

#### 4.2.2.1 Liability to tax

The ITA imposes taxes on the income of Canadian resident persons (regardless of geographical source) and the Canadian-sourced income of non-residents.[8] The use of residence and source as evidence of nexus or economic allegiance between the income and Canada is consistent with the economic allegiance theory, which was recently rephrased as the value creation principle in the OECD's Base Erosion and Profit Shifting (BEPS) Project.[9]

Corporate residence is determined by reference to the place of incorporation in Canada[10] and the place of central management and control for corporations incorporated outside Canada.[11] It is a tax fiction layered upon a legal fiction. There is no requirement of any substantial economic ties of a corporation to the country chosen by the corporation to be its residence country.[12]

#### 4.2.2.2 Corporate income

Corporations compute their income and taxable income in accordance with the same rules applicable to individuals. Income from business or property is the profit therefrom.[13] The computation of profit is generally based on, but not limited by, accounting rules. A corporation's income derived from both domestic and foreign sources is taxable. Foreign income earned by a foreign resident subsidiary of a Canadian parent is generally not taxable. Each corporation is taxed separately. There is no consolidation taxation of corporate groups. The

---

8 ITA (n 3) ss 2, 3, 212 and 219. Jinyan Li and Paul Lamarre, *International Taxation in Canada* (5th edn, LexisNexis, forthcoming 2024) ch 4.

9 Jinyan Li, Nathan Jin Bao and Huaning (Christina) Li, 'Value Creation: A Constant Principle in a Changing World of International Taxation' (2019) 67(4) Canadian Tax Journal 1107; Angelo Nikolakakis, 'Aligning the Location of Taxation with the Location of Value Creation: Are We There Yet!?!' (2021) 75(11/12) Bulletin for International Taxation 549.

10 ITA (n 3) s 250(4).

11 *Fundy Settlement v Canada* [2012] 1 SCR 520 [9]. The 'central management and control of a corporation will be exercised where its board of directors exercises its responsibilities'. For further reading, see Brian J Arnold, 'A Tax Policy Perspective on Corporate Residence' (2003) 51(4) Canadian Tax Journal 1559; Robert Couzin, *Corporate Residence and International Taxation* (IBFD Publications 2002); Michael J McIntyre, 'Determining the Residence of Members of a Corporate Group' (2003) 51(4) Canadian Tax Journal 1567; Geoffrey Loomer, 'The Disjunction between Corporate Residence and Corporate Taxation: Is Improvement Possible?' (2015) 63(1) Canadian Tax Journal 91.

12 *Canada v Alta Energy Luxembourg SARL* 2021 SCC 49.

13 ITA (n 3) s 9(1).

character of income as business income or non-business/passive investment income determines the application of anti-deferral rules.

Income may be taxed differently depending on the status of the corporation. For policy reasons, corporations are treated differently depending on whether they are public corporations and, if they are private corporations, whether they are Canadian-controlled private corporations ('CCPCs'), and whether their income is from carrying on business (technically, an 'active business') or not. Private corporations offer opportunities for the selective and self-interested separation of income from its economic owners. The same effect occurs with public corporations, but their 'publicness' generally means that they cannot be easily used by their shareholders to accomplish ulterior, highly personal planning objectives.

#### 4.2.2.3 Corporate tax rates

The general federal corporate income tax rate is 15%,[14] which is also the rate for personal income tax in the lowest income bracket.[15] It applies to public corporations and the business income of private corporations. The rate is reduced to 9% for active business income up to CAD 500,000 per year earned by a CCPC or a group of associated CCPCs.[16]

Additional taxes are imposed on a private corporation's investment income[17] and personal service business income. In effect, investment income is taxed at the rate of 38.67%, which is higher than the top personal tax rate of 29%. A portion of the corporate tax (currently 38.33%) is refunded to the corporation

---

14 Due to fiscal federalism and the fact that both the federal and provincial-level governments can tax corporations, the federal rules on corporate tax rates are complex. Under s 123(1), the general corporate tax rate for federal purposes is 38% of taxable income. This rate is reduced by 10% of the taxable income of a corporation earned in a province (the 'provincial abatement') (s 124(1)). A further reduction of 13% is available as the general rate reduction percentage under s 123.4(2) for business income not subject to the 'small business deduction' tax treatment described below (see the section 123.4(1) definitions of 'general rate reduction percentage' and 'full-rate taxable income', paras (a) and (b)). The federal rate on eligible income is thus 15%.

15 Ibid s 117 for individuals.

16 Ibid s 125.

17 Investment income (other than inter-corporate dividends) of a CCPC does not benefit from the 13% general rate reduction under s 123.4(1) and is subject to an additional special tax of (10 and 2/3)% under s 123.3. Consequently, a CCPC's investment income is taxed at a federal rate of (38 and 2/3)% (38% – 10% + (10 and 2/3)%).

when it distributes the investment income as a dividend.[18] A private corporation's income from a personal service business (i.e., an incorporated employee) is subject to tax at 33%,[19] which matches the top marginal personal tax rate.

#### 4.2.2.4 Dividends and shareholders

After-tax corporate income distributed to shareholders in the form of dividends is taxable to the shareholders. In the case of corporate shareholders, however, the dividends are technically included when computing income but fully deducted when computing taxable income and are thus, in effect, tax free. Such tax-free treatment of inter-corporate dividends applies when the payer is either a resident corporation[20] or a non-resident corporation. In the latter case, however, the dividends must be paid out of the 'exempt surplus' of the foreign corporation.[21] Dividends are taxable only when they are received by individuals or non-residents.

Individuals receiving dividends from Canadian corporations must include the amount of dividends in computing their income.[22] Assuming that the dividends are paid out of corporate after-tax income, the ITA effectively allows an individual shareholder a tax credit for the amount of corporate tax 'borne' by the dividends. The mechanism for achieving this effect is complex, consisting of dividend gross-up rules and tax credit rules.[23] Two corporate tax rates are assumed and indicated by distinguishing dividends as 'eligible dividends' (dividends paid out of income taxed at the general corporate tax rate) and dividends other than eligible dividends (non-eligible dividends). Public corporations and CCPCs earning business income over the small business deduction limit (CAD 500,000) pay tax at the general rate and can pay eligible dividends to shareholders. Private corporations earning non-business income or business

---

18 Ibid s 129(1). This dividend refund mechanism is part of the integration system in respect of investment income of private corporations.

19 Ibid s 123.5.

20 Ibid ss 82 and 112(1).

21 Ibid s 113 and supporting rules in the Income Tax Regulations.

22 Ibid ss 12(1)(j), 82(1)(a) and 82(1)(a.1).

23 Underpinning the design of the gross-up and dividend tax credit systems are the concepts of 'corporations resident in Canada', 'taxable dividends', 'eligible dividends' and 'dividends other than eligible dividends' (non-eligible dividends). A corporation is resident in Canada by reason of incorporation under Canadian laws (federal or provincial) or having its central management and control in Canada. Section 89(1) defines 'taxable dividends' to mean all dividends except for dividends that are exempt from tax, such as capital dividends. Section 89(14) defines a dividend as an 'eligible dividend' if the corporation designates it as such when it is paid. Eligible dividends can be designated by public and private corporations.

income eligible for the lower rate of corporate tax can only pay non-eligible dividends. The dividend tax credit rate is higher for eligible dividends.

The dividend gross-up and credit mechanism was designed to achieve fiscal unity in taxing the income earned through a corporation at a level of total taxation, as if the income were earned directly by the individual without using the corporate form. This mechanism is based on assumed corporate taxes and does not trace whether the underlying income is actually taxed. It does not account for the value of tax deferral and is not available to non-resident individual shareholders.

#### 4.2.2.5 Corporate tax reporting obligations

Corporations are required to withhold and remit taxes from payments of wages and salaries made to their employees[24] and payments of interest, rent, royalties and dividends made to non-residents.[25] They are also required to file information returns regarding payments of employment income, interest, royalties and dividends.[26] Corporate employers must also deduct payroll taxes, contributions to the Canada Pension Plan and premiums for the employment insurance programme.

### 4.2.3 Underlying Principles

#### 4.2.3.1 The separate entity principle and its justifications

There are various theories or principles justifying the taxation of corporations.[27] For example, the aggregate theory of the corporation posits that the corporate income tax is an indirect way of taxing the shareholders and backstops progressive personal income tax. If income earned by corporations is not taxed, unless tax law imputes corporate income to individual shareholders, shareholder-level tax would be deferred indefinitely, as corporate law does not require the annual distribution of profits to shareholders. Such an outcome would render progressive income tax elective, violating the fundamental principles of equity and neutrality. Imputing income to each and every individual shareholder is administratively difficult, especially in the case of publicly held, multinational corporations. Taxing corporate income is thus desirable and convenient. The benefit theory justifies the corporate tax on the grounds of the benefits of incorporation (e.g., limited liability protection) and the business

---

[24] ITA (n 3) s 153.

[25] Ibid ss 212(1) and (2).

[26] Regulations, ss 200–237.

[27] Richard M Bird, 'Why Tax Corporations?' (2002) 56(5) Bulletin for International Taxation 194; Reuven S Avi-Yonah, 'Corporations, Society, and the State: A Defense of the Corporate Tax' (2004) 90(5) Virginia Law Review 1193.

environment supported by public expenditures. It views the tax as a price paid for public expenditures that benefit businesses. This is particularly relevant when the business is carried on by a foreign corporation. There is also a regulatory rationale for taxing corporations: corporate income tax is necessary to control the excessive accumulation of power in the hands of corporate management.[28]

Even though none of the theories or rationales, in themselves, are conclusive as to why corporations should be taxed as separate taxpayers, the reality is that not taxing corporations is hard to justify in a country governed by the rule of law and reliant on the income tax system as a main source of revenue.

#### 4.2.3.2 The fiscal unity principle

The Canadian corporate tax system contains many anti-avoidance rules. Most of the rules in the corporate tax regime are designed to neutralize the otherwise 'natural' tax-avoiding effect of the corporate form. 'Much of the Act, and the IWTA before it, has been effectively devoted to eliminating corporations as taxpayers – that is, erasing their autonomous fiscal significance.'[29] The desires for achieving tax equity and neutrality as well as redistributive justice through progressive taxation on the basis of ability to pay dictate the taxation of income of human persons, not the legal fictions that own the income on behalf of individuals. It reflects the notion of fiscal unity.

The fiscal unity principle is consistent with the aggregate theory mentioned above. It seeks to tax the income earned through a corporation at a level parallel to that of the individual shareholder, albeit with allowance for deferral for societal benefit reasons. The ITA reflects this principle through integration mechanisms, especially in regard to income earned through private corporations. There is a pervasive thread of 'putting Humpty Dumpty' back together again – in more prosaic terms, to overcome the separation of income from its owners, notably in the case of passive income.[30]

In essence, individuals are free to use corporations as their alter egos in commercial and investment arrangements, but they should not use these alter egos to reduce their tax liability. Since 1917, large swathes of the Act have been dedicated to overcoming, even ignoring, the legal separation of income from its owners without actually overturning the private law that has created the

---

28 Avi-Yonah (n 27) 1244–9.

29 Scott Wilkie, 'Three Spirits of Canadian Corporate Income Tax: The Relic, the Remnant, and the Reflection' in Jinyan Li, J Scott Wilkie and Larry Chapman (eds), *Income Tax at 100 Years: Essays and Reflections on the Income War Tax Act* (Canadian Tax Foundation 2017), 8:1–8:32 at 8:7.

30 Jinyan Li, Joanne Magee and J Scott Wilkie, *Principles of Canadian Income Tax Law* (10th edn, Thomson Reuters 2022) 443–9.

legal fictions of corporations that enable this separation. The ITA also accepts the 'fiscal' separateness of corporations when they exist primarily for commercial purposes, and this is typically the case with public corporations and private corporations carrying on business in Canada.

## 4.3 TAX DEFERRAL

### 4.3.1 'Natural' Consequence of the Separate Entity Principle

Because each corporation is a separate taxpayer, shareholder-level tax is deferred when corporate income is not immediately distributed to shareholders. There is no requirement for mandatory annual distributions under corporate law. The extent of such tax deferral is determined by the gap between corporate tax and personal tax and the length of deferral.

### 4.3.2 Business Income and Societal Benefits of Tax Deferral

As noted above, business income of corporations is taxed at the general rate of 15%, which corresponds to the personal tax rate for the lowest bracket.[31] As an added incentive, the ITA provides a special, lower CCPC tax rate of 9% for business income.[32] The gap between personal and corporate tax rates is thus 18% in general and 24% in the case of private corporations. Such preferential taxation of corporate income is a form of tax subsidy: the 'free use' of the deferred tax dollars helps the corporation to lower the cost of capital. Why?

The tax deferral is the way in which the ITA recognizes corporations as quintessential vehicles for carrying on business, and the limited liability principle as important in encouraging entrepreneurs to take risks and raise capital. The success of business corporations contributes to the success of the Canadian economy in terms of innovation, risk-taking and job creation.

Tax deferral is not limited to domestic business income. Foreign business income of a foreign subsidiary is, in effect, exempt from Canadian tax when the income is earned as well as when the income is distributed to a Canadian parent. This treatment makes sense under the theory of tax neutrality (capital export neutrality) and the assumption that the income is subject to corporate income tax comparable to the Canadian tax. In practice, such an assumption is misplaced when the income is not taxed at all or taxed at a level below the Canadian tax rate. If Canada implements Pillar Two rules and imposes a

---

[31] ITA (n 3) ss 123 and 117(2).

[32] Ibid s 125. This is known as the small business deduction. The current rate is 9%, applicable to taxable income up to CAD 500,000 per year.

global minimum tax on the Canadian parent under the IIR (income inclusion rule) in respect of low-taxed foreign business income earned by foreign subsidiaries, the benefit of tax deferral will be lost.[33]

### 4.3.3 Passive Income and Anti-Deferral Rules

When corporations are largely the alter egos of their legal owners, the ITA adopts various measures to remove the fiscal effect of using the corporate form to defer taxation. Private corporations and controlled foreign corporations must employ more than five full-time employees to qualify their investment business as active businesses.[34] Tax deferral is denied in the case of passive income.

In the case of domestic private corporations, the ITA contains several types of anti-deferral rules. For example, passive income and personal service business income of private corporations are taxed at a rate on a par with the top marginal personal income tax rate.[35] More importantly, refundable tax is imposed on corporate passive income and portfolio dividends. There is an elaborate mechanism for tracking the passive income through a 'refundable dividends tax on hand' (RDTOH) account in respect of eligible dividends and non-eligible dividends, refunding the tax upon distribution of dividends, tracking the RDTOH and tax refund through the chain of corporate holdings, and integrating personal income tax on the dividends and the corporate tax on the passive income.[36] Portfolio dividends received by a resident private corporation that are otherwise excluded from income (i.e., tax-free inter-corporate dividends) are subject to an additional, refundable tax, effectively erasing the relevance of the corporate status of the holding company.[37]

When passive or non-business income is earned through controlled foreign corporations (CFCs), the CFC rules impute the income to the Canadian resident shareholder for tax purposes. In effect, these rules look through the foreign corporation. The choice of taxing such imputed income as 'income from a share' as opposed to 'dividend' reinforces the fiscal unity idea. In other words,

---

33 See Jinyan Li, 'Introducing a Global Minimum Tax (Pillar Two) in Canada: Some Knowns and Unknowns' (2023) 71(1) Canadian Tax Journal 103.

34 ITA (n 3) ss 125(7) and 95(1).

35 Ibid s 123.3 (tax rate on passive income of private corporations is 33.67%) and s 117(2) (the top marginal rate for individuals is 33%).

36 Ibid s 89(1) (defining 'refundable dividend tax on hand'), s 129 (dividend tax refund), and ss 82 and 112 (dividend gross-up and dividend tax credit, forming the integration regime for resident individual shareholders).

37 Ibid s 186. This tax is refunded when the holding company distributes the income to individual shareholders (s 129).

these rules do not recognize the foreign corporation as the earner of the passive income and deem a distribution of such income as a dividend. Instead, they tax the income directly as if the corporation did not exist.[38]

## 4.4 TAX SHIFTING

### 4.4.1 Benefits of Tax Shifting

Tax shifting through the use of the corporate form can be achieved by having low-income family members subscribe to shares for nominal consideration or by acquiring a foreign residence. In the case of family-owned corporations, tax savings arise from the shifted income being taxed at a lower rate and enabling the family member to benefit from non-refundable tax credits. Because the tax unit is each individual or corporation and personal tax rates are progressive (currently ranging from 15% to 33%), splitting or shifting of income from high-income taxpayers to low-taxed related taxpayers results in tax savings for the economic unit. The corporate form is one of the common means to this end.

### 4.4.2 Family-Owned Corporations

Family-owned private corporations are convenient vehicles for shifting income from the person who operates the business of the corporation to passive family shareholders (e.g., spouse and/or children who hold preferred shares of the corporation). This is known as the 'sprinkling' strategy. For example, in *Neuman v R* (1998),[39] the wife of a taxpayer had made no contribution to the company other than her subscription to the shares on which the dividend was paid. The Supreme Court of Canada held that the dividends were taxable to the wife, not the taxpayer.[40] Iacobucci J of the Supreme Court of Canada stated: '[T]axpayers are entitled to arrange their affairs for the sole purpose of achieving a favourable position regarding taxation'; that, his Honour explained, included the use of 'corporate structures which exist for the sole purpose of avoiding tax'.[41]

The ITA provides for several anti-splitting rules.[42] The tax-on-split-income rule (TOSI)[43] is the most recent addition to the anti-income splitting rules:

---

38 Ibid s 91 (the Canadian CFC rule).

39 *Neuman v Minister of National Revenue* [1998] 1 SCR 770 (SCC) (*Neuman*).

40 Ibid.

41 Ibid [63].

42 Li, Magee and Wilkie (n 30) 419–36.

43 ITA (n 3) s 120.4.

the tax on split income in section 120.4. This tax eliminates the advantage of 'sprinkling' dividends among low-tax family members. Effective from 2018, the TOSI rule imposes a special tax at the top rate (currently 33%) on 'split income', which is defined to include dividends from private corporations (except dividends that represent a reasonable rate of return on the capital).[44]

### 4.4.3 Foreign Residence

A foreign-resident corporation is not taxable in Canada in respect of its business income, even if its shareholders are resident individuals. Acquiring foreign residency is easily achieved by having the corporation incorporated under foreign law and the central management and control located outside Canada. A resident corporation can also migrate to a foreign jurisdiction and cease to be a Canadian resident. Off-shoring residence means off-shoring the Canadian tax base.

### 4.4.4 Transfer Pricing

Through pricing transactions and dealings, related corporations can shift their profit and tax base out of Canada. Canada has been concerned with transfer pricing since the beginning of the tax system. Section 3(2) of the IWTA 1917, contained the modern-day arm's length principle:

> Where an incorporated company conducts its business, whether under agreement or otherwise, in such manner as either directly or indirectly to benefit its shareholders … by selling its product or the goods and commodities in which it deals at less than the fair price which might be obtained therefor, the Minister may, for the purposes of this Act, determine the amount which shall be deemed to be the income of such company for the year, and in determining such amount the Minister shall have regard to the fair price which, but for any agreement … might be or could have been obtained for such product, goods and commodities.

The rule relied on a 'fair price', which can be regarded as a fiction, to test the contractual price and be the basis for determining the corporate income. Such a hypothetical test is now entrenched in the transfer pricing rules in section 247 of the ITA. It basically requires a determination as to whether, if the parties had not been related, they would have transacted as they ostensibly did. If the tested transactions had comparable arm's length counterparts, then the price of

---

[44] Reasonable return is determined as follows: if the adult is age 18–24, it means a return based on the prescribed rate or an arm's length rate; and if the adult is age 25 or older, it means a reasonable return based on work performed, capital, risk and other relevant factors.

the counterparts would be used – this scenario is addressed by sections 247(2)(a) and (c). If the transactions would not have occurred at all between arm's length parties, such as transferring potentially valuable intangibles, a further hypothetical is required: what would be the comparable transaction that would have been entered into by non-related parties, and what would be the price of such a hypothetical transaction – a scenario addressed by sections 247(2)(b) and (d)? In Rosenbloom's words, the question asked by this test is 'whether, if you had a brother, he would like cheese'.[45]

The arm's length principle is difficult to apply when transactions involve unique intangibles or services and there is information asymmetry between taxpayers and tax administrations. As pointed out by the Courts in *Canada v Cameco Corp*,[46] the transfer pricing rules do not mean piercing the corporate veil for tax purposes or regarding special purpose corporations located in low-tax jurisdictions (in this case, Salesco) as shams. The Federal Court of Appeal observed:

> For subsection 247(2) of the Act, the heading is 'Transfer Pricing Adjustment'. These headings support an interpretation of subsection 247(2) of the Act that would result in an adjustment in the pricing of the relevant transactions, rather than an interpretation that would allow the Minister to pierce the corporate veil of CEL [Salesco] and reallocate all of its profits to Cameco.

---

45 Rosenbloom (n 1) 996 (footnote omitted).

46 *Canada v Cameco Corp*, 2020 FCA 112, affirming the decision of the Tax Court of Canada (2018 TCC 195) that rejected the Minister's assessment of the transfer pricing transactions. In this case, the taxpayer created a subsidiary in a low-tax jurisdiction (Salesco), which bought and sold uranium, including uranium produced by the taxpayer in Canada. Salesco had two employees and relied on the taxpayer for administrative services under a services contract. The Federal Court of Appeal found that section 247(2)(b) applies when no arm's length persons would have entered into the transactions in question, under any terms and conditions, and it did not apply in this case. The profits of Salesco arose from buying and selling uranium, not shifted from Canada. The FCA noted that the Crown's interpretation of the provision was overly broad, and if correct, would result in being applied any time a Canadian corporation wanted to carry on business in a foreign country through a foreign subsidiary. Further, the FCA held (at [60]) that the Crown's interpretation effectively ignored the separate existence of Salesco and the transfer pricing rule does not allow the Minister to pierce the corporate veil and reallocate profits between members of a corporate group.

### 4.4.5 Related-Party Debt

Related-party debt is 'a principal tool of the tax planner'.[47] It is more 'fictional' than transactions involving goods, services or even intangible property, as capital can be circled among related corporations at will, anytime, anywhere. More importantly, it is utterly nonsensical in an economic or fiscal sense. Again, Rosenbloom explains:

> There seems to be only one serious problem with related-party debt: *by most standards of economics, substance, or common sense, it is not debt.* That is, related-party debt is generally not compensation for money lent by one person to another. Rather, it is a transfer of funds from one incorporated pocket to another, usually for tax-reduction purposes. Only a tax professional, considering indebtedness between commonly controlled entities, would perceive a similarity to raising funds from unrelated parties.[48]

The tax effect is tremendous. Under section 20(1)(c) of the ITA, a person can deduct interest expenses in computing profits.[49] To be deductible, there must be a legal obligation to pay interest on borrowed money used for the purpose of earning income. It goes without saying that one cannot contract with oneself to lend money to oneself. However, because a corporation is a separate person, one can lend money to one's company. Also, related corporations can lend money to one another. The fantastical tax effect can be seen in the 'money in the circle' case – *TDL Group Co v R.*[50] The relevant 'transactions' are:

- Wendy's International Inc (Wendy's), a US resident and the ultimate parent corporation of the Wendy's group of corporations, lent CAD 234 million to a US subsidiary, Delcan Inc, at a rate of interest not to exceed 7%.
- The same day, Delcan Inc lent the full amount to TDL, the taxpayer in this case, at an interest rate of 7.125%.
- Also, on the same day, TDL used the full amount of the loan to purchase additional common shares in its wholly-owned US subsidiary, Tim Donut US Limited, Inc (Tim's US).
- The next day, Tim's US lent the monies received on account of TDL's share subscription to Wendy's on an interest-free basis, evidenced by a promissory note.

---

47 Rosenbloom (n 1) 997.

48 Ibid.

49 ITA (n 3) s 20(1)(c).

50 *TDL Group Co v R*, 2016 FCA 67 (allowing TDL to deduct the interest on the loan from Delcan Inc even though TDL already owns 100% of Tim's US).

The effect of the above transactions is to enable the taxpayer to deduct the interest expense, thereby reducing profits for Canadian tax purposes. The interest payments to Delcan are free from Canadian withholding tax.[51] Tim's US may never pay dividends to TDL as it would attract US withholding tax. Even if it did, the dividends would be exempt from Canadian tax.[52]

In *TDL*, the Tax Court of Canada ruled against the taxpayer, holding that the sole purpose of the borrowed funds was to facilitate an interest-free loan to the parent company while creating an interest deduction in Canada, therefore failing the income-earning purpose test. The Federal Court of Appeal overruled that decision. It found that the temporary use of the subscription proceeds by Tim's US did not detract from TDL's income-earning purpose – the acquisition of additional shares.[53]

The ITA contains several anti-avoidance rules, including thin capitalization and the recent excessive interest and financing expenses limitation (EIFEL) rules. These rules recognize the validity of each corporate form and prescribe tax treatment to reflect the fiscal outcome in the absence of the special relationship between the parties. The thin capitalization rules, in effect, treat excessive related-party debt as equity and deny the deduction of interest on excessive debt.[54] The EIFEL (known in other countries as EBITDA) rules restrict the deduction for interest and financing expenses of Canadian corporations to 30% of their earnings before interest, taxes, depreciation and amortization computed for tax purposes (or adjusted taxable income).

## 4.5 TAX EXPENDITURES

### 4.5.1 Corporate Form in Tax Expenditure Provisions

The corporate form is used in tax expenditure provisions of the ITA. Canada adopts a broad notion of tax expenditures in the annual reporting on tax expenditures.[55] Any departure from the benchmark system is a tax expenditure. The benchmark system is defined by including only the most fundamental aspects of the system.[56] Typical tax expenditures are tax exemptions, lower tax rates,

---

[51] Per Canada–US tax treaty, Article X.

[52] ITA (n 3) s 113(1).

[53] This decision is consistent with the Supreme Court of Canada decision in *Ludco Enterprises Ltd v Canada* [2001] 2 SCR 1082.

[54] ITA (n 3) ss 18(4)–(6).

[55] Department of Finance, Canada, *Report on Federal Tax Expenditures: Concepts, Estimates and Evaluations 2022* (2022).

[56] For example, the unit of taxation is the individual for personal income tax and the single corporation for corporate income tax. The tax base for residents is

deferral rules (timing preferences), tax credits, rebates or refunds. For the purposes of illustrating the role of corporate form, tax expenditures are discussed in two groups: tax subsidies that represent spending programmes implemented through tax law; and technical or structural preferences, such as timing preferences in the case of corporate reorganizations.

### 4.5.2 Tax Subsidies

Tax subsidies aim at promoting certain investment or business activities; each corporation is the unit for qualifying for the subsidies. For example, the Scientific Research and Experimental Development Investment Tax Credit (SR&ED) was first introduced in 1948 and is available to every corporation in respect of eligible expenditures.[57]

Another example is the Canada Emergency Wage Subsidy (CEWS)[58] introduced as a COVID-19 pandemic fiscal response measure. It aimed to help prevent job losses due to lockdown and social distancing, which were introduced to slow down the spread of the coronavirus, and to encourage employers to quickly rehire workers previously laid off as a result of COVID-19. Given the nature of the emergency, the many unknowns at the beginning of the pandemic in March 2020, and the need to provide relief as quickly as possible, the income tax system became the natural choice for delivering fiscal relief. Corporations became tools of convenience. The CEWS was designed by reference to each corporation's revenues (whether the amount dropped due to COVID-19) and eligible remuneration paid to employees, including furloughed employees, in respect of a specified period.[59]

---

worldwide income, while it is only Canadian-sourced income for non-residents. The benchmark corporate tax rate is the statutory general rate. As such, taxing corporate income at 15% is not classified as a tax expenditure, even though, from a fiscal unity perspective, the correct benchmark should be the personal tax rate for the individual shareholder.

[57] ITA (n 3) s 127; the SR&ED aims to encourage businesses to conduct such research to develop new or improve existing methods, processes, services and products. It targets eligible expenses, including salaries, sub-contractor fees and materials.

[58] Ibid ss 125.7 and 164.

[59] The CEWS was available to other types of employers as well, such as individuals, partnerships, trusts and charitable organizations. It came into effect on 15 March 2020 and lasted until 23 October 2021. The estimated cost of CEWS was CAD 70,940 million in 2020 and CAD 29,555 million in 2021, and the number of beneficiaries was 458,000. See Department of Finance, Canada (n 55) 84–5; Government of Canada, 'CEWS Claims – Detailed Data' (22 May 2022) <https://

As fiscal spending instruments to achieve social and economic policy objectives, the design of SR&ED and CEWS relies on treating each corporation as a separate entity and identifying the corporation's 'Canadian-ness' by reference to its Canadian residence. The effect of SR&ED and CEWS is difficult to determine. In the case of CEWS, the money was used by the recipient corporations to pay increased executive compensation, dividends to shareholders or share buybacks. For example, one report claims that 37 companies that received the CEWS spent a combined CAD 81.3 billion on dividends, CAD 41.1 billion on share buybacks, and CAD 51.1 billion on acquisitions in 2020 and 2021.[60] The fiscal value of the corporate form is also difficult to assess.

In cases where a tax subsidy is intended to incentivize the entrepreneurs and owners of private corporations, such as the small business deduction,[61] the ITA uses the corporate form as well as an 'economic reality' test to ensure that one entrepreneur is entitled to the subsidy regardless of the number of corporate forms used in operating the business. Technically, associated corporations are required to share the tax subsidy (the 'associated corporations rule').[62] In other words, because small businesses are presumed to have difficulties in raising capital and are important in generating jobs and growing the Canadian economy, the ITA seeks to ensure that it is the business, not the corporate entity, that deserves the tax subsidy.

### 4.5.3 Tax-Free Reorganizations

The corporate form is malleable and mutable. It is different from a natural person. Rosenbloom describes the implications of this as follows:

> The corporation can be brought quickly into life and then transformed into a different corporation, loaded with features to support economic substance, or merged into other corporations by filing appropriate documents with appropriate authorities. … In the modern world, it can migrate to countries … facing no immigration

www.canada.ca/en/revenue-agency/services/wage-rent-subsidies/cews-statistics/cews-detailed-data.html>.

[60] DT Cochrane, *Public Funds for Private Gains: Canada's Most Profitable Corporations Received Pandemic Subsidies While Avoiding Billions in Taxes* (Canadians for Tax Fairness, February 2023) <https://www.taxfairness.ca/sites/default/files/2023-02/cews-final-2023-02-09.pdf>; Financial Post Staff, 'Canadian Companies that Received CEWS and Kept Paying a Dividend' *Financial Post* (7 December 2020) <https://financialpost.com/investing/canadian-companies-that-received-cews-and-kept-paying-a-dividend> accessed 20 August 2024.

[61] ITA (n 3) s 125.

[62] Department of Finance, Canada (n 55) 259.

issues, with fiscal authorities in the new motherland welcoming the corporate citizen without extensive inquiries into its lineage, substance, or purpose.[63]

Whenever a corporate person is created, merged, divided or terminated, it involves legal transfers of assets, and each transfer can give rise to a taxable event, resulting in the recognition of paper gains.

The ITA contains several rollover rules to allow the deferral of recognition of capital gains for tax purposes.[64] Under these rules, transfers of assets to a taxable Canadian corporation for consideration that includes at least one share of the corporation may be made on a tax-deferred basis. Shareholders and the corporation itself are also permitted tax deferrals under corporate reorganization rules applicable to amalgamations, windings up and divisive reorganizations. The rationale is that the transactions are purely paper transactions in that the exchanges represent merely changes in form and not in substance. The substance is unchanged because of the continuity in ownership or business activity.[65] These rules are also justified as measures 'to support business activity'.[66]

## 4.6 LIMITING THE TAX EFFECT OF THE CORPORATE FORM THROUGH ANTI-AVOIDANCE RULES

### 4.6.1 Specific Anti-Avoidance Rules

The ITA provides for specific anti-avoidance rules (SAARs) to limit the fiscal effect of the corporate form. These include anti-deferral rules (see section 4.3.3 above), anti-shifting rules (see section 4.4.2), the EIFEL rules (see section 4.4.5) and the associated corporations rule (see section 4.5.3). These rules generally identify the use of the corporate form in a specific situation and remove the tax benefit of such use when the fiscal outcome was not contemplated by the legislature.

---

63 Rosenbloom (n 1) 991.

64 ITA (n 3) ss 55, 85, 86, 87 and 88.

65 Stephen E Shay, 'Legal Fictions, Elections and Tax Law Boundaries' in Georg Kofler, Ruth Mason and Alexander Rust (eds), *Thinker, Teacher, Traveler: Reimagining International Tax, Essays in Honor of H. David Rosenbloom* (IBFD Publications 2021) 513, 520. (The basic idea is that under certain conditions of continuing ownership and business activity these entities and their shareholders may exchange assets of the entity or their stock for stock of another corporation without recognizing gain or loss.) For further information, see Yariv Brauner, 'A Good Old Habit, or Just an Old One? Preferential Tax Treatment for Reorganizations' (2004) (1) Brigham Young University Law Review 1.

66 Department of Finance, Canada (n 55) 128.

### 4.6.2 The General Anti-Avoidance Rule

The general anti-avoidance rule (GAAR) in section 245 of the ITA was enacted in 1987 and amended in 2024. The GAAR provision states that it:

> (a) applies to deny the tax benefit of avoidance transactions that result directly or indirectly either in a misuse of provisions of the Act … or an abuse having regard to those provisions read as a whole, while not preventing taxpayers from obtaining tax benefits contemplated by Parliament; and
> (b) strikes a balance between
>
> (i) the Government of Canada's responsibility to protect the tax base and the fairness of the tax system, and
> (ii) taxpayers' need for certainty in planning their affairs.[67]

Through the use of the concepts of 'misuse' and 'abuse', the GAAR provision requires a purposive analysis of the ITA provisions and the taxpayers' transactions and arrangements, including the use of the corporate form. If the corporate form is used primarily for tax purposes, the resulting tax benefit can be denied.

The protean nature of corporations enables taxpayers to use the corporate form to take advantage of the legislative ambiguities and gaps inherent in taxing statutes. To the extent that the use of the corporate form is considered offensive from a policy perspective and not addressed by any specific anti-avoidance rule, the GAAR functions as the last weapon against the tax-induced use of the corporate form.[68] Through the GAAR, Parliament reiterates the basic fact that income tax law is about reality, even though it is a matrix of organizational and transactional fictions. Lacking significant economic substance in the corporate form (and other legal arrangements) may be presumed to be abusive and subject to the GAAR.

However, the application of the GAAR hinges on the intent or purpose of Parliament in enacting the pertinent provisions relied upon to obtain the tax benefit. Of course, legislative purpose and intent are also legal fictions.[69] The specific fate of the corporate form or corporate law fiction is uncertain under the GAAR because the application of the fiction of legislative purpose or intent is unclear.

---

67 ITA (n 3) s 245(0.1).

68 Ibid s 245.

69 See John Prebble, 'Fictions of Income Tax' (2011) Victoria University of Wellington Legal Research Paper 29/2011, <https://ssrn.com/abstract=1604978>; Andrew Burrows, *Thinking about Statutes: Interpretation, Interaction, Improvement* (Hamlyn Lectures) (Cambridge University Press 2018) 38.

### 4.6.3 The Global Minimum Tax

Canada has introduced a Global Minimum Tax (GMT) that is based on the OECD Pillar Two Model Rules.[70] The GMT is governed by a different statute but is interlinked with the ITA in both design and implementation in many respects. It functions as a backup tax to prevent large multinational enterprises (MNEs) from shifting profits to lower-taxed foreign jurisdictions.

The GMT aims to create a global floor (15% effective tax rate) for taxing large MNEs' profit, regardless of where the profit is earned. It deals with the problem of race-to-the-bottom tax competition among countries. In terms of technical design, the corporate form is relevant as an accounting unit and tax-paying unit. More specifically, the amount of GMT payable in Canada by the Canadian parent of foreign low-taxed entities is computed by reference to the amount of top-up tax of each foreign low-taxed entity. However, for the purposes of determining if an MNE group is subject to the GMT and whether the effective tax rate in a country is below 15%, it is the corporate group that matters.

Does the GMT point to a future of the corporate form as a convenient accounting unit as opposed to the basis for determining tax liability on corporate income?

## 4.7 THE FUTURE OF THE CORPORATE FORM IN INCOME TAXATION

'It is tough to make predictions, especially about the future.'[71] The future of the corporate form in income tax law may be gleaned from the past and present.

Since the inception of the Canadian income tax system, the IWTA 1917 anticipated and addressed the use of the corporate form to deflect or defer the tax otherwise payable by individual shareholders[72] and the use of contractual arrangements between related corporations to manipulate prices for tax

---

70 Canada's Global Minimum Tax Act, which received Royal Assent on 20 June 2024, sets out the GMT rules and applicable reporting and filing requirements. It is based on the OECD's Global Anti-Base Erosion (GloBE) (or Pillar Two) model rules. However, this Act does not contain the model under-taxed profit rules (UTPR).

71 This is attributed to Yogi Berra.

72 IWTA (n 4) s 3(4) in effect applied progressive rates of taxation to undistributed corporate profits unless the Minister found that the accumulation was not for the purpose of evading tax or in excess of the reasonable requirements of the business. For further information, see Wilkie (n 29).

purposes.[73] Section 3(4) of the IWTA dealt with the fiscal effect of corporate personality – deferring individual-level taxation on income earned through a corporation by not distributing corporate profits. In effect, it applied progressive tax rates to undistributed corporate profits unless the Minister found that the accumulation was not for the purpose of evading tax or in excess of the reasonable requirements of the business. In other words, the IWTA regarded the corporation and individual shareholder as a fiscal unit in determining the tax in respect of the income. This is reflected in the ITA's persistent concern with surplus stripping and tax deferral. These concerns are centred around private corporations, and they are present in today's ITA.

At present, the corporate form is respected by tax law when it is used to earn active business income and when the corporation is a public corporation. Such respect for the corporate form can be justified on economic grounds – a significant portion of the Canadian economy is conducted by corporations, and the government can regulate the economy through regulating corporate activities.

Large MNEs have been singled out in recent tax reforms, including EIFEL rules and the GMT, because they present unique tax policy challenges. They earn excessive amounts of profit from everywhere and nowhere, which defies the entity-based taxation by reference to residence and source of income. These tax reforms generally treat members of the firm as parts of an economic unit or corporate family as opposed to independent entities or orphans.

In the near future, it is reasonable to predict that the ITA will continue to recognize the existence of private corporations in regarding passive income but downplay the fiscal effect of the corporate form in order to implement progressive income taxation. The respect for the corporate form in regard to active business income will continue in general but decline or disappear in the case of large MNEs. To paraphrase Rosenbloom, a tax world in which legal fictions are abandoned altogether is probably not possible, but there is no good reason to employ them except when they are truly necessary.[74]

## ACKNOWLEDGEMENTS

The research topic was inspired by insights from research for a bigger project designed to study the lessons to be learnt from fiscal responses during the COVID-19 pandemic. The author acknowledges funding received from

[73] IWTA (n 4) s 3(2). It applies to cases where a company 'conducts its business, whether under agreement or otherwise, in such manner as either directly or indirectly to benefit its shareholders … by selling its product … at less than the fair price which might be obtained therefor'. This rule has evolved into the present transfer pricing rules.

[74] Rosenbloom (n 1) 996.

the Social Sciences and Humanities Research Council, Canada. The author recognizes the assistance of Shelley Zhang, a JD/MBA student, and Luke Chao, a JD student, at York University. She thanks J Scott Wilkie for comments on an earlier draft and participants at a symposium, 'Taxing Income and Consumption: Past, Present and Future', 11–13 April 2023, Coimbra, Portugal.

# 5. Twenty years since GST reform in Australia: a critical assessment

**Binh Tran-Nam and Mahmoud Abdellatif**

## 5.1 INTRODUCTION

The Goods and Services Tax (GST) was introduced in Australia with effect from 1 July 2000. After more than 20 years, many transitional issues have been settled and there now exists a considerable body of empirical data that is readily available for reflecting upon the performance of Australia's GST. The principal aim of this chapter is therefore to provide a critical and comprehensive assessment review of the GST-based tax reform in Australia.[1] The assessment is more comprehensive than similar past exercises[2] in two respects. First, it goes beyond the traditional tax policy principles in considering other dimensions of tax policymaking such as political and administrative aspects of the GST. Secondly, as explained below, it adopts various approaches for evaluating the success or otherwise of the GST.

For convenience, the terms 'GST reform' and 'GST-based reform' are used interchangeably in this chapter. The chapter is not concerned with some elements of the GST package such as the Luxury Car Tax, the Wine Equalisation Tax and changes to tobacco excise. However, some associated policy measures (such as the distribution of GST revenue to State governments) will be considered.

[1] Note that the term 'reform' is used throughout this chapter merely for convenience, as the case for GST as an indirect tax improvement has not yet been established.

[2] See, for example, Binh Tran-Nam, 'The Goods and Services Tax (GST): The Public Value of a Contested Reform' in Joannah Luetjens, Michael Mintrom and Paul 't Hart (eds), *Successful Public Policy: Lessons from Australia and New Zealand* (ANU Press 2019); Denis McCarthy, 'Twenty Years Later: Australia's GST Design, Digitisation and Disruption – Old and New Challenges' (2020) 18(1) eJournal of Tax Research 168.

Before proceeding further, it is helpful to note that there are different ways to evaluate the GST reform. The first (and traditional) approach employs the tax policy design principles of equity, efficiency, simplicity, sustainability and policy consistency.[3] Strictly speaking, such assessment should compare GST against the taxes that it has replaced, e.g., the complexity of GST vs the complexity of the Wholesale Sales Tax (WST) and a number of indirect State taxes, rather than the complexity of the GST in its own right. The second approach is to examine the impact of the GST on two fundamental characteristics of any modern tax system, namely, tax level and tax mix in the context of stated government policy objectives, e.g., to reduce the reliance on direct taxation. The third approach is to compare the GST in Australia with value-added taxes (VATs) in member countries of the Organisation for Economic Co-operation and Development (OECD). The present chapter will combine these three approaches for assessing the GST reform in Australia.

The remainder of the chapter is organized as follows. Section 5.2 provides a succinct historical review of the GST reform in Australia. The review demonstrates that the GST reform was a long, unpredictable process, fraught with political obstacles. Section 5.3 assesses the GST from public policy and implementation perspectives. It is argued that the GST reform can be clearly considered a success as a public policy measure and in terms of its implementation. Section 5.4 examines the revenue impact of the GST on Australia's tax level and tax mix. It is shown that the GST reform is revenue reducing. Somewhat surprisingly, the GST reform has not reduced the reliance on direct taxation as intended by the then Howard government. Further, because of its various exemptions, the revenue from the GST has steadily fallen as a percentage of gross domestic product (GDP), causing some doubts as to the sustainability of the GST in its current form. Section 5.5 evaluates the GST under the traditional good tax policy principles of equity, efficiency and simplicity. This assessment produces a low scorecard for the GST on all three principles of tax policy. Section 5.6 considers future GST reform in Australia. It is suggested that while revenue-expanding GST reform in Australia is overdue, the current political and socio-economic environment may not be conducive to such reforms. Section 5.7 concludes.

## 5.2 HISTORICAL REVIEW OF THE AUSTRALIAN GST

Relative to other comparable countries such as Canada, New Zealand and the United Kingdom (UK), Australia is a newcomer to the broad-based

---

[3] Australia's Future Tax System Review Panel (Ken Henry, chair), *Australia's Future Tax System: Report to the Treasurer* (2009) pt 1, 18 (Henry Review).

consumption tax (BBCT).[4] The late start to Australia's GST arises from its very long gestation period, spanning three decades from initial policy conception (1970) to final adoption (2000). Since the evolution of the GST debate has been well discussed in the literature,[5] it is sufficient to present a brief discussion here. It seems helpful to start with some context for the GST debate.

The WST, Australia's first general consumption tax at any governmental level, was introduced in 1930 to reduce large budget deficits arising from the onset of the Great Depression. It was a single-stage consumption tax levied on a wide range of non-essential goods, initially at the uniform rate of 2.5%. Over time, the WST gradually grew into an unwieldy tax with a narrow base, a multiple rate structure and a cascading effect upon production. By 1995, there were seven different rates (counting the zero rate which applied to excluded items), while the share of private consumption subject to the WST fell to only 22%.[6] The pressure for indirect taxation reform in Australia had thus been ongoing.

Table 5.1 summarizes some of the milestones in the GST debate in Australia.

The history of the GST debate in Australia was full of trials, failures, pragmatism and political opportunism coupled with electoral unpredictability. Two illustrative examples suffice. First, throughout 1992, the then Prime Minister Paul Keating successfully mounted a campaign against the *Fightback!* GST proposal despite the fact that the Federal Treasury under his leadership had proposed a BBCT at the National Tax Summit seven years earlier. Secondly, after the 1993 debacle, subsequent Opposition Leader John Howard ruled out a GST as part of the Coalition's policy[7] despite his earlier personal commitment to a BBCT.[8] However, when his approval rating as preferred Prime Minister

---

[4] VAT was first implemented in France in 1954. Subsequently, over 50 years ago, it was introduced in the UK in 1973. The modern model of the GST with a broad base and single rate (with which Australians are familiar) was introduced in New Zealand with effect from 1986. Canada implemented its GST in 1991.

[5] See, for example, John Harrison and Marilyn Stretton, *The GST Debate* (Department of the Parliamentary Library 1999); Richard Eccleston, *Taxing Reforms: The Politics of the Consumption Tax in Japan, the United States, Canada and Australia* (Edward Elgar Publishing 2007); Tran-Nam (n 2).

[6] Sam Reinhardt and Lee Steel, 'A Brief History of Australia's Tax System' (2006) (Winter) Economic Roundup 1, 20.

[7] Howard declared: 'There's no way the GST will be part of our policy. It's dead. Never ever. It's dead'; see Michelle Grattan, 'Howard Bans GST "Forever"' *The Age* (3 May 1995) 5.

[8] For example, Howard wrote in 1984: 'I have long believed that the single most important reform which is needed to the Australian taxation system is a broadening of the taxation base towards a greater reliance on general consumption taxes with a corresponding reduction in our current over-reliance on personal

*Table 5.1* *Milestones in the GST debate in Australia*

| Year | Proposer | Proposal/Recommendation | Outcome |
|---|---|---|---|
| 1970 | Leslie Bury, Federal Treasurer (Coalition)[a] | An early advocate of BBCT | No coherent tax reform statement |
| 1975 | Asprey Report[b] | Value added tax (VAT) or another BBCT | Ignored by the Whitlam and Fraser governments |
| 1981 | John Howard, Federal Treasurer (Coalition)[c] | Cabinet proposal for a BBCT | Rejected by the Coalition Cabinet |
| 1985 | Paul Keating, Federal Treasurer (ALP)[d] | Draft White Paper's Option C: a 12.5% broad-based Retail Sales Tax | Rejected at the National Tax Summit |
| 1991–1992 | John Hewson, Opposition Leader (Liberal Party)[e] | *Fightback!* package: a 15% GST | Coalition's loss of 1993 'unloseable' Federal election |
| 1998 | Howard government (Coalition)[f] | A New Tax System (ANTS): a 10% GST | Narrow electoral victory on the platform of a GST reform |

| Year | Proposer | Proposal/Recommendation | Outcome |
|---|---|---|---|
| 1999–2000 | Howard government, A New Tax System (Goods and Services Tax) Act 1999 passed (after compromises with the Australian Democrats party on GST exemptions for many items such as fresh food, education and health) | A 10% GST with a narrower base than that in the original ANTS | GST commenced on 1 July 2000 |
| 2001 | Kim Beazley, ALP Opposition Leader | Limited GST rollback[g] | ALP's election loss effectively ended its opposition to the GST |

*Notes:* A table showing the key milestones in the Australian GST debate over the years 1970 to 2001, including the proposer of the reform, the proposal/recommendation and the outcome. [a] John Hawkins, 'Leslie Bury – from Treasury to Treasurer' (2012) (3) Economic Roundup 113, 121; [b] Taxation Review Committee (Justice Kenneth W Asprey, chair), *Full Report* (1975) 515; [c] Harrison and Stretton (n 5); [d] Australian Treasury, *Reform of the Australian Tax System, Draft White Paper* (1985); [e] Liberal Party of Australia, *Fightback! Taxation and Expenditure Reform for Jobs and Growth* (Liberal Party of Australia 1991); Liberal Party of Australia, *Fightback! Fairness and Jobs* (Liberal Party of Australia 1992); [f] Australian Treasury, *Tax Reform: Not a New Tax, a New Tax System – The Howard Government's Plan for a New Tax System* (1998); [g] David Clune, 'Back to the Future? The November 2001 Federal Election' (2002) 17(1) Australasian Parliamentary Review 3, 8.

fell to 20% in 1997,[9] and under pressure from many quarters, especially senior members of the business community,[10] Howard was pragmatic enough to decisively reverse his 1995 declaration and proceed with GST-based reform.

The change in Australian electoral attitude from 1993 to 1998 was also remarkable. This was attributable to an array of factors, including:

- Keating's unsuccessful indirect tax policy after 1993;[11]
- a change in attitude of the social welfare sector;[12]
- the High Court's decision in the *Ha v New South Wales and Walter Hammond v New South Wales* (1997) 189 CLR 465 case against the States, which enunciated a broad scope of the term 'duties of excise' prohibited to the States under s 90 of the Constitution and thus invalidated State business franchise fees, which were important to State revenue at that time;[13]
- an innovative link between GST reform and Commonwealth–State financial relations reform (at least in practical terms);[14]
- a comprehensive compensation package for the perceived 'losers' from the introduction of GST;[15]

---

taxation as a source of revenue'; see John Howard, 'Taxation Reform' (1984) 1(1) Australian Tax Forum 8, 12.

[9] Tracey Aubin, *Peter Costello: A Biography, The Full and Unauthorised Story of the Man Who Wants to Be PM* (Harper Collins 1999) 216.

[10] Eccleston (n 5) 79.

[11] Ibid 78.

[12] Ibid.

[13] Gareth Griffith, 'The Future of State Revenue: The High Court Decision in Ha and Hammond' (1997) NSW Parliamentary Library Briefing Paper No 16/97.

[14] All GST revenue is distributed to the States, thus lessening the enduring vertical fiscal imbalance at the State level.

[15] There was a one-off 4% increase in aged and service pensions under the new system (see Australian Treasury, *Tax Reform: Not a New Tax, a New Tax System – The Howard Government's Plan for a New Tax System* (1998) 18 (*Tax Reform: Not a New Tax, a New Tax System*) (this document sets out the details of the A New Tax System (ANTS) package) and the A New Tax System (Compensation Measures Legislation Amendment) Act 1999), whereas the one-off increase in the rate of inflation due to the GST was estimated to be about 2.8% across Australia; see Abbas Valadkhani and Allan P Layton, 'Quantifying the Effect of the GST on Inflation in Australia's Capital Cities: An Intervention Analysis' (2004) 37(2) Australian Economic Review 125, 125.

- promised income tax reductions (which were subsequently implemented by the Coalition Government in 2000–2001, 2004–2005, 2005–2006, 2006–2007 and 2007–2008);[16] and
- Howard's personal conviction, pragmatism and willingness to negotiate (although, as discussed later, the compromises he made have caused a fundamental weakness in the GST as introduced).

## 5.3 GST FROM PUBLIC POLICY AND IMPLEMENTATION PERSPECTIVES

This section considers two issues: the success of GST-based reform as a public policy measure, and the Australian experience in implementing its GST.

### 5.3.1 Public Policy Perspective

The introduction of the GST in Australia can be considered a public policy success from political, programmatic and process perspectives, each of which will be briefly considered in turn below.[17]

First, in political terms, the Australian GST convincingly passed the test of public policy legitimacy.[18] The 1998 re-election of the Howard government on the platform of GST-based tax reform was unprecedented in Australian Federal history[19] and gave the Coalition government a historic mandate for indirect taxation reform. Unlike several other new taxes in recent times,[20] the GST is also enduring and has become an established major tax and an integral part of the political landscape in Australia. Nevertheless, the legitimacy of the GST as a Commonwealth tax was undermined by the Australian Treasury's

---

16 Tax reductions included both bracket widening (for personal income tax) and rate cuts. For company tax, the rate decreased from 34% to 30% in 2000–2001 and has stayed at that level since, apart from a recent further phased reduction in the rate for small enterprises from the 2017–18 year, which has resulted in a 25% rate applying from the 2021–22 year.

17 The discussion in this section draws heavily from Tran-Nam (n 2).

18 This contrasts with the Canadian experience, in which the introduction of its GST lacked policy transparency and political legitimacy.

19 The Howard government's electoral victory was nevertheless a narrow one. It suffered a swing of 4.61% against it and achieved a two-party preferred vote of only 49.02%, compared with the ALP's 50.98%; see Scott Bennett, Andrew Kopras and Gerard Newman, 'Federal Elections 1998' (1999) Parliamentary Library Research Paper No 9 1998–99.

20 Examples of recent short-lived tax reforms in Australia include the Minerals Resource Rent Tax introduced in 2012 and repealed in 2014, and the 'carbon tax' introduced in 2011 and also repealed in 2014.

(unsuccessful) short-lived attempt to portray the GST as a State tax in the early 2000s.

Secondly, in programmatic terms, it can be argued that there is a well-developed and empirically feasible public value proposition that underpins the GST-based reform.[21] The reform sought to replace the outdated, inefficient and distorted system of State and Federal indirect taxes with a new and better tax system. To achieve that end, the means was a BBCT, preferably with a single standard rate. Among the menu of feasible alternatives, the GST was chosen as an appropriate policy instrument. Further, the GST is flexible enough to enable incremental adjustments to address changing macroeconomic conditions. However, as discussed in section 5.6, there are certain legal and political constraints to such changes, thus reducing the flexibility of the GST as a tax policy instrument.

Thirdly, in process terms, the GST-based reform demonstrated thoughtful and effective tax design and policymaking practices. The reform was formulated on the basis of rational, evidence-based decision-making. Its process also exhibited the iterative nature of public policy under which policymakers learn from the experience of previous trials and failures. The choice of a broad-based, relatively low, single-rate GST (especially as proposed in the original ANTS package) not only complemented the Keating-era income tax reforms (broadening the base and lowering the rate) but also brought Australia into line with countries such as New Zealand. The associated measures of income tax cuts and a compensation package made the GST-based reform attractive to voters, while the unanticipated intergovernmental financial agreement received strong support from State governments. The Howard government's compromises with the Australian Democrats Party prevented a period of policy paralysis, but the resulting narrowing of the GST base would have adverse, long-term consequences as discussed in the next section.

### 5.3.2 Implementation

As a late follower of the GST, Australia experienced a relatively smooth implementation of the GST. Several independent factors helped ease the transition to the new tax system. They are succinctly elaborated below.

#### 5.3.2.1 Macroeconomic environment

The Australian economy was performing strongly in the years leading up to the introduction of the GST in 2000. This contrasts with the introduction of the Canadian GST, which was hampered by poor timing as the Canadian economy

[21] Tran-Nam (n 2) 237.

was in recession in 1991. While Australia experienced a sharp slowdown in the second half of 2000, this was only temporary, and the economic growth rate recovered well in 2001–2002.[22] It seems reasonable to attribute Australia's reduced growth rate in the second half of 2000 to the lower business profitability that arose from the transitional adjustments to the GST. Inflationary pressure from the introduction of the GST in Australia was contained within one year. Consumer price index (CPI)-based annual inflation rose from 3.1% in 1999–2000 to 6.0% in 2000–2001, before falling back to the pre-GST level of 2.8% in 2001–2002.[23]

#### 5.3.2.2 Australian government's preparedness

Unlike the experiences of other countries, the Australian government sectors, including both the Federal and State governments, had about two years from the announcement of ANTS in 1998 to the commencement of the GST in 2000 to prepare for its implementation. More importantly, the Howard government had the advantage of inheriting the required administrative and technical details to implement the GST from John Hewson's revised 1992 *Fightback!* package. These details are contained in the unpublished report of the then GST Planning and Co-ordination Office.[24]

#### 5.3.2.3 GST payers' preparedness

Unlike the WST, the GST is broad based and involves a very large number of GST payers. This includes not only ordinary businesses but also non-profit organizations, government business enterprises and even government entities. However, as mentioned above, the two-year time lag between ANTS announcement and GST commencement provided GST payers in Australia with sufficient time to learn about the GST and its start-up and recurrent requirements. Naturally, these preparations were costly. There exists a very wide range of estimates of aggregate GST start-up compliance costs.[25] The lowest estimate

---

[22] Time series data on real GDP provided by the Australian Bureau of Statistics (ABS) show the annual growth rate in Australia fell from 3.7% in 1999–2000 to 1.9% in 2000–2001 (a relative decline of almost half), rising to 4.5% in 2001–2002: see ABS, *National Income, Expenditure and Product, Cat 5206.0* (June 2018) Table 1: Key National Accounts Aggregates.

[23] ABS, Consumer Price Index, Australia, March Quarter 2024 (April 2024) Tables 1 and 2: CPI: All Groups, Index Numbers and Percentage Changes.

[24] This unpublished report can be obtained from Michael Evans, who was the Technical Director in charge of the GST Planning and Co-ordination Office in 1992–93.

[25] For a summary of estimates, refer to Binh Tran-Nam and John Glover, 'Estimating the Transitional Compliance Costs of the GST in Australia: A Case

at AUD 2.2 billion (at 2000 prices) was provided by the Australian Treasury. Other estimates varied considerably, ranging from AUD 2.6 billion to AUD 24 billion, although the lower-end estimates were more credible.[26] The first author of this chapter's own estimate of AUD 2.8 billion (at 2000 prices) indicated that implementation costs incurred by businesses represented more than 10% of the initial estimate of GST revenue in 2000–2001.

#### 5.3.2.4 The Australian Taxation Office's role

The Australian Taxation Office (ATO) efficiently handled the administration of the introduction of the GST. Key elements of the ATO's responses included the following:

- resources: adequate additional resources were offered to the ATO for coping with the administrative challenges of introducing the new tax system from 1998 to 2001;[27]
- organizational structure: a new division called GST was established within the ATO (later renamed Indirect Tax and now absorbed into the Client and Engagement Group);
- the 'education first, enforcement later' approach: an 'extensive awareness, education and compliance programme' for GST implementation was conducted by the ATO over two years.[28] The aggregate GST start-up administration costs were estimated to be about AUD 405 million (at 2000 prices);[29]

Study Approach' (2002) 17(4) Australian Tax Forum 499, 507.

[26] Binh Tran-Nam, 'The Implementation Costs of the GST in Australia: Concepts, Preliminary Estimates and Implications' (2000) 3(5) Journal of Australian Taxation 331, 338–40 ('The Implementation Costs of the GST').

[27] Michael D'Ascenzo, 'Administration and Tax Reform' (2005) 1(2) Journal of the Australasian Tax Teachers Association 25.

[28] Ibid 31–2; Australian Treasury, 'Preliminary Assessment of the Impact of *The New Tax System*' (2003) (Autumn) Economic Roundup 1, 29 ('Preliminary Assessment').

[29] This total consisted of AUD 200 million (the ATO's own estimate of its transitional GST administration costs), AUD 180 million in subsidies to businesses, and AUD 25 million to the Australian Competition and Consumer Commission for monitoring GST-related price rises; see Binh Tran-Nam, 'Assessing the Tax Simplification Impact of Tax Reform: Research Methodology and Empirical Evidence from Australia' (2004) 97 Proceedings of the Annual Conference on Taxation and Minutes of the Annual Meeting of the National Tax Association 376, 381 ('Assessing the Tax Simplification Impact of Tax Reform').

- strategic targeting: the ATO targeted the education and charitable sectors that would be brought into the tax system for the first time and small businesses with less-sophisticated accounting systems;
- government subsidies administered by the GST Start-Up Assistance Office within the Treasury: the Federal government allocated AUD 500 million 'to assist small and medium enterprises (SMEs), community organizations and education bodies prepare for the GST'.[30]

In view of the above discussion, the Australian GST can be considered a success from public policy and implementation perspectives. Perhaps the most illustrative example is the number of businesses that registered for GST, which exceeded expectations. It was estimated that 1.4 million businesses would register for GST by 1 July 2000, with an additional 200,000 registrants expected the following year. However, over 2.2 million businesses ultimately registered for GST.[31]

## 5.4 THE REVENUE IMPACT OF THE GST

This section examines the impact of the GST on the tax level (tax-to-GDP ratio) and tax mix in Australia. In addition, it also discusses a proposed key benefit for introducing the GST, namely, revenue sustainability. The discussion includes a brief review of the evidence concerning the GST gap.

### 5.4.1 Tax Level

The ANTS document articulated some principles of the GST-based tax reform as being 'lower tax burden'[32] or 'no increase in the overall tax burden'.[33] This can be verified by looking at Australia's tax levels from 2000 (when GST was introduced) to 2008 (after the Coalition government lost office in November 2007, following the announcement of the personal income tax cut for 2008–2009 and later years[34]). Strictly speaking, tax level depends on both tax policy and general macroeconomic conditions. Given that Australian

---

30 Australian Treasury, 'Preliminary Assessment' (n 28) 28.

31 ATO, *Compliance Program 2002–03* (2002) 22.

32 Australian Treasury, *Tax Reform: Not a New Tax, a New Tax System* (n 15) iii.

33 Ibid 14.

34 Hon Peter Costello (Treasurer), 'Personal Income Tax Reform' (Media Release, 15 October 2007) <https://ministers.treasury.gov.au/ministers/peter-costello-1996/media-releases/personal-income-tax-reform> accessed 3 April 2023.

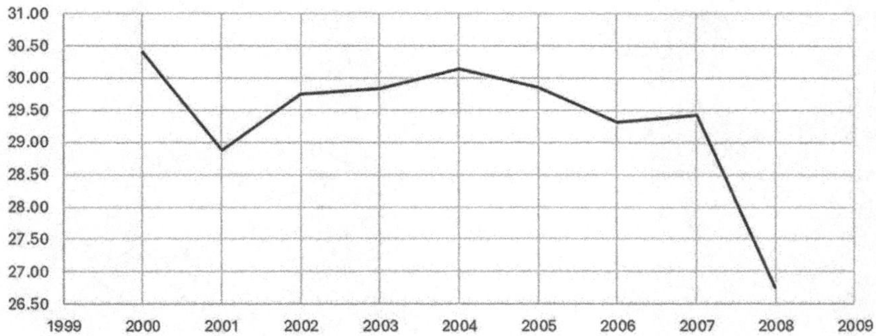


*Note:* The OECD data were used for consistency in comparing Australia with other OECD member countries. Using the taxation revenue data from the Australian Bureau of Statistics may yield some immaterial differences.
*Source:* OECD, 'Tax Revenue, Total, % of GDP, 2000–2020' <https://data.oecd.org/tax/tax-revenue.htm#indicator-chart> accessed 3 April 2023.

*Figure 5.1 Australia's tax-to-GDP ratio, 2000–2008*

macroeconomic conditions remained fairly stable from 2000 to 2008,[35] the changes in Australia's tax level during this period can be primarily attributed to the GST and subsequent income tax cuts. Figure 5.1 illustrates Australia's tax level from 2000 to 2008, using data from the OECD.

The data used in Figure 5.1 indicate that the GST-based tax reform has been revenue decreasing. Extending the time series from 2009, Australia's tax level went up in 2009 (29.5%) but then generally declined (as low as 25.5% in 2018) in subsequent years.[36] These findings are consistent with the lower tax level envisioned in the ANTS reform. Note that considering the revenue impact of GST and the taxes it replaced (WST and a range of indirect State taxes) alone is not a meaningful exercise, as there would have been no income tax reductions had the WST continued to operate in Australia.

The real question here is whether Australian tax reform should indeed be considered revenue decreasing or not. Australia has always been a low-tax country relative to the OECD, even before the introduction of its GST. From 2000 to 2020, the difference between the OECD's average tax-to-GDP ratio and that of Australia increased from 2.9% to 4.6%,[37] i.e., Australia's deviation

---

35 During the 2007–2009 global financial crisis, the Australian economy performed relatively well compared to most other countries.

36 Ibid.

37 OECD, 'Revenue Statistics 2022 – Australia' ('Tax-to-GDP Ratio') <https://www.oecd.org/tax/revenue-statistics-australia.pdf> accessed 3 April 2023

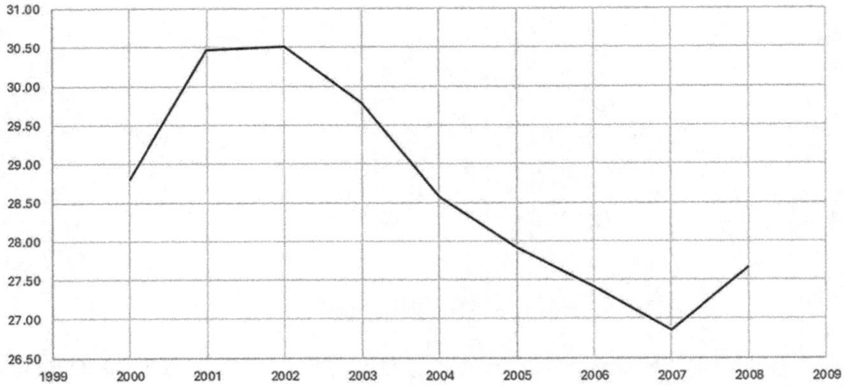


*Source:* OECD, 'Details of Tax Revenue – Australia' <https://stats.oecd.org/viewhtml.aspx?datasetcode=REVAUS&lang=en#> accessed 3 April 2023.

*Figure 5.2 Australia's share of indirect taxes in total tax revenue, 2000–2008*

from the OECD norm has been growing over the years. Currently, Australia ranks as the ninth-lowest tax country in the OECD, with only South Korea and the United States as industrialized nations with a lower tax burden.[38] Policy preferences for potential efficiency gains from low taxation over adequate revenue for satisfying current needs and future development goals should not be taken for granted. It deserves a thorough analysis, which can serve as a productive source for future evidence-based studies.

### 5.4.2 Tax Mix

In terms of tax mix, the ANTS package aimed to prevent a 'greater reliance on direct taxation'[39] and sought to substantially expand the indirect tax base via the GST. As a result, it is expected that the share of indirect taxes in total tax revenue in Australia would increase in the years following the introduction of the GST in 2000, assuming stable macroeconomic conditions. Figure 5.2 depicts Australia's indirect taxes as a percentage of total tax revenue from 2000 to 2008.

('Revenue Statistics 2022 – Australia').

38 Ibid.

39 Australian Treasury, *Tax Reform: Not a New Tax, a New Tax System* (n 15) 7.

It can be seen from Figure 5.2 that, after some initial increases in 2001 and 2002, the share of indirect taxes in total tax revenue in Australia declined over five consecutive years. Specifically, Australia's indirect taxes as a percentage of total tax revenue decreased from 28.8% in 2000 to 27.7% in 2008. Extending the time series for subsequent years from 2009 to 2020, in every year except 2009, Australia's share of indirect taxes in total revenue consistently fell below the 2000 figure of 28.8%.[40] Without a more detailed investigation, it is tentatively concluded that, on the basis of macro tax statistics, the GST-based reform has not reduced Australia's continuing reliance on direct taxation as was proposed in the ANTS package.

### 5.4.3 Revenue Sustainability of the GST

The ANTS package referred to the benefit of 'sustainability of both Commonwealth and State government finances'[41] without defining financial sustainability. A seemingly reasonable approach is to define GST revenue sustainability as the situation under which GST revenue remains a stable proportion of GDP over the long run. To examine GST revenue sustainability, it is useful to express the GST-to-GDP ratio as follows:

$$\begin{aligned} GST / GDP &= (GST / Household\ Final\ Consumption) \\ &\quad \times (Household\ Final\ Consumption / GDP) \\ &= t \times (GSTbase / Household\ Final\ Consumption) \\ &\quad \times (Household\ Final\ Consumption / GDP) \end{aligned} \tag{5.1}$$

where $t$ is the effective GST rate, which is very close to but smaller than the standard GST rate.

The ratio of the GST base to household final consumption expenditure is called the VAT revenue ratio (VRR).[42] Since the GST standard rate has remained 10% since 2000, the change in the GST-to-GDP ratio is determined

---

40 Ibid.

41 Australian Treasury, *Tax Reform: Not a New Tax, a New Tax System* (n 15) 155.

42 Strictly, *VRR* is defined as: *VRR* = *GST* / (*Potential Base* × *Standard VAT rate*); see OECD, *Consumption Tax Trends 2022: VAT/GST and Excise, Core Design Features and Trends* (OECD Publishing 2022) 56 (*Consumption Tax Trends 2022*).

by how the VRR and the ratio of household final consumption spending over GDP change over time.

First, Australia's VRR has declined over time because expenditure on GST-exempt (GST-free or zero-rated) items (particularly health and education) and input taxed items (involving a lower effective rate of GST, particularly rent and financial services) has grown more quickly than household final consumption spending. According to Smith, over the 15 years from 2002–2003 to 2017–2018, the consumption share of exempt or more lightly taxed categories of goods and services increased from 33.6% to 39.8%.[43] Available estimates suggest that Australia's VRR correspondingly fell from 57% in 2005[44] to 47% in 2018.[45] Secondly, during the same period, Australia's increased household saving rate has resulted in a small decline in the household consumption share of GDP. Combining these two effects, Australia's GST-to-GDP ratio has decreased over the years, from a peak of about 4% in the early 2000s to about 3.4% in recent years.[46]

Another factor that may erode the GST base relates to GST-related fraud, evasion and avoidance. A priori, we would expect increasing erosion of the GST base through non-compliance over time in view of taxpayers' greater familiarity with the operation of the GST. However, the GST non-compliance gap can be mitigated through the ATO's proactive measures, e.g., Operation Protego.[47] It is thus important to differentiate between gross (pre-audit) and net (post-audit) GST gaps. The ATO's estimations reveal that over the six-year period spanning from 2016–2017 to 2021–2022, the net GST gap exhibited a fluctuating pattern, with a rising trend followed by a subsequent decline, which was associated with the impact of the Covid-19 pandemic.[48] Overall, it appears

---

[43] Greg Smith, 'GST as a Secure Source of Revenue for the States and Territories' (2020) 18(1) eJournal of Tax Research 27, 40, citing ABS national accounts data.

[44] Henry Review (n 3) pt 2, vol 1, 273, 285 citing OECD, *Consumption Tax Trends: VAT/GST and Excise Rates, Trends and Administration Issues* (OECD Publishing 2008).

[45] OECD, *Consumption Tax Trends 2022* (n 42) 57.

[46] Smith (n 43) 40 citing Commonwealth government Budget Paper No 1 (various years).

[47] Operation Protego is an ATO-led investigation into large-scale GST frauds; see ATO, 'Operation Protego' <https://www.ato.gov.au/General/The-fight-against-tax-crime/Our-focus/Refund-fraud/GST-refund-fraud-attempts/Operation-Protego/> accessed 5 November 2023.

[48] The net GST gaps as a percentage of GST revenue in 2016–17, 2017–18, 2018–19, 2019–20, 2020–21 and 2021–22 were 5.7%, 6.3%, 7.2%, 4.5%, 2.7% and 3.6% respectively; see ATO, 'Goods and Services Tax Gap, Latest Estimate and Trends' (last updated 30 October 2023) <https://www.ato.gov.au/About-ATO/

reasonable to infer that GST fraud, evasion and avoidance would have a negligible impact on the sustainability of GST revenue.

The above examination implies that Australia's GST, in its current form, is not revenue-sustaining in the long run. To make the situation worse, expenditure required to maintain current levels of health, education and other social programmes is likely to increase at a rate faster than increases in GDP. Thus, the ANTS package's policy objectives of GST revenue sustainability and State revenue security will not be achieved without further reform.

## 5.5 GST AND ANTS POLICY OBJECTIVES

This section evaluates the GST with reference to ANTS' policy claims, which are in turn based on principles of tax policy. In particular, we consider three traditional criteria for good tax policy, namely, equity, efficiency and simplicity.

### 5.5.1 Equity

ANTS claim: 'Coalition Government is committed to … fairer … taxes'.[49]

Fairness or equity in taxation is concerned with distributive justice, focusing on the distribution of tax burdens among individuals in society. Under the widely accepted 'capacity to pay' principle, vertical equity requires that individuals commanding different levels of resources should pay different amounts of tax. Under the maxim of equity, Adam Smith stated that tax should be proportional to income, but he did not explicitly spell out whether this proportion should be constant (a flat tax) or increasing (a progressive tax).[50] Adding to vertical equity the condition that an equitable tax system should reduce income inequality, the average tax rate should increase with income; i.e., the tax system should be progressive. Has ANTS increased or decreased tax progressivity in Australia? To answer this question, we need to consider both elements of ANTS: the replacement of WST by GST and the subsequent income tax reductions.

Income-related measures under ANTS would have countervailing effects on the progressivity of the personal income tax system in Australia. The one-off 4% increase in aged and service pensions would improve personal income

---

Research-and-statistics/In-detail/Tax-gap/Goods-and-services-tax-gap/?anchor=Latestestimatesandtrends#Latestestimatesandtrends> accessed 5 November 2023.

49 Australian Treasury, *Tax Reform: Not a New Tax, a New Tax System* (n 15) 9.

50 Adam Smith, *An Inquiry into the Nature and Causes of the Wealth of Nations* (Strahan 1776) Bk V, Ch II, Pt II.

tax progressivity. However, the subsequent income tax reductions (both company and individual) and increase in family benefits following the introduction of the GST would relatively favour high-income individuals. In view of Australia's marked decline in tax level since 2000, it seems plausible to expect that personal income tax cuts and family benefits would dominate the compensation to pensioners, resulting in a decline in personal income tax progressivity. This theoretical speculation is supported by a study of Australia's personal income tax progressivity from 2000 to 2018, which found that tax progressivity has declined for most of the years under study.[51]

The GST is a regressive tax since individual/household consumption spending as a fraction of income decreases as income increases. In a 2015 distributional analysis of the GST, the Parliamentary Budget Office found that, with the exception of the fourth household income decile, GST as a percentage of household disposable income steadily decreased from over 12% for the first decile to 4% for the tenth decile.[52] But, since the repealed WST and a range of indirect State taxes were also regressive, the real issue that needs to be addressed is, how regressive is the GST compared to those taxes that it replaced? The WST is likely to have been less regressive than a revenue-equivalent GST since the GST imposed on most business inputs will ultimately flow to all goods and services, including some zero-rated items such as food, health and education services. A study examining Australian indirect taxation incidence over the period 1994–1995 to 2001–2002 found that 'the broad-based indirect tax reforms implemented over this period have become marginally more regressive'.[53] This is consistent with a comparable overseas finding which suggested that the Canadian GST is more regressive than the revenue-equivalent Manufacturers' Sales Tax that it replaced.[54]

The combined distributional impacts of the GST and income tax cuts have thus decreased the overall tax progressivity of the Australian tax system. Thus, the ANTS policy objective of a fairer tax system has not been achieved.

---

[51] Chung Tran and Nabeeh Zakariyya, 'Tax Progressivity in Australia: Facts, Measurements and Estimates' (2021) 97(316) Economic Record 45, 57.

[52] Parliamentary Budget Office, *Goods and Services Tax: Distributional Analysis and Indicative Reform Scenarios*, Report No 05/2015 (2015) 10, Figure 3-3.

[53] Neil Warren, Ann Harding and Rachel Lloyd, 'GST and the Changing Incidence of Australian Taxes: 1994–95 to 2001–02' (2005) 3(1) eJournal of Tax Research 114, 114 and 130.

[54] GC Ruggeri and K Bluck, 'On the Incidence of the Manufacturers' Sales Tax and the Goods and Services Tax' (1990) 16(4) Canadian Public Policy/Analyse de Politiques 359 and 369.

### 5.5.2 Efficiency

ANTS claim: 'Coalition Government is committed to … more efficient taxes'.[55]

When markets are working well, taxes distort the economic behaviours and decisions of taxpayers, consumers and producers, causing a loss in social welfare. Such losses are alternatively called deadweight losses, excess burden of taxation or efficiency costs of taxation. The principle of efficiency in taxation calls for the minimization of efficiency costs in raising any given level of tax revenue.

From the efficiency perspective, the GST has several advantages over the WST, such as a broad base and a non-cascading effect on the supply chain. It has often been asserted that the GST is a neutral (or non-distorting) tax in the sense that it does not alter the price ratio after taxation so that there is no substitution effect that distorts the purchaser's behaviour. This assertion is generally not true. Since the after-tax prices of different goods increase by different percentages, their post-GST price ratio will not be the same as their pre-GST price ratio; i.e., GST is not a neutral tax. This is well known from Ramsey's theory of optimal indirect taxation, according to which an efficient commodity tax rate should be inversely proportional to its price elasticity of demand.[56] Despite its administratively cumbersome nature, the multi-rate WST can be adjusted to reflect the Ramsey rule.

Estimating the efficiency costs of taxation is a complex process, requiring computable general equilibrium (CGE) modelling and various assumptions, sometimes strong ones, about the economy. There is an extensive Australian CGE modelling literature on taxation and its efficiency.[57] However, most of

---

[55] Australian Treasury, *Tax Reform: Not a New Tax, a New Tax System* (n 15) 9.

[56] FP Ramsey, 'A Contribution to the Theory of Taxation' (1927) 37(145) Economic Journal 47.

[57] See, for example, Peter B Dixon and Maureen T Rimmer, 'The Government/ Democrats' Package of Changes in Indirect Taxes' (2000) 44(1) Australian Journal of Agricultural and Resource Economics 147; KPMG Econtech, *CGE Analysis of the Current Australian Tax System, Final Report* (KPMG 2010); Liangyue Cao, Amanda Hosking, Michael Kouparitsas, Damian Mullaly, Xavier Rimmer, Qun Shi, Wallace Stark and Sebastian Wende, 'Understanding the Economy-Wide Efficiency and Incidence of Major Australian Taxes' (2015) Treasury Working Paper No 2015-01; Chris Murphy, 'Efficiency of the Tax System: A Marginal Excess Burden Analysis' (2016) Tax and Transfer Policy Institute Working Paper 4/2016; James A Giesecke and Nhi H Tran, 'The National and Regional Consequences of Australia's Goods and Services Tax' (2018) 94(306) Economic Record 255; Jason Nassios, John Madden, James Giesecke, Janine Dixon, Nhi Tran, Peter Dixon, Maureen Rimmer, Philip Adams and John Freebairn, 'The

these studies are concerned with either the efficiency of the GST as part of the Australian tax system or the efficiency gains/losses from GST reform, such as a rate rise or a base expansion. The relevant analysis for the purpose of this chapter is of the efficiency gains/losses from adopting the ANTS package proposals, i.e., the efficiency consequences of switching from WST and some indirect State taxes to GST.

The available evidence casts doubt on the assumed efficiency gains from ANTS. Using the MM303 model, Murphy estimated a long-run annual welfare gain of 0.2% of household final consumption spending (corresponding to AUD 0.6 billion at 2000 prices) from the original ANTS measures.[58] Using the MONASH model and taking into account the terms of trade and GST compliance costs, Dixon and Rimmer anticipated that the actual ANTS (not the original ANTS) would generate a net long-run annual welfare loss between 0.6% and 0.8% of household expenditure (corresponding to AUD 1.8 billion to 2.4 billion at 2000 prices).[59] There are two differences in the above analyses. First, Murphy analysed a generic GST based on the original ANTS while Dixon and Rimmer examined the actual GST derived from the revised ANTS. Secondly, Dixon and Rimmer explicitly took GST compliance costs into consideration, but Murphy did not.

In summary, net efficiency gains from the GST-based reform, if any, appear to be negligible.

### 5.5.3 Simplicity

ANTS claim: 'The current tax system is unnecessarily complex'.[60]

It is useful to distinguish between legal complexity and effective complexity.[61] Legal complexity is concerned with the intrinsic nature of tax complexity and embraces both statutory and procedural complexity. Statutory complexity refers to the difficulties involved in reading, interpreting, applying and resolving disputes in practical situations. Procedural complexity refers to the difficulties for taxpayers and tax administrators in meeting tax administrative requirements. Effective complexity deals with the consequences of legal com-

---

Economic Impact and Efficiency of State and Federal Taxes in Australia' (2019) Centre of Policy Studies Working Paper No G-289.

58 Senate Select Committee on a New Tax System, *Main Report* (1999) ch 2.

59 Dixon and Rimmer (n 57) 155.

60 Australian Treasury, *Tax Reform: Not a New Tax, a New Tax System* (n 15) 8.

61 Binh Tran-Nam, 'Tax Reform and Tax Simplification: Some Conceptual Issues and a Preliminary Assessment' (1999) 21(3) Sydney Law Review 500, 505–7.

plexity, referring to the value of resources expended in raising a given level of revenue from a particular tax. It is measured by the operating costs (sum of tax compliance and administration costs) of the tax under study.

Despite having only two rates (the standard rate and the zero rate) compared with the seven rates of the WST, the GST legislation is nevertheless more complex than the WST legislation, mainly because the GST has a broad base with many variable exemptions. Further, the GST is also effectively more complex than the WST for three key reasons:

- the operation of the GST involves a very large number of registered businesses and tax administrators compared with a revenue-equivalent WST;[62]
- registered businesses, especially GST-registered businesses without any employees, act as tax collectors on behalf of the government;
- under the credit-invoice method, the Australian GST is a transactional tax imposed on every sale (while WST was levied on the total wholesale value at the end of each tax period).

There is unambiguous evidence indicating that the GST has become the most burdensome tax in terms of compliance for Australian SMEs.[63] One of the factors contributing to the high GST compliance costs for small businesses is the low and stagnant GST-free threshold, which has remained at AUD 75,000 since 2007.[64]

---

62 There were about 2.2 million GST-registered businesses in Australia in 2000–2001; see ATO (n 31). The number of GST-registered businesses has grown rapidly over the years. For comparison, 'at the end of June 1999 there were 38,568 businesses operating in the wholesale trade industry': ABS, *Wholesale Industry, Australia, 1998–99*, *Cat 8638.0* (2000) <https://www.abs.gov.au/AUSSTATS/abs@.nsf/Lookup/8638.0Main+Features11998-99?OpenDocument> accessed 12 August 2023. The large number of GST-registered businesses is sometimes attributed to Australia's relatively low GST threshold of AUD 75,000 (initially AUD 50,000). However, it is interesting to note that Australia ranks second in terms of GST threshold among comparable countries: the UK (GBP 90,000 from April 2024), Australia (AUD 75,000), New Zealand (NZD 60,000) and Canada (CAD 30,000).

63 Phil Lignier, Chris Evans and Binh Tran-Nam, 'Tangled up in Tape: The Continuing Tax Compliance Plight of the Small and Medium Enterprise Business Sector' (2014) 29(2) Australian Tax Forum 217, 239.

64 The authors would like to thank Professor Richard Krever for suggesting this point.

It is not straightforward to determine the change in tax system operating costs as a result of ANTS. Using various sources of secondary data and under plausible assumptions, the following estimates were obtained for 2002–2003:[65]

- Saving in operating costs due to the abolition of WST and some indirect State taxes = Saving in tax compliance costs + Saving in tax administration costs = AUD 1,435 million + AUD 142 million = AUD 1,577 million;
- Increase in operating costs due to the introduction of GST = Increase in tax compliance costs + Increase in tax administration costs = AUD 2,400 million + AUD 266 million = AUD 2,666 million;
- GST implementation costs = Sum of GST start-up compliance and administration costs = AUD 2,800 million + AUD 405 million = AUD 3,205 million.

The GST implementation costs can be converted into a perpetual stream of annual costs using present value arithmetic. Assuming an interest rate of 5% per year, the GST implementation adds AUD 160.25 million (0.05 × 3,205 million) to the annual operating costs of the tax system. Thus, the combined increase in tax operating costs was AUD 2,826.25 million (AUD 2,666 million + AUD 160.25 million). Deducting the saving in operating costs, the GST increased tax operating costs in 2002–2003 by a net amount of AUD 1.25 billion (2.83 billion – 1.58 billion).[66]

In short, ANTS has not simplified the Australian tax system. In fact, GST has increased the operating costs of the tax system by a non-trivial amount. However, from a comparative perspective, it has been shown, using the diagnostic tool approach, that Australia's GST compliance burden is relatively low in comparison to those of member countries of the Forum on Tax Administration.[67]

[65] Tran-Nam, 'The Implementation Costs of the GST' (n 26); Tran-Nam, 'Assessing the Tax Simplification Impact of Tax Reform' (n 29) 381.

[66] This increase did not include a likely rise in tax dispute resolution costs. No data were available to estimate the magnitude of this likely increase.

[67] The Forum on Tax Administration brings together tax administrations from over 50 OECD and non-OECD countries. Australia's GST compliance burden is shown to belong to the second-lowest group of countries; see Chris Evans, Richard Highfield, Binh Tran-Nam and Michael Walpole, 'Diagnosing the VAT Compliance Burden: A Cross-Country Assessment' (2020) 31(2) International VAT Monitor 84, 87.

## 5.6 FUTURE GST REFORM

The discussion on revenue sustainability of GST in section 5.4 suggests that GST expansion reform is not only desirable but also inevitable. While a strong case for such reform can be made on the basis of economic rationalism, it is not politically easy to achieve such a reform. This section considers various aspects of a potential revenue-expanding GST reform in Australia. These include overall tax level and tax mix, rate increase, base broadening, regressivity and compensation, and institutional constraints.

### 5.6.1 Tax Level and Tax Mix

Since government expenditures on health, education and other social programmes tend to grow faster than GDP, it is sensible to recommend a revenue-expanding GST reform, at least to restore Australia's pre-GST tax level to 30% of GDP. Even so, the Australian tax level would still be well below the OECD's average tax level, which stood at 33.6% in 2020.[68] However, it would be politically more acceptable to propose a revenue-neutral (or very slightly revenue-expanding) GST reform in Australia. This implies that any increase in GST revenue collection would be matched by personal income tax cuts of the same (or slightly less) magnitude. In both cases, especially in the revenue-neutral GST reform, there would be a corresponding increase in Australia's reliance on indirect taxes.

### 5.6.2 GST Rate Increase

A very strong case can be made for raising the GST rate. First, the GST was introduced in Australia at a low rate, which has not changed for more than 20 years. Secondly, Australia's GST rate is just over half the average of the standard GST/VAT rates across the OECD, which was 19.2% in 2022.[69] With respect to the appropriate magnitude of the GST rate increase, we can be guided by past BBCT reform proposals such as the Draft White Paper in 1985 (12.5%) or the *Fightback!* 1992 package (15%). To raise the GST rate from its current level (10%) to an ultimate new level (e.g., 12.5%), the government could adopt either the 'big bang' or the incremental approach. While there are certain advantages in a big bang reform, it may be more politically tolerable, especially in the present economic climate of inflation, to raise the GST rate from its current level to a new ultimate level in several steps.

---

[68] OECD, 'Revenue Statistics 2022 – Australia' (n 37).

[69] OECD, *Consumption Tax Trends 2022* (n 42) 9.

To understand the impact of a rate increase on GST revenue sustainability, we need to refer to equation (5.1). Suppose that the GST rate increases from 10% to 12.5%, holding the GST base constant. Under the naïve assumption of no behavioural responses, the GST-to-GDP ratio would experience a one-off increase of 25%. Assume further that the GST-to-GDP ratio before the rate increase is 3.5%. After the rate increase, the GST-to-GDP ratio will be 4.4% $(= 3.5 \times 1.25)$. But, without base broadening, the new GST-to-GDP ratio will gradually decline over time.

### 5.6.3 GST Base Broadening

Most tax experts support an Australian GST reform that would result in a comprehensive tax base with minimal exemptions, along the lines of the original 1998 ANTS or New Zealand model. This would involve the removal of the GST zero-rated status that currently applies to a range of consumption items, including fresh food, health and education. Such a move would not only raise Australia's VRR substantially but also eliminate wasteful lobbying and harmful rent-seeking behaviours.

The benefits of GST base broadening on its revenue sustainability can be illustrated using equation (5.1). Suppose that, as a result of base broadening, Australia's VRR increases from 45% to 65%, holding the GST rate constant. Under the naïve assumption of no behavioural responses, the GST-to-GDP ratio would experience a one-off increase of 44%. Assume that, before base broadening, GST-to-GDP = 3.5%. After base broadening, the GST-to-GDP ratio will rise to about 5.1% $(= 3.5 \times 1.44)$. Unlike a GST rate increase, the VRR will not decrease over time, thus allowing the initial increase in the GST-to-GDP ratio to be maintained over time.

There tends to be very strong public opposition and resistance to GST base broadening. This is mainly connected to the perceived unfairness or regressivity of the GST, which will be addressed in the next section. Historically speaking, very few countries have succeeded in broadening the GST/VAT base substantially after the introduction of their GST/VAT.

### 5.6.4 Regressivity and Compensation

A revenue-expanding GST through rate increase or base broadening (and personal income tax cuts) would make the GST even more regressive and worsen the overall progressivity of the Australian tax system. The traditional approach is to provide (ongoing) compensation to lower-income households. An innovative alternative to make the GST 'progressive' is to provide every adult Australian with a 'GST-free' spending threshold of AUD 7,500 each year, so that their first AUD 7,500 of consumption expenditure would attract no GST.[70] Beyond the threshold, all goods and services would be taxed at the rate of, say, 15%, including those that are currently exempted, such as fresh food, health, education, etc. This interesting proposal would impose tremendous compliance costs (on individuals to claim their GST-free spending) and administration costs (on the government to refund the GST to individuals). In fact, several countries have already applied this idea by exempting from GST/VAT some low levels of household expenditures on telephone/internet and utilities.

### 5.6.5 Institutional Constraints

Although the GST is a Commonwealth tax, the Australian Federal government cannot unilaterally change the GST base or rate without consulting subnational governments. According to the A New Tax System (Commonwealth–State Financial Arrangements) Act 1999 (renamed the A New Tax System (Managing the GST Rate and Base) Act 1999), any changes in the existing GST base or rate require unanimous agreement from State and Territory governments. This requirement imposes legal and political constraints on any GST reform proposals.

Under existing arrangements, it would be extremely difficult for any State/Territory government to initiate GST revenue-expansionary proposals without incurring severe voter backlash. This is particularly true in the post-Covid-19 environment where the economy has slowed and there has been mounting inflationary pressure. The constraint is thus severe, but not insurmountable. Under appropriate conditions and with sufficient political will, it is conceivable that the Australian Federal government could pass legislation to make the GST a truly Federal tax, i.e., a tax the base and rate of which are solely controlled and determined by the Federal government. An alternative is to repeal the A New Tax System (Managing the GST Rate and Base) Act 1999. Either option would be very costly politically to the Federal government.[71]

---

[70] Rosalind Dixon and Richard Holden, 'The GST Can Be Progressive: Here's How' *Australian Financial Review* (7 July 2020) <https://www.afr.com/wealth/tax/the-gst-can-be-progressive-here-s-how-20200707-p559ph#:~:text=Our%20idea%20of%20a%20%E2%80%9Cprogressive,rate%20of%200%20per%20cent> accessed 3 April 2023.

[71] The current Federal Labor government in Australia is not receptive to any GST reform; see Matthew Cranston, 'Chalmers Rejects IMF Call for GST Increase' *Australian Financial Review* (13 April 2023) accessed 3 April 2023.

## 5.7 SUMMARY CONCLUSION

The GST reform in Australia has been a slow process, fraught with obstacles and uncertainties, and is, in fact, still ongoing. As Australia is a latecomer to BBCT, its GST contained no technical novelties. But, in addition to a low standard rate, tax burden reduction and an acceptable compensation package, there was also an innovative link between GST reform and intergovernmental financial reform. The Coalition government was thus able to localize the context for its indirect tax reform agenda.

The introduction of the GST can be regarded as a public policy success in terms of stakeholder support, political legitimacy, and a coherent and empirically feasible public value proposition. The GST reform can also be viewed as a public policy success in terms of its reasonably smooth implementation with minimal costs and disruptions. However, when it comes to more specific policy objectives, the GST has scored rather poorly:

- the GST-based change has been revenue reducing overall (although it is unclear whether this is an appropriate tax policy direction for relatively low-taxed Australia);
- the GST has not increased Australia's reliance on indirect taxation;
- the ANTS measures have made the Australian tax system neither fairer nor simpler;
- the efficiency gains from ANTS have been small at most and may even be negative.

These findings suggest that the term 'GST reform' cannot be employed without appropriate qualification.

The Coalition government's lack of control of the Senate after its 1998 electoral victory made compromises necessary to get the GST across the finishing line. However, it is that very political pragmatism which ensured that the GST reform is incomplete. As the GST-to-GDP ratio has been falling over the years, the GST is not revenue sustainable in the long run. Expansion of the GST base and, to a lesser extent, a rise in the standard GST rate are both desirable and inevitable. In view of the legal and political constraints on adjusting the GST, and given the inflationary pressure in the post-Covid-19 environment, there would be serious challenges facing any new champion of GST reform in Australia.

# PART II

# International tax abuse and corporate behaviour

# 6. International tax minimization: the role of corporate tax morality

**Kerrie Sadiq**

## 6.1 INTRODUCTION

Aggressive tax minimization strategies and corporate tax avoidance have become increasingly scrutinized in recent years. International bodies such as the Organisation for Economic Co-operation and Development (OECD) and domestic regulators have taken measures to address this behaviour. These measures have taken two forms: substantive regulatory reforms that attempt to close loopholes and address the strategies used by multinational entities (MNEs) to reduce taxes paid; and increased transparency measures, both voluntary and mandatory. These two forms of measures are generally viewed as working in concert and are seen as complementing each other. However, the underlying principles and policy rationales are often contradictory. The former, in the form of strict regulatory requirements demanding that an MNE follow the letter of the law, with legal sanctions where it fails to do so, suggests that where an MNE follows that law, it is complying with its tax obligations and is a good corporate citizen. The latter, in the form of transparency measures relating to an MNE's tax position and strategies, operates on the basis of coercion and suggests a corporate responsibility beyond legal compliance, to corporate morality. The former has no flexibility, whereas the latter allows the MNEs to provide a narrative.

This second measure of transparency stems largely from recent public and political outcry around corporate tax aggressiveness that has been brought to light mainly through the OECD's base erosion and profit shifting (BEPS) programme of reform. The call for such transparency measures suggests that, in addition to legal obligations, MNEs have a moral obligation to pay taxes beyond the level to which they could legally reduce the amounts payable. It is within this context that it can be argued that substantive regulatory reform and increased transparency measures are, in fact, in direct conflict with each other – on the one hand, compliance with the regulatory requirements with an obligation to pay a determined amount and punished by sanctions where obligations are not complied with, and on the other hand, tax practice disclosures which are often part of a voluntary business strategy, designed to be merely coercive, and generally applauded by stakeholders when provided. Given that tax regimes are grounded in regulatory systems, the question is one of what role transparency measures should play in the sphere of taxation and whether they should play a role at all if they are aimed at issues of ethics and morality.

The last decade has seen a heated debate on the role of ethics and morality in the payment of corporate tax, particularly where the corporation involved is an MNE. MNEs often point out that they pay all the taxes required by law and remind us through their transparency and corporate social responsibility (CSR) reports that they do not cheat on their taxes. Underlying their legal requirements to pay taxes are aggressive tax minimization strategies through profit shifting using transfer pricing, controlled foreign companies (CFCs), subsidiaries funded by excessive debt, and other related techniques. The piecemeal nature of legislative responses to these different techniques reduces only slightly the scope for profit shifting, with the result that the taxes required by law may be so low that consumers and often the broad stakeholder group, the public, regard the tax burden as socially unacceptable, prompting calls for citizen action such as boycotts unless higher taxes are paid. Consumers and the public are not the only stakeholder groups troubled by the low tax burdens faced by MNEs that legally shift profits to reduce their tax liability. Politicians regularly rail against and decry profit-shifting measures by MNEs that follow the letter of the law passed by those same politicians.[1] Beyond the question of whether transparency measures should play a role in addressing aggressive

---

[1] See, for example, parliamentary or congressional hearings held in the US, UK and Australia (Parliament of Australia, Senate Economics References Committee, 'Corporate Tax Avoidance' <https://www.aph.gov.au/Parliamentary_Business/Committees/Senate/Economics/Corporatetax45th>), along with relevant reporting. For example, Kristen A Parillo, 'HMRC Not Doing Enough on Corporate Tax Avoidance, UK Parliament Says' Tax Notes Today International (19 November 2014) <https://www.taxnotes.com/tax-notes-today-international/base-erosion-and-profit-shifting-beps/hmrc-not-doing-enough-corporate-tax-avoidance-u.k-parliament-says/2014/11/19/gxwc> accessed 19 July 2024; Dominic Rushe, 'Senators Accuse Apple of "Highly Questionable" Billion-Dollar Tax Avoidance Scheme' *The Guardian* (21 May 2013) <https://www.theguardian.com/technology/2013/may/20/apple-accused-tax-avoidance-billions-scheme> accessed 19 July 2024; Simon Santow, 'Google, Apple and Microsoft Deny Tax Avoidance at Senate Inquiry, Labor Says Australians Don't Accept Their Practices Are "Genuine"' *ABC News* (last updated 9 April 2015) <https://www.abc.net.au/news/2015-04-08/google-apple-microsoft-deny-tax-avoidance-senate-inquiry/6379024> accessed 19 July 2024.

tax practices, the disconnect in so many quarters with the tax behaviour of MNEs that break no laws also raises the question of whether it is possible, and even acceptable, to behave in a morally objectionable or socially irresponsible manner while meeting all requirements of the law. This chapter explores these questions.

## 6.2 INSTITUTIONAL FRAMEWORK AND CORPORATE RESPONSES

There is no doubt that MNEs have come under increasing public and political scrutiny, with the most prominent MNEs responding in various ways as broad stakeholder discontent poses a serious problem for those MNEs targeted. While MNEs such as the GAMMAs (Google, Amazon, Meta, Microsoft and Apple) faced various Senate inquiries and attention from the media and are eminently suitable for an analysis of their responses, their approach has tended to involve typical adversarial actions and ultimately reflects one of pointing out that they are following the letter of the law. These MNEs are so large that it is difficult for consumers and the public to influence their behaviour. However, other MNEs have faced a backlash that has made a difference. In contrast to examining defensive behaviour, this chapter considers two scenarios where neither a strict letter of the law nor an adversarial approach was adopted, but instead a perceived conciliatory response was made to public and political criticisms. The first is Starbucks in the United Kingdom (UK). The second is the settlement of extractive industry taxpayer cases in Australia.

Starbucks experienced potential public fallout in 2012 when faced with a UK consumer boycott following revelations of its low tax burden on high revenues. The revenues did not translate into profits following deductions for profits shifted abroad as various expenses of the UK company. HM Revenue and Customs (HMRC) confirmed that the company had paid all taxes required under the law and it could not raise an additional assessment against the company, leaving the company with no option to pay higher taxes. The public was not happy. To assuage public anger over its low tax burden, Starbucks announced a 'voluntary contribution' to the UK government as part of its business strategy.

The public scrutiny of Starbucks in 2012 over its aggressive tax practices highlighted that those practices were seen as a contradiction to its public commitment to being socially responsible and a good corporate citizen in the communities in which it operated.[2] Critics were quick to point out that Starbucks

[2] Katherine Campbell and Duane Helleloid, 'Starbucks: Social Responsibility and Tax Avoidance' (2016) 37 Journal of Accounting Education 38.

was very public in its commitment to social responsibility. Yet, it told investors that it made a profit in the UK but reported losses to the revenue authority. In 2008, Starbucks had set goals in relation to performance in ethical sourcing, environmental stewardship and community involvement, with a responsibility report produced annually[3] and a Global Responsibility Scorecard establishing goals and progress.[4] Goals included ethically sourced coffee, investment in farmers and communities, a reduction in energy consumption, improved recycling, and contributions to community service, but a fiscal commitment in terms of taxes paid was not included.

In the case of Starbucks, the public regarded paying taxes as a social responsibility, whereas the corporation regarded paying taxes as a legal requirement. Curiously, Starbucks' response was not to defend its position in terms of meeting the letter of the law but rather to legitimize the fallout by moving its tax obligations into the sphere of social responsibility. It shifted the rhetoric from tax obligations being an *ex post* legislated expense to one that was part of the cost of doing business to be treated like any other expense and, therefore, negotiable. Starbucks went further than suggesting that tax was a negotiable expense and engaged in impression management techniques to assuage consumers. It did not adopt an aggressive stance of arguing that it had paid all its due taxes, but viewed its tax obligations similarly to its commitment to ethically sourced coffee beans and reduced energy consumption. Starbucks' view of the public outcry was one of managing consumer expectations as part of their business strategy. Paradoxically, it is within this context that Starbucks made it clear that they were in the business of ensuring the best return for their investors rather than the coffee business.

More than ten years after Starbucks was brutally shamed in the media, other MNEs have adapted their behaviour to impression manage stakeholders' views of their tax positions and have embraced the notion that tax is a negotiable business expense rather than a statutory obligation to pay taxes due under regulatory requirements. This is obvious with the settlement of cases between MNEs and revenue authorities on international tax matters seen over the last decade. In Australia, there is a succession of reported cases dealing with large extractive industry MNEs, all of whom use offshore marketing hubs as part of their corporate structure. These hubs involve a related offshore entity or permanent establishment that acts as an agent or principal in relation to marketing

---

3 Starbucks Coffee Company, 'Committed to Transparency – People, Planet, Coffee' <https://www.starbucks.com/responsibility/reporting-hub/> accessed 18 July 2024.

4 Relevant Starbucks reporting documents from 2003 to the present can be found at: <https://www.starbucks.com/responsibility/reporting-hub/> accessed 18 July 2024.

and/or the procurement of non-core goods or services to support the operations of a related Australian business with little or no alteration.[5]

BHP and Rio Tinto, Australia's largest mining companies, disclosed that they had reached settlements with the Australian revenue authority regarding marketing hubs. In 2022, Shell was reportedly renewing its advance pricing arrangement.[6] In February 2023, Ampol was reported as the latest resources company to settle over the use of a marketing hub. The Ampol settlement dealt with transfer pricing outcomes of refined products and crude oil between a related Singapore marketing hub and the Australian taxpayer. The resulting extra tax was a mere AUD 5.6 million, with AUD 100,000 interest on earnings between 2014 and 2021. No penalties or anti-avoidance provisions were applied. The media reported the settlement as a 'win' for the public, yet the tax amounts compared to profits are small. A similar settlement was reached with Rio Tinto in 2022, following the 2018 settlement with BHP.[7]

---

[5] Australian Taxation Office (ATO), 'ATO Compliance Approach to Transfer Pricing Issues Related to Centralised Operating Models Involving Procurement, Marketing, Sales and Distribution Functions', Practical Compliance Guideline PCG 2017/1 (PCG 2017/1).

[6] Jacob Greber, Angela Macdonald-Smith and Mark Ludlow, 'Labor Escalates Fight Against "Tricky" Offshore Marketing Hubs' *Australian Financial Review* (8 August 2022) <https://www.afr.com/politics/federal/labor-escalates-fight-against-tricky-offshore-marketing-hubs-20220808-p5b86a>.

[7] See, respectively, Rio Tinto, 'Rio Tinto Settles All Tax Disputes with Australian Tax Office' (News Release, 20 July 2022) <https://www.riotinto.com/news/releases/2022/Rio-Tinto-settles-all-tax-disputes-with-Australian-Tax-Office>; BHP, 'BHP Settles Longstanding Transfer Pricing Dispute' (Media Release, 19 November 2018) <https://www.bhp.com/news/media-centre/releases/2018/11/bhp-settles-longstanding-transfer-pricing-dispute>. It has also been reported that settlements with Google, Apple, ResMed and Microsoft have been reached with the Australian Taxation Office: see, respectively, Hon Josh Frydenberg (Treasurer) and Hon Michael Sukkar (Assistant Treasurer and Minister for Housing), 'Government's Tax Avoidance Laws Sees Google Settle with the ATO for $481.5m' (Joint Media Release, 18 December 2019) <https://ministers.treasury.gov.au/ministers/josh-frydenberg-2018/media-releases/governments-tax-avoidance-laws-sees-google-settle-ato>; ATO, 'Tax Avoidance Taskforce Highlights 2021–22' (last updated 8 April 2024) <https://www.ato.gov.au/about-ato/tax-avoidance/tax-avoidance-taskforce/tax-avoidance-taskforce-highlights-2021-22>; Claire Bickers and AAP, 'Microsoft Makes Major Settlement with Australian Taxation Office' *news.com.au* (22 August 2017) <https://www.news.com.au/finance/business/microsoft-makes-major-settlement-with-australian-taxation-office/news-story/d52e5f6885b60830d128d79654d9db0f>.

The settlement amounts suggest that the legal tax due has little to do with the amount paid. Confidentiality means it is impossible to know the extent of the transfer pricing. However, in each case, settlement figures as a percentage of profits indicate that the payments are a mere fraction of the true tax obligation, and penalties and interest are generally waived as part of the settlement agreement. These cases are arguably not so much about a statutory obligation to pay tax at a particular rate or even a 'fair' amount of tax being paid, nor are they about enforcing the regulatory requirements of the tax system. Instead, while there were nuances to each settlement, the overarching narrative is that the taxpayers were in a position of power to effectively remove the legal obligation to pay tax and transform it into a business negotiation. The payment of tax moved from an *ex post* legislated expense determined according to the law to one that was part of the MNE's cost of doing business, which is *ex ante* negotiable and minimized to ensure the greatest return to shareholders. In each of the cases, the taxpayers achieved precisely this. As with Starbucks, the mining companies made it clear that they were in the business of ensuring the best return for their investors rather than the mining business.

The approach by the parties and the reconfiguration of the activity of paying taxes from an *ex post* legal obligation to an *ex ante* business transaction is evident in the statements made by corporate executives. Ampol Group Chief Financial Officer Greg Barnes was quoted as saying, 'We are pleased to have reached an agreement with the Australian Taxation Office (ATO) and to have certainty over the future tax treatment of Ampol Singapore earnings. The changes minimise operational disruption, while ensuring we fairly meet our tax obligations in Australia.'[8] This statement emphasized the business and shareholders' profits rather than the legal obligation to pay tax, following a trend that had been developing over recent years.

Peter Beaven, BHP's chief financial officer, stated in relation to its settlement in 2018 that it 'provides clarity for BHP and the ATO in relation to how taxes will be assessed and paid on the sale of Australian commodities. That certainty is good for business and for Australia.'[9] Again, the emphasis was on the settlement being good for business and seen as a business transaction for the benefit of stakeholders. The Rio Tinto settlement provided a similar narrative. Peter Cunningham, Rio Tinto's chief financial officer, said of its 2022 settlement, 'We are glad to have resolved these longstanding disputes and to have gained certainty over future tax outcomes relating to our Singapore marketing arrangements. Rio Tinto remains committed to our commercial activities in

---

[8] Quoted in Philip King, 'Ampol Pays $157m to Settle Transfer Pricing Dispute' *Accountants Daily* (20 February 2023) <https://www.accountantsdaily.com.au/tax-compliance/18183-ampol-pays-157m-to-settle-transfer-pricing-dispute>.

[9] BHP (n 7).

Singapore and the valuable role played by our centralised commercial team.'[10] In this statement, commerciality was emphasized in the same context as the payment of tax, a clear indication of the views of Rio Tinto that tax is a negotiable business expense.

This narrative is also supported by regulators and tax administrators who provide a discourse suggesting that aggressive tax strategies are being addressed and the outcomes of the settlements are positive for stakeholders, particularly the public. In response to the Ampol settlement, ATO Deputy Commissioner Rebecca Saint was quoted as saying, 'Locking in tax outcomes for the future has become an important feature of our settlements with multinationals as it provides us, taxpayers and the community with certainty that the multinational is meeting their tax obligations into the future, avoiding future disputes.'[11] She went on to say, 'We [the Australian Taxation Office] are keen to ensure that procurement hubs are not used as a mechanism to shift profit from Australia by charging excessive prices for imported goods and services in an effort to reduce tax paid in Australia.'[12] Ironically, marketing hubs are designed to achieve exactly what the Deputy Commissioner is suggesting the settlements are attempting to prevent – legal but aggressive tax minimization strategies through transfer pricing.

Within the political sphere, and along the same lines, Assistant Minister for Competition, Charities and Treasury Andrew Leigh stated that

> Ampol now joins BHP and Rio in agreeing to pay a major tax settlement for misuse of a Singaporean marketing hub. Importantly, these settlements also ensure that firms do the right thing in future years. The Albanese government will continue to reform multinational taxation laws and give the tax office the resources it needs to ensure that multinationals pay their fair share.[13]

This narrative was not new, with Deputy Commissioner Rebecca Saint stating in 2022 in relation to the Rio Tinto settlement that 'the resolution of these matters means that ordinary Australians can have confidence that even the biggest

---

[10] Rio Tinto (n 7).

[11] ATO, 'ATO Settles Dispute over Singapore Hub' (Media Release, last updated 20 February 2023) <https://www.ato.gov.au/Media-centre/Media-releases/ATO-settles-dispute-over-Singapore-hub/>.

[12] Ibid.

[13] Quoted in Tom McIlroy, 'Ampol Pays $157m in Tax Settlement over Singapore Hub' *Australian Financial Review* (20 February 2023) <https://www.afr.com/policy/tax-and-super/ampol-pays-157m-in-tax-settlement-over-singapore-hub-20230220-p5cluo>.

companies are held to account to pay their tax due'.[14] The public was simply told that their best interests were being looked after and that the social licence to operate that these corporations had with the Australian government and its people was legitimate. The inherent suggestion is that the MNEs act morally in meeting their tax obligations even though there is no discussion or questioning of their statutory requirements.

The result of cases such as Starbucks and the mining companies in Australia, along with many other MNEs, is that their behaviour is legitimized and accepted as appropriate, as is the revenue authorities' position on acceptance and/or settlements rather than litigation. The message is clear and is one of 'trust us'. Starbucks admitted no wrongdoing, and it seems that very little has changed in terms of its tax strategies, with reports that, in 2021, it paid GBP 5million UK corporation tax on GBP 95 million gross profit because the profits were substantially reduced through royalty and licensing fees.[15] Incorporating tax payments into its business operations and volunteering to pay an additional amount brought tax into its sphere of socially responsible actions, and the public was assuaged. While its legal obligations were met, they were not part of the narrative as coercion was the primary driver of the response, and any real reform and/or sanctions were removed.

In a similar vein, none of the companies in Australia admitted to tax avoidance, and those using marketing hubs made it clear that they would continue to do so in the future. There have been no proposed changes to legislation to attempt to prevent the use of marketing hubs, and the ATO continues to provide practical compliance guidelines to MNEs, setting out its compliance approach to transfer pricing issues related to the location and relocation of certain business activities and operating risks in a centralized operating model (marketing hub).[16] Again, coercive measures ensured the public was assuaged while legally aggressive tax strategies were relegated to the background and seemingly approved by the revenue authority. The MNEs were able to act in a morally repugnant manner and be rewarded for it.

These cases suggest that corporations accept that they have a social contract and a social licence to operate, with part of that contract being an obligation to pay taxes. However, genuine corporate morality regarding their aggressive

---

14 ATO, 'ATO Secures Settlement of Marketing Hub Tax Dispute' (Media Release, last updated 20 July 2022) <https://www.ato.gov.au/Media-centre/Media-releases/ATO-secures-settlement-of-marketing-hub-tax-dispute/>.

15 Rupert Neate, 'Starbucks Pays Just £5m UK Corporation Tax on £95m Gross Profit' *The Guardian* (31 March 2022) <https://www.theguardian.com/business/2022/mar/30/starbucks-uk-corporation-tax-profit-administrative-expenses-royalties>.

16 See, for example, ATO, PCG 2017/1 (n 5).

tax strategies seems not to be accepted. Instead, the approach uses impression management techniques and disclosure mechanisms to convince the disgruntled public that they are good corporate citizens. These same corporations provide a narrative that suggests their legitimacy is founded in their willingness to embrace tax payments as an act of CSR, thereby earning credibility and trust among the public. Paying taxes for a corporation is considered no different from sourcing coffee beans or digging minerals out of the ground; it is simply part of a business strategy. Through informal disclosure mechanisms, the corporations have made a compelling case that they are acting morally when it comes to international tax minimization.

These legitimacy and moral stances of MNEs are supported by revenue authorities and governments that also congratulate the behaviour of these corporations through rhetoric and by endorsing the use of aggressive tax practices and subsequently doing little in the way of addressing the substantive legal loopholes. The same politicians and revenue bodies that are railing against aggressive tax strategies also applaud MNEs that reveal information and act cooperatively, but do little to make substantive changes. Within this context, these MNEs have transposed what is a statutory obligation into one that is a business transaction deemed to be negotiable. Then, the same MNEs voluntarily disclose tax information in a manner that suggests they have met their statutory obligations.

Given the push for greater tax transparency over the last decade, the question is whether increased tax transparency measures, especially voluntary disclosure measures, are enabling tax behaviour of MNEs that, while breaking no laws, can still behave in a morally objectionable and socially irresponsible manner with the endorsement of the public, revenue authorities and politicians alike. This chapter, in the next section, explores how this position has been reached, where transparency measures are viewed as playing an important role in addressing aggressive tax practices. This allows a discussion on how it has become possible, and even acceptable, for MNEs to behave in a way that many argue is morally objectionable or socially irresponsible, while still meeting all requirements of the law.

## 6.3 TAXATION WITHIN THE SOCIAL CONTRACT

Corporations are artificial constructs that are legitimized through a social contract or what is commonly known as a public licence to operate. The traditional corporate social contract is between an entity and a nation's people, meaning that the contract sits at a domestic level. While MNEs are global entities, there is no global community with which a single social contract can be formed. Consequently, in the case of MNEs, the contract is not a global one but rather numerous contracts at a national level in each jurisdiction in which the entity operates, each with differing explicit and implicit terms. This group of contracts approach is entirely consistent with the current international tax regime, and therefore, its appropriateness is seldom questioned. The current international tax regime has a strong emphasis on sovereignty and jurisdiction to tax, which is founded on principles of residence and source. These individual social contracts support the elements of the current international tax regime, such as the arm's length pricing standard in the transfer pricing regime, excessive debt rules, and CFC rules, to name a few. What is not consistent, however, is the way that MNEs operate. Separate domestic-level social contracts are in direct contrast to the true nature of the MNE, which transcends national boundaries and operates to ensure it maximizes global profits. Yet, there is currently no mechanism to match the MNE's social contract with its global status. As such, tax policies revert to nation states.

Within each national jurisdiction, the separate social contracts provide nation states with the right to tax MNEs based on the ability-to-pay and benefits principle.[17] At a national level, governments also view the tax obligations of MNEs as part of the social contract or the MNE's social licence to operate in that jurisdiction. However, traditionally nation states tend to view the social contract as a requirement by corporate entities to legitimize their actions through disclosures to ensure the credibility and trust of the public. The effect is that the responsibility for corporate actions that occur internationally is reported at a domestic level. This makes sense with many actions that require legitimizing, such as ethically sourcing coffee beans or using labour production facilities with appropriate conditions. These types of corporate actions cannot be leveraged off each other across countries. Tax is a different matter. BHP, Rio Tinto and Ampol can disclose the tax they are paying where they are headquartered without regard to tax practices in other jurisdictions (marketing hubs), and the public is likely to be mollified if they believe it is an appropriate amount. Corporate entities take responsibility for paying taxes within the domestic social contract framework and leverage contracts in other jurisdictions off each other. Then, the MNEs disclose certain tax information and claim their responsibility is met, conflating reporting responsibilities and a statutory obligation to pay taxes.

The views of nation states, with the overarching support and encouragement of the OECD, are evident in proposed reform packages. Domestically, revenue authorities now view MNE disclosures as part of the social contract and see them as a way to ensure corporates pay their 'fair share' of tax. For

---

17 Sol Picciotto, 'Taxation of Transnational Corporations and the Social Contract' *Afronomicslaw* (Symposium Post, 18 July 2020) <https://www.afronomicslaw.org/2020/07/17/taxation-of-transnational-corporations-and-the-social-contract>.

example, recent reform proposals in Australia were couched in terms of ensuring the public understood that disclosure measures would mean that MNEs would be forced into a position where they met public expectations. In 2022, an Australian consultation paper expressly referred to the notion of the social contract, stating, 'The community is increasingly seeking more openness from business (and governments), to assist the public's understanding of MNEs' tax compliance and to better inform their assessment of MNEs' contributions to the community (in terms of tax paid) relative to their activities in the economy.'[18]

Disclosures were seen as a way to ensure the balance between business activities and payments of tax, not that statutory obligations were met. The paper further stated that

> [e]ssentially, this understanding reflects the social contract notion and the idea that the tax burden should be shared equitably; that is, MNEs should pay a fair share of tax. Public transparency allows civil society and the public to scrutinise the corporate behaviour of MNEs and judge whether it meets public expectations.[19]

Again, tax in this statement is clearly seen as a negotiable proposition whereby certain stakeholders are entitled to judge whether MNEs are acting morally and an appropriate amount of tax is being paid.

The views espoused by domestic revenue authorities prima facie support the notion that, somehow, disclosure mechanisms address aggressive tax practices and result in MNEs going beyond what they are legally required to pay in any given jurisdiction. It also implies that the two forms of reform measures, substantive regulatory reforms and increased transparency measures, complement each other. However, such a view is arguably inconsistent with the aims of the MNE and facilitates aggressive tax practices. This is demonstrated through the role that CSR plays within the social contract and the business of the firm.

## 6.4 CORPORATE SOCIAL RESPONSIBILITY

In 1970, Milton Friedman famously stated that 'the social responsibility of business is to increase its profits'.[20] Known as shareholder theory, the notion that the primary obligation of a company is to its shareholders and that profits

---

[18] Australian Treasury, *Government Election Commitments: Multinational Tax Integrity and Enhanced Tax Transparency, Consultation Paper* (August 2022) 19 <https://treasury.gov.au/sites/default/files/2022-08/c2022-297736-cp.pdf>.

[19] Ibid.

[20] Milton Friedman, 'A Friedman Doctrine – The Social Responsibility of Business Is to Increase Its Profits' *New York Times* (13 September 1970) <https://www.nytimes.com/1970/09/13/archives/a-friedman-doctrine-the-social-responsibility-of-business-is-to.html>.

must be maximized traditionally failed to take into account externalities. Around the same time, the concepts of corporate social responsibility (CSR) and the social contract for corporate entities took hold. While there is a lack of consensus on the origins of CSR,[21] the concept of the social contract in the corporate setting gained prominence in the 1970s,[22] particularly when it was articulated by the Committee for Economic Development in the United States (US) in 1971.[23] It established the idea that companies function and exist because of public consent and, therefore, have an obligation to contribute to society's needs. This premise that corporations were expected to assume responsibilities centred on what was seen as the impetus for CSR to gain prominence. In direct contrast to shareholder theory, these ethical and moral notions of the corporate entity led to what is known as stakeholder theory.

In 1984, R Edward Freeman detailed stakeholder theory to expand a company's obligation to all those who have a stake in the organization, including customers, employees, investors and communities.[24] A move from the traditional view of the corporation, that it exists primarily to make profits, to one where a broader stakeholder perspective is adopted brings with it the question of business ethics and the moral dilemmas that are generally managed outside a profit-driven framework. Essentially, it brought into the realm of the corporate world the notion that they, too, were part of the social contract network and that an ethical or moral obligation existed beyond profit maximization. However, the notion was one of the corporations legitimizing their business practices rather than meeting their statutory obligations. In the case of Starbucks, the moral obligation is aimed at ensuring coffee beans are ethically sourced, not meeting a statutory obligation to do so. In the case of the extractive industry, the moral obligation is to support the community where it is undertaking mining activities. These are not statutory obligations but rather

---

[21] Mauricio Andrés Latapí Agudelo, Lára Jóhannsdóttir and Brynhildur Davídsdóttir, 'A Literature Review of the History and Evolution of Corporate Social Responsibility' (2019) 4 International Journal of Corporate Social Responsibility 1.

[22] The concept of the social contract, developed by philosophers such as Locke, Rousseau and Hobbes, described the relationship between individuals and government with the notion that individuals delegate certain roles and responsibilities to the government, which in turn provides collective goods.

[23] See, for example, Committee for Economic Development, *Social Responsibilities of Business Corporations* (1971) <https://www.ced.org/pdf/Social_Responsibilities_of_Business_Corporations.pdf>.

[24] R Edward Freeman, *Strategic Management: A Stakeholder Approach* (Cambridge University Press 1984).

part of a business's strategy for sustainability. The question then is where statutory obligations fit within the social contract.

If we apply social contract theory to the obligation to pay tax, it suggests that MNEs have a CSR that goes beyond profit maximization for shareholder return to one where the corporation has an ethical or moral obligation to engage only in behaviour that is seen as palatable to the community and to pay a 'fair' amount of tax. This is because of their obligations to a broader stakeholder group, often considered the public at large or those who are part of a nation's social contract and a corporation's social licence to operate. What this creates, however, is a position where there is a societal expectation that a corporation has an obligation beyond its statutory duty to pay the taxes calculated according to the rules imposed by sovereign states under the principles established by that state.

It is no wonder that MNEs have begun to use CSR mechanisms to legitimize their aggressive tax practices. Within this context, the tax payments by MNEs have been incorporated into the social contract or their social licence to operate and are being promulgated through voluntary reporting mechanisms. However, doing so clearly works to the advantage of the MNE, where they can leverage individual social contracts with differing explicit and implicit terms against each other. Much of the discussion so far has focused on ad hoc disclosure measures. However, a discernible push exists for more consistent voluntary disclosures domestically and internationally. These reporting mechanisms and their role in the international tax regime are considered below.

## 6.5 TAXATION WITHIN A VOLUNTARY REPORTING FRAMEWORK

There is nothing new in corporate reporting generally, with mandatory financial reports required around the globe. Mandatory tax reporting is also increasingly being introduced. While mandatory country-by-country reporting introduced by the OECD in 2015 remains confidential to revenue authorities, a European Union (EU) directive that took effect in December 2021 makes publicly available country-by-country reporting mandatory for many businesses operating in the EU.[25] Other measures, such as the 2010 US Dodd–Frank Act, which requires extractive industries to publicly report all payments made to governments, the 2013 EU Accounting Directive requiring reporting of payments to

[25] European Parliament and Council of the European Union, Directive (EU) 2021/2101 of 24 November 2021 amending Directive 2013/34/EU as regards disclosure of income tax information by certain undertakings and branches (2021) OJ L 429/1 <https://eur-lex.europa.eu/legal-content/EN/TXT/PDF/?uri=CELEX:32021L2101&from=EN>.

the government from the extractive sector,[26] the 2014 EU Capital Requirement Directive IV requiring transparency for banks and capital markets,[27] and the 2016 HM Revenue and Customs requirement for UK businesses to publish a tax strategy,[28] are also mandatory tax reporting measures. However, these measures are generally not centred on the notion of corporate morality but rather address what are perceived as secret transactions. In the case of these reports, the information is quantitative and generally lacks a morality motivation as there is little scope for corporate impression management. As such, they are not within the scope of the current discussion.

In addition to mandatory reports, however, the traditional approach to addressing corporate morality from a stakeholder perspective has imposed some form of CSR expectations on corporations, generally through voluntary reporting measures. These reports, as traditionally developed, typically include information on a company's impact on economic, social and environmental imperatives and its efforts to operate ethically. Tax information may or may not be included in these general reports; however, there is an increasing call for MNEs to do so.

The tax positions and practices of MNEs are known only to the MNEs themselves, and the public has no right to access such information. This conundrum ultimately drives stakeholders' desire to address aggressive tax practices, or at least be able to report on them, and to seek disclosures from MNEs and revenue authorities about the tax positions of corporate taxpayers. It is generally believed that such knowledge will either provide a basis for naming and shaming the most significant offenders or offer some assurance that certain MNEs are good corporate citizens. Stakeholders simply ask MNEs to legitimize their tax practices and provide the public with information to ensure credibility and

---

[26] European Parliament and Council of the European Union, Directive 2013/34/EU of 26 June 2013 on the annual financial statements, consolidated financial statements and related reports of certain types of undertakings, amending Directive 2006/43/EC of the European Parliament and of the Council and repealing Council Directives 78/660/EEC and 83/349/EEC (2013) OJ L 182/19 <https://eur-lex.europa.eu/eli/dir/2013/34/oj>.

[27] European Parliament and Council of the European Union, Directive 2013/36/EU of 26 June 2013 on access to the activity of credit institutions and the prudential supervision of credit institutions and investment firms, amending Directive 2002/87/EC and repealing Directives 2006/48/EC and 2006/49/EC (2013) OJ L 176/338 <https://eur-lex.europa.eu/legal-content/EN/TXT/?uri=celex%3A32013L0036>.

[28] HM Revenue and Customs, 'Publish Your Large Business Tax Strategy' (Guidance, 24 June 2016, last updated 22 June 2018) <https://www.gov.uk/guidance/large-businesses-publish-your-tax-strategy>.

trust. In this sense, the stakeholders' desire for information and corporate entities' desire to be legitimized are in concert. Hence, it is prima facie difficult to see where any conflict lies. However, the answer lies in the nature of tax as a statutory obligation.

Traditionally, CSR disclosures aimed at revealing business practices and operating on a coercion model are generally matters of discretion. On the other hand, disclosures about mandatory statutory obligations that should sit outside any corporate business model and only operate on a sanctions model do not generally fall within CSR disclosures. Yet the latter, where the payment of corporate taxes sits, has moved into the sphere of the former category, with corporate tax practices being seen as part of the good corporate citizen narrative on a coercion-based model. The question of how this has occurred is arguably driven by the narrative that tax payments are somehow discretionary and open to negotiation, such as in the Starbucks and Australian mining companies cases. The fact that this has occurred, however, does not mean that it should.

The question of whether tax should be part of CSR reporting remains unanswered in the literature. CSR is an evolving concept that has increased in importance over the last few decades. A well-defined CSR description is simply impossible as it incorporates a diverse range of issues that have grown steadily over time.[29] Dozens of definitions of CSR exist, with the most widely cited being those of Carroll,[30] Visser[31] and the European Commission.[32] The last of these three defines CSR as 'the responsibility of enterprises for their impacts on society'.[33] This and other definitions are company led and leave responsibilities within the scope of impacts on society open to interpretation.

---

[29] Najeb Masoud, 'How to Win the Battle of Ideas in Corporate Social Responsibility: The International Pyramid Model of CSR' (2017) 2 International Journal of Social Responsibility 4.

[30] Archie B Carroll, 'A Three-Dimensional Conceptual Model of Corporate Performance' (1979) 4(4) Academy of Management Review 497 ('A Three-Dimensional Conceptual Model'); Archie B Carroll, 'The Pyramid of Corporate Social Responsibility: Toward the Moral Management of Organizational Stakeholders' (1991) 34(4) Business Horizons 39 ('The Pyramid of Corporate Social Responsibility').

[31] Wayne Visser, *The Age of Responsibility: CSR 2.0 and the New DNA of Business* (John Wiley & Sons 2011).

[32] European Commission, Communication from the Commission to the European Parliament, the Council, the European Economic and Social Committee and the Committee of the Regions, A renewed EU strategy 2011–14 for Corporate Social Responsibility, COM(2011) 681 final (25 October 2011) (A renewed EU strategy); Masoud (n 29) 2.

[33] European Commission, A renewed EU strategy (n 32) 6.

Carroll, who has designed models for assessing the responsibility of firms to disclose certain information, argues that corporate social performance requires certain elements to be assessed. First, a firm's social responsibilities need to be assessed, followed secondly by identifying the social issues that must be addressed. Third, a corporate entity chooses its response philosophy.[34] Carroll's three-part framework for social responsibility tends to form the basis of any modern description, is the most widely cited in the literature, and is used here to assess the role that tax plays in any reporting.[35] This three-part conceptual framework, labelled a social performance model, essentially consists of the definition of social responsibility, the social issues involved, and the philosophy of responsiveness.[36] Each element can be broken down into separate parts.

First, in assessing a corporation's social accountability, the definition is dissected into four interrelated responsibilities: economic responsibilities (to produce goods and services that society wants and to sell them at a profit); legal responsibilities (following the ground rules, the laws and regulations under which the business is expected to operate); ethical responsibilities (behaviours not codified into law but nevertheless expected of business by society's members); and discretionary responsibilities (social roles over and above those that fall within the first three categories).[37] Carroll has also framed the four responsibilities in a pyramid framework with economic responsibilities, including the fact that businesses have the legitimacy to make a profit during their activities as the foundation, and legal, ethical and philanthropic responsibilities.[38] While tax practices prima facie fall within the ambit of legal responsibilities, and no doubt the obligation to pay taxes due falls within the regulatory system, an analysis of 'what' is to be reported would suggest that accountability goes towards reporting the meeting of the legal obligations to pay taxes rather than reporting any moral obligation to go beyond what the letter of the law requires.

If, however, it is assumed that there is a corporate responsibility to report tax matters, the second issue to be identified involves the social issues tied to those responsibilities. Within this part of any CSR analysis, CSR has evolved over recent years, and those who purport that tax should be a part of the reporting process would argue that it is a pressing issue for corporations. The same argument presents itself, however, in that the social problem is simply whether an MNE has paid the taxes due under the regulatory regime. Yet, within this element of the framework, both the public and the corporate entities have

34 Carroll, 'A Three-Dimensional Conceptual Model' (n 30) 504.
35 Carroll, 'A Three-Dimensional Conceptual Model' (n 30).
36 Ibid 500.
37 Ibid.
38 Carroll, 'The Pyramid of Corporate Social Responsibility' (n 30).

extended the obligation to report to include both quantitative and qualitative data to provide a narrative designed by MNEs and known only to them as to whether it is accurate. These narratives are undoubtedly intended to 'impression manage' stakeholders and give legitimacy to the firms.

Given that some MNEs are using CSR disclosure mechanisms to report information on their tax positions and practices, the third element of Carroll's conceptual model, social responsiveness, also needs to be considered. Known as the philosophy, mode or strategy behind business responses to social issues, it has an acute presence in taxation reporting.[39] Along a continuum, this response can range from doing nothing to doing a great deal, an approach that is most evident in tax. While some MNEs refuse to provide any information on their tax practices, others offer the legal argument that they have paid what is due, while those such as Starbucks offer to pay more.

Davis and Blomstrom are among the many who provide a conceptual scheme for social responsiveness that ranges from withdrawal, through a public relations approach, a legal approach and bargaining, to problem solving.[40] MNEs have adopted each of these approaches. Starbucks, for example, adopted a public relations approach, while the extractive industry giants in Australia adopted a bargaining approach. Each was highly effective in its own way. Neither of these, however, adopted a legal approach, but diverted the narrative from the legality of what was occurring, suggesting that they were going beyond their legal obligations to assure the public that they engaged in ethical tax behaviours. The MNEs operated in a morally reprehensible fashion but were applauded because of the actions they took and the disclosures around them.

Logically, tax disclosures through CSR reporting mechanisms are an obvious part of the solution to determining the practices of these corporations. Hence, it makes sense that calls are made for such disclosures. Based on the same logic, it follows that international bodies such as the OECD, at the behest of their member states, embed disclosures in their recommendations, and nation states, in turn, pass domestic legislation requiring mandatory disclosures as well as offering guidance on recommended voluntary disclosures. What have failed to be recognized, however, are the different types of information that MNEs know only internally and how that information is reported. The fact that MNEs can then use the information that they selectively share and structure the narrative in such a way as to suggest they are acting in a morally appropriate manner removes the statutory obligation to pay taxes. It allows the MNEs to negotiate with the public. Once the public is satisfied that

---

39 Carroll, 'A Three-Dimensional Conceptual Model' (n 30) 501.

40 Keith Davis and Robert L Blomstrom, *Business and Society: Environment and Responsibility* (3rd edn, McGraw-Hill 1975), as cited in Carroll, 'A Three-Dimensional Conceptual Model' (n 30) 502.

the corporate behaviour is acceptable, the actual tax aggressive practices of the MNEs become irrelevant.

Despite this growing trend for MNEs to move their statutory tax obligations into the sphere of a morality narrative through either formal or informal social responsibility reporting, there is a counterintuitive growing trend towards encouraging the reporting of tax obligations in the social sphere rather than a mandatory legal requirement. The main voluntary reporting trends are discussed below.

## 6.6 VOLUNTARY REPORTING MECHANISMS IN TAXATION

CSR reporting mechanisms in the form of voluntary disclosures take many different forms. By their very nature, these reports are optional, and information on an array of activities can be located across various reporting mechanisms, ranging from formal reports to media and website statements. The most obvious reporting mechanism is the CSR Report, some of which include tax information, while most do not. Separately, some corporate entities produce voluntary tax disclosure statements like those recommended in Australia. Consistent with the discussion above, the profession is also increasingly encouraging corporate entities to provide public tax reporting. PwC, for example, has expressed the view that

> [a] company's approach to tax is no longer just a question of compliance. In the context of the environmental, social, and governance (ESG) imperative, it is becoming a powerful indicator of how a business views its role in society and its commitment to its purpose. It's a critical element of a business's social contribution – part of the 'S' in ESG.[41]

Again, the narrative is one of taxation being part of the corporate business with stakeholders to be managed through the narrative provided. From a moral obligation perspective, however, there is a question as to whether these reports affect corporate behaviour. In an attempt to answer this, various forms of disclosures have been subject to analysis by researchers. This section briefly looks at traditional CSR studies.

Researchers have previously investigated the relationship between CSR reporting and tax avoidance. The basis for this investigation is generally the

---

41 William Morris and Edwin Visser, 'Tax Is a Crucial Part of the ESG Conversation' *PwC* <https://www.pwc.com/gx/en/services/tax/publications/tax-is-a-crucial-part-of-esg-reporting.html> accessed 18 July 2024.

notion that morality is a common feature of both.[42] The theoretical basis for investigating the relationship is consistent with the discussion in this chapter and most commonly includes shareholder theory, stakeholder theory, legitimacy theory and the theory of the firm to analyse corporate behaviours. The literature, however, provides conflicting evidence as to the relationship between corporate tax payments and CSR reporting, with ambiguous findings and little consensus as to whether the reporting is simply a 'smoke and mirrors' tactic or a genuine attempt to demonstrate an ethical approach to corporate tax matters.

As Kovermann and Velte explain, much of this is due to the different approaches by the researchers themselves. They correctly point out that

> [w]hether the relationship between the two concepts is of positive or negative nature, mainly depends on the concept of CSR applied by the respective author and on the direction of the assumed causality. Whereas some studies conceive CSR as a determinant of tax avoidance … others conceive tax avoidance as a determinant of CSR.[43]

The same authors also highlight the fact that '[a]t least three major theoretical perspectives can be identified, namely (1) CSR as an expression of stakeholder-orientedness, (2) CSR as a risk-management device, and (3) CSR as an expression of agency problems, which lead to different predictions on the association between CSR (tax avoidance) and tax avoidance (CSR)'.[44]

At the core of the lack of consensus is that a study that investigates the relationship between CSR and tax aggressiveness 'requires a valid and reliable measurement of the phenomenon' being examined, that is, a measure of tax aggressiveness itself.[45] The tax practices of MNEs are highly confidential and known only to the MNEs themselves, which means that researchers use proxies such as effective tax rates, which can be calculated in many ways but do not take into account many of the more effective tax planning strategies such as transfer pricing and thin capitalization. Therefore, it is no wonder that there is a lack of consensus on the effect of voluntary disclosures on corporate tax aggressiveness. These contradictory results, however, tend to lead to the conclusion that, for example, '[t]o regulators, this reinforces the necessity to

---

42 Noorsakinah Abdul Wahab, Nurliana Md Rahin and Mohd Zulkhairi Mustapha, 'CSR Decoupling and Tax Avoidance' (2022) 16(3) Australasian Accounting, Business and Finance Journal 131, 131.

43 Jost Kovermann and Patrick Velte, 'CSR and Tax Avoidance: A Review of Empirical Research' (2021) 18(2) Corporate Ownership and Control 20, 22 (references omitted).

44 Ibid.

45 Ibid 23.

expand disclosure requirements on corporate taxes, to increase transparency, and to strengthen the reliability of CSR reporting'.[46]

Perhaps such a conclusion is warranted if tax reporting is to be considered part of an entity's CSR; however, researchers have not addressed the question of whether tax *should* be part of voluntary reporting. In this sense, investigations into the correlation between voluntary reporting and tax aggressiveness do little to address the fundamental problem of MNEs using legitimate tax measures to minimize their taxes. These investigations also divert attention from the key underlying issue – is tax avoidance through profit shifting consistent with positive corporate morality, good citizenship and social responsibility? Cases such as Starbucks and the Australian extractive industry giants would suggest that the answer is 'yes' and that it is, in effect, endorsed by governments and courts applying the laws passed by governments, notwithstanding the people who passed the laws sometimes railing against companies for doing precisely what they have been allowed to do.

Voluntary tax reporting measures are also encouraged in some jurisdictions, with Australia being a prime example. In May 2015, triggered by aggressive tax avoidance practices employed by 'a few high-profile companies' and as a part of the Australian Budget announcement, the then Treasurer, Joe Hockey, commissioned the Board of Taxation to work with businesses, the Treasury and the ATO to develop a voluntary code on increased public disclosure of tax information by companies, particularly multinationals, with a completion date of May 2016. The intent was to highlight companies paying their fair share of tax and to encourage companies not to engage in aggressive tax avoidance. The code's voluntary nature was expected to promote corporate leadership, build confidence in business, and strike an appropriate balance between promoting community confidence in the tax system and the release of commercially sensitive information.

In December 2015, following extensive public and confidential meetings, the Board of Taxation issued a consultation paper on the Tax Transparency Code.[47] This was promptly followed by a report to the Treasurer in February 2016,[48] which outlined a set of principles and minimum standards to guide the

---

[46] Ibid 35.

[47] For the relevant documents relating to the Tax Transparency Code, see Board of Taxation, 'Corporate Tax Transparency Code and Register' <https://taxboard.gov.au/current-activities/corporate-tax-transparency-code-and-register> accessed 18 July 2024.

[48] Board of Taxation, *A Tax Transparency Code: A Report to the Treasurer* (2016).

disclosure of tax information by businesses such that general[49] and interested[50] users, such as social justice groups, media, analysts, and shareholders, were better able to understand an entity's tax position.[51] These disclosures included reconciliations of accounting to taxable incomes, a summary of corporate taxes paid, information about related party dealings, an effective company tax rate for Australian and global operations, and the entity's tax strategy and governance. As of February 2023, there are 210 signatories to the voluntary tax transparency code, with the majority of those being large entities with an aggregated Australian turnover of AUD 500 million or more (80%) where the ultimate holding company is in Australia (76%).

Other voluntary reporting measures include the 2003 Extractive Industries Transparency Initiative and recommendations by the Global Sustainability Standards Board (GSSB),[52] the Global Reporting Initiative's (GRI)[53] independent standard-setting body responsible for overseeing the development of the standards. In 2017, the GSSB initiated a project to develop a disclosure regime related to tax and payments to the government. GRI207, the tax standard ultimately approved after broad consultation, was launched in 2021. The

---

49 '"General users" [are] the "person in the street" and the community at large … [These users] would be best served by a simplified, standardised disclosure, focusing on the tax contribution of a business to Australia': Board of Taxation (n 48) 13.

50 '"Interested users" [are] shareholders, analysts, investors, social justice groups, media and politicians … [These users] require more detailed information about a business's tax affairs', including 'more information about international dealings and tax paid': ibid.

51 Board of Taxation, 'Draft Appendix to The Tax Transparency Code' (2016), available at https://taxboard.gov.au/current-activities/corporate-tax-transparency-code-and-register accessed 18 July 2024.

52 The GSSB consists of 15 members, individuals from diverse sectors, backgrounds and locations. See Global Reporting Initiative, 'Global Sustainability Standards Board' <https://www.globalreporting.org/standards/gssb-and-standard-setting/gssb-members/> accessed 18 July 2024.

53 Founded in Boston in 1997 by the Coalition for Environmentally Responsible Economies, the Tellus Institute and the United Nations Environment Programme, the GRI is an independent organization tasked with developing global standards of sustainability reporting (accountability mechanisms to ensure companies follow responsible and sustainable conduct). The GRI assists businesses and governments worldwide to communicate their impact on sustainability issues such as climate change, human rights, governance and social well-being, using a set of global standards for sustainability reporting. See GRI, 'Our Mission and History' <https://www.globalreporting.org/about-gri/mission-history/> accessed 18 July 2024.

aim of the standard is to enable organizations to report on tax practices as part of their sustainability reporting, provide disclosures on tax strategy, governance and risk management that meet different stakeholder expectations of reporting, introduce public country-by-country reporting of business activities, revenues, profit and tax, and promote disclosure of the reasons for the difference between corporate income tax accrued and the tax due if the statutory tax rate is applied to profit/loss before tax.[54]

While the literature fails to answer whether tax should be part of any form of voluntary CSR reporting, the actions of the MNEs themselves appear to hold the key. Throughout this chapter, it has been demonstrated that MNEs are utilizing voluntary disclosure measures to move the statutory obligation of paying tax according to the law to one that is a negotiable business transaction. The payment of tax moves from being an *ex post* cost outside normal business practices and becomes an *ex ante* business decision, which is seen as something to be managed within the context of the business of the firm, with profits being the central driver and other behaviours requiring legitimization to fulfil the social contract(s). Once the public is convinced of a corporation's legitimacy, credibility and trust are guaranteed, and aggressive tax planning practices are no longer seen as a negative. Instead, the MNE manages to persuade those who need convincing that it is acting responsibly despite morally reprehensible tax strategies.

## 6.7 CONCLUSION

Jurisdictions fail to deter the aggressive tax planning behaviour of MNEs because these corporations act in ways that others cannot; they can sacrifice parts of the corporation for the benefit of the entity as a whole.[55] The reality is that, from a legal perspective, the MNE lacks a unitary corpus,[56] resulting in distinct social contracts and multinational choice. These separate contracts with differing explicit and implicit terms, coupled with multinational choice, allow MNEs to take advantage of different national systems, whether through different standards and wages or other possible arbitrages.[57] Tax is a prime example of the advantage of multinational choice, with the current transfer

[54] Global Reporting Initiative, *GRI 207: TAX 2019, A New Global Standard for Public Reporting on Tax* (Factsheet) <https://www.globalreporting.org/media/sfcpcrt4/gri-207-tax-standard-2019-factsheet.pdf>.

[55] E Palmer, 'Multinational Corporations and the Social Contract' (2001) 31(3) Journal of Business Ethics 245, 249.

[56] The phrase 'unitary corpus' is taken from Palmer (n 55) 249.

[57] Ibid.

pricing regime, the arm's length standard and local arrangements favouring specific behaviour and taxpayers.

For over a century, governments have had tools available to stop profit shifting by adopting a formulary apportionment system to allocate the profits of MNEs. Given the deliberate rejection by international organizations and governments of a rule that would stop profit shifting, and the endorsement by all these parties of the separate entity myth and arm's length pricing for transactions that would never take place between unrelated parties, is it fair to claim that MNEs are breaching a moral code when they pursue these arrangements? Is this perhaps instead an example of companies legitimately using legislatively (and consequently socially) endorsed rules that encourage profit shifting? This is precisely what is implicitly endorsed through voluntary tax reporting mechanisms.

Corporations are artificial constructs, and MNEs operate to ensure maximum global profits. This approach is inherently supported by the OECD, which remains wedded to an arm's length standard and a system that encourages a traditional view of sovereignty whereby nation states remain competitors. Palmer states:

> The OECD is also an artificial product, a consortium entity built by national governments. Its perspective is a product of those of its member nations, and we should not expect corporations to manifest the same priorities, because they maintain a different perspective. Nor should we expect them to conform to those priorities without justification.[58]

The MNE is in a position of power like no other, and it is a position they can abuse while remaining within the bounds of the legal requirements to pay tax. To change the behaviour of the MNE, a change in the underlying principles is needed, and the laws need to enforce that principle through sanctions. If making MNEs accountable for tax on their global profits is the aim, coercive measures such as reporting are much more likely to have the opposite effect. No matter what an MNE produces and/or sells, whether coffee or oil, corporate executives will consider themselves to be in the business of making profits for investors. Using reporting mechanisms to address aggressive tax practices and including tax as part of CSR or any other form of reporting is more likely to have the opposite effect and provide a rationale to corporations to treat the tax payments as a business transaction rather than a legal obligation. In doing so, MNEs can legitimize aggressive tax strategies and argue that they are good corporate citizens and pay their 'fair' share of tax.

---

[58] Ibid 255.

Many are discontented with the tax behaviour of MNEs, which nevertheless breaks no laws. This raises the question of whether it is possible for MNEs to continue to behave in what is perceived as a morally unacceptable or socially irresponsible manner, while still meeting all the requirements of the law. The answer seems to be that while the actions of MNEs are supported by a narrative centred on CSR, morally unacceptable behaviour will continue.

# 7. Applying exit taxes: issues in the financial valuation and accounting recognition of transferred assets

**António Martins**

## 7.1 INTRODUCTION

The European Union (EU) Anti-Tax Avoidance Directive (ATAD-1)[1] establishes that assets transferred between jurisdictions, under the conditions required by the Directive's rule[2] about exit taxation, must be valued at market prices. This rule implies the computation of potential capital gains. In many cases, companies' assets (especially intangibles) are of a unique nature and market prices are difficult to use as a valuation standard.[3]

This chapter discusses two accounting and financial issues related to exit taxation, one of a general nature, the other related to the Portuguese version of the tax. The first issue follows from the fact that most assets are not traded in active markets, comparable transactions are rarely available, and valuation is often based on discounted cash flow (DCF) models. When applying these models, both forecasting cash flows and estimating discount rates (cost of capital) are of paramount importance.[4] To exemplify DCF complexities, when an asset has reduced, or even null, tradability, financial theory recommends the increasing of the discount rate by the so-called discount for lack of tradability or liquidity.[5] Moreover, if an intangible asset is in its development stage,

---

[1] Council of the European Union, Directive 2016/1164 of 12 July 2016 laying down rules against tax avoidance practices that directly affect the functioning of the internal market (2016) OJ L 193/1 (ATAD-1).

[2] See ibid Art 5.

[3] James R Hitchner, *Financial Valuation: Applications and Models* (4th edn, Wiley 2017).

[4] Aswath Damodaran, *Applied Corporate Finance* (3rd edn, Wiley 2011).

[5] Linda H Chen, Edward A Dyl, George J Jiang and Januj A Juneja, 'Risk, Illiquidity or Marketability: What Matters for the Discounts on Private Equity

then forecasting its useful life is a challenging task. Applying DCF models in the context of exit taxes, the valuation of intangibles with unique traits may become a complex topic and one prone to litigation between companies and tax authorities, because small variations in financial assumptions that underlie DCF may induce significant changes in computed valuations, impacting the quantitative base of the exit tax.

The second issue is related to the Portuguese version of the tax, which calls for the computation of the market value of assets *even if they are not recognized in the balance sheet*. A complex issue arises: how to value internally generated assets that cannot (because of accounting standards) be recognized in financial statements. How, for example, should a customer list, the skills of employees, brand recognition, or research and development (R&D) projects be valued?[6] The receiving jurisdiction may question the existence of these 'assets' for tax purposes and their quantitative valuation (the supposed market value) carried out at the time they exited the former jurisdiction.

The chapter is organized as follows: section 7.2 offers a brief note on exit taxation; section 7.3 deals with the accounting recognition of intangibles; section 7.4 discusses the valuation of intangibles; section 7.5 presents a discussion of taxpayer and tax authority behaviour regarding the valuation issue, and section 7.6 concludes.

## 7.2 EXIT TAXATION: A BRIEF NOTE

A short view of exit taxation should start with its economic rationale. ATAD-1 of 12 July 2016 establishes rules against tax avoidance practices that have a direct impact on the functioning of the EU's internal market. It states that exit taxation has the function of ensuring, in the event that taxpayers transfer assets by changing location, that the state of residence taxes the economic value of any capital gains generated in its territory, even if these gains have not been realized at the time of exit. In order to calculate the tax base, it is essential to calculate a market value (or an acceptable proxy) for the transferred assets at the time of exit.

Taxing unrealized, or potential, gains embedded in certain corporate assets is a deviation from the principle of realization. The application of an exit tax is, therefore, based on the principle that a country has the right to tax the

---

Placements?' (2015) 57 Journal of Banking and Finance 41.

[6] W Todd Brotherson, Kenneth M Eades, Robert S Harris and Robert C Higgins, 'Company Valuation in Mergers and Acquisitions: How Is Discounted Cash Flow Applied by Leading Practitioners?' (2014) 24(2) Journal of Applied Finance 43.

economic gains of an entity that were generated in its territory.[7] Such a tax can generate serious concerns for taxpayers. It arises on the date of asset migration, not on the date of realization of any capital gain on the transferred assets, and liquidity may be a concern.[8] Additionally, possible future fluctuations in the value of the assets, after the exit, may not be considered for tax purposes. Such problems are important for companies and tax authorities.

Courts have been dealing with these issues. The European Court of Justice (ECJ), in the case *National Grid Indus BV*,[9] decided that:

(a) a Member State may impose an exit tax on the migration of tax residence of an entity subject to corporation tax to another Member State;
(b) an exit tax need not consider – in calculating the quantum of that exit tax – future decreases in asset values up to the realization date;
(c) national legislation should offer a choice between the immediate payment of tax, but without the exercise of administrative tracking of gains/losses, or tax deferral, although in this case with future tracking of gains/losses on the asset.

Adding a new layer of complexity in the application of the exit tax, article 83, section 1, of the Portuguese Corporate Income Tax Code (CITC) establishes that the market values of transferred assets must be determined even if they are not recognized in the balance sheet.

A general analysis of the valuation issues related to exit taxation must recognize that many business assets (e.g., tangible fixed assets, intangible assets, investment properties), even if recognized in the balance sheet, are not regularly traded and no observed market prices exist. Consequently, financial valuation models will be used to compute asset values. This may cause significant divergence with tax authorities regarding the computation of the exit tax base.

The potential disagreement between companies and tax authorities is reduced when valuing assets such as cash, receivables and inventory. In the case of long-term assets, key contributors to long-term competitiveness and value creation, complex issues arise related to their valuation.

Whether projecting cash flows, estimating discount rates, or forecasting growth rates for longer periods, value assessments are based on assumptions

[7] Andrew Parkes, 'Exit Taxes on Corporate Relocation', 4772 *Taxation* (8 December 2020) <https://www.taxation.co.uk/articles/exit-taxes-on-corporate-relocation> accessed 9 July 2024.

[8] The Directive (ATAD-1 (n 1)) establishes the option of paying the tax over five years, easing liquidity constraints.

[9] Case C-371/10 *National Grid Indus BV v Inspecteur van de Belastingdienst Rijnmond/kantoor Rotterdam* [2011] ECR I-12273.

that are often questioned by tax authorities. This is particularly relevant for intangibles.[10]

Determining the market value of items typically not recognized in the balance sheet (e.g., research and development expenses, customer lists, special skills of the management team and employees) can lead to serious disagreements with the tax auditors if the latter challenge exit taxation procedures and calculations.

Parkes underlines that the ECJ concluded that exit taxes are justified on the grounds of a balanced distribution of taxing powers between Member States, based on the principle of territoriality linked to a temporal activity component.[11] If a company benefited from the infrastructure of a country while being resident for tax purposes, then the country is authorized to tax any gains arising during that period. If the value of assets increases because of advantages provided by a jurisdiction, it is reasonable to share part of the value increase.

An area of complexity in the application of the exit tax relates to items that are recognized in accounting statements, but which, due to their unique nature, are difficult to value. Complexity increases when items are not recognized because accounting standards do not allow their inclusion in the balance sheet. Intangibles are an obvious source of potential problems as far as valuation for the purposes of exit taxation is concerned. Complexity in valuing intangibles arises from two major factors: market values are absent and many unrecognized items are important sources of company value creation.

## 7.3 INTANGIBLE ASSETS: SOME ISSUES IN THEIR RECOGNITION AND VALUATION

An intangible asset is an identifiable non-monetary asset without physical substance. As argued by Lev, it is often difficult to attribute corporate expenses directly to a specific intangible (by capitalizing the expenses) rather than allocating them to the business as a whole, so impacting net profit.[12] The recognition of intangibles, and their periodical valuation, is a difficult accounting topic.

---

[10] António Martins, 'The Portuguese Intellectual Property Box: Issues in Designing Investment Incentives' (2018) 17(3) Journal of International Trade Law and Policy 86.

[11] Parkes (n 7).

[12] Baruch Lev, 'Ending the Accounting-for-Intangibles Status Quo' <https://ideas.repec.org/a/taf/euract/v28y2019i4p713-736.html> (2019) 28(4) European Accounting Review 713. <https://ideas.repec.org/s/taf/euract.html>.

International Accounting Standard (IAS) 38, 'Intangible Assets', prescribes accounting recognition criteria.[13] Paragraphs 21 to 23 are important guidelines in recognizing and valuing intangibles:

21. An intangible asset shall be recognized if, and only if:
    (a) it is probable that the expected future economic benefits that are attributable to the asset will flow to the entity; and
    (b) the cost of the asset can be measured reliably.
22. An entity shall assess the probability of expected future economic benefits using reasonable and supportable assumptions that represent management's best estimate of the set of economic conditions that will exist over the useful life of the asset.
23. An entity uses judgement to assess the degree of certainty attached to the flow of future economic benefits that are attributable to the use of the asset on the basis of the evidence available at the time of initial recognition, giving greater weight to external evidence.

As stated in these paragraphs, the use of estimates, value judgements, probabilistic reasoning and similar approaches are crucial to determining the value of an intangible asset, introducing a certain degree of subjectivism. The valuation of recognized intangible assets is a task involving a high level of uncertainty.

The Portuguese CITC, requiring the valuation of intangible items that are not recognized for accounting purposes, increases the number of situations where valuation methods based on forecasts, expectations and value judgements influence the calculation of the tax base. Therefore, disagreements can happen between tax authorities and taxpayers when quantifying the exit tax due when a company is leaving Portugal.

If tax auditors disagree with valuation approaches taken by companies and adjust the taxable income through alternative methods (also dependent on estimates about a vast number of variables such as expected cash flows, expected useful lives and discount rates to be applied), disputes between taxpayers and tax authorities may conceivably increase.

IAS 38 does not allow the recognition in the balance sheet of intangible items that, although potentially contributing to the generation of future economic benefits, do not meet recognition criteria, especially if an entity does

---

[13] IFRS Foundation, 'Intangible Assets' (IFRS Accounting Standard IAS 38, May 2014) <https://www.ifrs.org/content/dam/ifrs/publications/pdf-standards/english/2021/issued/part-a/ias-38-intangible-assets.pdf> accessed 29 March 2024 (IAS 38).

not control those intangible elements and it is difficult to deal with them separately.[14]

Why do such expenses not lead to the recognition of assets if they are carried out internally and may, in the form of goodwill[15] in an acquisition process, be recognized by an acquiring company? The main reason is probably related to an external valuation process to which such intangible items are subjected in corporate acquisitions, less open to manipulation and sometimes derived from competitive bids between potential buyers. Conversely, it can be argued that an entity's management is better informed about the potential economic effects of invested sums and has an adequate basis to value internally generated intangible items. However, the approval of a market price would be missing as an objective source of valuation.[16] Thus, IAS 38 has established a restrictive view concerning the recognition of assets derived from internally generated intangible elements.[17]

---

[14] Tami Dinh, Helen Kang and Wolfgang Schultze, 'Capitalizing Research & Development: Signaling or Earnings Management?' (2016) 25(2) European Accounting Review 373.

[15] Goodwill is an intangible asset recognized in the context of corporate acquisitions. It is the difference between the price paid for a target company and the fair value of its identifiable net assets. Goodwill has an economic rationale based on the contribution to value creation made by unrecognized items (e.g., skills of people, brand prestige, innovative capacity, product reputation, unique production formulas) that the target company may have and whose value is included in the price to be paid, even if not accounted for in the balance sheet.

[16] Elena-Mirela Nichita, 'Intangible Assets – Insights from a Literature Review' (2019) 18(2) Accounting and Management Information Systems 224.

[17] As stated in paras 9 and 10 of IAS 38 (n 13):

> 9. Entities frequently expend resources, or incur liabilities, on the acquisition, development, maintenance or enhancement of intangible resources such as scientific or technical knowledge, design and implementation of new processes or systems, licences, intellectual property, market knowledge and trademarks (including brand names and publishing titles). Common examples of items encompassed by these broad headings are computer software, patents, copyrights, motion picture films, customer lists, mortgage servicing rights, fishing licences, import quotas, franchises, customer or supplier relationships, customer loyalty, market share and marketing rights.
>
> 10. Not all the items described in paragraph 9 meet the definition of an intangible asset, i.e., identifiability, control over a resource and existence of future economic benefits. If an item within the scope of this Standard does not meet the definition of an intangible asset, expenditure to acquire it or generate it internally is recognised as an expense when it is incurred. However, if the item is acquired in a business combination, it forms part of the goodwill recognised at the acquisition date.

One of the proponents of a substantial change in the accounting model for intangibles agrees that the risk level of these assets is high.[18] The causes are: (i) the absence of markets where such items are regularly traded impacts the degree of tradability and portfolio diversification; (ii) the sunk cost nature of many (intangible-related) cash outlays that do not reach the income generation stage, and (iii) the fact that intangibles often have spillover effects, with benefits not being restricted to their owners (e.g., reverse engineering or patent infringement).

Nonetheless, Lev sustains that intangibles meeting, cumulatively, the following conditions should be capitalized:

(a) the entity holds legal ownership of the asset through patents, copyrights or registered trademarks, or through restricting access for competitors;
(b) the asset is scarce (limited in supply) and cannot be easily imitated;
(c) the asset is capable of generating, and there are expectations that it will generate, future benefits;
(d) the entity is able to allocate periodic investments in the asset and has the means to complete its development.

Lev also sustains that certain intangible items, such as in-house employee training and the development of organizational capital, will often be excluded from capitalization, because companies do not regularly determine costs involved in their creation.

If an intangible element complies with the aforementioned conditions and is capitalized in the balance sheet, it must be subjected to regular impairment tests, or even written off, if it proves to be a complete economic failure. The convenience of not capitalizing these assets is especially appreciated by managers. By treating them as expenses, they do not leave a trace on the balance sheet and do not provide unpleasant future surprises when carrying out impairment tests. Changes in IAS 38 are strongly argued for by Lev, calling for modifications in the process of recognition of intangibles that are important sources of competitiveness and expected benefits for many firms.

The main argument against the capitalization of internally generated intangibles (high uncertainty about future benefits) cannot, according to Lev, be distinguished from the risk related to development projects that may be recognized as intangibles in corporate acquisitions. Many tangible fixed assets (e.g., hardware, robots, specialized laboratory equipment) present high levels of uncertainty regarding the ability to generate future benefits. This does not prevent their capitalization.

---

[18] Lev (n 12).

This agenda for intangible valuation and recognition is opposed by Skinner.[19] He argues that reasons for reforming intangible recognition criteria are weak and do not support the position according to which large-scale changes in IAS 38 are necessary. Skinner emphasizes that capital markets work well in financing companies that develop innovative, high-tech and knowledge-based activities without such items appearing on the balance sheet.

Furthermore, proposals to modify the current model of accounting in order to recognize certain items on the balance sheet are undesirable. Skinner notes that the existing model does not recognize many knowledge-based intangibles. In many cases, internally developed intangibles such as brands, customer relationships and employee training do not satisfy criteria for asset recognition. However, in Skinner's view, this does not mean that there is a problem with the accounting model, because the balance sheet was not designed to form the basis for valuing entities.

Most valuation approaches rely on information from the income statement and use that information to forecast future cash flows. Penman[20] shows that this approach works well for valuing companies, even in cases where a large part of the value is attributable to (unrecognized) intangibles.

If, on the accounting side, intangibles present thorny issues, when it comes to valuation of intangible items to compute the base on which the exit tax applies, these complexities are amplified.

## 7.4 INTANGIBLE ASSETS: VALUATION

### 7.4.1 Recognized Intangible Assets

Exit taxation requires the valuation of recognized intangible assets. The uniqueness of many intangibles implies the absence of market prices. Therefore, alternative valuation methods must be applied. According to Hitchner,[21] common methods for valuing intangibles fall into three broad categories: market value of similar assets, cost and DCF.

#### 7.4.1.1 Market value of similar assets

The value of an intangible asset is obtained by comparing it with the price actually paid for a similar asset in comparable circumstances. The problem with this method is the extreme difficulty in finding truly comparable intangible

---

[19] Douglas J Skinner, 'Accounting for Intangibles – A Critical Review of Policy Recommendations' (2008) 38(3) Accounting and Business Research 191.

[20] Stephen H Penman, 'The Quality of Financial Statements: Perspectives from the Recent Stock Market Bubble' (2003) 17(Supp) Accounting Horizons 77.

[21] Hitchner (n 3).

assets. Intangibles are, in many circumstances, unique to a particular company and distinctive in nature.

When selecting a valuation method, an appraiser will prefer comparable market transactions involving similar intangibles instead of cost or DCF methods. However, if market valuation is complex when used for *tangible* assets (such as machines or vehicles), in the case of *intangibles* this approach is unlikely to work, given the scarcity of comparable traded intangible assets.[22]

#### 7.4.1.2 Cost method

The cost approach is based on the expenditure that would be incurred to obtain an intangible similar to the one being valued. The cost for replacing intangible assets must be adjusted through factors such as the obsolescence rate in order to make the hypothetical new intangible asset comparable to what is intended to be valued. This approach is usually disregarded because it does not consider potential future earnings attributable to the intangible asset.

#### 7.4.1.3 Discounted cash flow method

The valuation of an entity using the DCF model usually supposes that there is a first period (e.g., five years) for which explicit cash flow forecasts are made and thereafter the entity grows at an estimated perpetual rate. Expected cash flows are discounted to the present time using the cost of capital.

In the case of intangibles, complexities in applying DCF are mostly related to cash flow estimation (quite often cash flows are derived from business lines and not from individual assets), the useful life of intangible resources (typically of a finite nature) and how to relate the higher riskiness of the intangible to the appropriate discount rate.

Damodaran mentions a major criticism of valuation models in general, and the DCF in particular: their low suitability to deal with intangible assets.[23] Economic resources that create competitive advantages such as brands, people's qualifications, customer relations, technical sophistication and patents are often neglected in the valuation of companies.

The valuation of recognized intangibles is a difficult step in exit taxation. Some issues are particularly complex when the valuation of intangibles is based on a DCF model. First, the useful life of technological intangible assets is unpredictable, rendering the time span of cash flow forecasting quite risky.

Secondly, the possibility of new entrants in information technology-based industries is a major factor contributing to the variation in the pricing power

---

[22] Robert F Reilly and Robert P Schweihs, *Guide to Intangible Asset Valuation* (rev edn, Wiley 2014).

[23] Damodaran (n 4).

of firms that have a high intensity of intangible elements as determinants of competitiveness and cash flow generation.

Thirdly, when firms are integrated in multinational groups, the value of an intangible asset located in a certain company may be dependent on the contribution of other intangible sources located in different jurisdictions.

Finally, in the case of litigation related to the quantitative base of the exit tax – when it includes intangibles – courts may not have the technological and financial skills to decide between the arguments of litigants.

If the valuation of recognized intangible assets often generates controversy, the case is more delicate when dealing with non-recognized intangible items. That is the specific issue raised by the Portuguese version of the exit tax.

### 7.4.2 Unrecognized Intangible Items

It is useful to classify assets into various classes. Karius considers productive assets such as tangible assets, and identifiable intangible assets, which the author calls intellectual property, like patents, trademarks and copyrights.[24]

On the other hand, firms may have non-identifiable, unrecognized intangible items that are divided into human capital (e.g., the quality and skills of people), organizational capital (e.g., leadership), and informational capital (e.g., information networks, databases).

Becker suggests a division between human capital (employee capabilities, innovation, adaptability and education), relational capital (relationships with customers and suppliers, company reputation, distribution channels) and structural capital (databases, organizational structure, business processes).[25]

Unrecognized intangible items usually do not have market prices. Additionally, the cost method is not often a viable alternative because management accounting does not focus on information to capitalize such intangible items, immediately expensing the monetary disbursements that increase these sources of competitiveness.

Karius emphasizes that DCF models generate several problems when valuing intangible elements such as the skills of people, the prestige of brand names, and the reputation of a company gained with its clientele and the providers of financial resources.[26]

---

[24] Tim Karius, *Intellectual Property and Intangible Assets: Alternative Valuation and Financing Approaches for the Knowledge Economy in Luxembourg* (European Institute for Knowledge and Value Management Research Report No 3, 2016).

[25] Gary S Becker, 'Foreword' in Alan Burton-Jones and J-C Spender (eds), *The Oxford Handbook of Human Capital* (Oxford University Press 2011).

[26] Karius (n 24).

A major problem is that the analysis of historical data and its extrapolation into the future, underlining the typical application of DCF, imply that the value of unrecognized intangibles will hardly be correctly calculated. Their life cycle is unpredictable and dependent on other assets, and the valuation phase is often quite far from the time of potential income generation, leading to high uncertainty in the valuation process.

The treatment given to unrecognized intangible items by accounting standards affects the financial management of companies whose activity depends mostly on intangible elements and which may have restricted access to different types of financing, especially bank credit. Bankers looking at balance sheets of these entities may restrict funding, given the absence of recognized assets that can guarantee loans.

Non-identifiable intangible assets are sometimes accompanied by intangible liabilities. The latter are generated by weak leadership or bad relationships with customers and suppliers. Non-identifiable intangible assets would constitute the positive part of goodwill, and non-identifiable intangible liabilities would be the negative part of goodwill.[27]

The forecasting pitfalls inherent in the DCF model are notorious. In the case of human capital, the estimated duration of a professional career in the service of a certain company is characterized by great uncertainty. Staff turnover rates are high, making predictions difficult. The cost model, based on expenses related to personnel admission and training, is an alternative approach.

As for structural capital, Pastor and co-authors identify some subtypes: organizational structure, organizational culture, and rules and norms of behaviour. Such items cannot be sold separately but may be acquired via franchising. The expected cash flows of a franchising arrangement can serve as a valuation basis. The value of other assets (contributory assets) would have to be deducted to arrive at the value of the structural capital.

Companies also have customer lists, databases and other relevant business information. If surrogate elements for these items can be obtained, then the cost method may be a solution for valuing this subtype. If not, DCF is the recommended alternative.

As for relational capital, it encompasses relationships with customers, suppliers and business partners, the company's image, reputation, customer satisfaction, and distribution channels. Pastor and co-authors note the extreme difficulty in valuing these items. In most cases, relational capital is measured by

[27] Damián Pastor, Jozef Glova, František Lipták and Viliam Kováč, 'Intangibles and Methods for Their Valuation in Financial Terms: Literature Review' (2017) 13(2) Intangible Capital 387.

non-financial indicators.[28] That is why quantitative and qualitative approaches for valuing intangibles are put forward by authors like Karius.[29] The first approach includes methods such as cost, market value and DCF. The second incorporates methods based on financial and non-financial indicators, resorting to analytical tools similar to the Balanced Scorecard.

There are cases in which traditional quantitative methods may prove to be complex and, therefore, limited in application. However, in the case of exit taxation, a quantitative assessment is needed. Qualitative methods can offer a first step when critical factors of competitiveness are selected and rated. But, at a later stage, a calculation of their contribution to a quantitative assessment is inevitable.

Karius, underlining the limitations of traditional, quantitative methods in the valuation of non-identifiable intangibles, proposes an intellectual property score.[30] It applies a qualitative approach that is focused on some characteristics, such as legal protection and potential uses of the intellectual property. The objective is not a quantitative valuation of the intangible items that constitute intellectual property but a qualitative-based scoring depending on the risk of obtaining the expected benefits from the intangible items under analysis. This approach does not eliminate the requirement of a quantitative valuation for the intangible.

The difference lies in the fact that the scoring values influence this assessment. A first step, qualitative, is followed by another, numerical, in which the inputs of the first enter into the determination of the computed value. In short, whatever the designation, whether the qualitative phase is more or less extensive, exit taxation inevitably implies calculating the value of these intangibles.

Criticisms directed at the DCF model regarding the influence of assumptions are not absent from qualitative models. The latter expand the number of factors influencing the assessment but do not replace quantitative techniques. In exit taxation, a quantitative basis is mandatory. Independently of the range of intangible unrecognized assets a firm may select, and the qualitative criteria that may help to assess future profitability, exit taxation requires a final quantitative valuation. Independently of the nature of the valuing models and the factors that influence unrecognized intangibles, it is impossible to avoid a final calculation that adopts either a backward-looking (cost) or forward-looking (DCF) foundation.

---

28 Anne Wyatt, 'What Financial and Non-Financial Information on Intangibles Is Value-Relevant? A Review of the Evidence' (2008) 38(3) Accounting and Business Research 217.

29 Karius (n 24).

30 Ibid.

Qualitative-based models present a logical basis for apprehending the sources of value derived from non-identifiable intangibles. It is likely that, in reality, companies and tax authorities will adhere to methods of valuation that are less extensive, but more easily applied, because in a possible litigation context, the more variables entering into the assessment of intangibles, the greater the range of possible disagreement.

According to recent research about the accounting rules for intangibles, present accounting practices are unlikely to change.[31] Accounting standard-setters place greater emphasis on how companies report and disclose the value of intangibles rather than changing recognition criteria. That means problems highlighted in this chapter are here to stay.

Are unrecognized intangible items effective sources of corporate competitiveness? The relationship between unrecognized intangible items and the competitiveness and value of companies was analysed for the Peruvian case.[32] That study investigated whether there is a relationship between intellectual capital (measured by a set of attributes) and the export performance of Peruvian companies. The study presented an empirical analysis relating intellectual capital to the export capacity of entities in the textile sector in Peru. In a sample of 207 textile manufacturing companies, it was found that human capital and organizational capital have a positive influence on export performance.

In financial analysis for banking purposes, or attracting venture capital, qualitative information allows a more complete appreciation of the business characteristics and the potential for generating cash flows. The disclosure of such intangible items, for example in notes to the financial statements, contributes to the improvement of information available to various interested parties. In the tax field, especially in exit taxation, a quantitative assessment is necessary. It can be based on the previous exposition of the elements that make up intellectual capital. But in the end, it will be necessary to quantify a tax base, not merely to present a qualitative description of intangible elements.

When a company changes its tax residence and exit taxation implies the valuation of unrecognized intangible items, as in Portugal, the set of items to be considered and the choice of valuation methods are complex issues. A potential way of computing the value of intangible assets is to apply the DCF

---

[31] Henry Hussinki, Tatiana King, John Dumay and Erik Steinhöfel, 'Accounting for Intangibles: A Critical Review' (2025) 47(5) Journal of Accounting Literature 27.

[32] Carlos Del Castillo Guardamino and José Ventura Egoávil, 'Export Performance in South America: Do Intangibles Affect Firms' Performance in Developing Countries such as Peru?' (2021) 61(2) Revista de Administração de Empresas 1.

model because, as noted by Skinner,[33] the DCF values unrecognized items, especially by determining the residual (going concern) value. Amounts calculated using DCF often deviate from book values, and this is largely due to the contribution of unrecognized intangible items companies may use when computing the exit tax in Portugal. In short, the exit tax, as it is legislated in Portugal, will often imply the computation of a company's goodwill, as the reflection of the intangible assets not recognized in the balance sheet.

## 7.5 EXIT TAXATION, TAX AUDITS AND COURTS

In the previous section, the difficult issues related to the valuation of intangibles in the process of exit taxation were stressed. For recognized intangibles, valuation methods such as cost, market value and DCF are available, albeit with ample margins of disagreement between tax authorities and corporations that change tax residence. The case is more complex regarding unrecognized intangible items. Qualitative-based models highlighted in this chapter must lead, at a final stage, to a quantification technique that values intangible items in terms of their contribution to the tax base.

The difficult exercise of applying exit taxation to intangible unrecognized assets is an issue that interested parties have to deal with. What mechanisms could be put in place to minimize the potential for legal disputes between companies and tax authorities in exit taxation?

On the side of companies, valuation reports should be carefully substantiated. Economic and business assumptions related to future benefits (or incurred costs) must be available and openly discussed with tax auditors. In many real-life situations, the openness of firms to supplying detailed information may not be high because unrecognized intangible items are important sources of competitiveness and constitute business-critical data that managers resist sharing with external parties.

Some major issues should also merit careful attention from tax authorities in auditing procedures. When compared to managers, tax auditors have less knowledge of businesses and, therefore, even if highly trained, they may overlook some specific and unique issues that impact comparability in finding similar intangibles used as benchmarks.

Carefully substantiated audit reports are of paramount importance in auditing exit taxation when intangibles are involved. Senior audit team leaders with extensive practical experience are required, particularly if a major case is at stake.

---

33 Skinner (n 19).

Additionally, high-ranking tax authority officers should not be afraid of conducting thorough reviews of tax audits, nudging junior auditors towards balanced conclusions. Junior auditors must be informed that their professional chances of promotion do not depend on significant tax adjustments emerging from superficially sustained reports but on the quality of the arguments and proofs that underpin an exit tax review.

The experience of tax authorities in transfer pricing, a frequent topic for auditing and litigation, may serve as an alert for avoiding errors in draconian audits. When dealing with transfer pricing, comparable market values are a core issue. Thus, exit tax auditors can be chosen based on a solid background in transfer pricing analysis.

Tax authorities could eventually produce internal rule books for auditing exit taxation by identifying the most common assets to be valued, delicate issues often found, and possible ways of overcoming them.

In cases of controversy between firms and tax authorities, calling in independent valuers who can broker a reasonable solution, acceptable to both parties, may significantly reduce litigation that is time consuming and generates tax uncertainty. A careful and collaborative approach by both parties, companies and tax authorities, is called for. In times of stringent public finances, this collaborative approach may be overlooked.

Additionally, in Portugal, tax litigation is an all-or-nothing process ('mere nullification process'). For example, if the tax authority argues for an adjustment of EUR ten million and the company sustains the position that no adjustment should take place, courts only analyse the legal grounds of the tax authority adjustment. If it is found to be correct, the tax authority wins; if not, the company wins. In exit taxation (as in other areas of corporate income tax), middle-ground solutions should be at the disposal of the courts. Based on expert testimony and the expertise of judges, more equitable outcomes could be envisaged in areas that are fuzzy and subjective.

As argued in subsection 7.4.2 of this chapter, the process of quantifying the value of unrecognized intangible assets is often similar to valuing goodwill. As will be known, a critical assumption in computing goodwill is the rate of perpetual growth that a company's asset base can sustain. However, a note of restraint for tax auditors in exit taxation should be underlined: in many cases, exited intangible items have finite lives, and the growth rate in perpetuity is dependent on future investments made by the company in the new jurisdiction. Therefore, in-depth discussions between firms and tax authorities are quite important when assessing the reasonableness of hypotheses underlying the quantification of the economic and financial basis of the exit tax.

To sum up, the interplay of IAS 38, financial valuation techniques and exit taxation calls for a collaborative and open procedure between firms and tax authorities that is not often observed.

## 7.6 CONCLUSION

The use of estimates, value judgements, probabilistic reasoning and similar approaches are crucial to determining the value of an intangible asset, introducing a certain degree of subjectivism. The valuation of recognized intangible assets is a task involving a high level of uncertainty.

The valuation of recognized intangibles is a difficult step in exit taxation. The useful life of technological intangible assets is unpredictable, and the possibility of new entrants in internet-based industries is a major factor contributing to the variation in the pricing power of firms that have a high intensity of intangible elements. When firms are integrated in multinational groups, the value of an intangible asset located in a certain company may be dependent on the contribution of other intangible sources located in different jurisdictions.

A major problem in valuing intangible unrecognized items is that the analysis of historical data and its extrapolation into the future, underlining the typical application of DCF, imply that the value of unrecognized intangibles will hardly be correctly calculated. Their life cycle is unpredictable, and dependent on other assets, and the valuation phase is often quite far from the time of potential income generation, leading to high uncertainty in the valuation process.

In-depth discussions between firms and tax authorities are quite important when assessing the reasonableness of hypotheses underlying the quantification of the economic and financial basis of the exit tax when unrecognized intangible items are involved. Intangible valuation in the context of exit taxation calls for a collaborative procedure between firms and tax authorities that is not often observed.

# PART III

# International tax: BEPS and beyond

# 8. What's the problem that prompted Pillar Two and is there a better solution?

**J. Clifton Fleming Jr, Robert J. Peroni and Stephen E. Shay**

## 8.1 THE ROAD TO TAX COMPETITION

In 1648, the major powers of Europe, exhausted by their efforts in the Thirty Years War to impose religious orthodoxy on each other while securing comparative geopolitical advantages, entered into the Treaties of Westphalia. These instruments brought peace for a time and, most importantly, are generally regarded as providing a seminal recognition of the concept of state sovereignty.[1] One of the bedrock elements of this sovereignty is the power to impose and control taxation within state borders.[2] In time, states discovered that their sovereign power to set tax rates within their borders gave them the capacity to use tax holidays or low or zero rates of tax to lure business activity and

[1] See generally John P Grant and J Craig Barker, *Parry and Grant Encyclopaedic Dictionary of International Law* (3rd edn, Oxford University Press 2009) 676 ('Westphalia, Peace of, Treaty of, 1648'); Sean D Murphy, *Principles of International Law* (Thomson/West 2006) 21; Hendrik Spruyt, *The Sovereign State and Its Competitors: An Analysis of Systems Change* (Princeton University Press 1994) 27.

[2] See, e.g., Organisation for Economic Co-operation and Development (OECD), *Action Plan on Base Erosion and Profit Shifting* (2013) 9 ('Taxation is at the core of countries' sovereignty') (*Action Plan*); Tsilly Dagan, *International Tax Policy: Between Competition and Cooperation* (Cambridge University Press 2018) 13 ('The implicit traditional conception of states sees them as powerful sovereigns that operate in a closed economy with the capacity to make and enforce mandatory rules, impose taxes, and set redistribution').

investment into their economies and away from other countries.[3] There was little that most affected countries could do unilaterally except to respond by offering their own tax concessions with respect to profits earned within their borders by foreign businesses and investors.[4] The result was international tax competition.

## 8.2 THE ROAD TO PILLAR TWO

Tax competition has eroded the control of nation states over their tax policies to such a degree that one scholar aptly describes the modern world of international income taxation as 'an increasingly elective marketplace, where states are often compelled to offer competitively priced deals'.[5] There is an appropriately robust and provocative debate regarding the costs and benefits of this tax competition.[6] That debate is outside the scope of this chapter. For present purposes, it is sufficient to observe that much of the commentary is generally, though not entirely, critical of the tax competition phenomenon, a critique with which we largely agree.[7]

---

[3] See, e.g., Avi Nov, 'The "Bidding War" to Attract Foreign Direct Investment: The Need for a Global Solution' (2006) 25(3) Virginia Tax Review 835, 842–3; Yariv Brauner, 'What the BEPS?' (2014) 16(2) Florida Tax Review 55, 64–5; Arthur J Cockfield, 'International Tax Competition: The Last Battleground of Globalization' (2011) 63(12) Tax Notes International 867, 868.

[4] See Mindy Herzfeld, 'The UK Embraces Tax Competition and BEPS' (2014) 75 Tax Notes International 85. Recently, the United States has employed section 301 of the Trade Act of 1974 to justify tariffs as a response to the taxation rules of other countries that are considered unreasonable foreign trade practices that harm the US economy. See, e.g., Office of the US Trade Representative, *Report on France's Digital Services Tax Prepared in the Investigation Under Section 301 of the Trade Act of 1974* (2019) 71–4. For a critical analysis of the use of this tool in taxation matters, see Stephen E Shay, 'Trade Enforcement Tools and International Taxation: A Digital Services Tax Case Study' in Julien Chaisse and Cristián Rodríguez-Chiffelle (eds), *The Elgar Companion to the World Trade Organization* (Edward Elgar Publishing 2023).

[5] Dagan (n 2) 23.

[6] See, e.g., Nov (n 3); Brauner (n 3); Cockfield (n 3).

[7] See, e.g., OECD, *Tax Effects on Foreign Direct Investment: Recent Evidence and Policy Analysis* (OECD Publishing 2007) 69–73, 79–86; International Monetary Fund (IMF), OECD, United Nations and World Bank, 'Options for Low Income Countries' Effective and Efficient Use of Tax Incentives for Investment' (2015) Working Paper 100756; OECD, *Programme of Work to Develop a Consensus Solution to the Tax Challenges Arising from the Digitalisation of the Economy* (OECD Publishing 2019) 25–6; Staff of the Joint Committee on

Reflecting the general disapproval of tax competition, in May 1996, heads of state of the G7 countries directed the Organisation for Economic Co-operation and Development (OECD)[8] to 'develop measures to counter the distorting effects of harmful tax competition on investment and financing decisions and the consequences for national tax bases, and report back in 1998'.[9] The result was the 1998 OECD report entitled *Harmful Tax Competition: An Emerging Global Issue*.[10] This report included a number of recommendations, among which were the creation of a list of tax havens, the strengthening of existing enforcement measures, and a call for greater international cooperation in curtailing tax competition.[11] However, there was a strong opposition lobbying campaign, plus stout objections from numerous Caribbean countries and an announcement by the United States that the harmful tax competition project should be limited to information exchange and should not extend to the setting of substantive international income tax standards. These obstacles led to the project's results being limited to bilateral tax information exchange agreements.[12] This led one prominent commentator to conclude that '[a]fter [these

---

Taxation, *US International Tax Policy: Overview and Analysis* (JCX-16R-21, 2021) 57; Pasquale Pistone and Belisa Ferreira Liotti, 'Tax Sparing' in Georg Kofler and others (eds), *Exemption Method and Credit Method: The Application of Article 23 of the OECD Model* (IBFD Publications 2022) 231–3; Allison Christians and Laurens van Apeldoorn, *Tax Cooperation in an Unjust World* (Oxford University Press 2021) 52–8; Nov (n 3); Cockfield (n 3); Peter Dietsch and Thomas Rixen, 'Tax Competition and Global Background Justice' (2014) 22(2) Journal of Political Philosophy 150; David C Elkins, 'The Merits of Tax Competition in a Globalized Economy' (2016) 91(3) Indiana Law Journal 905; Reuven Avi-Yonah and Young Ran (Christine) Kim, 'Tax Harmony: The Promise and Pitfalls of the Global Minimum Tax' (2022) 43(3) Michigan Journal of International Law 505, 511–15; Afton Titus, 'Global Minimum Corporate Tax: A Death Knell for African Country Tax Policies?' <https://ssrn.com/abstract=3975331> accessed 22 April 2024; Tyler Goodspeed, 'The Global Minimum Tax Crackup' *Wall Street Journal* (6 February 2023) A17.

8 See Martin A Sullivan, 'Lessons from the Last War on Tax Havens' (2007) 116 Tax Notes 327.

9 OECD, *Harmful Tax Competition: An Emerging Global Issue* (OECD Publishing 1998) 3 (*Harmful Tax Competition*).

10 See Sullivan (n 8) 327.

11 See OECD, *Harmful Tax Competition* (n 9) 37–62. The list of tax havens was widely understood to be a blacklist for use in coercing listed countries to cooperate with anti-tax competition efforts. See Sullivan (n 8) 327, 335, 337.

12 See Christians and van Apeldoorn (n 7) 54; Sullivan (n 8) 329; see also Reuven S Avi-Yonah, 'The OECD Harmful Tax Competition Report: A Retrospective after a Decade' (2009) 34(3) Brooklyn Journal of International Law

developments], the OECD efforts to curb "harmful tax competition" slowly dissolved into a series of toothless pronouncements, a mixture of cheerleading and scorekeeping that continues to this day'.[13]

The next major development in the attack on tax competition was a 2012 declaration from the G20 leaders encouraging the OECD's work on the topic.[14] In response, the OECD produced a report on 12 February 2013,[15] followed later that same year by an action plan that mandated the delivery of reports and proposals regarding 15 'action items'.[16] Work on these items gave rise to a

---

783, 784–7. The opposition included an assertion that the harmful tax competition project did disproportionate damage to developing countries with predominantly black populations. See member of the US House of Representatives Charles B Rangel (Ranking Democrat, Committee on Ways and Means), 'Rep Rangel Praises O'Neill's Action to Not Support of OECD "Harmful Tax Competition" Initiative' (News Release, 11 May 2001); see also Steven A Dean and Attiya Waris, 'Ten Truths about Tax Havens: Inclusion and the "Liberia" Problem' (2021) 70(7) Emory Law Journal 1659.

[13] See Sullivan (n 8) 329; see also Avi-Yonah and Kim (n 7) 525; Yariv Brauner, 'Serenity Now! The (Not So) Inclusive Framework and the Multilateral Instrument' (2022) 25(2) Florida Tax Review 489, 534, 541.

[14] G20, 'G20 Leaders Declaration' (18–19 June 2012) para 48; see also Jeffery M Kadet, 'BEPS: A Primer on Where It Came From and Where It's Going' (2016) 150(7) Tax Notes 793. In a related development, the European Union (EU) put forth a 2011 proposal for a 'Common Consolidated Corporate Tax Base' (CCCTB). See Teri Sprackland, 'EU's CCCTB Plan Draws Mixed Reviews' (2016) 84 Tax Notes International 441. This proposal has not made significant progress towards adoption, having been pre-empted by the OECD's Pillar Two minimum tax proposal, and effectively has been supplanted by work on the EU's 'Business in Europe: Framework for Income Tax' (BEFIT) proposal. See European Commission, Directorate-General for Taxation and Customs Union, *Annual Report on Taxation 2023* (2023) 98–9; Alexander Klemm, Shafik Hebous and Christophe J Waerzeggers, 'Capital Income Taxation in the Netherlands' (2021) 103 Tax Notes International 187, 201–2; Oliver Treidler and Tom-Eric Kunz, 'Why the OECD Should Take a Stance on the European Commission's BEFIT Proposal' (2021) 103 Tax Notes International 177.

[15] OECD, *Addressing Base Erosion and Profit Shifting* (OECD Publishing 2013).

[16] OECD, *Action Plan* (n 2). The BEPS project asserted that a principle exists requiring taxation of profits where value is created and that this principle is a normative basis for the project. See OECD/G20, *Tax Challenges Arising from the Digitalisation of the Economy – Consolidated Commentary to the Global Anti-Base Erosion Model Rules (2023)* (OECD Publishing 2024) 3 (*Commentary*). For discussions on whether this principle does exist and, if so, whether it provides useful guidance for structuring rules of international income taxation, see Werner

set of final reports released in October 2015.[17] This was followed in 2017 with the release for signature of a novel multilateral convention to accelerate the implementation of those items that would involve changes to bilateral income tax treaties.[18] This work ultimately became known as the OECD/G20 BEPS project,[19] involving more than 145 countries acting through an organization known as the OECD/G20 Inclusive Framework on BEPS.[20] In the summer and autumn of 2021, this work morphed into the OECD/G20 Inclusive Framework Agreement on the Two-Pillar Solution to Address the Tax Changes Arising from the Digitalization of the Economy, referred to colloquially by some as BEPS II.[21]

Pillar One (outside the scope of this chapter) is a complex system designed to expand source-based taxing jurisdiction by allowing source countries to reach certain so-called residual profits that would otherwise escape their taxing jurisdiction under the permanent establishment concept of current international tax law. Pillar Two (the subject of this chapter) is a regime for attacking tax competition by applying a minimum tax to the incomes of large multinational enterprises (MNEs).

---

Haslehner and Marie Lamensch, 'General Report on Value Creation and Taxation: Outlining the Debate' in Werner Haslehner and Marie Lamensch (eds), *Taxation and Value Creation* (IBFD Publications 2021); Werner Haslehner, 'Value Creation and Income Taxation: A Coherent Framework for Reform?' in Werner Haslehner and Marie Lamensch (eds), *Taxation and Value Creation* (IBFD Publications 2021); Clemens Fuest, 'Taxation in the Place of Value Creation: An Economic Perspective' in Werner Haslehner and Marie Lamensch (eds), *Taxation and Value Creation* (IBFD Publications 2021); Adolfo J Martín Jiménez, 'Value Creation: A Guiding Light in the Interpretation of Tax Treaties?' (2020) 74(4/5) Bulletin for International Taxation 197.

[17] See OECD/G20, *Inclusive Framework on BEPS, Progress Report: September 2021 – September 2022* (OECD Publishing, October 2022) 2 (*Inclusive Framework Progress Report*).

[18] OECD, Multilateral Convention to Implement Tax Treaty Related Measures to Prevent Base Erosion and Profit Shifting (adopted 24 November 2016).

[19] See OECD/G20, 'Statement on a Two-Pillar Solution to Address the Tax Challenges Arising from the Digitalisation of the Economy' (October 2021) 1 ('Statement on a Two-Pillar Solution').

[20] See OECD, *Inclusive Framework Progress Report* (n 17) 2.

[21] See G7, 'Finance Ministers and Central Bank Governors Communiqué' (5 June 2021) para 16; OECD/G20, 'Statement on a Two-Pillar Solution' (n 19).

## 8.3 THE STRUCTURE OF PILLAR TWO

The Pillar Two minimum tax regime has two parts: a global minimum tax (GloBE), calculated on a country-by-country basis and intended to ensure that MNE income bears a levy of at least 15%,[22] and a subject-to-tax rule that allows source countries to impose source taxation on royalties, interest and certain other payments at a rate sufficient to bring the total tax burden up to 9% when the tax rate in the recipient country is lower than that.[23] The subject-to-tax rule is outside the scope of this chapter.

The principal element of the GloBE is a top-up tax. It requires that an MNE with annual consolidated revenue of at least EUR 750 million in at least two of the four preceding fiscal years must be disaggregated into its constituent entities,[24] including the parent corporation and its subsidiaries and branches that are included in the MNE's consolidated financial statement.[25] Each constituent entity determines its GloBE income based on the jurisdictional financial statement income, as adjusted under the GloBE rules. An MNE group's effective income tax rate (ETR) is calculated in each country by aggregating the covered taxes and the in-country GloBE income or loss of each in-country constituent entity.[26]

Then, for each country with net GloBE income, the MNE group will subtract from the GloBE income a specified percentage of its tangible assets located in the country as well as a specified percentage of its in-country payroll.[27] The

---

[22] See OECD/G20, *Commentary* (n 16) 9–10, 147; OECD/G20, *Tax Challenges Arising from the Digitalisation of the Economy, Global Anti-Base Erosion Model Rules (Pillar Two)* (OECD Publishing 2021) 60; Jane G Gravelle and Mark P Keightley, *The Pillar 2 Global Minimum Tax: Implications for US Tax Policy* (Congressional Research Service Report R47174, updated 21 July 2023) 6.

[23] See OECD/G20, 'Statement on a Two-Pillar Solution' (n 19) 5.

[24] See OECD/G20, *Commentary* (n 16) 18–19.

[25] See ibid 18, 23–6; Gravelle and Keightley (n 22) 4–5. In certain circumstances, a QDMTT (see text at n 34) safe harbour may apply such that the GloBE rules will not apply even where the QDMTT does not fully match the top-up tax that would apply under the GloBE rules. OECD/G20, *Tax Challenges Arising from the Digitalisation of the Economy – Administrative Guidance on the Global Anti-Base Erosion Model Rules (Pillar Two)* (July 2023) 77–9.

[26] See OECD/G20, *Commentary* (n 16) 145; Gravelle and Keightley (n 22) 6–7.

[27] See OECD/G20, *Commentary* (n 16) 150–51; Gravelle and Keightley (n 22) 5–6. The Commentary (n 16) 114 notes a technical exception where an ETR must be calculated for a net GloBE loss jurisdiction if the local tax loss is greater than the loss that has been recorded for GloBE purposes and the additional tax loss

sum of these two items is the substance-based income exclusion (SBIE).[28] In order to phase in the effect of Pillar Two, the SBIE percentage with respect to tangible assets is initially 8% and declines over ten years to 5%. Similarly, the SBIE payroll percentage starts at 10% and declines over ten years to 5%.[29]

Finally, if the ETR calculated above is less than 15% for a jurisdiction, the top-up tax is derived by multiplying the excess of 15% over the ETR by the MNE's GloBE income remaining after subtracting the SBIE exclusion.[30] Thus, if in a jurisdiction the MNE's ETR is 10% and it has GloBE income of 1,000 and an SBIE of 200, it will have a top-up tax of 40.[31] As indicated above, a top-up tax is calculated separately for each country in which an MNE group's constituent entities earn net positive GloBE income.[32]

The next question is, which country will collect the top-up tax? First priority goes to the country in which the constituent entity operates (i.e., the country that is determined under the GloBE rules to under-tax the constituent entity).[33] Thus, it may impose a top-up tax, known as a qualified domestic minimum top-up tax (QDMTT), sufficient to increase the MNE group's country ETR to 15%.[34] The QDMTT would be computed on the net GloBE income of the MNE group as explained in the preceding paragraph.

Of course, a source country that hosts one or more of an MNE's constituent entities might fail to enact a QDMTT because it prefers a policy of continued tax competition. To deal with that scenario, the GloBE rules confer a backup taxing right on the country in which the ultimate parent entity of the MNE is located. This is known as the Income Inclusion Rule (IIR).[35] The IIR would include the MNE group's net GloBE income from the low-tax source country in the ultimate parent entity's (UPE's) income to an extent sufficient to increase

---

results from a deduction for a non-economic loss or similar permanent difference between the local tax base and GloBE.

[28] As a result of this subtraction, the SBIE is not a factor in calculating the ETR.

[29] See OECD/G20, *Commentary* (n 16) 150–54; Gravelle and Keightley (n 22) 6.

[30] See OECD/G20, *Commentary* (n 16) 147–8; Gravelle and Keightley (n 22) 6–7.

[31] $(1{,}000 - 200) \times 5\% = 40$. Stated differently, if 80% of the MNE's GloBE income in the country remains after subtracting the SBIE carve-out, the top-up tax would be 4% of in-country GloBE income as calculated before the SBIE ($5\% \times 80\% = 4\%$). See Gravelle and Keightley (n 22) 6–7.

[32] See ibid 5.

[33] See ibid 6–7.

[34] See OECD/G20, *Commentary* (n 16) 145–6; Gravelle and Keightley (n 22) 6.

[35] See OECD/G20, *Commentary* (n 16) 34–5; Gravelle and Keightley (n 22) 7.

the ETR to 15%.[36] The revenue from the IIR would be collected from the ultimate parent entity by the country in which the UPE is located and would be forgone by the low-tax source country in which the MNE group is operating.[37] It seems likely that low-tax source country hosts of in-scope MNE groups will be effectively forced to adopt QDMTTs and that the IIR ultimately will not play a significant role (except as a nudge to those low-tax source countries).

If a country of operation does not have a QDMTT and the host country of the MNE's ultimate parent entity does not have an IIR, the GloBE rules confer a second-level backup taxing right called the undertaxed payments rule (UTPR).[38] Specifically, if there is no applicable QDMTT or IIR, then any country in which an MNE group has at least one constituent entity may join with similarly situated countries to collect the top-up tax determined with respect to the low-tax source country by disallowing deductions or imposing additional tax.[39] Where multiple countries join in imposing the UTPR with respect to a particular MNE, the right to the top-up tax would be allocated among those countries based 50% on their share of the total tangible assets of the MNE group and 50% on their share of the MNE group's payroll.[40] Thus, both the country or countries that undertaxed an MNE's constituent entities, as well as the home country of the MNE's ultimate parent entity, could lose revenue to the countries that are not hosts of the undertaxed constituent entities.[41] This would reinforce the incentive for host countries of constituent entities to adopt QDMTTs and put considerable pressure on host countries of ultimate parent entities to adopt IIRs.

## 8.4 EVALUATING PILLAR TWO AS AN ANTI-TAX COMPETITION REGIME

An important point in evaluating the efficacy of Pillar Two is that it continues to allow a degree of tax competition. Specifically:

1. Pillar Two does not apply to any MNE having revenues below the EUR 750 million threshold. Thus, Apple, Microsoft, Google, Amazon and Tesla are within the scope of Pillar Two, but the benefits of tax competition remain

[36] See Gravelle and Keightley (n 22) 7.

[37] See ibid.

[38] See OECD/G20, *Commentary* (n 16) 42–9; Gravelle and Keightley (n 22) 7.

[39] See Gravelle and Keightley (n 22) 7; OECD/G20, *Commentary* (n 16) 47, 49–50, 274–5.

[40] See OECD/G20, *Commentary* (n 16) 49–50; Gravelle and Keightley (n 22) 7.

[41] See Gravelle and Keightley (n 22) 7.

fully available to the numerous 'smaller fish' entities that operate in the global economy today.

2. Moreover, tax competition by source countries remains available, even in the case of an in-scope MNE, with respect to GloBE income within the SBIE carve-out.[42] Since the carve-out is based on tangible assets and payroll located in a source country, its effect is to encourage in-scope MNEs to move real business operations and real jobs to countries that continue to engage in tax competition within the space created by the carve-out.[43]
3. Finally, tax competition by source countries remains available with respect to GloBE income of an in-scope MNE in excess of the SBIE to the extent of the spread between the 15% GloBE rate and the rates in high-tax developed countries.[44] Since the US corporate rate is 21%, the OECD average rate is 23%, and the G20 average rate is 29%,[45] a source country that wishes to continue in a tax competition vein can do so by imposing only a 15% rate on income above the SBIE, which will be 29% less than the US rate, 35% less than the OECD average rate, and 48% less than the G20 average rate.

In addition to facilitating tax competition at ETRs above 15%, Pillar Two is in many ways more complicated than the current international tax system. Furthermore, much of Pillar Two's complexity will be unfamiliar. Thus, the adoption of Pillar Two will entail significant transition costs, including increased taxpayer compliance costs and administrative costs both for governments of countries that adopt it and for governments of other countries, which will have to determine how to treat Pillar Two taxation of their taxpayers under

---

[42] See nn 26–32 and accompanying text.

[43] See Lilian V Faulhaber, 'Pillar Two's Built-In Escape Hatch' (2023) 76(1) National Tax Journal 167, 180–81.

[44] See Michael P Devereux, 'International Tax Competition and Coordination with a Global Minimum Tax' (2023) 76(1) National Tax Journal 145, 160 ('Pillar 2 introduces a floor on tax competition'). Preservation of tax competition above a floor is a characteristic that Pillar Two shares with the US GILTI regime. See J Clifton Fleming, Jr, Robert J Peroni and Stephen E Shay, 'Expanded Worldwide versus Territorial Taxation after the TCJA' (2018) 161 Tax Notes 1173, 1187–9 ('Expanded Worldwide versus Territorial Taxation').

[45] See Reuven S Avi-Yonah, 'What Does the United States Get from Pillar 2?' (2023) 49(2) International Tax Journal 29, 31.

their own international tax rules (e.g., to what extent will a Pillar Two tax paid by a US MNE be creditable for US foreign tax credit purposes?).[46]

Nevertheless, our conclusion is that if Pillar Two is adopted by enough countries,[47] as appears to be the case, it would be better than the status quo. However, we believe that there is another, better alternative for dealing with the international tax competition problem, and we will turn to that point after discussing the plight of low-income countries.

## 8.5 LOW-INCOME COUNTRIES AND PILLAR TWO

Low-income countries are particularly pressured to engage in tax competition by making tax concessions to MNEs to attract inbound investment. Pillar Two might provide relief by allowing low-income countries to raise revenue by taxing the inbound profits of MNEs at a rate up to 15% without compromising their capacity to engage in tax competition.[48] On the other hand, the pressure to attract inbound investment by MNEs may cause such low-income countries to effectively surrender much or all of the resulting revenue by providing

---

[46] Transfer pricing is a potential problem for Pillar Two. Addressed by only one paragraph in the Pillar Two Model Rules, the separate financial statements used as the starting point in most cases have not been pressure-tested for compliance with the arm's length standard because that standard is largely not relevant within a consolidated financial statement. Nonetheless, with reduced stakes from transfer pricing, in many (but certainly not all and perhaps not even most) cases the issue will not be front and centre. However, it will continue to be important when the amounts at stake justify it. See Joseph L Andrus and Richard S Collier, 'Transfer Pricing and the Arm's-Length Principle after the Pillars' (2022) 105 Tax Notes International 543, 554–5 (concluding that 'we do not see the [P]illar 2 measures as bringing any kind of fix of the arm's length principle that might restore stability to the system').

[47] Regarding the extent of Pillar Two adoption, see Mindy Herzfeld, 'A Pillar 2 Tour Around the World' (2023) 110 Tax Notes International 305. Regarding the unlikelihood of Pillar Two adoption by the United States, see member of the House of Representatives Ron Estes, 'OECD Pillar 2 Is a Bad Deal for America' (Letter to the Editor) (2023) 110 Tax Notes International 697; Mindy Herzfeld, 'How to Think about How the US Congress Thinks about International Tax Reforms' (2022) (5) British Tax Review 550; Stephanie Soong and Cady Stanton, 'House GOP Bill Aims to Hit Back at OECD Global Tax Deal' (2023) 110 Tax Notes International 1177.

[48] See Christians and van Apeldoorn (n 7) 43, 59–60; Avi-Yonah and Kim (n 7) 548–9.

land, buildings, infrastructure, utilities, employee training programmes, etc., to MNEs at below-market rates.[49]

## 8.6 IS THERE A BETTER SOLUTION?

We use the term 'expanded worldwide taxation' to refer to current taxation of consolidated worldwide MNE income by the residence country of each MNE's ultimate parent corporation, with a foreign tax credit limited to the residence-country tax, applied on a per-country basis.[50] For reasons that we have explored at length in previous articles,[51] we conclude that widespread adoption of expanded worldwide taxation is superior to Pillar Two as a regime for addressing source tax competition and its location-distortion effect.

Specifically, the widespread adoption of expanded worldwide taxation with a per-country limited foreign tax credit and a non-deferred tax on controlled foreign corporation (CFC) income at a rate equal to the regular domestic corporate tax rate has the following advantages over Pillar Two as an anti-tax competition regime:

1. It imposes a much simpler top-up tax. Source countries would simply impose their domestic tax on the domestic-source income of MNEs, and to the extent the source tax was less than the relevant residence-country tax, the residence country would collect a residual tax. Thus, in a less complicated way, this approach would eliminate the incentive for source countries to engage in tax competition, but by accommodating their

49 See generally Michael C Durst, 'BEPS, Pillar 2, and the Replacement of Tax-Based Incentives with Nontax Incentives' (2023) 110 Tax Notes International 349.

50 This approach seems to have been ignored in the process that led to Pillar Two. See Kadet (n 14) 804.

51 See Fleming, Peroni and Shay, 'Expanded Worldwide versus Territorial Taxation' (n 44); J Clifton Fleming, Jr, Robert J Peroni and Stephen E Shay, 'Defending Worldwide Taxation with a Shareholder-Based Definition of Corporate Residence' (2016) (6) Brigham Young University Law Review 1681, 1689–90; J Clifton Fleming, Jr, Robert J Peroni and Stephen E Shay, 'Formulary Apportionment in the US International Income Tax System: Putting Lipstick on a Pig?' (2014) 36(1) Michigan Journal of International Law 1, 18–20; J Clifton Fleming, Jr, Robert J Peroni and Stephen E Shay, 'Two Cheers for the Foreign Tax Credit, Even in the BEPS Era' (2016) 91(1) Tulane Law Review 1.

primary taxing right, it would allow source countries to collect needed revenue.[52]

2. It eliminates the remaining tax competition permitted by the SBIE and the spread between the 15% rate and the corporate tax rate in high-tax developed countries.
3. It eliminates the remaining tax competition permitted by the EUR 750 million threshold.
4. Because it employs familiar elements of the current international tax system, the transition costs of moving to expanded worldwide taxation should be lower than with adopting Pillar Two.

Granted, expanded worldwide taxation puts comparative pressure on the foreign tax credit by shifting to the foreign tax credit the burden of avoiding double taxation that, under Pillar Two, is accomplished by the implicit residency allocation approach of the QDMTT and the formulary approach of the UTPR. However, answers to most of the complexities of the foreign tax credit regime have been worked out over time[53] whereas, as mentioned above, the QDMTT and the UTPR present the significant costs of transitioning to a new, untested system.

Even exemption system countries are familiar with worldwide taxation and the foreign tax credit because they often apply worldwide taxation to income bearing a low foreign tax and to foreign-source income of resident individuals. But what if moving to expanded worldwide taxation is simply a bridge too far for exemption system countries? Alternatives other than Pillar Two for improving the ability of an exemption system to significantly mitigate international tax competition include the incorporation of a minimum tax or subject-to-tax requirement in an exemption system.[54]

The UTPR serves as a defence against capital-exporting countries continuing to resist worldwide taxation. We acknowledge that our view that full worldwide taxation is superior to the limited and complex Pillar Two rests in material part on the support for Pillar Two translating into support for full worldwide taxation to take advantage of its strengths.

---

52 See Scott Wilkie, 'Pillar 2 – "What's It All About?"' (2023) 110 Tax Notes International 499, 500–502.

53 See Christians and van Apeldoorn (n 7) 99.

54 See J Clifton Fleming, Jr, Robert J Peroni and Stephen E Shay, 'Incorporating a Minimum Tax in a Territorial System' (2017) 157 Tax Notes 73; J Clifton Fleming, Jr, Robert J Peroni and Stephen E Shay, 'Designing a US Exemption System for Foreign Income When the Treasury Is Empty' (2012) 13(8) Florida Tax Review 397, 413–41.

## 8.7 CONCLUSION

Pillar Two partially mitigates tax competition, which is a step in the right direction. A better approach would be for countries that are hosts to MNEs to adopt expanded worldwide taxation at their respective regular corporate rates.

# 9. BEPS, Pillar Two and developing countries: combating the race to the bottom

**Catherine Brown**

## 9.1 BASE EROSION, PROFIT SHIFTING AND GLOBAL TAX REFORM

The Organisation for Economic Co-operation and Development (OECD) in 2021 proposed a global minimum tax for in-scope multinational enterprises (MNEs) to reduce tax competition and profit shifting.[1]

According to the OECD/G20 Inclusive Framework on Base Erosion and Profit Shifting agreement, the Pillar Two rules would ensure all global profits of multinational enterprises are taxed at least at a minimum effective tax rate (ETR) of 15%.[2]

To achieve this result, countries may implement either the income inclusion rule (IIR), the qualified domestic minimum top-up tax (QDMTT), or both to ensure the appropriate rate of tax is paid by targeted multinational enterprises.[3]

---

[1] OECD, 'OECD Releases Pillar Two Model Rules for Domestic Implementation of 15% Global Minimum Tax' <https://www.oecd.org/newsroom/oecd-releases-pillar-two-model-rules-for-domestic-implementation-of-15-percent-global-minimum-tax> accessed 23 June 2024. The new rules will apply to multinational corporations with gross revenues over EUR 750 million.

[2] It is expected that the new tax will result in annual global revenue gains of around USD 220 billion, or 9% of global corporate income tax revenues. See OECD, 'Revenue Impact of International Tax Reform Better than Expected: OECD' (18 January 2023) <https://www.oecd.org/en/about/news/press-releases/2023/01/revenue-impact-of-international-tax-reform-better-than-expected.html> accessed 21 June 2024.

[3] Pillar Two also includes the undertaxed payment rule (UTPR) as a backstop in case the IIR and QDMTT are not applied. In general terms it allows Country A to collect the revenues from the top-up tax from Country B if Country B has either

If the IIR is adopted by a particular country, it will allow revenues from the required top-up tax to be collected by the parent country if the effective tax rate (ETR) falls below 15%. The ETR is calculated on a country-by-country basis.[4] As a result, if a subsidiary's ETR is below the 15% minimum globally agreed rate, its parent pays a 'top-up tax' on its proportionate share of the income of the low-taxed subsidiary to the country where the parent is located.[5] In contrast, if the QDMTT is adopted, it will result in the additional tax being collected by the host country where the subsidiary is located. It follows that a country with a large number of multinational enterprises operating abroad in low-tax jurisdictions would benefit under the IIR. Conversely, a country could gain from the QDMTT if it hosts many foreign multinational enterprises that are taxed below 15% – assuming a QDMTT can be imposed.

Tax incentives, including tax holidays, preferential tax rates, tax credits, investment allowances or income exemptions, will clearly affect the ETR in a host country and are targeted by the Pillar Two reforms.

The result is that, once implemented, Pillar Two will render many of these incentives ineffective because any multinational corporation that benefits from such an incentive and has an ETR of less than 15% will directly or indirectly be subject to a top-up tax under the IIR or QDMTT rules.

It follows that countries that have agreed to be bound by Pillar Two will be required to review and in some cases repeal tax incentives in their domestic law and under investment agreements to ensure the effective tax rate is in line with the global tax rate. But at what cost?

While some tax incentives can be undone unilaterally by legislative amendments, others may be subject to tax rulings, fiscal stabilization provisions or other protections under long-established investment agreements and treaties. Developing countries are particularly subject to legal limitations under international agreements, national laws or private contracts that will prevent them

---

not implemented Pillar Two or has failed to collect the full amount. The amount that Country A could collect from Country B is based on the number of employees and assets that MNEs of Country B have in Country A.

4 This is calculated as the total taxes on corporate profits paid to government authorities, or 'cash tax' (the numerator), as a proportion of the tax base, which is based on accounting profits (the denominator) expressed as a fraction.

5 For example, if a parent in Country A has subsidiaries in Countries B and C that do not pay tax at global minimum rate, the difference between the ETR and the global minimum rate is collected by the parent in Country A under the IIR. As a result, the primary beneficiaries of a global minimum tax will often be capital exporting countries, where multinational companies are typically headquartered.

from unwinding tax incentives that were promised to investors.[6] Many developing countries also face significant legal limitations that will prevent them from collecting the QDMTT under Pillar Two.[7]

Therefore, the most predictable outcome under the Pillar Two rules is that any additional tax will be collected by another jurisdiction, generally that of the parent corporation under the IIR. The developing country will therefore lose both the benefit of the foreign investment that it hoped to gain by providing the tax incentive as well as the tax revenue.

---

6 See OECD, *Tax Incentives and the Global Minimum Corporate Tax: Reconsidering Tax Incentives after the GloBE Rules* (OECD Publishing 2022) <www.oecd.org/tax/tax-incentives-and-the-global-minimum-corporate-tax-25d30b96-en.htm> accessed 21 June 2024 (*Tax Incentives and the Global Minimum Corporate Tax*). According to a 2023 report by the United Nations Conference on Trade and Development (UNCTAD), 'The Global Minimum Tax and Investment Treaties: Exploring Policy Options' (International Investment Agreements Issues Note Issue 4, November 2023) <https://unctad.org/system/files/official-document/diaepcbinf2023d7_en.pdf>, four BIT standards are most likely to cause tensions: the fair and equitable treatment (FET) provision, the umbrella clause, non-discrimination rules, and the expropriation provision. The first three could, depending on their interpretation and individual investor circumstances, discourage countries from collecting taxes. Especially the existence of negotiated and contractually stabilized tax incentives, for example, as part of the admission to a special economic zone, may prove sensitive under the FET standard and the umbrella clause. Frictions may similarly arise from the different treatment of the constituent entities of enterprises that are covered by the minimum tax and those that are not.

7 See Mindy Herzfeld, 'Could Bilateral Investment Treaties Kill Pillar 2?' (2023) 110 Tax Notes International 1701, 1702.

## 9.2 THE PERFECT STORM

Is this problem real? The answer is yes.[8] Many countries have either implemented or agreed to implement the Pillar Two proposals with effect from 1 January 2024.[9]

One hundred of the 140 countries listed in the OECD's Inclusive Framework agreement on the Two-Pillar reforms as of June 2023 are referenced by the World Bank and UNCTAD as developing countries.[10]

Characteristic of many of these countries is that:

(i) they require significant foreign direct investment (FDI) to facilitate infrastructure and resource development;
(ii) they have implemented tax incentives to encourage FDI; and
(iii) they have entered investment or trade agreements or private contracts that limit their ability to change national tax laws or policies.

---

[8] See UNCTAD (n 6). According to the report, even newer investment treaties with tax carve-outs may allow investors to challenge Pillar Two reforms. According to the report (at 5),

> more than half of all MFN, NT and FET clauses in this sample of treaties are applicable to tax measures. They thus generally apply to the types of measures that are likely to be adopted to implement the global minimum tax, such as top-up taxes, the withdrawal of corporate income tax incentives or an increase of the headline corporate income tax rate. Thus, tax measures could be challenged by foreign investors even under the majority of recent IIAs.

[9] See PwC, 'PwC's Pillar Two Country Tracker' (3 June 2024) <www.pwc.com/gx/en/tax/international-tax-planning/pillar-two/pwc-pillar-two-country-tracker-summary-v2.pdf> accessed 21 June 2024 for a list of countries that have either announced plans to implement or have implemented Pillar Two reforms in their domestic law.

[10] OECD, 'Members of the OECD/G20 Inclusive Framework on BEPS joining the October 2021 *Statement on a Two-Pillar Solution to Address the Tax Challenges Arising from the Digitalisation of the Economy* as of June 9 2023' <https://www.oecd.org/tax/beps/oecd-g20-inclusive-framework-members-joining-statement-on-two-pillar-solution-to-address-tax-challenges-arising-from-digitalisation-october-2021.pdf> accessed 24 June 2024. The reality is that the GloBE rules are likely to affect all countries, even those deciding not to adopt Pillar Two. This is because if one jurisdiction does not tax an MNE entity at the minimum rate, the tax jurisdictions of parent or sibling entities may enforce the minimum by imposing top-up taxes. Consequently, even non-participating countries may lose out on the benefits of corporate income tax incentives they grant to investors.

### 9.2.1 Contractual Obligations

For example, many developing countries have offered tax concessions for large investment projects such as mining or oil and gas exploration, either through special provisions in their domestic law or in investment contracts with foreign investors. Often these tax concessions include tax incentives and tax holidays that are locked in by fiscal stabilization clauses.[11] These clauses generally freeze any applicable tax measures so that no changes can be made by the host government that would impact an existing investment project, at least for a defined period.[12]

As discussed further below, the promised tax concessions may also be protected by investment treaties under an 'umbrella clause'.[13] An umbrella clause is designed to impose an international treaty obligation on a host country that requires it to respect contractual or other obligations it has entered into with respect to investments.[14] These clauses therefore also provide access

---

[11] The literature describes the use of stabilization clauses in BITs with developing countries as widespread, especially in non-OECD countries. See Katja Gehne and Romulo Brillo, 'Stabilization Clauses in International Investment Law: Beyond Balancing and Fair and Equitable Treatment' (2014) Swiss National Centre of Competence in Research Working Paper 2013/46 <www.wti.org/media/filer_public/c7/83/c783ecf8-11cf-4e3c-88c4-6214f8f7b51e/stab_clauses_final_final.pdf> accessed 21 June 2024.

[12] See, for example, *Duke Energy International Peru Investments No 1 Ltd v Peru*, ICSID Case No ARB/03/28, Award, dated 18 August 2008, para 2 as cited in Danielle Morris, Yarik Kryvoi, Sam Winter-Barker and Tunç Savaş, 'Empirical Study: Tax-Related Measures in Investor–State Arbitration' (British Institute of International and Comparative Law and WilmerHale Report, 2024) 1, 27 <https://papers.ssrn.com/sol3/papers.cfm?abstract_id=4704750> accessed 21 June 2024. In *Duke* a claim was brought under an agreement that was concluded between the government of Peru and a subsidiary of Duke known as DEI Bermuda. Peru imposed a tax assessment on the subsidiary in violation of a tax stabilization clause in its agreement that provided that no changes would be made to the tax provisions in effect for a term of ten years.

[13] J Nna Emeka, 'Anchoring Stabilization Clauses in International Petroleum Contracts' (2008) 42(4) The International Lawyer 1317.

[14] One of the main difficulties with 'umbrella' clauses is that they effectively expand the scope of the BIT by incorporating non-treaty obligations of the host state into the treaty, which may increase the risk of being faced with costly legal proceedings, and they have given rise to conflicting interpretations by investor–state tribunals resulting in a high degree of unpredictability. See UNCTAD (n 6).

to binding arbitration for the investor if the host country does not honour its commitments.[15]

It follows that if a developing country has entered into an agreement that provides protection to investors, any attempt to collect the Pillar Two tax may violate the agreement. It may also expose the country to costly international arbitration under an investment treaty if the measure is challenged by an aggrieved investor.[16]

If the developing country does not collect the proposed minimum tax, Pillar Two provides rules for other jurisdictions, including that of the parent, to do so and to keep the tax.

### 9.2.2 Investment Agreements: Other Protections for Investors

In addition to private agreements with a host government and the safeguard of umbrella clauses, the investor may also be protected under other provisions in an investment treaty or under the investment provisions in a free trade agreement.

The reason for these additional provisions is understandable.

The protection of foreign investment is a central objective of most developed countries. This goal has been aggressively pursued through the negotiation of investment treaties, particularly with developing countries.[17] There are currently more than 2,500 bilateral investment treaties (BITs) in force globally as well as more than 700 bilateral and regional free trade agreements that include investment provisions.[18]

A BIT is one of the most common types of treaties used to attract foreign investment. These agreements are negotiated between governments and

---

[15] The Poland–US BIT, for example,

> states that 'each Party shall observe any obligation it may have entered into with regard to investments'. This umbrella clause could also be relevant to a tax-related proceeding under a BIT if a new law overrides commitments a state made in a contract with an investor, in a stabilization agreement, or through the grant of preferential tax rates. (Herzfeld (n 7) 1702)

[16] International Centre for Settlement of Investment Disputes <https://icsid.worldbank.org/> accessed 21 June 2024.

[17] Approximately 90% of these are old-generation agreements that were concluded in the 1980s, 1990s and 2000s. They generally contain unrefined treaty standards and grant broad access to investor–state dispute settlement (ISDS) in the form of binding international arbitration. See UNCTAD (n 6).

[18] See for example, the US–Mexico–Canada Agreement (USMCA), the Comprehensive and Progressive Agreement for Transpacific Partnership (CPTPP) and the ASEAN Comprehensive Investment Agreement (ACAI).

provide investors with significant guarantees such as fair and equitable treatment, full protection and security, protection from expropriation, and most-favoured-nation and national treatment. More importantly, BITs generally allow an investor to resolve disputes with a host country through independent international arbitration.[19]

### 9.2.3 Fair and Equitable Treatment

Of the protections offered under a BIT, a violation of the fair and equitable treatment (FET) standard is most often cited as the basis for challenging changes to tax measures.[20] This treaty obligation requires the host country to 'ensure fair and equitable treatment to investments'. Its scope is wide enough for investors to challenge decisions taken by states in the exercise of their regulatory power, even where they are pursuing public interest goals, and has been the basis for claims against tax measures in a number of cases about withdrawal of incentives, suspension of tariff adjustments for public utilities or refusal to reimburse.[21] As discussed, the withdrawal/amendment of a tax-specific incentive in a stabilization clause may also constitute a breach of this provision.[22]

---

[19] BIT claims are generally resolved through arbitration, usually under the auspices of the International Centre for Settlement of Investment Disputes (ICSID) (n 16).

[20] UNCTAD (n 6) 27. The report indicates that investors invoked the FET standard, either as a standalone claim or in combination with other standards, in over two-thirds of all tax-related claims under investment agreements.

[21] Some bilateral investment treaties include provisions that analogize fair and equitable treatment (FET) to stabilization clauses. These could be interpreted by some arbitral tribunals as requiring the stability of the legal framework and therefore potentially broadening the number of tax incentives that cannot be changed unilaterally by host governments. Countries may also need to review their treaties for overly broad FET clauses.

[22] As Herzfeld has noted:

> Tribunals have examined a range of factors in assessing an investor's claim that a host country violated this requirement, but they generally focus on stability (which may protect against retroactive law changes) and investors' legitimate expectations. Also relevant is whether changes in a country's legal framework complied with its contractual obligations; the transparency of those changes; whether the changes included due process and procedural propriety; whether the investor was free from coercion and harassment; whether the government behaved arbitrarily; and whether it behaved in a discriminatory fashion. An early case – *Neer v United Mexican States*, Claims Commission, 4 RIAA 60 (1926) – set some standards. It said that

The legitimate expectations of investors also play a significant role in establishing a violation – especially if an investor can establish that it expected the conditions applicable at the time of investment would not change.[23]

#### 9.2.3.1 Expropriation

Another of the primary protections provided in investment treaties is the guarantee that foreign investors will not fall victim to uncompensated expropriations. While the language of such clauses varies, they generally ensure that investors are protected against direct takings (or direct expropriations), which involve the transfer of title or outright physical seizure of an investor's property. Foreign investors are also protected from measures that fall short of direct takings but are considered indirect expropriations. Taxation measures may constitute an indirect expropriation where they lead to substantial deprivation of the foreign investor's investment.[24] As Herzfeld has noted, 'A country's assertion of its taxing power may amount to an indirect expropriation under this definition.'[25] A 2024 report indicates that investors invoked the indirect expropriation standard in almost half of tax-related treaty claims in recent years.[26]

#### 9.2.3.2 Other protections

BITs also protect foreign investors from discrimination, including national treatment and most-favoured-nation treatment. The US Model BIT, for example, provides that it 'shall accord to investors of the other Party treatment no

---

> to constitute a delinquency, a country's treatment of a non-resident investor should amount 'to an outrage, to bad faith, to willful neglect of duty, or to an insufficiency of governmental action so far short of international standards that every reasonable and impartial man would readily recognize its insufficiency'.

See Herzfeld (n 7) 1701–2.

[23] See generally UNCTAD, 'Facts on Investor–State Arbitrations in 2021: With a Special Focus on Tax-Related ISDS Cases' (International Investment Agreements Issues Note 1, July 2022) <https://unctad.org/system/files/official-document/diaepcbinf2022d4_en.pdf> accessed 21 June 2024, and OECD, *Tax Incentives and the Global Minimum Corporate Tax* (n 6) 22–3. A new tax law that reverses an investor's expectations might seem an obvious case for a claim under a BIT.

[24] See Catherine Brown and Elizabeth Whitsitt, 'Implementing Pillar Two: Potential Conflicts with Investment Treaties' (2023) 71(1) Canadian Tax Journal 189.

[25] Herzfeld (n 7) 1702.

[26] Morris and others (n 12) 20.

less favorable than that it accords, in like circumstances, to its own investors' or 'to investors of any non-Party'.[27] There are also other BIT obligations that a country may violate if it seeks to suddenly change the essential rules of the game upon which an investor relied when making the investment.[28]

### 9.2.4 BITs and Tax Carve-Outs

An investor's rights under a BIT may also be impacted by a tax carve-out that would allow the imposition of the QDMTT without violating an investment treaty obligation.

According to a 2024 report,[29] about 10% of all BITs worldwide now include a tax carve-out. However, these are mostly BITs entered into by capital-exporting states such as Canada, the United States, Japan and the United Kingdom. In contrast, most investment treaties, including those with developing countries, do not exclude taxation from their scope of application. As a result, a foreign investor can challenge a wide range of taxation measures imposed by a host state. This is particularly true for the older-generation investment treaties that were negotiated in the 1990s and remain in force today. Most of these treaties contain broadly worded investor protections with few exceptions. As a result, developing countries may face increased liability for violating investment treaty protections, particularly under FET and expropriation provisions.

Even in investment treaties that include a general tax carve-out, there are often exceptions that explicitly allow an investor to bring a claim relating to a taxation measure (i.e., tax clawbacks), if the conditions in the exception are met. Expropriation is one common area where investor claims are often permitted, as are breaches of contractual commitments made by a host government. Both are frequent sources of tax disputes submitted by investors to international arbitration.

In summary, not all BITs are the same or provide the same investor rights. Some, notably those that include developed countries, also include tax carve-outs that may limit some tax challenges under Pillar Two.[30] But the evidence is clear that there are increasing numbers of claims by investors against

---

[27] See US Department of State, '2012 US Model Bilateral Investment Treaty' arts 3 and 4.

[28] These standards, however, have not been invoked with the frequency of the FET standard and indirect expropriation in taxation matters: ibid (Chart 17).

[29] Ibid 8 (Chart 4).

[30] The tax carve-outs in investment agreements are complex but can be categorized into main types that include a general exclusion, a limited exclusion, a tax veto in expropriation cases, the prioritization of tax treaties over investment agreements, or some combination.

developing countries for tax measures under BITs. These include challenges under umbrella clauses (that would protect fiscal stabilization agreements), or more general claims that the host country has violated its fair and equitable treatment obligations or indirectly expropriated investor assets. These treaty obligations provide ample room for an international arbitration body to review a new Pillar Two tax and frequently survive the most rigorous tax carve-outs in an investment treaty.

The fact that there may be a tax carve-out and/or a tax clawback in a BIT will also create significant challenges for many developing countries in interpreting and applying the treaty provisions and create further tensions with developed countries.[31]

## 9.3 THE PATH AHEAD FOR DEVELOPING COUNTRIES

One of the most significant challenges for developing countries may be navigating the complex and competing international laws, obligations and norms converging on them.

---

[31] The tax carve-out and clawbacks in Canada's BITs (known as Foreign Investment Protection Acts, or FIPAs) provide an excellent example. The tax carve-out in Canada's FIPAs permits challenges to tax measures where Canada or its investment treaty partner implements a taxation measure in breach of an agreement they have with an investor. Canada's tax carve-out also leaves open the possibility that a foreign investor or Canadian investor could make an expropriation claim against Canada or a foreign government, respectively, for imposing a tax measure. The investor's claim can only be avoided under these provisions if the taxation authorities of Canada and its treaty counterparty agree that the impugned tax measure is not a violation of either an agreement with the investor or the relevant expropriation provision. Consider the following scenario: Canada and Mali have entered an FIPA. A Canadian subsidiary has secured a 15-year commitment from Mali for a tax holiday in Mali (an ETR of 5%) in return for a major capital investment in Mali. It is now year four of that agreement. The government of Mali notifies the directors of the Canadian subsidiary of its intention to withdraw the promised tax holiday in response to its Pillar Two commitments. Under the FIPA procedure, the impacted Canadian subsidiary will refer the breach of their agreement with the government of Mali to the Canadian tax authority. The Canadian tax authority must make a choice. It must either deny the Canadian investor a right to arbitration by determining that there was no breach of the investment agreement with Mali or agree that the measure is in breach of the FIPA and is therefore subject to arbitral challenge. This will require the government of Mali to endure potentially costly arbitration and damages or allow Canada to collect a top-up tax under the IIR rules.

Pillar Two seeks to impose a global minimum tax. That goal can only be achieved if countries, especially developing countries, make changes in their current tax regimes.

BITs provide individual investors with a powerful remedy to initiate arbitration when promises made to them are violated. Countries that choose to implement Pillar Two, and in particular the QDMTT in their domestic law, will no doubt violate BIT obligations and trigger investor rights to initiate ISDS proceedings.

Nonetheless, it has been argued[32] that an aggrieved investor may not do so. The reasoning is that from the investor's perspective, since it will be paying the tax somewhere, 'it is not clear … whether it is worth suing the host country, especially since a successful suit that results in a payment could be treated as a further tax reduction that triggers additional tax elsewhere'.[33]

The OECD, in its July 2023 administrative guidance on Pillar Two, also appears to discourage an investor from making a claim under a BIT by explicitly disregarding the status of a QDMTT as a QDMTT payable whenever a multinational enterprise group legally challenges it.[34] The OECD's message to investors is clear: do not challenge the QDMTT, as you will pay a UTPR or IIR instead.

But neither the logic that tax must be paid somewhere, nor the OECD guidance provides a clear path forward for a developing country. The investor has a right to sue, and the developing country will be concerned about its reputation for safe investment as well as the costs (time and money) to defend the claim. It will also want the top-up tax.

One obvious tactic for a developing country in these circumstances is to promise other incentives to persuade impacted investors to forgo an arbitration

---

32 Reuven Avi-Yonah, 'Pillar 2 and the BITs' (Correspondence) (2023) 71(3) Canadian Tax Journal 949, 949.

33 There is some appeal to this logic. A 'multinational group' that is faced with a global minimum tax that is to be paid somewhere may be indifferent about which country receives the funds. It will, however, be an issue for the developing country, especially if the developing country is losing the benefit of attracting foreign direct investment through tax incentives. At a minimum, the developing country will no doubt want to keep the tax revenue collected.

34 OECD, 'QDMTT Payable' in *Tax Challenges Arising from the Digitalisation of the Economy – Administrative Guidance on the Global Anti-Base Erosion Model Rules (Pillar Two)* (OECD Publishing July 2023) ch 4, paras 73–81, in particular paras 74–6.

claim.[35] Despite its obvious appeal, it will also create significant challenges for a developing country.

Vietnam provides an excellent example.

The government of Vietnam has been actively engaged in negotiating BITs and investment provisions in free trade agreements since the 1990s as part of an ambitious programme to attract foreign direct investment.[36] Vietnam also announced its intention to adopt the Pillar Two provisions and to add an IIR and QDMTT to its domestic law effective 1 January 2024.[37]

Vietnam reportedly made public in 2023 that it was considering granting subsidies to large multinational enterprises, including Korean technology giants Samsung Electronics and LG Electronics, US chipmaker Intel and Germany's Bosch (which had direct investments in the country), to compensate them for the higher taxes they would face when Vietnam implemented the Pillar Two QDMTT provisions in 2024.[38] Under the proposed compensation plan, companies with large investments in Vietnam would be allowed

---

[35] For example, a host country could reduce taxes that are not covered by Pillar Two, such as value added tax (VAT) or import tariffs. It could offer business facilitation measures such as simplified import and export procedures, single-window mechanisms for permits and licences, or streamlined procedures for employment visas. Expenditure-based incentives might also be substituted, i.e., rewarding investment or reinvestment by reducing the after-tax cost of capital expenditures through allowances, accelerated depreciation or tax credits, as they are less impacted by Pillar Two. According to UNCTAD, multinational enterprises subject to the global minimum tax are unlikely to initiate formal proceedings. Instead, they could utilize BITs (IIAs) as a bargaining chip to bring governments to the negotiating table to partially replace corporate income tax incentives with economically similar benefits, while officially being taxed at the effective minimum rate: UNCTAD (n 6). This will put more pressure on developing countries.

[36] See Tran Viet Dung, 'Vietnam's Experiences with International Investment Agreements Governance: Issues and Solutions' (2019) 25 Asian Yearbook of International Law 84.

[37] It did so on 23 November 2023. See KPMG, 'Vietnam: Resolution Adopting Pillar Two Global Minimum Tax' (29 November 2023) <https://kpmg.com/us/en/home/insights/2023/11/tnf-vietnam-resolution-adopting-pillar-two-global-minimum-tax.html> accessed 21 June 2024.

[38] Francesco Guarascio, 'No Handouts to Big Firms to Offset Global Tax, OECD Tells Vietnam' *Reuters* (7 June 2023) <www.reuters.com/markets/asia/no-handouts-big-firms-offset-global-tax-oecd-tells-vietnam-2023-06-07/> accessed 21 June 2024. This announcement was apparently the result of demands for compensation by these multinational enterprises in private talks with the government. The four companies were among half a dozen large investors who pushed for compensation, according to the source who attended the meeting.

to receive after-tax cash handouts or refundable tax credits to support their manufacturing or research outlays.

According to the news report, the firms cited 'have invested tens of billions of dollars in the country and are major employers. Samsung, for example, is the biggest single foreign investor in Vietnam, employs 160,000 people and produces half of its smartphones in the country, accounting for nearly one fifth of the nation's total exports'.[39]

The response by the OECD was swift. It warned the Vietnamese government that if subsidies were provided to multinational enterprises to compensate for higher taxes under Pillar Two, 'the domestic top-up tax would be disqualified', with the result that the parent entity's home jurisdiction would tax under the IIR (income inclusion rule).[40]

The basis for the OECD threat is an anti-abuse rule in Pillar Two that imposes a no benefit requirement (NBR).[41] In summary, the rule applies if the

---

[39] Francesco Guarascio and Khanh Vu, 'Exclusive: Vietnam Eyes Multi-Million-Dollar Handouts to Samsung, Others to Offset Global Tax' *Reuters* (31 May 2023) <https://www.reuters.com/world/asia-pacific/vietnam-eyes-multi-million-dollar-handouts-samsung-others-offset-global-tax-2023-05-30/> accessed 12 August 2024.

[40] OECD officials, according to a source quoted in Guarascio (n 38). In the meantime, Vietnam has responded by establishing an investment support fund to support research and development in the country with the top-up tax collected under the QDMTT. Dezan Shira and Associates, 'Draft Global Minimum Tax Support Fund Unveiled' *Vietnam Briefing* (2 January 2024) <www.vietnam-briefing.com/news/draft-global-minimum-tax-support-fund-unveiled.html> accessed 21 June 2024.

[41] The definition of Qualified Domestic Minimum Top-up Tax is contained in Article 10.1 of the Pillar Two Model Rules (defined terms):

> [It] means a minimum tax that is included in the domestic law of a jurisdiction and that: (a) determines the Excess Profits of the Constituent Entities located in the jurisdiction (domestic Excess Profits) in a manner that is equivalent to the GloBE Rules; (b) operates to increase domestic tax liability with respect to domestic Excess Profits to the Minimum Rate for the jurisdiction and Constituent Entities for a Fiscal Year; and (c) is implemented and administered in a way that is consistent with the outcomes provided for under the GloBE Rules and the Commentary, provided that such jurisdiction does not provide any benefits that are related to such rules.

See OECD, *Tax Challenges Arising from the Digitalisation of the Economy – Global Anti-Base Erosion Model Rules (Pillar Two)* (OECD Publishing 2021) <www.oecd.org/tax/beps/tax-challenges-arising-from-the-digitalisation-of-the-economy-global-anti-base-erosion-model-rules-pillar-two.htm> accessed 21 June 2024.

host country provides any benefits to multinational enterprises related to the implementation of the Pillar Two top-up rules in their domestic tax system.

A violation of the NBR results in that country not having a *'qualified'* QDMTT. As a result, any income produced in that country is subject to top-up taxation in other jurisdictions. Further, whether a benefit runs foul of Pillar Two can be determined by the country that can impose the top-up tax. One can only imagine the tension between countries that will result from this form of global scrutiny and the pressure on developing countries attempting to attract and keep FDI while complying with the Pillar Two requirements.

Meanwhile other countries may have the capability or be at a stage of development where they can create incentives for multinational enterprises to offset the QDMTT but not run foul of Pillar Two.

For example, Singapore announced that it will be offering refundable tax credits under a new refundable investment credit (RIC) programme.[42] According to the Singapore Inland Revenue Authority government website,[43] the RIC will be awarded on qualifying expenditures incurred in respect of a qualifying project, during the qualifying period of up to ten years. The credits will be offset against corporate income tax payable and unutilized credits will be refunded in cash. According to news reports, this incentive, unlike the one offered by Vietnam, will align with the Pillar Two rules for qualified refundable tax credits (QRTCs) and offset any QDMTT tax imposed.[44]

## 9.4 CONCLUSION

Developing countries frequently offer tax incentives to investors to encourage foreign direct investment. Commitments to investors are also included in

---

[42] The RICs will include refundable credits against tax liabilities and cash refunds. It is intended to attract MNEs looking to make substantial, future-focused investments.

[43] Inland Revenue Authority of Singapore, 'Refundable Investment Credit (RIC)' <https://www.iras.gov.sg/schemes/disbursement-schemes/refundable-investment-credit-%28ric%29> accessed 12 August 2024.

[44] See Martin A Sullivan, 'Will Singapore's Refundable Investment Credit Trigger Pillar 2 Tax?' (2024) 114 Tax Notes International 995; Uma Devi, 'Budget 2024: Quick Takes on Refundable Investment Credit Scheme' *The Business Times* (16 February 2024) (citing expert observers on the proposal) <https://www.businesstimes.com.sg/singapore/budget-2024-quick-takes-refundable-investment-credit-scheme> accessed 13 August 2024. Not surprisingly, the new credits target sectors and projects identified as pivotal to future growth in Singapore, such as advanced manufacturing, digital innovation, green technologies, and research and development, which often require significant upfront investment.

investment or trade agreements that limit the country's ability to change tax laws and policies. Further, many developing countries have limited capacity to comply with Pillar Two obligations or the investor claims for binding arbitration or demands for other forms of compensation that may result from compliance.

In the short term it thus appears that Pillar Two will operate to increase the tax revenue in the country of the foreign parent. It will also remove the benefit of any tax incentives provided by the developing country. For developing countries, this seems the worst of all possible outcomes.

Finding a global solution will not be an easy task. In the interim the following suggestions are offered.

First, developed countries should review the financial impact on developing countries as the result of constraints posed by a BIT to which they are a party. UNCTAD has suggested, '[a]s a stopgap measure, establish[ing] a mechanism to return any top-up revenues raised by developed home countries that should have accrued to developing host countries, but that they were unable to raise because of capacity or treaty constraints'.[45]

Second, the broader international community should address the constraints on developing countries and especially less developed countries (LDCs) as the result of investment agreements, which clearly place these countries at a disadvantage under the Pillar Two proposals. This could include, at a minimum, technical assistance to developing countries to support BEPS implementation and make investment policy adjustments.[46]

Third, the matter of dispute resolution should be carefully considered and whether challenges to Pillar Two reforms should be heard in an investment treaty arbitration or through tax authority/tax treaty arbitration. As it stands, investment treaty arbitrators, who may have little knowledge of tax mechanisms, will be making decisions about the legality of such measures under investment treaties.

---

[45] See UNCTAD, *World Investment Report 2022: International Tax Reforms and Sustainable Investment* (United Nations 2022) xvi <https://unctad.org/system/files/official-document/wir2022_overview_en.pdf> accessed 21 June 2024.

[46] UNCTAD previously proposed a multilateral instrument that clarifies the relationship between the global minimum tax and IIAs to create legal certainty and ensure that the latter do not impede the implementation of the former: ibid 152. This instrument could be adopted in a self-standing manner or as part of a larger package of treaty-based measures for the implementation of Pillars One and Two. Table 1 of its 2023 report (n 6) further sets out some of the relevant short-term considerations to avoid any potential friction between the minimum tax and IIAs.

Finally, the interaction of Pillar Two with other international legal agreements should be more carefully explored.[47]

The purpose of Pillar Two was to prevent a 'race to the bottom'. According to the OECD this was a race to lower tax rates. This chapter considers the impact of the Pillar Two rules differently. Will they result in a race to the bottom for developing countries in their ability to compete globally for foreign investment?

[47] Błażej Kuźniacki, 'Pillar 2 and International Investment Agreements: "QDMTT Payable" Seals an Internationally Wrongful Act' (2023) 112 Tax Notes International 159.

# 10. Global tax governance in international tax law-making: in search of legitimacy and inclusiveness

**Irma Mosquera Valderrama**

## 10.1 INTRODUCTION

In 2016, Thomas Rixen and Peter Dietsch, in their book *Global Tax Governance: What Is Wrong with It and How to Fix It*, defined global tax governance as

> consist[ing] of the set of institutions governing issues of taxation that involve cross-border transactions or have other international implications. This definition implies that global tax governance need not, but could, involve a *full or partial shift of the power to tax, that is, the right to impose taxes on citizens, to the international level.*[1]

As will be further elaborated in section 10.2 below, since the 2008 financial crisis, the Organisation for Economic Co-operation and Development (OECD), with the political mandate of the G20, has introduced standards: first the standard of exchange of information, thereafter a number of standards under the Base Erosion and Profit Shifting (BEPS) Project and the BEPS four minimum standards to tackle tax avoidance by multinational enterprises, and more recently the proposals to address taxation of highly digitalized businesses (Pillar One) and to introduce a global minimum tax rate to tackle tax competition (Pillar Two). These standards are applicable to OECD, G20 and non-OECD, non-G20 countries, including developing countries.

In the author's view, addressing these international tax developments from the perspective of global tax governance and using the definition put forward

[1] Peter Dietsch and Thomas Rixen, 'Global Tax Governance: What It Is and Why It Matters' in Peter Dietsch and Thomas Rixen (eds), *Global Tax Governance: What Is Wrong with It and How to Fix It* (ECPR Press 2016) 3 (emphasis added).

by Rixen and Dietsch referred to above, the process means then that there is a shift of the power to tax from countries to international organizations (the OECD) and to a political forum (the G20). The questions that the research team has explored in the framework of the GLOBTAXGOV Project (of which the present author is the principal investigator)[2] involve identifying the conditions under which this shift of power can be legitimate and feasible vis-à-vis non-OECD, non-G20 countries.

To define legitimacy, the GLOBTAXGOV Project has used the concepts developed respectively by Scharpf[3] and Schmidt[4] of input/output and throughput legitimacy, which have been used in areas other than tax law. In short, legitimacy provides a framework to evaluate the participation and representation in decision-making (i.e., input legitimacy), the outcome being useful for all stakeholders (output legitimacy), and the process being transparent, inclusive, accountable and open (throughput legitimacy).

---

2 Information on the GLOBTAXGOV Project is available at <https://globtaxgov.weblog.leidenuniv.nl/a-new-model-of-global-governance-in-international-tax-law-making-globtaxgov/> accessed 16 June 2024.

3 For this purpose, the definition of Scharpf, including the distinction between input legitimacy, i.e., government by the people, and output legitimacy, i.e., government for the people, has been taken into account: Fritz Scharpf, *Governing in Europe: Effective and Democratic?* (Oxford University Press 1999) 7. See, for an analysis in international tax law-making, Irma Johanna Mosquera Valderrama, 'Legitimacy and the Making of International Tax Law: The Challenges of Multilateralism' (2015) 7(3) World Tax Journal 343–82 ('Legitimacy and the Making of International Tax Law').

4 Schmidt introduces throughput legitimacy as a new intermediary concept to fill in the gap between input and output legitimacy and to ensure the trustworthiness of the processes. Schmidt argues that the concepts related to this throughput legitimacy are the efficacy of the many different forms of governance processes and the adequacy of the rules they follow in policymaking. In this context, accountability involves responsiveness to participatory input demands and being held responsible for the output decisions, transparency involves demands for some form of scrutiny by a specific forum, and inclusiveness involves the openness of the institutions to civil society: Vivien A Schmidt, 'Democracy and Legitimacy in the European Union Revisited: Input, Output *and* "Throughput"' (2012) 61(1) Political Studies 2, 14. The analysis of throughput legitimacy has been conducted by the present author in an article on the implementation of the four BEPS Minimum Standards in seven countries (Congo, Cameroon, Costa Rica, Jamaica, Peru, Sri Lanka and Viet Nam): Irma Mosquera Valderrama, 'Throughput Legitimacy of the Peer Review Process of the Four BEPS Minimum Standards: A Case Study' (2024) 52(3) Intertax 171 ('Throughput Legitimacy of the Peer Review Process').

Scholars, civil society and countries have expressed in articles and meetings at the international and regional levels their concerns regarding the legitimacy of the BEPS Project vis-à-vis non-OECD, non-G20 countries (see section 10.3.1 below).

In order to address these concerns, the OECD created the BEPS Inclusive Framework, in which countries were invited to participate as BEPS Associates and to commit to the implementation of the BEPS four minimum standards. This implementation is on equal footing and subject to the consensus minus one rule. This rule means that upon review of the implementation, the peer review of the country can be adopted even if one country does not agree with it (minus one rule). This country is most likely the country that is being peer reviewed.[5] The system of peer review and consensus minus one rule was adopted based on the experience of peer review of the standard of transparency and exchange of information.[6]

Despite the participation of countries in the BEPS Inclusive Framework, countries, civil society,[7] regional tax organizations (e.g., the African Tax

---

[5] The OECD in the Progress Report July 2016–June 2017 stated that '[t]hese reviews will be adopted subject to a "consensus minus one" rule, aimed at ensuring that no one jurisdiction, whether the jurisdiction under review or another jurisdiction with an isolated position, can block consensus on the adoption or publication of a report': OECD, *Inclusive Framework on BEPS: Progress Report, July 2016–June 2017* (OECD Publishing 2017) 22.

[6] Irma Mosquera Valderrama, Addy Mazz, Luís Eduardo Schoueri, Natalia Quiñones, Jennifer Roeleveld, Pasquale Pistone and Frederik Zimmer, 'The Rule of Law and the Effective Protection of Taxpayers' Rights in Developing Countries' (2017) WU International Taxation Research Paper Series No 2017-10.

[7] Alex Cobham, 'New UN Tax Handbook: Lower-Income Countries vs OECD BEPS' *Tax Justice Network* (11 September 2017) <https://www.taxjustice.net/2017/09/11/new-un-tax-handbook-sets-lower-income-countries-oecd-beps/> accessed 16 June 2024. See for instance Action Aid, *Levelling Up: Ensuring a Fairer Share of Corporate Tax for Developing Countries* (2015); BEPS Monitoring Group, 'Overall Evaluation of the G20/OECD Base Erosion and Profit Shifting (BEPS) Project' ([5 October 2015]) <https://www.bepsmonitoringgroup.org/news/2018/5/10/overall-evaluation>; Sol Picciotto, 'Briefing on Base Erosion and Profit Shifting (BEPS) Implications for Developing Countries' (Tax Justice Network Briefing, February 2014) <https://www.taxjustice.net/wp-content/uploads/2013/04/TJN-Briefing-BEPS-for-Developing-Countries-Feb-2014-v2.pdf> accessed 16 June 2024.

Administration Forum (ATAF))[8] and scholars[9] have highlighted the fast pace of the BEPS Project,[10] and the limited capacity of developing countries to allocate resources (technical, personnel) efficiently to address the implementation of BEPS minimum standards (see section 10.3.1 below). These concerns highlight the importance of addressing the feasibility of the BEPS Project vis-à-vis developing countries.

In addition to legitimacy and feasibility, there are other concerns from developing countries regarding the inclusiveness (equal footing) of the BEPS Inclusive Framework. These concerns have resulted in scholars, regional tax organizations and civil society highlighting that the main role in international tax law-making should shift from the OECD towards the United Nations. In November 2022, Nigeria, with the support of other African countries, submitted a proposal for a draft resolution at the UN Second Committee on the 'Promotion of Inclusive and Effective International Tax Cooperation' by means of developing a framework or instrument. This resolution was approved by

---

[8] See presentation by Logan Wort (ATAF) at the UN High-Level Panel on International Financial Accountability, Transparency and Integrity for Achieving the 2030 Agenda (FACTI Panel), 'Improving Cooperation in Tax Matters' (Virtual Consultation, 5 May 2020) <https://www.factipanel.org/events/virtual-consultation-session-improving-cooperation-in-tax-matters> accessed 16 June 2024.

[9] Irma Johanna Mosquera Valderrama, 'Output Legitimacy Deficits and the Inclusive Framework of the OECD/G20 Base Erosion and Profit Shifting Initiative' (2018) 72(3) Bulletin for International Taxation 160 ('Output Legitimacy Deficits'); Ivan Ozai, 'Institutional and Structural Legitimacy Deficits in the International Tax Regime' (2020) 12(1) World Tax Journal 53; Allison Christians and Laurens van Apeldoorn, 'The OECD Inclusive Framework' (2018) 72(4/5) Bulletin for International Taxation 226; Yariv Brauner, 'BEPS: An Interim Evaluation' (2014) 6(1) World Tax Journal 10; Richard Collier and Nadine Riedel, 'The OECD/G20 Base Erosion and Profit Shifting Initiative and Developing Countries' (2018) 72(12) Bulletin for International Taxation 704.

[10] Some of these challenges have also been addressed, for instance, by OECD representatives at international organizations (World Bank/International Monetary Fund (IMF)) meetings. See the presentation by Ben Dickinson, Head of the Global Relations and Development Division, OECD at the OECD BEPS Inclusive Framework Online Conference 27–28 January 2021 and Tax Development Day 29 January 2021. See also the Tax Sunday Conference organized by the World Bank and IMF, 'International Tax Avoidance – What Has BEPS Accomplished for Developing Countries?' (Virtual Conference, 18 October 2020) Panel 2 (from 16:53) <https://www.worldbank.org/en/events/2020/10/08/tax-Sunday-conference-2020#2>. See also Irma Mosquera Valderrama, 'Global Tax Governance' in Florian Haase and Georg Kofler (eds), *The Oxford Handbook of International Tax Law* (Oxford University Press 2023).

the General Assembly in December 2022.[11] This resolution gives the United Nations a more important role in the setting of international tax standards. Since then, an Ad Hoc Committee has been created to draft the Terms of Reference for a United Nations Framework Convention on International Tax Cooperation. At the time of writing, discussions on these Terms of Reference are being held (see section 10.3.2.2 below).

Regional organizations such as the African Union[12] and CARICOM[13] and regional tax organizations such as ATAF have also addressed the concerns of inclusiveness by questioning whether the rules provided for in Pillar One and Pillar Two are what developing countries need or whether new rules should be introduced to achieve a global fair deal.

Against this background, this contribution aims to provide, in light of the analysis of legitimacy and inclusiveness, the conditions under which a new governing body in international tax law (such as the OECD and/or the UN) can be legitimate and inclusive for both OECD and non-OECD countries, including developing countries. The main argument is that both the OECD and the UN should give attention not only to the content of the rules but also to the decision-making process to enhance legitimacy and inclusiveness in international tax law-making.

This contribution will address the current discussion of the BEPS Project, BEPS Pillar One and BEPS Pillar Two in the framework of global tax governance, legitimacy and inclusiveness. Section 10.2 will address the political developments that influence taxation at the international level. Thereafter, section 10.3 will address legitimacy and inclusiveness. Finally, a short conclusion with some recommendations to address legitimacy and inclusiveness by the OECD and the UN will be provided.

---

[11] See United Nations, Resolution Adopted by the General Assembly on 30 December 2022, Promotion of Inclusive and Effective Tax Cooperation at the United Nations, A/RES/77/244 <https://financing.desa.un.org/document/general-assembly-resolution-promotion-inclusive-and-effective-tax-cooperation-united>.

[12] African Union, 'Africa Calls for International Taxation Systems Reforms as It Forges a Common Position on Digital Taxation' (Press Release, 8 December 2020) <https://au.int/en/pressreleases/20201208/africa-calls-international-taxation-systems-reforms-it-forges-common-position> accessed 16 June 2024.

[13] CARICOM, 'Caricom Wants Inter-Governmental Tax Body to Set Standards, Rules' (Press Release, 20 February 2020) <https://caricom.org/caricom-wants-inter-governmental-tax-body-to-set-standards-rules/> accessed 16 June 2024.

## 10.2 INTERNATIONAL POLITICAL DEVELOPMENTS

Since the 2008 financial crisis, countries and international organizations have been searching for ways to collect revenue. The proposed solution at that time was to facilitate transparency and exchange of information among countries. Bank secrecy needed to be repealed, and tax havens needed to facilitate the exchange of information on the assets and financial accounts owned by residents and non-residents (individuals and businesses).

In response, the OECD, with a political mandate from the G20 (a political forum with some OECD and non-OECD countries such as China, Russia, Indonesia and India), introduced international tax standards such as the standard on the exchange of information and transparency. This standard was also later implemented by other countries (non-OECD, non-G20) participating in the Global Transparency Forum (currently more than 170 tax jurisdictions[14]).

Later on, due to tax scandals involving large multinational enterprises such as Starbucks and Google, among others, the OECD (again), with the political mandate of the G20, decided to introduce the Base Erosion and Profit Shifting (BEPS) Action Plan and Project to tackle aggressive tax planning by multinational enterprises and to ensure that multinational enterprises pay their fair share. This Project contains 15 Actions, i.e., four minimum standards (Actions 5, 6, 13 and 14),[15] ten best practices and one Multilateral Instrument. The BEPS Multilateral Instrument includes two of the BEPS four minimum standards and some of the BEPS best practices.

As has been argued by this author previously, the decision-making regarding the content of the BEPS Project and its Actions took place in the so-called BEPS 44 Group (the OECD, OECD Accession countries and G20 countries).[16] Non-OECD, non-G20 countries were invited to participate as BEPS Associates in the implementation of the four minimum standards. The result was the creation of the BEPS Inclusive Framework, with more than 145 tax jurisdictions (as of June 2024).[17]

---

[14] OECD, 'Global Forum Members' (last updated January 2024) <https://www.oecd.org/tax/transparency/who-we-are/members/> accessed 16 June 2024.

[15] Action 5 deals with countering harmful tax regimes and the exchange of rulings; Action 6 deals with preventing treaty abuse; Action 13 deals with transfer pricing documentation and country-by-country reporting; and Action 14 deals with making dispute resolution mechanisms more effective.

[16] Mosquera Valderrama, 'Legitimacy and the Making of International Tax Law' (n 3).

[17] OECD, 'Members of the OECD/G20 Inclusive Framework on BEPS' (updated 28 May 2024) <https://www.oecd.org/tax/beps/inclusive-framework

Furthermore, more than 100 tax jurisdictions have signed the BEPS Multilateral Instrument which amends their bilateral tax treaties.[18] Since the BEPS Project, the aim of tax treaties is not only to prevent double taxation and tax avoidance, but also to prevent double non-taxation, where income is taxed nowhere.

At the time of writing, the BEPS Multilateral Instrument has been ratified by more than 70 of the more than 100 jurisdictions that have signed the Instrument.[19] However, even where a country signs and ratifies the BEPS Multilateral Instrument, the country must explicitly mention the tax treaties that will be covered by the Instrument. The country has the possibility to opt in or opt out of the provisions provided in the BEPS Multilateral Instrument.[20]

In both cases, the result is the OECD, with the political mandate of the G20, introducing international tax standards that non-OECD, non-G20 countries are implementing throughout their membership, in networks (Global Transparency Forum and BEPS Inclusive Framework) or by signing multilateral instruments (Common Reporting Standard, the Multilateral Convention on Mutual Administrative Assistance in Tax Matters and the BEPS Multilateral Instrument).

Countries participating in the BEPS Inclusive Framework have also agreed to be reviewed by their peers (peer review) on their commitment to these standards. However, unlike treaties where a country signs the treaty, and it has an effect for both or multiple parties, the BEPS four minimum standards are regarded as soft law since these standards are not binding for countries. So,

-on-beps-composition.pdf> accessed 16 June 2024 ('Members of the OECD/G20 Inclusive Framework on BEPS').

[18] There are also multilateral tax treaties concluded by more than two countries, for instance, the Andean Community Multilateral Tax Treaty. These multilateral tax treaties are outside the scope of this contribution. See Irma Mosquera Valderrama, 'How Can Regional Cooperation Help the Enhancement of Regional Economic Development and Strengthen the Voices of Developing Countries in Global Tax Negotiations?' (2024) 25(2) Journal of World Investment and Trade 201.

[19] OECD, 'Signatories and Parties to the Multilateral Convention to Implement Tax Treaty Related Measures to Prevent Base Erosion and Profit Shifting' <https://www.oecd.org/tax/treaties/beps-mli-signatories-and-parties.pdf> accessed 16 June 2024.

[20] This is different from tax treaties concluded by countries where parties agree bilaterally (or multilaterally) to specific provisions to prevent double taxation and tax avoidance and to facilitate the exchange of information, among other things. In this case, there are no opt-in, opt-out provisions. Countries can only provide reservations, for instance, reservations to provisions of the OECD or UN Models.

in principle, countries are not required to implement these standards; but they do so. Why?

Some articles published by the present author elsewhere have addressed some of the reasons.[21] For instance, three main reasons are:

(i) chance and necessity (technical assistance by developed countries and/or OECD, and twinning projects between developed and developing countries);
(ii) expected efficacy of the law (access to information by tax administrations on multinational enterprises);
(iii) political, economic and reputational incentives (commitment to the EU Standard of Tax Good Governance in trade, partnership agreements to receive EU funding, and to be excluded from the list of non-cooperative jurisdictions).

Due to the increase in digital business prior to the Covid-19 pandemic, countries decided to address this issue, without any success until 2021.[22] For instance, at the start of the discussions in 2018–2019 on Pillar One (taxation of highly digitalized businesses), it was clear that there were three positions: (i) user participation from OECD countries; (ii) marketing intangibles from the United States; and (iii) significant economic presence from G24 (developing) countries.[23] Because no consensus was reached, the OECD Secretariat submitted a proposal (at the end of 2019[24]) that was a combination of the OECD and the United States' proposals, leaving behind the G24 (developing) countries' proposal (i.e., focusing on significant economic presence).[25]

---

[21] Mosquera Valderrama, 'Output Legitimacy Deficits' (n 9).

[22] See Irma Johanna Mosquera Valderrama, 'Trade Digitalization and Taxation' in Julien Chaisse and Cristián Rodríguez-Chiffelle (eds), *The Elgar Companion to the World Trade Organization* (Edward Elgar Publishing 2023) ('Trade Digitalization and Taxation').

[23] OECD, *Programme of Work to Develop a Consensus Solution to the Tax Challenges Arising from the Digitalisation of the Economy*, OECD/G20 Inclusive Framework on BEPS (OECD Publishing 2019).

[24] OECD, *Secretariat Proposal for a 'Unified Approach' under Pillar One, Public Consultation Document (9 October 2019 – 12 November 2019)* (OECD Publishing 2019).

[25] G24, 'Comments of the G-24 on the OECD Secretariat Proposal for a Unified Approach to the Nexus and Profit Allocation Challenges Arising from the Digitalisation (Pillar 1)' (2019) <https://g24.org/comments-of-the-g-24-on-the-oecd-secretariat-proposal-for-a-unified-approach-to-the-nexus-and-profit-allocation-challenges-arising-from-the-digitalisation-pillar-1-2/> accessed 16 June 2024.

Nevertheless, the present author has noted that the significant economic presence approach has been adopted unilaterally by countries such as Nigeria, Israel and Indonesia (a G20 country), and Colombia (an OECD country) in 2022, which 'shows that countries have decided to follow unilaterally the rules that they consider are more convenient for their own economy. This is the case [with] the significant economic presence [approach] and the digital service tax (e.g., Kenya) for taxation of highly digitalized business'.[26]

Amid these discussions, the United States asked countries to refrain from introducing unilateral measures such as digital service taxes and that, if they did not, the US would start Section 301 US trade investigations, which would result in trade retaliation measures.

Consultations and discussions took place in 2020, but there was no progress on the adoption of the OECD Secretariat proposal. However, the situation changed in 2021 with the Biden presidency of the United States. The United States decided to implement the Global Anti-Base Erosion (GLoBE) (Pillar Two) proposal and endorse the Pillar One OECD Secretariat proposal. This proposal was discussed at the G7 and G20 and thereafter in the BEPS Inclusive Framework.

In 2021, 137 of the 141 tax jurisdictions[27] then belonging to the BEPS Inclusive Framework reached a political agreement to introduce measures to tax highly digitalized businesses (Pillar One) and to introduce a global minimum tax rate of 15% (GloBE Pillar Two).

In July 2023, 138 of the 143 jurisdictions committed to the standstill (freeze) of digital taxes while global agreement is being reached and agreed on the introduction of an implementation package for Pillar One and Pillar Two.[28] Belarus, Canada, Pakistan, Russia and Sri Lanka did not support this political

---

[26] Irma Mosquera, 'Global Tax Governance: Legitimacy and Inclusiveness, Why It Matters' *GLOBTAXGOV* (30 June 2023) <https://globtaxgov.weblog.leidenuniv.nl/2023/06/30/global-tax-governance-legitimacy-and-inclusiveness-why-it-matters/>.

[27] Except Nigeria, Sri Lanka, Pakistan and Kenya: OECD, 'Statement on a Two-Pillar Solution to Address the Tax Challenges Arising from the Digitalisation of the Economy' (8 October 2021) <https://www.oecd.org/tax/beps/statement-on-a-two-pillar-solution-to-address-the-tax-challenges-arising-from-the-digitalisation-of-the-economy-october-2021.pdf> accessed 16 June 2024 ('Statement on a Two-Pillar Solution').

[28] OECD, 'Outcome Statement on the Two-Pillar Solution to Address the Tax Challenges Arising from the Digitalisation of the Economy' (11 July 2023) <https://www.oecd.org/tax/beps/outcome-statement-on-the-two-pillar-solution-to-address-the-tax-challenges-arising-from-the-digitalisation-of-the-economy-july-2023.pdf> accessed 16 June 2024 ('Outcome Statement on the Two-Pillar Solution').

statement. The reasons why are not clear, except in the case of Canada, which is not in agreement with the standstill of digital taxes.[29] The number committed to the standstill has now increased to 141 tax jurisdictions since the Inclusive Framework has increased to more than 145 tax jurisdictions (including more than 100 non-OECD, non-G20 countries).[30]

The concerns regarding the legitimacy and inclusiveness of these developments will be addressed in the following section.

## 10.3 GLOBAL TAX GOVERNANCE

### 10.3.1 Legitimacy

The BEPS four minimum standards have been accepted by countries participating in the BEPS Inclusive Framework, which includes OECD, G20 and non-OECD, non-G20 countries. At the time of writing, more than 145 tax jurisdictions have committed to implementation, and most of these jurisdictions have been peer reviewed (and assessed positively) in their implementation.[31]

As the present author highlighted in 2015, non-OECD, non-G20 countries, including developing countries, need to participate in the agenda setting of international tax standards (input legitimacy) and to benefit from these standards (output legitimacy).[32] Therefore, there was a lack of input and output legitimacy.

Subsequently, in a 2018 article, after the creation of the BEPS Inclusive Framework, the author continued to question the legitimacy and feasibility of the BEPS four minimum standards. At that time it was not clear, and it is still not clear, whether these BEPS four minimum standards are what developing countries need. How much revenue has the implementation of the BEPS four minimum standards raised for developing countries? The author's 2018 article concluded (and it is a conclusion which also continues to apply) that the fast pace of the implementation of the BEPS four minimum standards has resulted in developing countries focusing on these standards while diverting their attention from other priorities, such as taxation of the informal economy,

---

29 Reuters, 'Countries Agree to Extend Digital Services Tax Freeze through 2024' (13 July 2023) <https://www.reuters.com/business/finance/countries-agree-extend-digital-services-tax-freeze-through-2024-2023-07-12/> accessed 16 June 2024.

30 OECD, 'Members of the OECD/G20 Inclusive Framework on BEPS' (n 17).

31 OECD, *OECD/G20 Inclusive Framework on BEPS, Progress Report July 2019–July 2020* (OECD Publishing 2020).

32 Mosquera Valderrama, 'Legitimacy and the Making of International Tax Law' (n 3).

tax evasion, digitalization of tax administration and improving taxpayer compliance, among other things.

More recently, in light of the developments involving Pillar One and Pillar Two, countries have also addressed the lack of legitimacy of both of these Pillars. Regarding Pillar One, the question is whether the political outcome agreed upon by most of the countries of the BEPS Inclusive Framework is legitimate vis-à-vis developing countries. In this 2021 political outcome, it was required for countries to commit to the repeal of the digital service tax.[33]

Four countries did not endorse this political statement, i.e., Nigeria, Kenya, Sri Lanka and Pakistan. Nigeria has expressed the view that the political outcome is not fair, and therefore, they will continue with their own rules (e.g., significant economic presence to tax digital business). Kenya has a digital service tax, so at that time policymakers in Kenya did not consider that the country should commit to this political statement. However, in the framework of the negotiations of a trade agreement, the US has asked Kenya to repeal the digital service tax and to commit to the political outcome for Pillar One and Pillar Two. Kenya's government has recently indicated that they will follow that path.[34]

In the midst of the discussions, Logan Wort, General Secretary of ATAF, addressed in September 2021[35] the need to obtain an effective and equitable agreement on the Pillar One and Pillar Two rules, and in November 2021,[36] the difficulties countries faced to be included in the discussions, and the need to consider the pace and technicality of the discussions that were being carried out regarding the Pillar One and Pillar Two rules. According to Logan Wort:

> Africa's readiness has a number of elements and I will focus on two. First, if you look at the recently concluded Inclusive Framework discussions on the tax challenges of the digitalisation of the economy, you need to ask is Africa ready for that

---

33 OECD, 'Statement on a Two-Pillar Solution' (n 27).

34 Kepha Muiruri, 'President Ruto Drops Digital Service Tax against Multinationals' *Business Daily Africa* (30 March 2023) <https://www-businessdailyafrica-com.cdn.ampproject.org/c/s/www.businessdailyafrica.com/bd/economy/ruto-drops-digital-service-tax-against-multinationals--4179322?view=htmlamp> accessed 16 June 2024.

35 Quoted in 'The G7 Global Tax Deal: Where To From Here?' *ATAF News* (September 2021) 1 <https://irp.cdn-website.com/a521d626/files/uploaded/ATAF%20News%20Sept.%202021-3.pdf> accessed 16 June 2024.

36 ATAF, 'ATAF's Executive Secretary Logan Wort Calls for Greater Transparency in the Granting of Tax Incentives at Mazars Conference' (ATAF Communication, 26 November 2021) <https://www.ataftax.org/atafs-executive-secretary-logan-wort-calls-for-greater-transparency-in-the-granting-of-tax-incentives-at-mazars-conference> accessed 16 June 2024.

> level of technicality and pace of the conversation? The past three years have been incredibly complex and continues to be incredibly complex. The proposed Pillar One and Pillar Two rules raise a huge range of technical design and implementation issues such as the design of a Multilateral Convention for Amount A that countries will need to sign and ratify, drafting of domestic Legislation, the creation of the so-called Review Panel and Determination Panel for Amount A and related issues, the revenue sourcing rules and tax credit rules and then a Multilateral Instrument and domestic legislation for Pillar Two. All of this will create very significant implementation challenges for African tax administrations with limited capacity.[37]

Furthermore, regarding Pillar Two, the October 2021 Statement and the template for domestic implementation of Pillar Two have received criticism from scholars, mainly regarding the consequences of these proposals for tax treaties and the added complexity for the international tax regime. Additionally, there is concern that these proposals are putting developing countries in a situation of disadvantage.[38] More recently, the conformity of the Pillar Two rules, in this case the undertaxed profits rule (UTPR), with international law obligations has also been addressed.[39]

More recently, in a political statement on the Two-Pillar Solution published in July 2023 initiated by the OECD, 138[40] members of the BEPS Inclusive Framework delivered a package to further implement the Two-Pillar Solution to Address the Tax Challenges Arising from the Digitalisation of the Economy. These measures include the introduction of a Multilateral Convention on Amount A of Pillar One, some guidance for Amount B on Pillar One, the framework for the implementation of the subject to tax rule under Pillar Two to be introduced under a multilateral instrument, and a plan to support the coordinated implementation of the Two-Pillar Solution.[41]

The question is whether the OECD will address the criticism from scholars, and if so, how this will be done in the forthcoming consultations, since the

---

37 Ibid.

38 Maarten de Wilde, 'Towards a "2020s Compromise" in International Business Taxation: Reflections on an Emerging New Tax Paradigm' (2022) 76(4) Bulletin for International Taxation 207. See also Vikram Chand, Alessandro Turina and Kinga Romanovska, 'Tax Treaty Obstacles in Implementing the Pillar Two Global Minimum Tax Rules and a Possible Solution for Eliminating the Various Challenges' (2022) 14(1) World Tax Journal 3; Filip Debelva and Luc De Broe, 'Pillar 2: An Analysis of the IIR and UTPR from an International Customary Law, Tax Treaty Law and European Union Law Perspective' (2022) 50(12) Intertax 898.

39 Peter Hongler, Irma Mosquera, Filip Debelva, Vikram Chand and Julien Chaisse, 'UTPR – Potential Conflicts with International Law?' (2023) 113 Tax Notes International 141.

40 See section 10.2 above.

41 OECD, 'Outcome Statement on the Two-Pillar Solution' (n 28).

rules for domestic implementation of Pillar Two have already been introduced. It seems from the wording that the focus will be more on guidance and interpretation to ensure compliance with these rules than on providing an opportunity for countries to effectively be heard in their views regarding the problems of implementation of Pillar Two. This is also true in light of the new July 2023 political statement on Pillar One and Pillar Two, where countries have decided to agree on an implementation package of Pillar One and Pillar Two despite the current developments at the United Nations level. These developments will be addressed in section 10.3.2.2 below. The following section will address the inclusiveness of countries participating in the BEPS Inclusive Framework regarding the BEPS Project.

### 10.3.2 Inclusiveness

#### 10.3.2.1 Inclusiveness of the BEPS Inclusive Framework in the BEPS Project

In the BEPS Inclusive Framework, the OECD has invited non-OECD, non-G20 countries to participate on an equal footing in the implementation of the BEPS four minimum standards. The then Director of the OECD Centre for Tax Policy and Administration mentioned in the first meeting of the BEPS Inclusive Framework (Kyoto, 30 June 2016) that '[t]hrough their participation in the decision-making as well as the technical working groups of the OECD's Committee on Fiscal Affairs, the members of the inclusive framework will now have a direct influence in shaping international tax rules to tackle BEPS and ensuring a level playing field'.[42]

However, scholars have highlighted the problems of governance of the BEPS Inclusive Framework. Much attention has been given to the lack of 'true equal footing' of the countries participating in the BEPS Inclusive Framework.[43] For instance, in 2018, Christians and van Apeldoorn rightly stated that:

> The Inclusive Framework continues the OECD's expansion of tax cooperation beyond its member countries, but it unfortunately also continues an OECD tradition of institutional and procedural opacity. As such its emphasis on inclusivity is intuitively appealing but elusive. The question for non-member states is whether, in the long term, the Inclusive Framework can adequately define and then deliver

[42] OECD, 'First Meeting of the New Inclusive Framework to Tackle Base Erosion and Profit Shifting Marks a New Era in International Tax Co-operation' (30 June 2016) (quoting Pascal Saint-Amans, Director of the OECD Centre for Tax Policy and Administration) <https://web-archive.oecd.org/2016-11-08/407519-first-meeting-of-the-new-inclusive-framework-to-tackle-base-erosion-and-profit-shifting-marks-a-new-era-in-international-tax-co-operation.htm> 16 June 2024.

[43] Christians and van Apeldoorn (n 9).

> on the promise of inclusivity on an equal footing. Since it is not possible to experiment without significant costs, the decision to move forward with the Inclusive Framework is fundamentally an act of trust in the OECD as an institution. However, better assessment of the likely costs and benefits of participation could be achieved with greater transparency from the OECD as well as the governments that are or seek to be affiliated with it.[44]

In a 2020 working paper, Christensen and co-authors analysed the problems with developing countries' participation in the decision-making process of the BEPS Inclusive Framework.[45] In this paper, the authors argue that the Plenary Meeting led by the OECD Secretariat leaves little room for developing countries to participate in the decision-making. The authors addressed the decision-making process, including also the views of some developing countries, stating that behind the statements of the BEPS Inclusive Framework Plenary meeting

> lies a three-tiered structure of decision making: plenary, Steering Group and working parties. At the top political level, plenaries convene senior tax officials from almost every IF member, alongside observers from regional and international organisations. Plenaries evaluate progress and take final decisions, on a consensus basis, on proposals prepared by subordinate bodies. The plenary is the formal decision-making body, and the final step in a process which identifies and resolves disagreements between countries in advance. Many interviewees described its meetings as choreographed:
>
>> It is a room of approval where everything has been well prepared and orchestrated … the sauce has been made, the dish is served. If you say that the salt is missing, you want to add something … they will tell you that the dish is done. It is at the Steering Group level that the dish is prepared. (Lower-income country)[46]

One of the conclusions in the working paper relates to the limitations of the 'one size fits all' consensus model. The authors stated:

> The limitations of the consensus model have already led the OECD to follow a 'minilateral' approach when it delivered a mandatory binding arbitration solution for only those countries choosing to opt in. This model could create flexibility to move beyond the lowest common denominator approach, and aid the prioritisation

---

44 Ibid 233.

45 This analysis was based on the decision-making process at the OECD as well as on interviews with representatives of developing (low-income) countries: Rasmus Corlin Christensen, Martin Hearson and Tovony Randriamanalina, 'At the Table, Off the Menu? Assessing the Participation of Lower-Income Countries in Global Tax Negotiations' (2020) International Centre for Tax and Development Working Paper 115, 10–11.

46 Ibid.

> of limited capacity. A first step could be to reconsider the universality of the minimum standards.[47]

The OECD has addressed some of these problems in the participation of developing countries in the 2021 report to the G20 on BEPS and developing countries. The OECD stated:

> *While recent developments are encouraging, developing countries with limited capacities continue to face challenges to their active participation in the Inclusive Framework*, particularly due to the pace of the work over multiple workstreams which have been progressed simultaneously. Many are on a steep learning curve, having to adapt to new ways of intergovernmental co-operation. There is also a view that the agenda is not sufficiently reflective of developing countries' interests.[48]

In this report, the OECD acknowledged the different needs of developing countries and the limited capacity of developing countries to (actively) participate in the decision-making process that takes place within the BEPS Inclusive Framework.

In order to address these concerns, the OECD has, since February 2022, institutionalized the creation of two chairs of the BEPS Inclusive Framework, one from an OECD/G20 country and one from a non-OECD/non-G20 country. The OECD recommended that:

> The Inclusive Framework stakeholders should, as a priority, reflect on governance arrangements to ensure a broad and systematic inclusion of developing countries. This could include consideration of representation in the leadership of the Inclusive Framework and its subsidiary bodies, and updating the mandate of the Advisory Group for Co-operation with Partner Economies.[49]

In November 2021, in a Ministerial Dialogue on Tax and Developing Countries[50] hosted by the Minister of Finance of Jamaica, the countries stated their concerns regarding

---

47 Ibid 31.

48 OECD, *Developing Countries and the OECD/G20 Inclusive Framework on BEPS: OECD Report for the G20 Finance Ministers and Central Bank Governors, October 2021, Italy* (OECD Publishing 2021) 13 <https://www.oecd.org/tax/beps/developing-countries-and-the-oecd-g20-inclusive-framework-on-beps.pdf>.

49 Ibid 45.

50 Countries participating were Barbados, Côte d'Ivoire, Egypt, Georgia, Honduras, Jamaica, Jordan, Senegal, Thailand and Viet Nam and the three countries hosting the G20 Presidency between 2020–2022, i.e., the United Kingdom, Italy and Indonesia: Office of the Minister of Finance and the Public Service, Jamaica, 'Chair's Statement of Outcomes, Ministerial Dialogue on Tax and

> governance of the Inclusive Framework, including the representation of developing countries in leadership positions, and ways to maximise our voice and influence over international tax rule making. We noted the diversity of the membership of the Inclusive Framework and that the practicalities of participating effectively in international taxation discussions are often significant constraints, particularly for small lower capacity countries.[51]

In order to enhance governance, the countries participating in the Ministerial Dialogue also recommended that a developing country's representative be included as co-chair of the BEPS Inclusive Framework.[52]

The question is whether the proposed co-chair by one developing country of the BEPS Inclusive Framework recommended in the OECD report to the G20 and the Ministerial Dialogue would be enough for developing countries' participation in the decision-making process and to enhance the legitimacy of the OECD vis-à-vis developing countries. This question is even more relevant in light of the concerns raised by developing countries and regional (tax) organizations and the current role of the United Nations in these discussions. The following section will address some of the concerns regarding the participation of developing countries in the Pillar One and Pillar Two discussions.

#### 10.3.2.2 Inclusiveness of the BEPS Inclusive Framework in Pillar One and Pillar Two

The OECD and the G20 have stated that the decisions regarding the proposals to tax highly digitalized businesses (Pillar One) and to introduce a minimum tax for multinational enterprises above a EUR 750 million threshold (Pillar Two) are being taken within the BEPS Inclusive Framework. However, as in the BEPS Project, developing countries have stated that the decision-making process in the BEPS Inclusive Framework is not inclusive and does not address the needs of developing countries.

---

Developing Countries, Hosted by the Minister of Finance of Jamaica, Hon Nigel Clarke, DPhil, MP, 10 November 2021' <https://mof.gov.jm/wp-content/uploads/chair-statement-of-outcomes-ministerial-dialogue-on-tax-and-developing-countries.pdf> accessed 16 June 2024.

[51] Ibid 1–2.

[52] Ibid 2.

Some of these concerns have also been addressed by representatives of the OECD,[53] IMF[54] and tax administrations at several conferences.[55] These concerns have also resulted in countries developing unilateral rules to deal with the taxation of the digital economy[56] and regional tax organizations such as ATAF presenting their own proposal[57] which departs from the solution adopted by the OECD and the G20.

As was mentioned in section 10.2 above, most of the tax jurisdictions participating in the BEPS Inclusive Framework (more than 140 of the 147 as of June 2024) have endorsed the 2021 and 2023 political statements.[58] Furthermore, administrative guidance and model rules have been published by the OECD with several consultation processes.[59]

Despite the participation of developing countries in the political statement, at the end of 2022, Nigeria, with the support of some other African countries, stated that the current Pillar One and Pillar Two rules are not inclusive enough

---

53 See Dickinson (n 10); Tax Sunday Conference (n 10) Panel 2 (from 20:22).

54 Ernesto Crivelli, Ruud De Mooij and Michael Keen, 'Base Erosion, Profit Shifting and Developing Countries' (2015) International Monetary Fund Working Paper WP/15/118.

55 See for instance, OECD BEPS Inclusive Framework Online Conference (n 10). See also Tax Sunday Conference (n 10) Panel 2, Future Directions presentations by representatives of Jamaica and Viet Nam.

56 Examples are the digital services tax and significant economic presence, among others. See Mosquera Valderrama, 'Trade Digitalization and Taxation' (n 22).

57 ATAF, '130 Inclusive Framework Countries and Jurisdictions Join a New Two-Pillar Plan to Reform International Taxation Rules – What Does This Mean for Africa?' (ATAF Communication, 1 July 2021) <https://www.ataftax.org/130-inclusive-framework-countries-and-jurisdictions-join-a-new-two-pillar-plan-to-reform-international-taxation-rules-what-does-this-mean-for-africa> accessed 16 June 2024. See also ATAF, *The Place of Africa in the Shift towards Global Tax Governance: Can the Taxation of the Digitalised Economy Be an Opportunity for More Inclusiveness?* (2019) <https://events.ataftax.org/index.php?page=documents&func=view&document_id=35> accessed 16 June 2024.

58 OECD, 'Statement on a Two-Pillar Solution to Address the Tax Challenges Arising from the Digitalisation of the Economy' (1 July 2021) <https://www.oecd.org/tax/beps/statement-on-a-two-pillar-solution-to-address-the-tax-challenges-arising-from-the-digitalisation-of-the-economy-july-2021.pdf> accessed 16 June 2024.

59 OECD, 'Tax Challenges of Digitalisation: OECD Invites Comments on Compliance and Tax Certainty Aspects of Global Minimum Tax' (20 December 2022) <https://www.oecd.org/tax/oecd-invites-comments-on-compliance-and-tax-certainty-aspects-of-global-minimum-tax.htm> accessed 16 June 2024.

and therefore proposed a draft UN resolution on the 'promotion of inclusive and effective international tax cooperation at the United Nations'.

This proposal has also been also supported by ATAF, which stated that

> the current global tax rules do not result in a fair allocation of taxing rights between source and residence countries to the detriment of source countries and do not effectively address the risks of base erosion and profit shifting (BEPS) in low-capacity developing countries. This outcome requires support from governments around the world to establish a fair global tax order. ATAF commends the work that has been done to date by the United Nations Committee of Experts on International Tax Cooperation which has helped developing countries start to tackle some of these challenges. The establishment of a Member State-led, open-ended, ad hoc intergovernmental committee to recommend actions on the options for strengthening the inclusiveness and effectiveness of international tax cooperation provides the opportunity to take forward and build on the work of the United Nations Committee of Experts on International Tax Cooperation and significantly enhance the role of the United Nations in the global standard-setting process.[60]

In March 2023, at the United Nations Special Meeting on International Cooperation in Tax Matters, Ahmed Zainab, Minister for Finance, Budget and National Planning of Nigeria, was recorded to have

> expressed concern about the lack of inclusiveness and equal footing in the development of taxation frameworks, both in terms of the weight attributed to inputs from the developing countries, and their capacity to make such inputs. Tax cooperation architecture should address mutual accountability measures through a fair process, she said, adding that developing countries are being punished by unilateral declarations and 'blacklisting by forums and bodies in which they have no voice'.[61]

These concerns resulted in the UN General Assembly's approval in December 2022 of the resolution to create an instrument or framework for international tax cooperation under the auspices of the United Nations. Following this resolution, input has been sought (i) on the content of this framework convention or instrument and (ii) on the role of the United Nations in achieving inclusive and

---

[60] ATAF, 'ATAF Statement on the Success of the Africa Group Resolution for the Creation of a United Nations Convention on International Tax Cooperation' (ATAF Communication, 24 November 2022) <https://www.ataftax.org/ataf-statement-on-the-success-of-the-africa-group-resolution-for-the-creation-of-a-united-nations-convention-on-international-tax-cooperation> accessed 16 June 2024 ('ATAF Statement on the Success of the Africa Group Resolution').

[61] UN, 'Inclusive International Tax Systems Crucial in Strengthening Developing Countries' Fiscal Policies, Green Transition, Speakers Tell Economic and Social Council' (Meetings Coverage, 31 March 2023) <https://press.un.org/en/2023/ecosoc7116.doc.htm> accessed 16 June 2024.

effective international tax cooperation.[62] At the end of May 2023, a virtual consultation with UN countries and other stakeholders took place. International organizations, regional organizations, civil society, academia and business, among others, have provided input to the content of this instrument or framework.[63] Following the report by the Secretary-General in September 2023[64] and the choice of a framework convention in November 2023,[65] a UN Ad Hoc Committee was created, which at the time of writing was in the process of drafting the terms of reference of a framework convention. It was expected to finalize its work by August 2024.[66]

This is not the first time that efforts have been made to give importance to the United Nations in tax matters. At the 2015 Addis Tax Initiative, it was proposed to give the UN Tax Committee the status of an intergovernmental body. The Civil Society Forum advocated 'a forum where every country has the right to participate, not just the richest'.[67] The Civil Society Forum stated in the declaration that '[a] key reason why the global tax system has failed is

---

[62] See for instance the present author's input with Dirk Broekhuijsen and Ezgi Arik in the letter to the Secretary-General of the Department of Economic and Social Affairs of 9 March 2023, available at <https://globtaxgov.weblog.leidenuniv.nl/2023/03/09/input-to-the-un-public-consultation-on-promotion-of-inclusive-and-effective-tax-cooperation-at-the-united-nations/>.

[63] UN, 'Inputs, Tax Report 2023, Promotion of Inclusive and Effective Tax Cooperation at the United Nations' <https://financing.desa.un.org/inputs> accessed 16 June 2024.

[64] UN, Promotion of Inclusive and Effective International Tax Cooperation at the United Nations: Report of the Secretary-General, A/78/235 (26 July 2023) <https://financing.desa.un.org/secretary-generals-tax-report-2023>. Information on the Seventy-Eighth Assembly available at International Institute for Sustainable Development, '78th Session of the UN General Assembly (UNGA 78)' <https://sdg.iisd.org/events/78th-session-of-the-un-general-assembly-unga-78/> accessed 16 June 2024.

[65] UN, Revised Draft Resolution of the General Assembly, Nigeria on behalf of the Group of African States, Promotion of Inclusive and Effective International Tax Cooperation at the United Nations, 15 November 2023, A/C.2/78/L.18/Rev.1 <https://digitallibrary.un.org/record/4027784?v=pdf> accessed 16 June 2024 (Revised Draft Resolution).

[66] UN, 'Ad Hoc Committee to Draft Terms of Reference for a United Nations Framework Convention on International Tax Cooperation' <https://financing.desa.un.org/un-tax-convention/second-session> accessed 29 June 2024 ('Ad Hoc Committee to Draft Terms of Reference').

[67] CIDSE, 'Declaration from the Addis Ababa Civil Society Forum on Financing for Development' (12 July 2015) 4 <https://www.cidse.org/wp-content/uploads/2015/07/Addis_Ababa_CSO_FfD_Forum_Declaration_-_12_July_2015.pdf> accessed 16 June 2024.

that more than half of the world's countries are currently excluded from the decision-making process on global tax standards'.[68]

Accordingly, the Civil Society Forum stressed that '[w]e need to fundamentally change the tax rules, and not having every country represented in writing those rules to make sure they work for everyone is not only undemocratic but also unfair'.[69] '[D]eveloping countries, as a precondition to agreeing to the universal financing agenda, are asking for a more inclusive mode of discussion and a seat at the table in the policy decision-making on financing for development'.[70] Developed countries rejected the proposed upgrade. These countries argued that the OECD should play the leading role in all tax issues.[71] Since then, civil society groups, as well as developing countries, have continued calling for a more predominant role of the UN, including during the current discussions on Pillar One and Pillar Two.

In addition, in the January 2023 meeting of the World Economic Forum, José Antonio Ocampo, the Minister of Finance of Colombia (at that time), called for Latin American and Caribbean ministers to rethink global taxation.[72] For Ocampo,

> The two-pillar solution delivered by the OECD/G20 Inclusive Framework is a step forward, but does not fully address the concerns developing and emerging countries have raised. Latin American and Caribbean countries face common challenges when it comes to cross-border taxation, from the role of tax havens to taxing the digitalized economy. We share the same problems, but we have not shared our views and technical strengths to come up with common solutions. Therefore, our interests have not been visible enough in the international tax policy debate so far, and this must change.[73]

---

68 Ibid.

69 Ibid.

70 UN, 'UN Negotiations Resume on Financing Framework to Advance Global Development' (News, 14 July 2015) (quoting Alexander Trepelkov, Director of the Financing for Development Office in the UN Department of Economic and Social Affairs) <https://www.un.org/development/desa/en/news/financing/negotiations-resume-on-financing.html> accessed 29 June 2024.

71 See UN, Resolution Adopted by the General Assembly on 27 July 2015, Addis Ababa Action Agenda of the Third International Conference on Financing for Development (Addis Ababa Action Agenda), A/RES/69/313, paras 28 and 29 <https://www.un.org/en/development/desa/population/migration/generalassembly/docs/globalcompact/A_RES_69_313.pdf> accessed 29 June 2024.

72 José Antonio Ocampo, 'Calling All Latin American and Caribbean Ministers to Rethink Global Taxation' *International Centre for Tax and Development* (17 January 2023) <https://www.ictd.ac/blog/calling-all-ministers-rethink-global-taxation/> accessed 16 June 2024.

73 Ibid.

Following the May conference, in July 2023 at the First Latin American and Caribbean Summit for an Inclusive, Sustainable and Equitable Global Tax Order, which was initiated by Colombia, Chile and Brazil, finance ministers and high-level officials from 16 Latin American and Caribbean countries approved the creation of a regional tax cooperation platform for Latin America and the Caribbean. This agreement has been supported by the United Nations Economic Commission for Latin America and the Caribbean, known as ECLAC (in Spanish, CEPAL), which will act as the 'technical secretariat' for this platform.[74]

In the joint declaration the signatory countries

> affirm their commitment to generating knowledge, sharing experiences, contributing to the forging of shared positions and non-binding concrete solutions that would guide ministerial decision-making in addressing the region's tax policy challenges. Furthermore, they seek to build in a participatory way and through consensus a space for integrating Treasury, Economy and Finance ministers to foster dialogue with the aim of ensuring that international and regional tax policies be inclusive, equitable, environmentally and socially sustainable and favorable to growth, the reduction of inequalities and the achievement of the Sustainable Development Goals (SDGs).[75]

To sum up, the description above shows that countries in Africa, Central America, the Caribbean and Latin America are questioning the legitimacy, feasibility, and inclusiveness of the initiatives to achieve international tax cooperation developed by the OECD and G20 and the need to establish a fair global tax order.[76] In addition, countries such as Colombia, under the auspices of the United Nations (CEPAL), are proposing a new regional cooperation framework in Latin America and the Caribbean to address the needs of the region and to agree on common solutions tailored to the region.

Given the political developments and the voices raised by scholars, civil society organizations and countries (unilaterally or in regional settings), this new development at the United Nations could shift the decision-making process from the OECD–G20 towards the United Nations. However, it is not yet clear whether this will happen, and therefore, any developments in global tax

---

[74] UN, 'Authorities from 16 Countries Approve the Creation of the Regional Tax Cooperation Platform for Latin America and the Caribbean' (Press Release, 27 July 2023) <https://www.cepal.org/en/pressreleases/authorities-16-countries-approve-creation-regional-tax-cooperation-platform-latin> accessed 16 June 2024.

[75] Ibid.

[76] ATAF, 'ATAF Statement on the Success of the Africa Group Resolution' (n 60).

governance will need to take into account this new role of the United Nations as well as the importance of addressing the concerns of legitimacy and inclusiveness in international tax law-making.

## 10.4 CONCLUSION

To conclude, international taxation nowadays is not only about technical rules. Political developments need to be taken into account. In addition, to participate in the international tax law-making process and to introduce tax rules, countries should not only have technical knowledge, but also resources and the political will to change the rules. The findings of this contribution show that more research is needed on how these international tax developments have been influenced by political developments.

In the past, the author has argued that for OECD countries, the BEPS Project was an opportunity to advance projects that were not broadly implemented, e.g., measures against harmful tax competition, and to take the leading role in international tax matters with the OECD Secretariat and the Committee of Fiscal Affairs deciding on the agenda and topics to be addressed in the BEPS Project.[77]

The present author has also argued in 2015 that there is a lack of input and output legitimacy of the OECD and G20 BEPS Project vis-à-vis non-OECD, non-G20 countries. Even if countries wanted to participate in this decision-making process, it was not possible. As the author argued in 2015, membership of the OECD is on an invitation-only basis, and it requires an accession process. It is even more difficult to become a member of the G20, which is a political forum in which very few emerging economies participate (e.g., Indonesia, India, China, Brazil, Argentina, etc.).[78] Despite the existence of other political forums with developing countries, e.g., the G24 and G77, these forums were not invited to take part in the decision-making process of the BEPS Project.

This is also true in respect of the Pillar One and Pillar Two discussions, as shown in section 10.3 above. For instance, even in the case of a proposal submitted by developing countries, e.g., G24 countries in Pillar One opting for significant economic presence, the proposal was left behind in the OECD Secretariat's proposal, which combined the OECD and the United States' approaches.

---

[77] Mosquera Valderrama, 'Output Legitimacy Deficits' (n 9). See also Irene Burgers and Irma Mosquera, 'Corporate Taxation and BEPS: A Fair Slice for Developing Countries?' (2017) 10(1) Erasmus Law Review 29.

[78] Mosquera Valderrama, 'Legitimacy and the Making of International Tax Law' (n 3).

As addressed in section 10.3.2.2 above, regional tax organizations, such as the African Tax Administration Forum (ATAF), have remarked on the fast pace of the BEPS Project's implementation and the need to provide effective and equitable Pillar One and Pillar Two rules. Latin American and Caribbean countries have also questioned whether there is a global fair tax deal that benefits both developed and developing countries.

Regarding the decision-making process, the discussions on Pillar One and Pillar Two within the BEPS Inclusive Framework have also shown that there is limited participation of non-OECD, non-G20 countries in decision-making. This limited participation was addressed by the OECD in the report to the G20 under the 2021 Italian Presidency (see section 10.3.2 above).

Despite the legitimacy concerns highlighted by countries, scholars and regional organizations and the recent reforms by the OECD in introducing a co-chair of the BEPS Inclusive Framework, countries continue to comply with the BEPS minimum standards and participate in the peer review process. However, due to the recent developments at the United Nations and the call of developing countries for more inclusive and effective international tax cooperation, it is important that further research is carried out on why and how countries participate[79] and whether the reasons for participation are sufficient to ensure the inclusiveness of developing countries in the decision-making process under the auspices of the OECD, the G20 and the BEPS Inclusive Framework.

In some articles published elsewhere, the present author has addressed some of the reasons for participation,[80] for instance: (i) chance and necessity (technical assistance by developed countries and/or OECD, and twinning projects between developed and developing countries); (ii) expected efficacy of the law (access to information by tax administrations on multinational enterprises); and (iii) political, economic and reputational incentives (commitment to the EU

[79] The reason for countries to comply with the standards has been dealt with by the present author in another article, which has analysed the peer review and (throughput) legitimacy of the BEPS four minimum standards in a case study of seven countries (Congo, Cameroon, Costa Rica, Jamaica, Peru, Sri Lanka and Viet Nam). Since these seven countries were non-members of the BEPS 44 group (OECD, OECD Accession, and G20 countries), these countries did not participate in the agenda-setting and decision-making process of the content of the BEPS Project and its 15 Actions, including the BEPS four minimum standards. Since then, one country, Costa Rica, has become an OECD member and another country, Peru, is in the accession process to become a member of the OECD: Mosquera Valderrama, 'Throughput Legitimacy of the Peer Review Process' (n 4).

[80] Mosquera Valderrama, 'Output Legitimacy Deficits' (n 9).

Standard of Tax Good Governance in trade, partnership agreements to receive EU funding and to be excluded from the list of non-cooperative jurisdictions).

Since the 2015 Addis Ababa Conference, some developing countries, civil society groups and regional tax organizations (e.g., ATAF) have called for a more decisive role of the United Nations in tax matters. This proposal was rejected in 2015 due to the argument of some developed countries as to the predominant role of the OECD in international tax matters. However, times have changed since November 2022, when Nigeria, with the support of some other African countries, asked the UN to create an instrument or framework for international tax cooperation under the auspices of the United Nations.

As addressed in section 10.3.2.2, following the 2022 resolution, further progress has been made by the UN to strengthen international tax cooperation and make it more effective and inclusive. This has included, among other things, the report by the Secretary-General in September 2023,[81] the choice of a framework convention in November 2023,[82] and the creation of a UN Ad Hoc Committee to draft the terms of reference of a framework convention, the work of which was expected to be finalized by August 2024.[83]

At the time of writing, even though there are references in the objectives of the zero draft of the Terms of Reference for a UN Framework Convention[84] (i) to establish an inclusive, fair, transparent, efficient, equitable, effective international tax system (para 7(c)) and (ii) to enhance legitimacy, certainty, resilience and fairness of international tax rules (para 7(c)), in the present author's view, by using so many terms without clear definition, there is a lack of a clear path in what this UN Framework Convention wants to achieve in order to strengthen international tax cooperation and make it fully inclusive and more effective. For instance, in the past, the present author has addressed (in a jointly authored contribution with Irene Burgers) the different approaches to fairness (political, economic, philosophical, juridical), which may result in different outcomes for citizens, countries and organizations.[85]

---

81 See Tax Report 2023 and information on the Seventy-Eighth Assembly (n 64).

82 UN, Revised Draft Resolution (n 65).

83 UN, 'Ad Hoc Committee to Draft Terms of Reference' (n 66).

84 Bureau of the Ad Hoc Committee, 'Introductory Note to the Bureau's Proposal for Zero Draft Terms of Reference for a United Nations Framework Convention on International Tax Cooperation by the Chair of the Ad Hoc Committee, Mr Ramy M Youssef, 7 June 2024' <https://financing.desa.un.org/post-news/bureaus-proposal-zero-draft-terms-reference-un-framework-convention-international-tax> accessed 29 June 2024.

85 IJJ Burgers and IJ Mosquera Valderrama, 'Fairness: A Dire International Standard with no Meaning?' (2017) 45(12) Intertax 767.

The use of so many words without a clear definition or path will not help to ensure legitimate, inclusive and effective international tax cooperation. In the present author's view, the UN could benefit from making this process effectively legitimate by addressing not only input legitimacy (participation in agenda-setting and decision-making processes) and output legitimacy (outcomes linked to the Sustainable Development Goals) but also throughput legitimacy (accountability, transparency, inclusiveness and openness). These are clear objectives and principles that can strengthen the legitimacy and inclusiveness of the UN in international tax law-making.

For any global international tax body to function, either at the UN or as a separate international tax body or any international or regional tax organization, it is important to keep in mind that the need is not only for input and output legitimacy, but also throughput legitimacy, i.e., transparency, accountability, responsiveness and openness. Agenda setting and decision-making should be transparent. Furthermore, this body should be held accountable for the decisions taken. The process should be open to all stakeholders and responsive to the needs of all countries.

The analysis of throughput legitimacy of the BEPS four minimum standards has been carried out by the present author elsewhere, with a comparison of the peer review process in seven countries (Cameroon, Congo, Costa Rica, Jamaica, Peru, Sri Lanka and Viet Nam). The analysis concluded that there are throughput legitimacy deficits in the peer review process of the BEPS four minimum standards.

As in the peer review process, the analysis of the roles of the OECD and the UN through the perspective of throughput legitimacy can help to ascertain which problems of legitimacy and inclusiveness the OECD, the BEPS Inclusive Framework and the UN may encounter during the drafting and implementation of international tax law rules and how these issues might be resolved. This analysis is also necessary to ensure that the content of the OECD and/or BEPS Inclusive Framework initiatives in international tax law-making (exchange of information, BEPS Project, Pillar One and Pillar Two) is valid and that countries and multinational enterprises comply voluntarily with the implementation of these rules. This analysis is also necessary for the UN and the UN Ad Hoc Committee when deciding on the content of the UN Framework Convention.

To conclude, the current draft of the terms of reference for the UN Framework Convention is broad and general and lacks a specific approach to improve governance and decision-making within the UN. Therefore, the UN should also give attention (i) to the way that decision-making is going to take place in this new UN setting of more than 190 countries, and (ii) to a better understanding of the conditions under which OECD and non-OECD countries would be open to agreement to a UN Framework Convention.

# 11. Domestic judicial transplants of OECD interpretive solutions or principles

**Carlo Garbarino**

## 11.1 INTRODUCTION

Convergence or divergence in respect of the Organisation for Economic Co-operation and Development (OECD) Model of tax treaties is achieved at the level of individual treaties concluded by countries through the adoption of provisions that are, or are not, based on the OECD Model. This convergence or divergence can also be achieved through law in action, and specifically through judicial decisions or administrative guidelines that may be 'inspired by' or 'refer to' the OECD Commentary. In particular, interpretive solutions or principles advanced by the OECD Commentary can be considered by national judges in the application and interpretation of specific treaties. This chapter focuses on how this occurs, proposing a model in which OECD interpretive solutions or principles circulate through 'judicial transplants' activated by domestic courts. Section 11.2 of this chapter analyses in this light the OECD Model and Commentary and their role in judicial interpretation, while section 11.3 briefly introduces the concept of 'judicial transplants' and discusses their role as vehicles of convergence or divergence. Section 11.4 develops considerations about gaps in the Commentary, which have prompted an interesting legal phenomenon of a new tax treaty judicial activism. Section 11.5 concludes by summarizing the findings of this chapter: changes in tax systems can also be introduced through a peculiar phenomenon in which different actors in different systems (for example judges of different countries) introduce a new set of rules, basing their decisions on OECD principles.

## 11.2 THE OECD MODEL AND COMMENTARY AND THEIR ROLE IN JUDICIAL INTERPRETATION

The Commentary to the OECD Model Tax Convention on Income and on Capital (referred to respectively as the Commentary, and the Model or Convention[1]) in its introduction summarizes the evolution of a model for specific double tax conventions (treaties) concluded by states on a bilateral basis.[2] The work by international law scholars commenced in 1921 at the League of Nations, which in 1928 issued the first model, followed by the model treaties of Mexico (1943) and London (1946). The Council of the Organisation for European Economic Co-operation (OEEC) issued the first Recommendation concerning double taxation on 25 February 1955, and from 1958 to 1961, the Fiscal Committee released four interim reports, which led in 1963 to the Draft Double Taxation Convention on Income and Capital, taking the form of a recommendation by the Council of 30 July 1963 for member states to conform to that Draft Convention.[3]

The elaboration of standards then shifted to the OECD, which is a forum where governments can compare policy experiences, seek answers to common

---

[1] OECD, *Model Tax Convention on Income and on Capital 2017* (OECD Publishing 2019) (OECD Model Tax Convention).

[2] In relation to tax treaties, see generally Reuven S Avi-Yonah, 'Double Tax Treaties: An Introduction' in Karl P Sauvant and Lisa E Sachs (eds), *The Effect of Treaties on Foreign Direct Investment: Bilateral Investment Treaties, Double Taxation Treaties, and Investment Flows* (Oxford University Press 2009); Ekkehart Reimer and Alexander Rust (eds), *Klaus Vogel on Double Taxation Conventions* (4th edn, Kluwer Law International 2015); Philip Baker, *Double Taxation Conventions and International Tax Law, A Manual on the OECD Model Tax Convention on Income and on Capital* (Sweet and Maxwell 2001); Philip Baker, *Double Taxation Conventions* (Sweet and Maxwell 2010); Alex Easson, 'Do We Still Need Tax Treaties?' (2000) 54(12) Bulletin for International Taxation 619; Kevin Holmes, *International Tax Policy and Double Tax Treaties: An Introduction to Principles and Application* (2nd rev edn, IBFD Publications 2014); Michael Lang, *Introduction to the Law of Double Taxation Conventions* (2nd edn, Linde Verlag and IBFD Publications 2013); Klaus Vogel, *Klaus Vogel on Double Taxation Conventions: A Commentary to the OECD-, UN- and US Model Conventions for the Avoidance of Double Taxation of Income and Capital, with Particular Reference to German Treaty Practice* (3rd edn, Kluwer International 1997); Michael Lang and Heinz Jirousek (eds), *Praxis des Internationalen Steuerrechts, Festschrift für Helmut Loukota zum 65. Geburtstag* (Linde Verlag 2005); Jean-Claude Martinez, *Les Conventions de Double Imposition* (Litec 1986).

[3] OECD Model Tax Convention (n 1) Commentary, Introduction, paras 4–11.1.

problems, identify good practices and work to coordinate domestic and international policies.[4] The OECD has worked extensively on the issues of tax treaties. In 1977, a new Model Convention and Commentary were released by the OECD. Working Party No 1 prepared reports related to the 1977 Model Convention and recommended amendments. In 1991, the Committee on Fiscal Affairs adopted the concept of an ambulatory Model and Commentary to which periodic updates and amendments are regularly made.[5] This revision process enabled input from non-member countries, other international organizations, and other interested parties. In 1992, the OECD released a Model Convention in a looseleaf format, which was the first step of an ongoing revision process and which constitutes the Model in the proper sense. In 1997, the Committee on Fiscal Affairs added positions of non-member countries.[6]

The Model has become the standard reference for the application of bilateral treaties effectively entered into by countries.[7] The main purpose of the Model is the application by all countries of common solutions to identical cases of double taxation. The introduction to the Model notes that the Council of the OECD has recommended that

> member countries ... should conform to this Model Convention as interpreted by the Commentaries thereon and having regard to the reservations contained therein and their tax authorities should follow these Commentaries, as modified from time

---

[4] Ken Messere, 'Expansion of the OECD's Tax Activities' (2003) 57(2) Bulletin for International Taxation 75; Peter Carroll and Aynsley Kellow, *The OECD: A Study of Organisational Adaptation* (Edward Elgar Publishing 2011); Richard Woodward, *The Organisation for Economic Co-operation and Development (OECD)* (Routledge 2009); Jeffrey Owens, 'International Taxation: Meeting the Challenges – The Role of the OECD' (2006) 46(12) European Taxation 555.

[5] With regard to the impact of the changes to the OECD Model, see for example Brian J Arnold, 'An Introduction to the 2014 Update to the OECD Model' (2014) 68(10) Bulletin for International Taxation 526; Edward Barret, 'The Changes Introduced by the 2014 Update to the OECD Model Tax Convention' (2014) 68(10) Bulletin for International Taxation 529; Fernando Serrano Antón, '*La Modificación del Modelo de Convenio de la OCDE para Evitar la Doble Imposición Internacional y Prevenir la Evasión Fiscal: Interpretación y novedades de la versión del año 2000: la eliminación del artículo 14 sobre la tributación de los servicios profesionales independientes y el remozado trato fiscal a las partnerships*' (2002) Universidad Complutense de Madrid working paper.

[6] See Guglielmo Maisto, 'The Observations on the OECD Commentaries in the Interpretation of Tax Treaties' (2005) 59(1) Bulletin for International Taxation 14.

[7] Michael Lang and others (eds), *The Impact of the OECD and UN Model Conventions on Bilateral Tax Treaties* (Cambridge University Press 2012).

> to time and subject to their observations thereon, when applying and interpreting the provisions of their bilateral tax treaties that are based on the Model Convention.[8]

The Commentary and other OECD reports and documents constituting 'soft tax law' are often implemented in domestic tax systems by legislative measures or administrative guidelines that essentially transplant OECD policies. For example, tax treaties often reproduce the exact wording of the clauses of the Model, while tax authorities have implemented the OECD cost-sharing and transfer pricing policies in regulations and other normative documents.

There is no doubt that the Model has a primary impact on the negotiation and development of tax treaties entered into by individual countries. According to the introduction to the Commentary, since 1963 the Model has had wide repercussions on the negotiation, application and *interpretation* of tax treaties.

The activity of 'interpretation' is at the core of the analysis conducted here and requires a few clarifications. Legal interpretation in general is developed and propounded by different agents or 'actors' within a domestic tax system, each of them advancing different interests and supporting different values. These actors are essentially the following: tax authorities, tax courts, tax scholars and tax practitioners. So, tax interpretation varies depending on the type of actor who propounds it, with the result that there is so-called 'authentic interpretation' enacted by tax authorities, judicial interpretation developed by tax courts, doctrinal interpretation propounded by tax scholars, and practical interpretations advanced by tax practitioners.

'*Authentic interpretation*' enacted by tax authorities can be explicitly found in interpretive regulations, but also encompasses the positions taken by auditing offices on a case-by-case basis when motivating their tax assessments, advancing their arguments in tax litigation, or replying to specific questions posed by taxpayers in private letter rulings. Authentic interpretation is generally binding on a case-by-case basis unless overturned by a judge, but interpretive regulations are generally not binding. Authentic interpretation should be impartial, but tax authorities often de facto advance a specific set of strategic and practical interests – namely revenue-raising – so that the interpretation propounded by them is almost invariably that which is more favourable to the Treasury.

Finally, *judicial interpretation* developed by tax courts is generally binding on a case-by-case basis. Courts had traditionally taken an overly legalistic approach in taxation that downplayed purposive interpretation; but recently, trends of judicial substantive interpretation have emerged and percolated up to supreme national courts, establishing judicial principles.

---

8 OECD Model Tax Convention (n 1) Commentary, Introduction, para 3.

To understand the structure of domestic tax laws, one must analyse the complex relationship between the various types of interpretations advanced by different actors within the tax system. Tax law is a complex institutional process, not just the mere collection of validly enacted legislation. The analysis of actor-based interpretations provides a dynamic approach to taxation and focuses on tax law as the result of the social activity of groups or communities institutionally involved in creating it. Thus the tax interpretation process can be seen as an arena in which different philosophical views compete, a view that belies the idea that tax law is unitary.

These groups, identified above, produce different kinds of texts: statutes, regulations, opinions, briefs and articles, and they each have an archive (previously written documents) and a professionally tested style to transform old documents and produce new ones. These texts and documents, and the way in which they are produced, interrelated, reused and cited, become key features in understanding the structure and evolution of national systems of 'tax law in action'. Each national tax system can therefore be understood as a set of interlocked documents used by the involved actors according to their respective interpretive strategies. Thus, one must look at the so-called 'operative rules', i.e., at the actual rules implemented by tax law in action as the result of actor-based interpretations.

Within domestic tax systems there is often competition among actor-based interpretations, as these interpretations do not necessarily coincide in determining the operative tax rules. For example, guidelines of tax authorities may conflict with case law and scholarly opinions, or case law can generate conflicting trends. Also, the operative tax rules may not be uniform because one operative rule may be provided by case law, another by scholars, and yet another by statutes, etc. As a result of competition among different interpretive strategies, there is often an underlying dialectic process within domestic tax systems.

However, when different actor-based interpretations work together, they contribute to defining an institutional cooperative arrangement that comes in two basic patterns: a 'top-down pattern' in which tax statutes are enacted and subsequently interpreted and implemented by administrative guidelines and/or case law, as well as supported by the opinions of tax scholars; and a 'bottom-up pattern' in which administrative guidelines in conjunction with case law and opinions of legal scholars shape tax law in action with virtually no recourse to legislation.

This matrix of interactions has reversed a traditional trend in which scholarly interpretations, generally opposed to interpretations advanced by tax authorities, influenced judicial interpretations. In that previous scenario of actor-based interpretation, there was a tension between, on the one hand, scholarly and judicial interpretations aimed at protecting taxpayers' rights, and, on the other hand, interpretations advanced by tax authorities, in most cases advancing the practical interests of tax offices.

These considerations about the actors of tax interpretation in general also apply to the interpretation of tax treaties, where the role of courts is particularly relevant. There is a huge literature on this topic that cannot be recounted here.[9] Essentially interpretation of treaties, including tax treaties, is governed by Articles 31 to 33 of the Vienna Convention on the Law of Treaties (VCLT), which advance *two basic types* of interpretation (*strict interpretation* and *purposive interpretation*), but Article 3(2) of the Model is also relevant in this matter.[10]

---

[9] On the interpretation of tax treaties, see generally Klaus Vogel and Rainer Prokisch, 'General Report' in International Fiscal Association (ed), *Cahiers de Droit Fiscal International: Vol 78a, Interpretation of Double Taxation Conventions* (1993); Michael Edwardes-Ker, 'Tax Treaty Interpretation' (PhD thesis, University of London 1994); Frank Engelen, *Interpretation of Tax Treaties under International Law* (IBFD Publications 2004); Johannes Heinrich and Helmut Moritz, 'Austria – Interpretation of Tax Treaties' (2000) 40(4) European Taxation 142; Jinyan Li, 'Beneficial Ownership in Tax Treaties: Judicial Interpretation and the Case for Clarity' in Philip Baker and Catherine Bobbett (eds), *Tax Polymath: A Life in International Taxation – Essays in Honour of John F. Avery Jones* (IBFD Publications 2011); Michael Schilcher and Patrick Weninger (eds), *Fundamental Issues and Practical Problems in Tax Treaty Interpretation* (Linde Verlag 2008); Frank A Engelen and Frank PG Pötgens, 'Report on "The Application of the OECD Model Tax Convention to Partnerships" and the Interpretation of Tax Treaties' (2000) 40(7) European Taxation 250; John F Avery Jones and others, 'The Interpretation of Tax Treaties with Particular Reference to Article 3(2) of the OECD-Model – I' (1984) (1) British Tax Review 14; Raffaele Russo, 'The 2005 OECD Model Convention and Commentary: An Overview' (2005) 45(12) European Taxation 560; John F Avery Jones, 'Understanding the OECD Model Tax Convention: The Lesson of History' (2009) 10(1) Florida Tax Review 1; Robert Danon and others (eds), *Modèle de Convention fiscale OCDE concernant le revenu et la fortune: Commentaire* (Editions Francis Lefebvre 2014); Hugh J Ault, 'The Role of the OECD Commentaries in the Interpretation of Tax Treaties' (1994) 22(4) Intertax 144.

[10] Article 3(2) of the OECD Model Tax Convention (n 1) provides that:

> As regards the application of the Convention at any time by a Contracting State, any term not defined therein shall, unless the context otherwise requires or the competent authorities agree to a different meaning pursuant to the provisions of Article 25, have the meaning that it has at that time under the law of that State for the purposes of the taxes to which the Convention applies, any meaning under the applicable tax laws of that State prevailing over a meaning given to the term under other laws of that State.

First, Article 3(2) points to 'any term not defined in the treaty' and clarifies that these terms have the meaning that they have under the law of that state for the purposes of the taxes to which the Convention applies, and this is the so-called *renvoi* method. Second, Article 3(2) points at 'terms that are defined in the treaty', and for which the context does not require another interpretation, leading to the so-called *autonomous interpretation*. Third, Article 3(2) points at 'terms that are defined in the treaty, but for which the context requires another interpretation', setting the stage for the so-called *contextual interpretation*.

The analysis of the interpretation of tax treaties is generally developed by describing how the two basic types of interpretation of tax treaties advanced by Articles 31 to 33 of the VCLT (that is, strict interpretation and purposive interpretation) operate in combination with three approaches of interpretation of tax treaties advanced by Article 3(2) of the Model (the *renvoi* method, autonomous interpretation and contextual interpretation).

In spite of the fact that the interpretation of tax treaties is potentially a very powerful vehicle for legal change, traditionally OECD member countries have conformed to the Model by actually concluding or revising bilateral treaties.[11] The Commentary also notes that the impact of the Model Convention has extended beyond the OECD area: 'It has been used as a basic document of reference in negotiations between member and non-member countries and among non-member countries, as well as in the work of other worldwide or regional international organisations in the field of double taxation and related problems.'[12] The Model is used as the basis for the original drafting and the subsequent revision of the United Nations Model Double Taxation Convention between Developed and Developing Countries and reservations of certain member countries on some provisions of the Convention.[13]

The Model is a Convention-Model and is accompanied by the extensive Commentary, a document issued by the Committee on Fiscal Affairs, which provides an explication and interpretation of the Model. As the Commentary has been drafted and agreed upon by the experts appointed to the Committee

---

11 OECD Model Tax Convention (n 1) Commentary, Introduction, para 12.

12 OECD Model Tax Convention (n 1) Commentary, Introduction, para 14. On the role of tax treaties in shaping the global system, see Eric CCM Kemmeren and others (eds), *Tax Treaty Case Law around the Globe 2012* (IBFD Publications 2013); Richard Vann, *Tax Treaties: Linkages between OECD Member Countries and Dynamic Non-Member Economies* (OECD 1996); Kees van Raad, 'International Coordination of Tax Treaty Interpretation and Application' (2001) 29(6/7) Intertax 212.

13 OECD Model Tax Convention (n 1) Commentary, Introduction, para 14.

on Fiscal Affairs by the governments of member countries, it is of special importance in the development of international tax law.[14]

Convergence or divergence with respect to the Model is achieved at the level of individual treaties concluded by countries through the adoption of provisions that are, or are not, based on the Model.[15] One should, however, bear in mind that convergence or divergence with respect to the Model can also be achieved through law in action, for example, through judicial decisions or administrative guidelines which may be 'inspired by' or 'refer to' the Model.[16]

The Model is, however, accompanied by a Commentary, and this fact highlights the importance of the interpretation of tax treaties. Not only is the formal status currently being debated,[17] but also the practical impact of such a Commentary on actual interpretive approaches taken by domestic tax courts.[18] The claim that is made here is that *convergence or divergence with respect to the Model is often achieved through judicial interpretation when national courts use the Commentary to interpret the treaties*.[19] So there can be

---

[14] Peter J Wattel and Otto Marres, 'The Legal Status of the OECD Commentary and Static or Ambulatory Interpretation of Tax Treaties' (2003) 43(7) European Taxation 222.

[15] See, for example, Lang and others (eds) (n 7).

[16] On the role of the OECD Model in tax treaty interpretation, see David A Ward, 'The Role of the Commentaries on the OECD Model in the Tax Treaty Interpretation Process' (2006) 60(3) Bulletin for International Taxation 97; Thomas Ecker and Gernot Ressler (eds), *History of Tax Treaties: The Relevance of the OECD Documents for the Interpretation of Tax Treaties* (Linde Verlag 2011).

[17] On the legal status of the OECD Commentaries, see Sjoerd Douma and Frank Engelen (eds), *The Legal Status of the OECD Commentaries* (IBFD Publications 2008); Frank Engelen, 'Some Observations on the Legal Status of the Commentaries on the OECD Model' (2006) 60(3) Bulletin for International Taxation 105.

[18] See, for example, Frank van Brunschot, 'The Judiciary and the OECD Model Tax Convention and its Commentaries' (2005) 59(1) Bulletin for International Taxation 5; Guglielmo Maisto (ed), *Courts and Tax Treaty Law* (IBFD Publications 2007); John F Avery Jones and others, 'The Origins of Concepts and Expressions Used in the OECD Model and their Adoption by States' (2006) 60(6) Bulletin for International Taxation 220; John F Avery Jones, 'Tax Treaties: The Perspective of Common Law Countries' in Guglielmo Maisto (ed), *Courts and Tax Treaty Law* (IBFD Publications 2007); Linda Favi and Andrea Parolini, 'Italian Case Law and International Taxation' (2010) 64(8/9) Bulletin for International Taxation 429; Linda Favi, 'Italy' in Guglielmo Maisto (ed), *Courts and Tax Treaty Law* (IBFD Publications 2007).

[19] See, for example, Hans Pijl, 'The OECD Commentary as a Source of International Law and the Role of the Judiciary' (2006) 46(5) European Taxation 216.

situations in which the same provision of different individual treaties, based on the Model, are interpreted differently by national courts, leading to divergent outcomes. By the same token, there can be situations in which different provisions of different individual treaties that diverge from the Model are interpreted uniformly by national courts, leading to convergent outcomes.

The OECD has taken a very proactive position on the role of the Commentary on treaty interpretation. For example, according to the OECD '[t]he tax administrations of member countries routinely consult the Commentaries in their interpretation of bilateral tax treaties' and '[t]ax officials give great weight to the guidance contained in the Commentaries'.[20] Moreover, in the view of the OECD, 'taxpayers make extensive use of the Commentaries in conducting their businesses and planning their business transactions and investments'.[21]

These statements raise an important question that has a twofold aspect: (i) *normatively, whether the Commentary should have a binding impact on national tax authorities*, and (ii) *descriptively, how and to what extent such an impact has unfolded in countries' practices*. An additional research question is *whether and to what extent the Commentary creates rights or duties for taxpayers in their domestic tax systems*. Another important issue is *how judges use the Commentary in their domestic tax systems*. This chapter aims to address these questions by identifying the exact use of the Commentary in judicial application of tax treaties – often based on the Model – by national courts.

According to the OECD,

> courts are increasingly using the Commentaries in reaching their decisions. Information collected by the Committee on Fiscal Affairs shows that the

---

[20] OECD Model Tax Convention (n 1) Commentary, Introduction, para 29.1. On the role of the OECD Commentary in tax treaty interpretation, see Klaus Vogel, 'The Influence of the OECD Commentaries on Treaty Interpretation' (2000) 54(12) Bulletin for International Taxation 612; Maarten J Ellis, 'The Influence of the OECD Commentaries on Treaty Interpretation – Response to Prof Dr Klaus Vogel' (2000) 54(12) Bulletin for International Taxation 617; Maarten J Ellis, 'The Role of the Commentaries on the OECD Model in the Tax Treaty Interpretation Process – Response to David Ward' (2006) 60(3) Bulletin for International Taxation 103; Ekkehart Reimer, 'Interpretation of Tax Treaties' (1999) 39(12) European Taxation 458; David A Ward and others (eds), *The Interpretation of Income Tax Treaties with Particular Reference to the Commentaries on the OECD Model* (International Fiscal Association 2005); David A Ward, 'Is There an Obligation in International Law of OECD Member Countries to Follow the Commentaries on the Model?' in Sjoerd Douma and Frank Engelen (eds), *The Legal Status of the OECD Commentaries* (IBFD Publications 2008).

[21] OECD Model Tax Convention (n 1) Commentary, Introduction, para 29.2.

> Commentaries have been cited in the published decisions of the courts of the great majority of member countries. In many decisions, the Commentaries have been extensively quoted and analysed, and have frequently played a key role in the judge's deliberations.[22]

In spite of the fact that the Committee on Fiscal Affairs 'expects this trend to continue as the worldwide network of tax treaties continues to grow and as the Commentaries gain even more widespread acceptance as an important interpretative reference',[23] one should assess whether this is really the case. There is a need to review accurately to what extent and how the Commentary has an impact at the level of domestic internalization. This can be done by relying on the transnational legal process approach. More precisely, the main focus of this study revolves around interpretive techniques adopted by national courts when using the Commentary in the interpretation of tax treaties.

The key question in fact is exactly *how the courts use the Commentaries*, when they abide by the OECD positions, when they advance local solutions, or when they pursue other goals. Even if there is no doubt that the Commentary is 'referred to' or 'used' by national judges in applying the treaties, the interpretive solutions advanced by the Commentary are not strictly binding on them. For example, according to the Model:

> Although the Commentaries are not designed to be annexed in any manner to the conventions signed by member countries, which unlike the Model are legally binding international instruments, they can nevertheless be of great assistance in the application and interpretation of the conventions and, in particular, in the settlement of any disputes.[24]

A few definitional remarks are required at the outset to clearly define the scope of the judicial use of the Commentary. The *first remark* is that the Model is viewed as a set of rules or norms (often allocation rules) which are generally posed in a conditional form, such as, for example: *(if F, then G)*. These rules often are subject to multiple detailed requirements arranged in a complex structure, such as for example: *[if F, and (F2 or F3) but not F4, then G]*, so that one of the purposes of the Commentary is to attribute a certain meaning to the rules of the Model.[25] The 'interpretation' of the Model by the Commentary is meant here to be the *attribution by the Commentary of a meaning to the text*

22 Ibid para 29.3.
23 Ibid.
24 Ibid para 29.
25 A structure like that is found in Article 15 of the Model, for example.

*of a rule included in the Model.*[26] This attribution of a meaning leads to a so-called '*interpretive solution*' which is advanced in the Commentary.

This approach to interpretive solutions advanced in the Commentary, however, does not imply a full interpretive scepticism according to which interpretation can lead to any outcome: according to a well-established approach, there is a *framework of potential interpretive solutions* available, from which the judge in an individual domestic tax system can select one by using particular '*interpretive techniques*' based on clusters or arrangements of '*arguments*' that essentially advocate the persuasiveness of the interpretive outcome.[27]

The *second remark* is that a given interpretive solution advanced by the Commentary does not 'reveal' the actual, unique and pre-existing meaning of the rule of the Model, so a distinction is made between the 'text' of a rule of the Model in prescriptive language and the 'meaning' of that rule, which is attributed to it by the Commentary, and which amounts to an interpretive solution. In this context it should be understood that such an interpretive solution is one of many potentially available outcomes of diversified, competing interpretive strategies, which may also emerge at the national judicial level.

The *third remark* is that the interpretive solutions advanced by the Commentary often take the form of '*principles*' which are *not* posed in a conditional form (like the rules of the Model), but rather: (i) have a 'foundational' nature, and (ii) are indeterminate in their scope. The 'foundational nature' of those principles of the Commentary is that they are value based. The 'indeterminacy' of the principles of the Commentary has three features. First, the scope of principles is not subject to requirements enumerated *ex ante*. Second, principles are defeasible, in the sense that the list of derogations is open ended. Third, principles are non-self-executing insofar as they require other norms to be applied, or because they express policies that can be applied in different or alternative ways.

There are many instances of these principles within the Commentary, and it is beyond the scope of this chapter to identify all of them; the following is just one example of such principles. The Commentary to Article 1, in a previous version, when discussing the treaty entitlement of partnerships, provided that if the partnership is treated as a company resident in the country where profits

---

26 The term 'interpretation' in American neo-constitutionalism and generally in the Anglo-Saxon legal tradition is often used with a wider, and more vague, meaning; see for example Ronald Dworkin, *Law's Empire* (Harvard University Press 1986). That approach to 'interpretation' is not used in this chapter.

27 On the framework of possible available interpretations, see, for example, Hans Kelsen, *Reine Rechtslehre: Einleitung in die rechtswissenschaftliche Problematik* (Deuticke 1934) Ch VIII, but also Herbert LA Hart, *The Concept of Law* (2nd edn, Clarendon Press 1961).

are produced and is 'liable to tax' therein (Article 4(1)), then the partnership is entitled to treaty benefits as a person; for example, the profits are subject to the dividends Article when distributed.[28] This principle still has a 'foundational nature' because it establishes a norm on the basis of a practical value. This principle is also 'indeterminate' because: (i) its scope is not subject to requirements enumerated *ex ante* but potentially applies to an indeterminate set of situations; (ii) it is defeasible because the list of derogations is open ended, and (iii) it is non-self-executing because it expresses a policy that can be applied in different or alternative ways.

Finally, it should be noted that the Commentary does not always provide interpretive solutions or principles, as in many instances it simply suggests *alternative policies* which may be adopted by states, thereby not creating any binding principle. Here are a few examples. The Commentary to Article 1 addresses the issues raised by the current treatment of collective investment vehicles (CIVs) and advances five approaches proposing possible treaty clauses.[29] Likewise the Commentary before the changes made in 2017 addressed the policy issues raised by improper use of the treaties and advanced five approaches proposing treaty clauses (look-through approach; subject-to-tax approach; channel approach; bona fide safeguard clauses; and limitation-of-benefits approach).[30]

In a more general way, the Commentary to Article 18 on pensions evaluates different alternative provisions that can be adopted to deal with the misalignment of national systems.[31] With regard to royalties, the Commentary observes that Article 12(2) requires that software be classified as a literary, artistic or scientific work, but also notes that none of these categories is 'entirely apt'. For this reason, the copyright laws of many countries specifically classify software as *a literary or scientific work*.[32] This issue has been addressed in particular in cases decided in Spain.[33]

Another example of policy discussion by the Commentary is whether dividends received by a permanent establishment (PE) in the source country in respect of participations owned by that PE in foreign companies should be

[28] OECD, *Model Tax Convention on Income and on Capital 2014* (OECD Publishing 2014) Commentary on Art 1, para 5.

[29] OECD Model Tax Convention (n 1) Commentary on Art 1, paras 22–48.

[30] OECD, *Model Tax Convention on Income and on Capital 2014* (n 28) Commentary on Art 1, paras 13–20.

[31] OECD Model Tax Convention (n 1) Commentary on Art 18, paras 12–21.

[32] Ibid Commentary to Art 12, para 13.1.

[33] Spain, Tribunal Económico Administrativo Central (Central Economic–Administrative Court), 3604/2006, 17 April 2008, *Jurisprudencia Tributaria*, 2008, 819.

subject, in the same source country, to the same treatment afforded to dividends received by domestic companies in the source country in respect of participations owned by those companies in foreign companies. The Commentary does not take a position and weighs the arguments for and against the extension of dividends exemption to PEs.[34]

## 11.3 JUDICIAL TRANSPLANTS AS VEHICLES OF CONVERGENCE OR DIVERGENCE

The conclusion of the previous section is that interpretive solutions or principles advanced by the Commentary are among those that can be considered by local judges in the application and interpretation of specific treaties. So the question is how this occurs. A way to approach this problem is to posit that OECD interpretive solutions or principles may circulate through '*judicial transplants*' activated by domestic courts.

In a broad sense, judicial transplants occur when interpretive solutions or principles are imported from a given source, which can be a domestic tax system or an authoritative international authority ('source'), into one or more countries ('destination') through the judicial position taken by their domestic courts. For example, the tax courts of one country can accept judicial principles developed by case law in another country, and this can be done explicitly by citing the foreign judicial authority.

In this perspective, the courts of one or more countries ('destination') can be said to import the interpretive solutions or principles advanced by the Commentary, which is thus considered to be the international source of reference for national judicial solutions.[35] One therefore needs to place the

[34] OECD Model Tax Convention (n 1) Commentary on Art 24, paras 48–54.

[35] On interpretive practices and guidelines, there are different threads based on national approaches. With regard to the US, for example, see American Law Institute, *Federal Income Tax Project, International Aspects of United States Income Taxation II: Proposals on United States Income Tax Treaties* (American Law Institute 1992); Juan Angel Becerra, *Interpretation and Application of Tax Treaties in North America* (2nd edn, IBFD Publications 2013); Reuven S Avi-Yonah and Martin B Tittle, 'The New United States Model Income Tax Convention' (2007) 61(6) Bulletin for International Taxation 224; Richard L Doernberg and Kees van Raad, *The 1996 United States Model Income Tax Convention: Analysis, Commentary and Comparison* (Kluwer Law International 1997). With regard to the UK, see John F Avery Jones, 'The United Kingdom's Influence on the OECD Model Tax Convention' (2011) (6) British Tax Review 653; with regard to Italy, Carlo Garbarino, *Le Convenzioni dell'Italia in Materia di Imposte sul Reddito e Patrimonio: Commentario* (Egea 2002); with regard to Germany, Jens Shönfeld and Xaver Ditz (eds), *Doppelbesteuerungsabkommen DBA- Kommentar* (Schmidt

transplants by national judges of interpretive solutions or principles of the Commentary within a wider model of the transnational legal process. This model, in a broad manner, looks at how public/private actors interact in various forums at domestic and international levels to make, interpret, apply, enforce and internalize international norms – in the present case OECD interpretive solutions or principles, as reflected in bilateral tax treaties.

When several countries are involved in a process that may span several decades, the pathways of diffusion of judicial transplants may be complex and indirect, and influences may be reciprocal. Moreover, judicial transplants of OECD interpretive solutions or principles may take place through informal interactions among judiciaries without involving formal adoption or enactment of foreign decisions. In these cases, diffusion occurs through a drawn-out process, which, even if there were some critical moments, cannot be understood without reference to events that may have occurred before or after such moments.

More importantly, the idea that imported OECD interpretive solutions or principles retain their identity in the transplanting domestic tax system without significant change is often misleading, as one is often faced with locally idiosyncratic modifications of the original purpose of the imported interpretive solution or principle.[36] Important qualifications of this model of judicial transplants of OECD interpretive solutions or principles are also that: (i) diffusion of these interpretive solutions or principles may take place between many kinds of legal orders at and across different geographical levels and not just horizontally between national tax systems, and (ii) formal governmental institutions are not the only agents of diffusion of those solutions because of the operation of networks, epistemic communities and local elites.

The study of judicial transplants of OECD interpretive solutions or principles, enriched by these qualifications, shows that changes in domestic tax systems are often the result of a wide global process of *circulation* of such solutions. Comparative analysis is meaningful insofar as it detects which characteristics of a given interpretive solution or principle have developed domestically and which have developed through judicial transplants using the Commentary as a source. This analysis provides a 'conjectural history' of national interpretive solutions or principles adopted in a given country by domestic judges because

2013); Thomas Reith, *Internationales Steuerrecht: Handbuch zum Doppelbesteuerungs und Aussenseuerrecht und zu Gestaltungen grenzüberschreitender Investitionen* (Verlag Vahlen 2004); Klaus Vogel and Moris Lehner (eds), *Doppelbesteuerungsabkommen* (5th edn, CH Beck 2008).

[36] See, in general, William Twining, 'Diffusion of Law: A Global Perspective' (2004) 36(49) Journal of Legal Pluralism and Unofficial Law 1; Esin Örücü, 'Law as Transposition' (2002) 51(2) International and Comparative Law Quarterly 205.

it connects them to interpretive solutions or principles previously developed at the level of the source, the Commentary.

The fact that judicial transplants are an important vehicle for the circulation of OECD interpretive solutions or principles thus highlights three important features. First, judicial transplants can create *convergence* as well as *divergence* among different domestic tax systems. Secondly, when judicial transplants create convergence, they may contribute to the explanation of *common features of domestic tax systems* based on the Commentary. Thirdly, when judicial transplants create divergence, they may contribute to the explanation of *how competition among national judicial solutions unfolds in spite of the uniforming solution (if any) advanced by the Commentary.* Finally, judicial transplants by national courts of OECD interpretive solutions or principles offer a strong challenge to the idea that tax laws are exclusively a local response to social demands felt by specific national communities.

In the taxonomy proposed here, there are two basic types of domestic judicial transplants of OECD interpretive solutions or principles: *judicial transplants*, which operate as vehicles of judicial convergence, and *judicial pseudo-transplants*, which operate as vehicles of judicial divergence.

*Judicial transplants* occur when the source OECD judicial interpretive solutions or principles are imported into one or more destination countries through judicial decisions retaining the OECD's purported meaning. In these cases the OECD's interpretive solution imported into the destination countries has a *common origin* as it comes from an identified source (the Commentary) and has the same content, as it retains the content originally found in the source. In this situation, after the judicial transplant, the interpretive solution adopted in the importing countries is the same as that proposed at the OECD level, so one can safely say that judges have faithfully aligned to an external interpretive solution or principle.

Canadian cases offer good examples of these judicial transplants of OECD judicial interpretive solutions or principles. For example, in the leading case *Prévost*, the Court noted that a definition of 'beneficial ownership' could be interpreted in the light of the OECD Conduit Companies Report (1987) and the Commentary.[37] In other cases, courts have addressed situations in which the issue was whether a taxpayer *was effectively liable to tax* and therefore entitled to the benefits of the treaty. For example, in *TD Securities* the Court held that the expression 'liable to tax' had to be interpreted, according to paragraph 8 of the Commentary on Article 4, as the description of those who are subject

---

37 *Prévost Car Inc v Her Majesty the Queen* [2008] 5 CTC 2306 (Tax Court of Canada).

to comprehensive taxation (i.e., full liability to tax).[38] In *Garcia*, the taxpayer was a dual resident and the Court applied the tiebreak rules of the residence Article, relying on paragraphs 11, 12 and 13 of the 2005 Commentary.[39]

*Knights of Columbus*, a case about the concept of the right of use test to determine whether there is a PE, relied on paragraph 4.3 of the Commentary to Article 5 about the supervising work by the parent company where it affirms that this situation occurs when, for example, employees of a company are allowed (for a sufficiently long period of time) to use an office in the headquarters of another company to ensure that the company complies with contracts.[40] Likewise, in *American Income Life Insurance*, the Court referred to paragraph 38 of the Commentary to Article 5 (detailed instructions) and paragraph 38.3 of the Commentary (responsibility to a principal for the results of work) to evaluate legal and economic indicators of independence.[41]

These cases are typical examples of judicial transplants of OECD interpretive solutions or principles because, in their reception by domestic courts, Commentary paragraphs are cited and faithfully followed. It should, however, be pointed out that these judicial transplants merely constitute a paradigm case in which reception involves a direct one-way transfer from the source to the destination, carried out by courts through the formal enactment of judicial decisions. This paradigm case also assumes that the object of reception retains its identity without significant change after the date of reception.

By contrast, *judicial pseudo-transplants* of OECD interpretive solutions or principles are a peculiar type of transplant that should be distinguished from straightforward judicial transplants of those solutions. In judicial pseudo-transplants, the imported OECD interpretive solution is modified substantially in the process of being transplanted by judges in a given domestic tax system. These transplants have a peculiar feature in which the authority of the Commentary is used as justification for what is in reality a – sometimes idiosyncratic – national solution. In this case, the judicial transplants lead to an interpretive solution or principle at the national level that is different from that advanced by the Commentary. So in a judicial pseudo-transplant, while the OECD-divergent solution is presented by the national court as the outcome

38 *TD Securities (USA) LLC v Her Majesty the Queen* [2010] 5 CTC 2426 (Tax Court of Canada).

39 *Garcia v Her Majesty the Queen* [2008] 1 CTC 2215 (Tax Court of Canada); *Crown Forest Industries Ltd v Canada* [1995] 2 SCR 802 (Supreme Court of Canada).

40 *Knights of Columbus v Her Majesty the Queen* [2009] 1 CTC 2163 (Tax Court of Canada).

41 *American Income Life Insurance Co v Her Majesty the Queen* [2009] 2 CTC 2114 (Tax Court of Canada).

of the application of the OECD Commentary as an authoritative source, in practice, the solution is the outcome of autonomous judicial reasoning by that same court.

In judicial pseudo-transplants, the interpretive solutions or principles adopted in the destination countries do have a common origin as they both come from the same source institution (the Commentary), yet they do not have a common content, because the transplanted solution is modified in a relevant aspect and thus acquires *new content.* In practice, in these judicial pseudo-transplants, the transplant is used as a vehicle, sometimes even as a mere pretext, for domestic change.

Judicial pseudo-transplants are identified through the internal perspective of each individual tax system on a case-by-case basis. What follows are merely a number of examples of judicial pseudo-transplants, which in effect constitute an underlying force in the internalization process of OECD interpretive solutions or principles that unfold in manifold manifestations.

Judicial applications of the Commentary to Article 5 provide good examples of judicial pseudo-transplants which express the pressure by national courts to protect the interest of the source country. For example, in respect of preparatory/auxiliary activities, the Commentary before the changes made in 2017 observed that under the exception provided by Article 5(3), activities carried out through a fixed place of business are not PEs if these activities are 'remote from the actual realization of profits'; but national courts included in the core activities of the PE the preparatory or auxiliary activities carried on through a fixed place of business.[42] Likewise, storage space fell under this exception of Article 5(3)(a), but judicial trends denied that storage space, as such, constitutes an exception.[43]

---

[42] See, for example, Austria, Verwaltungsgerichtshof (Supreme Administrative Court), 98/14/0026, 19 March 2002, <ris.bka.gv.at/Dokument.wxe?Abfrage=Vwgh&Dokumentnummer=JWT_1998140026_20020319X00>.

[43] See, for example, Spain, Tribunal Económico Administrativo Central (Central Economic–Administrative Court), 0657/2003, 2 March 2006, <http://serviciosweb.meh.es/apps/doctrinateac/>; Germany, Finanzgericht of Schleswig-Holstein (Court of First Instance), II 1224/97, 6 September 2001, Entscheidungen der Finanzgerichte, 2001, 1535; India, Income Tax Appellate Tribunal (ITAT) Delhi, *Pioneer Overseas Corp v Assistant Director of Income Tax*, Nos 1868, 1869, 1870 and 1871/Del/2005, 24 December 2009, [2010] 37 SOT 404; Italy, Corte Suprema di Cassazione (Supreme Court), 7682, 25 May 2002 (Italy, Corte Suprema di Cassazione (Supreme Court), 7682); Germany, Bundesfinanzhof (Federal Tax Court), IR 292/81, 23 January 1985, Bundessteuerblatt, 1985, II, 13, 417.

The Commentary to Article 5 observed at that time that the mere fact that a person has attended or participated in negotiations is not by itself authority to conclude contracts that creates an agency PE. National courts instead established that persons who have attended or participated in negotiations constitute an agency PE.[44]

The Commentary to Article 5 affirms that the existence of a subsidiary company does not, of itself, constitute that company as a PE of its parent company because the subsidiary company is an independent legal entity,[45] but national courts have held that a subsidiary may be considered a dependent agent by application of the same tests applied to unrelated companies.[46]

In other cases, national courts, instead of resorting to judicial pseudo-transplants, simply do not apply the interpretive solution offered by the Commentary and introduce an autonomous local solution. Examples of this kind of judicial reasoning are found, for example, in respect of the Commentary to Article 13 (capital gains), Article 24 (non-discrimination) and Article 25 (mutual agreement procedure).

The Commentary to Article 13 provides a guideline for the redemption of securities, according to which differences between the selling price and the par value of the shares attributed by a shareholder to the issuing company, in connection with the liquidation of such company or the reduction of its paid-up capital, may be treated in the state of which the company is a resident as a distribution of accumulated profits and not as capital gains realized by them.[47] Judicial decisions, however, do not follow this approach and treat redemptions under the capital gains Article.[48]

---

44 See, for example, Italy, Corte Suprema di Cassazione (Supreme Court), 8488, 9 April 2010. See Giovanni Rolle, 'Cass n 8488 del 9 aprile 2010 – La Cassazione si pronuncia sulla stabile organizzazione "personale" e "materiale"' (2010) 20 Il Fisco 3154; Ennio Vial, 'Cass n 8488 del 9 aprile 2010 – Stabile organizzazione personale anche in presenza di rappresentante vincolato' (2010) 17 Il Fisco 2713; Diego Avolio and Benedetto Santacroce, 'C'è stabile organizzazione anche se l'agente segue le direttive della società' (2010) 27 Corriere tributario 2155.

45 OECD Model Tax Convention (n 1) Commentary on Art 5, paras 105 and 115.

46 See, for example, Italy, Corte Suprema di Cassazione (Supreme Court), 7682 (n 43).

47 OECD Model Tax Convention (n 1) Commentary on Art 13, para 31 and Commentary on Art 10, paras 3 and 28.

48 The Netherlands, Hoge Raad der Nederlanden (Supreme Court), 29.531, 15 March 1995, Beslissingen Nederlandse Belasting Rechtspraak, 1995, 150c*; 29 296, 15 December 1993, Beslissingen Nederlandse Belasting Rechtspraak, 1994, 259*; 38.461, 12 December 2003, Beslissingen Nederlandse Belasting

The Commentary to Article 24 takes the position that the non-discrimination standard does not apply to payments of interest to resident/non-resident taxpayers as opposed to payments of interest to resident taxpayers because such payments are outside the scope of Article 24(5).[49] National courts have not applied this interpretive solution and instead have held that the non-discrimination standard does apply to payments of interest to resident/non-resident taxpayers and therefore established that domestic thin capitalization rules that adversely affect foreign lenders are therefore discriminatory.[50]

Finally, with respect to the mutual agreement which can be reached pursuant to Article 25, the Commentary takes the view that the obligation of implementing such an agreement is unequivocally stated in the last sentence of Article 25(2) insofar as it provides that any agreement reached shall be implemented in spite of any time limits in the domestic laws of the contracting states,[51] but national courts have taken the position that mutual agreements are not binding on the basis of constitutional domestic constraints.[52]

Judicial pseudo-transplants of OECD interpretive solutions or principles occur when certain areas are 'transplant resistant' because domestic tax cultures have developed barriers, when a potentially efficient interpretive solution is deprived of its impact because it is introduced in an incompatible setting of tax procedural arrangements, or when the court expressly refers to Article 3(2) of the treaties to make reference to domestic laws to determine the meaning of a treaty term or to interpret a treaty provision. How, and to what extent, any particular OECD interpretive solution or principle imported through a judicial transplant retains its identity or is accepted, ignored, used, assimilated, adapted, rooted, resisted, rejected, interpreted, enforced selectively, and so on, depends largely on local conditions.

These types of judicial pseudo-transplants are a critical area of evolution in international tax law in which the vehicle of diffusion appears to be a transplant that introduces a domestic solution that diverges from the original OECD

Rechtspraak, 2004, 123c*; 36.773, 6 December 2002, Beslissingen Nederlandse Belasting Rechtspraak, 2003, 285c*; Germany, Bundesfinanzhof (Federal Fiscal Court), IR 11/85, 22 February 1989, Bundessteuerblatt, 1989, II, 794.

49 OECD Model Tax Convention (n 1) Commentary on Art 24, para 79.

50 Spain, Tribunal Supremo (Supreme Court), 5871/2006, 17 March 2011; France, Conseil d'État (Supreme Administrative Court), 233894, 14 November 2001, Droit Fiscal, 2002, 29, 620.

51 OECD Model Tax Convention (n 1) Commentary on Art 25, para 29.

52 See, for example, Germany, Bundesfinanzhof (Federal Fiscal Court), IR 111/08, 2 September 2009, Internationales Steuerrecht 2009, 814. Germany, Bundesfinanzhof (Federal Fiscal Court), IR 90/08, 2 September 2009, Internationales Steuerrecht, 2009, 817.

interpretive solution or principle. A naïve or simplified model of judicial transplants mistakenly assumes that national judicial decisions are straightforward and direct applications of OECD interpretive solutions or principles. By contrast, in a judicial pseudo-transplant of OECD interpretive solutions or principles, the object of reception often does *not* retain its identity.

In conclusion, judicial pseudo-transplants of OECD interpretive solutions or principles show that the naïve model of judicial transplants of the Commentary is unable to account for the real processes of change, and are evidence of the fact that diffusion often involves a long, drawn-out process, which leads to divergence rather than convergence.

## 11.4 GAPS IN THE COMMENTARY AND TAX TREATY JUDICIAL ACTIVISM

In certain cases the Commentary neither provides an interpretive solution nor adopts a principle concerning a particular issue, creating a *normative gap* in the Model–Commentary integrated system. For example, the treatment of foreign PE losses is not covered by the Commentary[53] and this has left room for the development of two opposing national judicial approaches: according to the former approach, foreign PE losses can be deducted in the residence country, but according to the latter approach, they cannot. Moreover, depreciation and devaluation of the PE's assets are not treated by the Commentary, leading to judicial decisions clarifying that capital losses are not covered by the capital gains Article.[54] Moreover, neither Article 13 nor the Commentary settles the question of exchange gains, which is entirely left to domestic laws.[55]

Normative gaps in the Model–Commentary integrated system leave space for the exercise of judicial activism at the national level. There are essentially three instances of this activism: (i) courts develop frameworks for *factual analysis*; (ii) courts create *indicators* to determine the application of a provision of the Model; and (iii) courts rely on *domestic laws* to solve treaty issues.

A good example of courts developing *frameworks for factual analysis* is the cases concerning the tiebreak rules of Article 4. Article 4(2)(a) adopts the centre of vital interests test, and the Commentary observes that the state where the 'centre of vital interests' is located is the state with which the personal and

53 OECD Model Tax Convention (n 1) Commentary on Arts 23A and 23B, para 44.

54 See, for example, Denmark, Østre Landsret (High Court of Eastern Denmark), 14 May 2012, B-307-10; France, Conseil d'État (Supreme Administrative Court), 351702, 12 June 2013, Droit Fiscal, 2013, 46, 511.

55 OECD Model Tax Convention (n 1) Commentary on Art 13, paras 16–17; Commentary on Art 10, paras 31 and 28.

economic relations of the individual are closest and provides several indicators of that.[56] National courts have applied this tiebreak rule through detailed substantial analysis of the actual conduct of life,[57] focusing on family ties closely connected to cultural and social factors,[58] or conducting an analysis which balances the economic and the personal ties in a kind of global view.[59]

Good examples of *indicators* developed by courts to determine the application of a treaty provision are those relating to the 'beneficial owner' of dividends defined in broad strokes by the Commentary to Article 10.[60] These indicators are found in judicial applications focused on intricate patterns (for example, of private equity deals) that clarified that narrow powers to act were not in themselves sufficient for a company to be disregarded as the beneficial owner of the dividends.[61] With respect to the 'restricted force of attraction of PE' to determine in which cases interest is not attracted and therefore subject to isolated treaty treatment, courts have established a counterfactual argument: interest was not attributable to a fixed base in Switzerland of a taxpayer resident in Germany (and so was taxable in Germany, i.e., the residence country of the recipient) because the interest could have been realized in the residence country irrespective of the fixed base.[62] Another court attributed relevance to the involvement of the PE in the decision process leading to the payment of interest.[63]

Finally, a good example of judicial activism within gaps in the Model–Commentary integrated system is the *reliance by courts on domestic laws* to solve treaty issues about the application of foreign tax credit (FTC) rules.[64]

---

56 Ibid Commentary on Art 4, paras 14–15.

57 *Gaudreau v Her Majesty the Queen* [2005] 1 CTC 2702 (Tax Court of Canada).

58 France, Conseil d'État (Supreme Administrative Court), 28,831, 13 May 1983, Bulletin Fiscal Francis Lefebvre, 1983, 7, 430; 8,046, 14 March 1979, Droit Fiscal, 1980, 32, 409.

59 France, Conseil d'État (Supreme Administrative Court), 76,534, 19 May 1972, Droit Fiscal, 1975, 27, 116.

60 OECD Model Tax Convention (n 1) Commentary on Art 10, paras 12.4 and 12.6.

61 See, for example, Denmark, Østre Landsret (High Court of Eastern Denmark), B-2152-10, 20 December 2011; Denmark, Landsskatteretten (National Tax Tribunal), 09-01478, 3 March 2010.

62 Germany, Finanzgericht Bayern (Tax Court Bayern), 9 K 3576/01, 10 December 2003, Entscheidungen der Finanzgerichte, 2004, 634.

63 Belgium, Hof van Beroep Gent (Court of Appeals Gent), 1995/FR/59, 1 April 2003, Jurisprudence Fiscale, 2004, 42, 138.

64 See, for example, Austria, Verwaltungsgerichtshof (Supreme Administrative Court), 2000/14/0172, 28 September 2004, <ris.bka.gv.at/JudikaturEntscheidung

In a similar manner, the application of Article 6 on income from immovable property is based on domestic laws of the contracting states, particularly with respect to how the income from immovable property is actually taxed.[65] Domestic laws are also applied to determine the amount of taxable income from immovable property, which is assessed as 'notional income'.[66]

## 11.5 CONCLUSIONS

It is now possible to draw some conclusions from the analysis conducted in this chapter. It is well known that in general there are relevant instances of tax transplants where the function of the transplanted operative rule is maintained without mere reproduction of the same legal formant. For example, the solution of one country, included in a piece of legislation (the legislative legal formant), is reproduced using the same legal formant (the legislative legal formant) through mere reproduction of legislation. By contrast, there are other instances that are defined here as *blended tax transplants*: these transplants occur when there is a shift from one formant of the tax law to another. For example, a country can transplant the operative rule resulting from statutory materials by way of judicial decisions. In this case, although the formant in the two countries is different, the operative rule is the same.

Tax change in these cases is thus explained as a complex set of routines carried out by different actors performing different institutional roles. This is the legal phenomenon that occurs through the domestic judicial transplants of OECD interpretive solutions or principles, which is the topic of this chapter. In these specific instances, the shift from one formant to another is developed through the judiciary when judges convey a general principle or broad standard of taxation – that is allegedly provided by the OECD Model or Commentary – into a judicial decision.

This chapter has evidenced that changes in tax systems are the result of a peculiar phenomenon in which different actors in different systems (for example judges of different countries in the examples above) decide to introduce a new set of rules, basing their decisions on OECD principles. In certain cases

.wxe?Abfrage=Vwgh&Dokumentnummer=JWR_2000140172_20040928X02>.

65 OECD Model Tax Convention (n 1) Commentary on Art 6, para 4.

66 See, for example, the Netherlands, Gerechtshof 's-Hertogenbosch (Court of Appeal of 's-Hertogenbosch), 07/00088, 17 October 2008, Vakstudie-Nieuws, 2009, 13.14.

these blended judicial transplants morph into a kind of 'pseudo-transplant', which is a peculiar type of transplant characterized by substantial modification of the *imported operative rule during the process of being transplanted.* This process belongs to 'transportation with transformation', a process in which imitation does not necessarily lead to conformity.

# PART IV

# Tax specifics

# 12. Taxing and not taxing: the problematic nature of tax concessions for charities and not-for-profit entities in Australia

**Ann O'Connell**

## 12.1 INTRODUCTION

Australia, like most other countries, provides a range of tax concessions for 'charities' (as defined in the Charities Act 2013 (Cth)) and a range of other not-for-profit (NFP) entities. These concessions include an exemption from income tax (for all income – including commercial and investment income) and a deduction for gifts to qualifying entities. But there are also other concessions: a refund of franking credits for charitable entities,[1] some goods and services tax (GST) concessions[2] and an exemption or rebate from fringe benefits tax (FBT) for benefits provided to employees of qualifying entities.[3] Membership-based entities can also apply the common law concept of mutuality to disregard receipts from members when calculating taxable income.[4] There are also a number of concessions under State and Territory taxing regimes.[5]

---

[1] Income Tax Assessment Act 1997 (Cth) Divs 207 and 67 (ITAA 1997). A franking credit is a type of tax credit paid by corporations to their shareholders along with their dividend payments to reflect the tax paid by the corporation. Australia and some other countries allow franking credits as a way to reduce or eliminate double taxation.

[2] This includes a higher registration threshold and an exemption for 'non-commercial' activities of charities: see Ann O'Connell, *Taxation of Charities and Not-for-Profits* (LexisNexis 2020) ch 10.

[3] Fringe Benefits Tax Assessment Act 1986 (Cth) ss 57A (exemption) and 65J (rebate) (FBTAA 1986).

[4] See O'Connell (n 2) ch 11.

[5] Such as payroll tax, stamp duty, land tax and rates concessions. For a discussion of the State and Territory concessions, see ibid ch 12.

The federal income tax regime commenced in 1915, but its antecedents can be found in earlier legislation imported from Britain.[6] The system has been added to in fits and starts over time, often at the whim of a politician, and certainly not as the result of carefully considered tax policy.[7] The generally accepted rationale for providing these concessions is that the government is providing support for 'worthy' causes, some of which might relieve the government of its own fiscal responsibilities.[8] There has been discussion from time to time about how this support might be given more directly,[9] or in the case of gift relief, more equitably,[10] but ultimately such significant changes have been eschewed.

In the 110 years since the enactment of the first Income Tax Assessment Act in 1915 (ITAA 1915), there have been a number of reviews that have touched on the appropriateness of the concessions,[11] but surprisingly only one review dedicated to examining the tax measures applying to the NFP sector – what was described as 'the envelope of tax support provided to the sector'.[12] Unfortunately, the recommendations of that review were not fully considered when there was a change of government in 2013. This review is considered further below.

The concessions introduced in 1915 – the income tax exemption and the gift deduction – have endured with very little change. What has changed over that period is an expansion of the type and number of entities that are eligible to access the concessions. Another change worth noting is that when the concessions were introduced, eligible entities were unlikely to have had significant revenue and in many cases were reliant on donations. Many income tax-exempt entities now have significant income streams, meaning that there

---

6 For the history of the federal concessions, see ibid ch 4.

7 Ibid.

8 Ibid ch 1.

9 See, for example, Not-for-Profit Sector Tax Concession Working Group (Linda Lavarch, chair), *Fairer, Simpler and More Effective Tax Concessions for the Not-for-Profit Sector, Final Report* (May 2013). (The present author was a member of the Working Group.) The Productivity Commission has recently completed a report on philanthropy that considers, inter alia, the tax regime: <https://www.pc.gov.au/inquiries/completed/philanthropy#report>.

10 Not-for-Profit Sector Tax Concession Working Group (n 9).

11 This includes two Royal Commissions (1920–23 and 1932–34), Asprey Review (Justice Kenneth W Asprey, chair, 1975), Charities Definition Inquiry (Ian Sheppard, chair, 2001), Productivity Commission, *Contribution of the Not-for-Profit Sector* (2010), and Australian Future Tax System Review (Ken Henry, chair) (2009–10).

12 Not-for-Profit Sector Tax Concession Working Group (n 9).

is a larger cost to the revenue of not taxing some or all of that income.[13] This raises the possibility of considering whether the rationale for providing concessions is still valid.

It is also instructive to note that Australia has one of the most generous regimes compared to other jurisdictions – it exempts all income and allows a deduction for the whole amount of the gift to eligible entities, although it should be noted that the gift deduction is only available to a more restricted group of entities ('deductible gift recipients' or DGRs).[14] In 2020 the Organisation for Economic Co-operation and Development (OECD) produced a report on taxation and philanthropy that considered the tax regimes applying in 40 countries.[15] The regime in Australia, by comparison, was one of the most complex and the most difficult to justify by reference to underlying principle.[16]

This chapter will consider a number of examples where either the circumstances of different entities or the rationale for providing support have changed. These include the exemption for agricultural trading companies and professional sporting entities, and the gift deduction for school building funds.

Before doing so, it is instructive to consider the provisions enacted in 1915, which were blissfully concise[17] (and, it should be noted, in a form still used by many other countries):

(i) the exemption from income tax was available for 'the income of a religious, scientific, charitable or public educational institution'[18] (the only other exemptions for entities were for friendly societies and trade unions[19]);
(ii) the gift deduction was available for individual gifts of £20 (approximately AUD 2,300 in current terms[20]) or more to 'public charitable institutions'.[21]

---

[13] For a discussion of the cost of the concessions, see O'Connell (n 2) 22–26.

[14] The 'cost' of these concessions, i.e., revenue forgone, is estimated in the Tax Expenditures and Insights Statement produced by Treasury annually: see <https://treasury.gov.au/sites/default/files/2024-01/p2024-489823-teis.pdf>, although there is no accurate way of measuring the benefit provided to society by an active NFP sector.

[15] OECD, *Taxation and Philanthropy*, OECD Tax Policy Studies No 27 (OECD Publishing 2020) 23–5 (OECD Report).

[16] Ann O'Connell, 'The OECD on Taxation and Philanthropy: An Australian Report Card' (2021) 75(5) Bulletin for International Taxation 202.

[17] Indeed, the Income Tax Assessment Act 1915 (Cth) (ITAA 1915) was only 22 pages in length.

[18] Ibid s 11(d).

[19] Ibid ss 11(b) and (c).

[20] Reserve Bank of Australia pre-decimal inflation calculator: <https://www.rba.gov.au/calculator/annualPreDecimal.html>.

[21] ITAA 1915, s 18(h).

> The only other gift deduction was for individual contributions to the war effort of £5 (approximately AUD 578 in current terms[22]) or more.[23]

So in 1915, being a public charitable institution meant that the institution could access both concessions. But income tax exemption was also available to religious, scientific and public educational institutions, whether or not they were charitable. Two comments can be made: first, the scope of the term 'charity' has expanded (and occasionally contracted[24]) over time and secondly, at the same time, the concessions have been extended to many non-charitable NFPs. It is worth pausing for a moment to consider that we now have more than 200,000 entities known to the Australian Taxation Office (ATO) as accessing one or more tax concessions,[25] but only approximately 60,000 of them are charities (that report to the Australian Charities and Not-for-profits Commission (ACNC)).[26] That means that there are 140,000 to 145,000 entities with access to significant tax concessions that we know very little about.[27]

In relation to gift deductibility, there was a significant change to eligibility in 1927 as a result of the Privy Council decision in *Chesterman v Federal Commissioner of Taxation*,[28] which held that 'charity' had a legal meaning set

---

22 Ibid.

23 Ibid.

24 See Myles McGregor-Lowndes and Frances M Hannah, 'National Rifle Association' (note on Charity Commission for England and Wales, Charity Compliance Decision, 7 February 2020) (Australian Centre for Philanthropy and Nonprofit Studies Legal Case Report 2020-07, February 2020), where it was held that a gun club to train the young to defend the realm was no longer charitable.

25 ATO, 'Straight from the Source – February 2023' (2 February 2023) <https://www.ato.gov.au/Non-profit/Newsroom/General/Straight-from-the-Source---February-2023/>, which states that '[t]here are just under 207,000 not-for-profits registered in the Australian tax system. The vast majority, about 70%, self-assess income tax exemption, about one third are endorsed tax concession charities and about 3% are taxable not-for-profits'.

26 As at 1 April 2024 there were 60,259 registered charities: Australian Government, 'ACNC Registered Charities' <https://data.gov.au/dataset/ds-dga-b050b242-4487-4306-abf5-07ca073e5594/details?q=>.

27 As part of the 2021–22 federal Budget, self-assessing entities with an active ABN are required to undertake a self-assessment review and lodge an annual return from 1 July 2023: see ATO, 'Reporting Requirements to Self-Assess Income Tax Exemption' (last updated 2 May 2024) <https://www.ato.gov.au/businesses-and-organisations/not-for-profit-organisations/statements-and-returns/in-detail/reporting-requirements-to-self-assess-income-tax-exemption>.

28 *Chesterman v Federal Commissioner of Taxation* (1925) 37 CLR 317, reversing the High Court of Australia in *Chesterman v Federal Commissioner of*

out in the House of Lords decision in the *Pemsel* case.[29] As a result, the legislation was amended so that the concession was only available to a category of charity described as a 'public benevolent institution'. The intention of the legislature appears to have been to limit the gift deduction to entities more closely aligned to the popular meaning of charity, i.e., giving to those in need.[30]

Another point to note is that the ability of entities to access grants from ancillary funds puts pressure on them to bring themselves within the DGR categories even when they will not be seeking public donations and, it follows, achieving DGR status in those circumstances will not impact the revenue. This, of course, raises the question of whether executive or judicial decisions about charitable status should or could have regard to the fiscal consequences.[31] There have been calls in the past to separate questions of fiscal privilege from those relating to what is charitable, although as Dal Pont notes, those calls have 'largely fallen on deaf ears'.[32]

Another big-picture issue is whether there should be greater symmetry between the income tax exemption and deductible gift recipient (DGR)

---

*Taxation* (1923) 32 CLR 362.

[29] *Commissioners for Special Purposes of Income Tax v Pemsel* [1891] AC 531 (*Pemsel*).

[30] The Charities Definition Inquiry Report in 2001 recommended that there be a subset of charity, to be known as Benevolent Charity, that would replace public benevolent institutions. The Report stated: 'Benevolent Charities are entities that meet all the requirements to be a charity and whose dominant purpose is to benefit, directly or indirectly, those whose disadvantage prevents them from meeting their needs': Inquiry into the Definition of Charities and Related Organisations (Ian Sheppard, chair), *Report of the Inquiry into the Definition of Charities and Related Organisations* (2001) 9 (Charities Definition Inquiry Report).

[31] See the Canadian case *Amateur Youth Soccer Association v Canada Revenue Agency* [2007] 3 SCR 217 and criticism of it: Adam Parachin, 'The Role of Fiscal Considerations in the Judicial Interpretation of Charity' in Matthew Harding, Ann O'Connell and Miranda Stewart (eds), *Not-for-Profit Law: Theoretical and Comparative Perspectives* (Cambridge University Press 2014).

[32] GE Dal Pont, *Law of Charity* (3rd edn, LexisNexis 2021) [21.5]. Kirby J alluded to the 'special privilege' of income tax exemption in his dissent in *Federal Commissioner of Taxation v Word Investments Ltd* (2008) 236 CLR 204, [107] in relation to a religious entity claiming an exemption from income tax, given that many citizens may not support the particular religion. In his view, this meant that '[a]ny ambiguity as to the ambit of an exemption for such an institution should therefore be construed against the claimed exemption and in favour of liability of that body to pay otherwise generally applicable tax obligations' [111]. See also *Central Bayside General Practice Association Ltd v Commissioner of State Revenue (Vic)* (2006) 228 CLR 168, [86]–[87].

provisions. This would certainly simplify the operation of the provisions and is the model adopted in a number of other countries,[33] but it begs the question: how do we define which entities should get some or all concessions? This question is complicated by the fact that there are now many more concessions available beyond income tax exemption and gift deductibility.

And so, to examples of the current operation of the concessions where either the entities accessing the concessions have changed or where societal circumstances have changed so that the concession may no longer be justified.

## 12.2 AGRICULTURAL TRADING COMPANIES

Tax concessions for entities that promote agriculture can be traced back to the beginning of the twentieth century. However, it may surprise some people to learn that at least two large agricultural companies – Co-operative Bulk Handling Ltd (CBH), which operates in Western Australia, and Queensland Sugar Ltd (QSL)[34] – are now charities registered with the ACNC. This means that those entities are income tax exempt, entitled to the FBT rebate and – significantly – eligible for franking credit refunds. QSL is also entitled to exemption from State taxes such as payroll tax,[35] although Western Australia amended its legislation in 2015 so that CBH does not obtain State payroll tax or duties exemptions.[36]

It is important to note that even in the absence of registration as charities, entities that promote the development of primary and secondary resources, including agricultural resources, may be entitled to income tax exemption provided they are not carried on for the purpose of profit or gain to individual members.[37] A specific provision providing income tax exemption for promoting the development of agriculture and other resources was included in the Income Tax Assessment Act 1922. It provided an exemption for:

---

33 OECD Report (n 15).

34 Both entities are companies limited by guarantee under the Corporations Act 2001 (Cth). In the absence of an exemption, the income of these entities is likely to have been taxed as co-operatives under ss 118–120 of the Income Tax Assessment Act 1936 (Cth) (ITAA 1936).

35 Queensland Sugar Ltd, *QSL: Working for YOU: Annual Report 2014/15* (2015) 3 (*Annual Report 2014/15*).

36 See Pay-roll Tax Assessment Act 2002 (WA), amended in 2015 to include s 42A (definition of 'relevant body').

37 Such an exemption would not entitle the entity to claim refunds of franking credits as this concession is confined to 'exempt institutions [that] are eligible for a refund' – defined in ITAA 1997 (n 1) s 207-115 as limited to, inter alia, exempt charities (and DGRs).

> any society or association not carried on for the purposes of profit or gain to the individual members thereof, established for the purpose of promoting the development of the agricultural, pastoral, horticultural, viticultural, stock-raising, manufacturing or industrial resources of Australia.[38]

This was in addition to the exemption for religious, scientific, charitable and public educational institutions,[39] so the legislature did not believe all these entities were charities. The provision, in a slightly modified form, is now in section 50-40(1), Item 8.2 of the ITAA 1997.

It is perhaps not surprising that the legislature wanted to encourage and support agriculture in the early days of the Federation. The Commonwealth Year Book for 1922 notes that there had been a persistent decline in the acreage under cultivation in the early part of the century[40] and that this had been addressed, inter alia, by the making of loans to farmers by the Commonwealth and State governments.[41] The introduction of the tax exemption may well have been part of this programme of encouragement.

A few years later, in the United Kingdom, a society for the promotion of agriculture was recognized as a charity in *Commissioners of Inland Revenue v Yorkshire Agricultural Society* in 1927.[42] The Society was formed in 1837 by a group of agriculturalists to hold an annual show for the exhibition of farming stock, implements, etc., and for 'the general promotion of agriculture'. It was, and is, similar to agricultural societies formed in each of the Australian colonies in the 1800s, which continue to perform an educative function.[43]

---

38 Income Tax Assessment Act 1922 (Cth) s 14(1)(j).

39 Ibid s 14(1)(d).

40 Commonwealth Bureau of Census and Statistics, *Official Year Book of the Commonwealth of Australia, No 15* (1922) 240.

41 Ibid 294.

42 *Commissioners of Inland Revenue v Yorkshire Agricultural Society* [1928] 1 KB 611 (*Yorkshire Agricultural Society* (Court of Appeal)). The Society has recently won an appeal against the imposition of value-added tax on the profits of its annual show: *Yorkshire Agricultural Society v HM Revenue and Customs* [2023] UKFTT 389 (TC). HM Revenue and Customs was granted permission to appeal to the Upper Tribunal, and the case was listed for hearing in October 2024.

43 See, for example, *Brisbane City Council and Myer Shopping Centres Pty Ltd v Attorney-General (Queensland)* [1979] AC 411 (Privy Council, 23 May 1978), where the Council was unable to sell some land to Myer as it was subject to a charitable trust, i.e., to enable a show to be held annually. Various Royal Agricultural Societies for each of the Australian States and Territories are registered as charities with the ACNC.

Although the judge at first instance thought the society was for the benefit of its members (and so not charitable),[44] the Court of Appeal took a different view.[45] It should also be noted that the only issue in the case was whether the investment income of the Society was subject to tax as the trading income was taxable in any event.

At this point, it might be thought that entities concerned with the promotion of agriculture might be charitable in the United Kingdom, but that in Australia, the question would be whether they came within the specific exemption.

There was not much judicial consideration in Australia of the position of agriculture as a charity, probably for this reason. There was an obiter reference to the promotion of agriculture in the case of *Incorporated Council of Law Reporting (Qld) v Federal Commissioner of Taxation*,[46] a case concerned with whether the production of law reports came within the fourth head of charity under the *Pemsel*[47] case. Barwick CJ considered the Preamble to the Charitable Uses Act of 1601 and noted:

> Consistently with the spirit and width of this concept of charity the promotion of agriculture is seen to be charitable (*Inland Revenue Commissioners v Yorkshire Agricultural Society*) … Agriculture partakes of that fundamental social quality which can give a charitable nature to a trust or purpose relating thereto which is beneficial to the community.[48]

Before 2000, the procedure relating to eligibility for income tax exemption was not very robust – entities that believed they were eligible simply self-assessed. In 2000 a system of endorsement was introduced, which required entities that were charities, or which could be charities, to be endorsed by the Commissioner of Taxation to be income tax exempt.[49] This did not include entities under section 50-40(1), Item 8.2 (or some other specific exemptions), presumably because they were not viewed as charities, although the reason for different treatment is not obvious. In 2010, the Commissioner of Taxation, following a review in 2008, determined to remove the exemption from CBH, and

---

[44] *Yorkshire Agricultural Society* (Court of Appeal) (n 42) 612 (per Rowlatt J).

[45] Ibid.

[46] *Incorporated Council of Law Reporting (Qld) v Federal Commissioner of Taxation* (1971) 125 CLR 659 (*Incorporated Council of Law Reporting (Qld)*).

[47] *Pemsel* (n 29).

[48] *Incorporated Council of Law Reporting (Qld)* (n 46) 669.

[49] ITAA 1997 (n 1) Subdiv 50-B, introduced by the A New Tax System (Tax Administration) Act 1999 (Cth). See also Explanatory Memorandum to the A New Tax System (Tax Administration) Bill 1999 (Cth) [6.7].

the case came before the Federal Court of Australia.[50] It is important to note that the Court was confined to determining the application of section 50-40(1), Item 8.2 based on the facts set out in the private ruling application submitted by CBH in 2008 rather than at the time of the hearing. On those facts, the judge at first instance,[51] and a majority on appeal (Siopis J dissenting)[52] held that CBH was entitled to the specific exemption. There was some discussion in the Full Court of the notion of what amounted to promotion of 'development of agriculture'[53] but the more important issues were whether CBH had the purpose of promotion (the purpose issue) and whether CBH was carried on for the profit of the individual members (the not-for-profit issue). In relation to the not-for-profit issue, although it was clear that the growers did benefit, the majority held that as not all the growers were members and as growers who were not members received the same benefits as member growers, the exemption applied.[54] The majority described the benefits to members as being 'incidental'.[55] The majority also noted that the rules of CBH and s 35A of the Bulk Handling Act 1967 (WA) precluded a distribution of profit to members.[56] Siopis J, in dissent, noted that members comprised 95% of growers and would have found the exemption did not apply.[57] In his view, the essential purpose of CBH was the conduct of its grain bulk handling business for the benefit of growers rather than any broader purpose of promotion of development of agricultural resources.[58]

The finding by the Full Federal Court meant that CBH was entitled to the income tax exemption in section 50-40(1), Item 8.2. As a result, CBH was also entitled to the FBT rebate in relation to any fringe benefits provided to employees.[59] However, in March 2014, CBH was retrospectively endorsed by the ATO as a charitable institution, with effect from 1 July 2000.[60] The effect of this change in status is that as a charity, CBH became entitled to tax concessions that it would not have been entitled to as an exempt entity under section

---

50 *Federal Commissioner of Taxation v Co-operative Bulk Handling Ltd* (2010) 189 FCR 332 (*Co-operative Bulk Handling Ltd* (Full Federal Court)).

51 *Co-operative Bulk Handling Ltd v Federal Commissioner of Taxation* (2010) 79 ATR 582, [123] (Gilmour J).

52 *Co-operative Bulk Handling Ltd* (Full Federal Court) (n 50).

53 Ibid [71]–[84] (Mansfield and McKerracher JJ).

54 Ibid [112].

55 Ibid [94].

56 Ibid [36].

57 Ibid [152].

58 Ibid [122].

59 FBTAA 1986 (n 3) s 65J.

60 CBH Group, *Annual Report 2019* (2019) 71.

50-40(1), Item 8.2(a), namely refunds of franking credits.[61] The timing of this endorsement is curious – it appears to be after the commencement of the ACNC (which occurred on 3 December 2012). It may be that it was the ACNC that accepted that CBH had a charitable purpose – the promotion of agriculture may be regarded as a charitable purpose,[62] and the ATO accepted that fact in granting endorsement. This would be consistent with the ACNC registering various 'royal' agricultural societies as charities.[63]

It could be asked whether CBH should continue to be recognized as a charity (or indeed be eligible for exemption under section 50-40(1), Item 8.2). In this regard, it could be noted that the profitability of the business operated by CBH indicates that it is no longer in need of the support provided by either section 50-40(1), Item 8.2, or the charitable exemption which it currently receives. CBH runs a business that is an end in itself. The size of the business is remarkable – for the year ended 30 September 2022, CBH had gross revenue of AUD 1.1 billion,[64] and a 'surplus' of AUD 216 million.[65] CBH also has assets of AUD 1.9 billion.[66] This puts it in the very highest category of registered charities by size – 'extra-large' – with only 0.4% of charities having revenue in excess of AUD 100 million.[67] Of course, many charities run businesses and then apply the profits or surplus towards charitable objects. For example, the entity in *Word Investments*[68] applied the profits to advance a religious purpose, but CBH does not apply its revenue for a charitable purpose – it is simply a grain supply co-operative run for the benefit of members/growers.

Another reason for reassessing the charitable status of CBH is that it appears to be operating differently now compared to when it was before the Federal Court. In that case, it was noted that CBH was prohibited by its rules and by statute from paying dividends.[69] However, CBH has operated a programme,

---

61 ITAA 1997 (n 1) Divs 67, 207.

62 See, for example, *Ziliani v Sydney City Council* (1985) 56 LGRA 58.

63 The ACNC Charity Register lists more than 150 entities with the word 'agricultural' in their name and 16 with the words 'royal agricultural'. The designation as a royal society indicates that at some stage the entity had royal patronage.

64 Co-operative Bulk Handling Limited, 'Annual Information Statement 2022' (Statement, Australian Charities and Not-for-Profits Commission, 30 March 2023) <https://www.acnc.gov.au/charity/charities/b9ef6be7-39af-e811-a95e-000d3ad24c60/documents/1cf6522a-e5ce-ed11-a7c7-00224893bd39>.

65 Ibid.

66 Ibid.

67 Australian Charities and Not-for-Profits Commission, *Australian Charities Report, 8th Edition* (7 June 2022) 7.

68 *Federal Commissioner of Taxation v Word Investments Ltd* (n 32).

69 *Co-operative Bulk Handling Ltd* (Full Federal Court) (n 50) [93] (Mansfield and McKerracher JJ).

now called the Grower Patronage Rebate Programme, since June 2013 (and a variation on this programme in the 2009–11 income years) where amounts are distributed to growers (including the small percentage of non-member growers) to effectively reduce the amount they pay for the service CBH provides.[70] In 2019, CBH announced that it had returned more than AUD 440 million to growers under the programme.[71] Although the payment of rebates would not be unusual in a distributing co-operative, it seems anomalous that these distributions would not indicate that there is a gain or benefit to members that is more than incidental.

A further reason for reassessing the position of CBH arises from the interaction with other members of the CBH Group. CBH has 12 wholly owned subsidiaries and two associated companies.[72] The Full Federal Court noted that those subsidiaries were subject to tax.[73] However, as a result of the recognition of CBH as a charity, CBH can claim a refund of franking credits with respect to franked dividends[74] it receives from those entities. The effect of this is that effectively the CBH Group – with revenue of AUD 6.2 billion and a surplus of AUD 497 million[75] – is not paying any tax. As noted above, the refund would not be available if the exemption in section 50-40(1), Item 8.2 applied.

Another large agricultural trading company, Queensland Sugar Limited (QSL), is also registered as a charity with the ACNC. QSL commenced as a statutory marketing authority in 1923 (called the Queensland Sugar Board, which became the Queensland Sugar Corporation in 1991).[76] It became QSL, a company limited by guarantee, in 2000[77] and has been income tax exempt

---

70 Grain Central, 'CBH Group Delivers $16 Million Operations Rebate' (30 September 2019) <https://www.graincentral.com/news/agribusiness/cbh-group-delivers-16-million-operations-rebate/> accessed 26 June 2024.

71 CBH Group, 'CBH Group Delivers $16 Million Operations Rebate' (Media Release, 27 September 2019) <https://www.cbh.com.au/media-releases/2021/06/cbh-group-delivers-$16-million-operations-rebate>. It was reported in October 2022 that CBH would not pay a rebate for the 2021/2022 season: Cally Dupe and Adam Poulsen, 'CBH Rebate Divides Opinion among WA Growers', *Countryman* (20 October 2022) <https://www.countryman.com.au/countryman/news/wa-growers-furious-as-cbh-rebate-debate-flares-up-c-8584597> accessed 26 June 2024.

72 CBH Group, *Annual Report 2022* (2022) 90–91 (CBH *Annual Report 2022*).

73 *Co-operative Bulk Handling Ltd* (Full Federal Court) (n 50) [56], [78], [84], [114] (Mansfield and McKerracher JJ) and [133] (Siopis J), where references to the tax status of the subsidiaries can be found.

74 ITAA 1997 (n 1) Divs 67, 207.

75 CBH *Annual Report 2022* (n 72) 66.

76 Australian Cane Farmers, 'Historical Events' <https://www.acfa.com.au/sugar-industry/historical-events>.

77 Ibid.

since 1 July 2000.[78] QSL was granted charity status by the ACNC in late 2015, backdated to 3 December 2012.[79] QSL's stated purpose is to 'promote the development of the sugar industry'.[80] In its Annual Information Statement, it describes its beneficiaries as the 'general community in Australia' (as well as the sugar industry and associated businesses).[81] However, its website states that it is '[o]wned by its members, with net sale proceeds returned to those who choose to use its services'.[82] QSL has also reported that it is entitled to an exemption from payroll tax in Queensland – in 2014/15 it stated that the exemption was worth AUD 1 million per year.[83] Furthermore, as the exemption was backdated to 2010, it was entitled to a significant refund.[84] In 2021 QSL had revenue of more than AUD 900 million, a surplus of more than AUD 4 million[85] and assets of AUD 423 million.[86] QSL also received a refund of franking credits of AUD 765,000 in the 2022 year.[87]

In 2017, the Productivity Commission was critical of the granting of charitable tax concessions to agricultural trading companies such as CBH and QSL. The Productivity Commission recommended that 'The Australian Government should legislate to exclude agricultural commodity trading companies from being granted charity status and receiving the associated tax concessions.'[88]

There is a strong argument for saying that these entities are simply providing private benefits and should not be classified as charities or indeed be

---

78 Australian Business Register, 'Current Details for ABN 76 090 152 211', *ABN Lookup* (last updated 20 October 2021) <https://abr.business.gov.au/ABN/View/76090152211>.

79 Ibid.

80 Queensland Sugar Ltd, *Constitution of Queensland Sugar Ltd (ACN 090 152 211)* (approved 16 November 2010) cl 6.

81 Queensland Sugar Ltd, 'Annual Information Statement 2023' (Statement, Australian Charities and Not-for-Profits Commission, 27 November 2023) <https://www.acnc.gov.au/charity/charities/0b064a67-3aaf-e811-a963-000d3ad244fd/documents/1c8b94dd-d88c-ee11-be36-002248110683>.

82 Queensland Sugar Ltd, *Annual Report 2014/15* (n 35); Queensland Sugar Ltd, 'About QSL' <https://www.qsl.com.au/content/about-qsl>.

83 Queensland Sugar Ltd, *Annual Report 2014/15* (n 35) 3.

84 Ibid 13. Noted by the Productivity Commission, *Regulation of Australian Agriculture*, Inquiry Report No 79 (2016) 510.

85 QSL reported a loss of AUD 605 million for the 2022 income year: Queensland Sugar Ltd, *QSL: Your Trusted Partner: Annual Report 2021–2022* (2022) 22.

86 Ibid 22 and 23.

87 Ibid 31.

88 Productivity Commission, *Regulation of Australian Agriculture* (n 84) recommendation 12.3.

entitled to exemption under section 50-40(1), Item 8.2.[89] But an issue arises as to how to distinguish these types of entities from other agricultural societies that arguably do promote the development of agriculture. One possibility would be to exclude entities that make distributions to members. This seems to have been intended by the exemption in section 50-40(1), Item 8.2, and the not-for-profit requirement in relation to charity. Another possibility would be to limit the exemption to entities that have income below a certain threshold, or to adopt the reform introduced in Western Australia that excluded entities that promote 'trade, industry or commerce' from the notion of charity.[90]

The position in other countries is worth considering. In the UK, where the *Yorkshire Agricultural Society* case in 1927 held that an agricultural society was a charity, there is now a specific provision that exempts from corporation tax the profits of an agricultural society that arise from an exhibition or show held for the purposes of the society, and are applied solely for the purposes of the society.[91] Nevertheless, such entities are subject to tax on 'trading income' except where it is derived from the 'primary purpose of the charity',[92] although many avoid this tax by conducting commercial or trading activity through a wholly owned trading subsidiary.[93] In the US, there is a specific exemption for an 'agricultural organization', provided that the net earnings do not inure to the benefit of any member, and it has as its objects the betterment of the conditions of those engaged in agricultural pursuits, the improvement of the grade of agricultural products, and the development of a higher degree

---

89 The author has addressed possible reform elsewhere: see Ann O'Connell, 'Is It Really a Charity? Membership-Based Entities as Charities: The Australian Experience' in Henry Peter and Giedre Lideikyte Huber (eds), *The Routledge Handbook of Taxation and Philanthropy* (Routledge 2021) ('Is It Really a Charity?'); Ann O'Connell, 'Stretching the Concept of Charity in the Tax Context: Membership-Based Entities as Charities' (2021) 50(2) Australian Tax Review 121 ('Stretching the Concept of Charity in the Tax Context').

90 See O'Connell, 'Is It Really a Charity?' (n 89) 133; O'Connell, 'Stretching the Concept of Charity in the Tax Context' (n 89) 135.

91 Corporations Tax Act 2010 (UK) s 989. An 'agricultural society' is defined as any society or institution established for the purpose of promoting the interests of – (a) agriculture, (b) horticulture, (c) forestry, or (d) the breeding of any kind of animal: s 989(2).

92 Ibid s 478.

93 See Charity Commission for England and Wales, 'Trustees Trading and Tax: How Charities May Lawfully Trade' (Guidance, 24 February 2016) <https://www.gov.uk/government/publications/trustees-trading-and-tax-how-charities-may-lawfully-trade-cc35/trustees-trading-and-tax-how-charities-may-lawfully-trade>.

of efficiency in agriculture.[94] Section 501(g) of the IRC provides that the term 'agricultural' includes the art or science of cultivating land, harvesting crops or aquatic resources, or raising livestock. Such entities may be subject to unrelated business tax on profits from commercial operations.[95] It seems unlikely that a large agricultural trading company would qualify for exemption in either the UK or the US.

## 12.3 PROFESSIONAL SPORTING BODIES

### 12.3.1 Introduction

The inclusion of tax concessions for entities in Australia that encourage the promotion of sport can be traced back to the middle of the twentieth century. However, it is somewhat surprising that professional[96] sporting bodies in Australia, such as the Australian Football League (AFL), National Rugby League (NRL) and Victorian Racing Club (VRC), to name a few, are income tax exempt.[97] Unlike many equivalent overseas sporting bodies, each of these entities operates as a 'not-for-profit' entity. Being not-for-profit should mean that the entity does not operate for the profit, personal gain or other benefit of members or other individuals. However, the AFL and NRL both make significant distributions to member clubs and players, and the VRC provides significant benefits to members in the form of hospitality.

Being income tax-exempt entities means that, like CBH and QSL, these sporting entities are entitled to a rebate in relation to fringe benefits provided to employees[98] so that they pay approximately half of the amount of FBT that most other entities are required to pay. However, as they are non-charitable, they are not entitled to franking credit rebates or State tax concessions.

Again, like the agricultural company cases, the income tax exemption for sporting clubs is a result of a specific exemption from income tax inserted into the ITAA 1936 in 1952.[99] An earlier proposal in 1922 to exempt cricket

---

94 Internal Revenue Code, 26 USC s 501(c)(5) (2006).

95 Ibid s 512.

96 The term 'professional' in this context is used to refer to sports where players receive remuneration for their performance, as opposed to 'amateur' sports, where they do not.

97 Each of these entities is incorporated as a company limited by guarantee under the Corporations Act 2001 (Cth). Even without incorporation, in the absence of an exemption, they would be taxed as companies under the ITAA 1997 (n 1).

98 FBTAA 1986 (n 3) s 65J(1), Item 11.

99 Income Tax and Social Services Contribution Assessment Act (No 3) 1952 (Cth).

associations was rejected by the Federal (Commonwealth) Parliament on the basis that sport 'was not important enough'. The Treasurer stated: '[W]e do not take the view that sporting associations are so essential, or require such encouragement in this country, that special provision must be made for their exemption under an Income Tax Assessment Bill.'[100]

One of the reservations expressed was that some of the players were paid, and so tax relief seemed inappropriate.[101] But in 1952, with the announcement that the next Olympic Games would be held in Melbourne, legislators were keen to talk up the importance of sport and to provide a specific exemption.[102]

Given the importance of sport in the Australian psyche, it is perhaps surprising to note that there was no federal recognition of sport until 1972, when a Minister was appointed for Tourism and Recreation,[103] and not until 1983 that a standalone Ministry for Sport was created.[104] It is also interesting to note that sport is currently within the Department of Health,[105] reflecting perhaps the perceived significance of sport to health and well-being, although the tax concession is not currently limited to sports that have such impacts.

The specific exemption for sporting and other bodies can be found in section 50-45 of the ITAA 1997. The corresponding provision in the ITAA 1936 originally provided an exemption for:

> the income of a society, association or club which is not carried on for the purposes of profit or gain to its individual members and is –
>
> …
>
> (iii) a society, association or club established for the encouragement or promotion of an *athletic game or athletic sport* in which *human beings are the sole participants*.[106]

The reference to human beings was removed in 1990[107] so that it now provides an exemption for entities established for the encouragement or promotion of any game or sport, provided it is not carried on for the purposes of profit or gain to its individual members.[108] The Explanatory Memorandum in 1990 did

---

100 Commonwealth, *Parliamentary Debates*, House of Representatives (10 October 1922) 3445 (Stanley Bruce, Treasurer).

101 Ibid.

102 Commonwealth, *Parliamentary Debates*, House of Representatives (24 September 1952) 2019 (Winton Turnbull).

103 Frank Stewart, Labor, 1972–75.

104 John Brown, Labor, 1983–87.

105 Albeit with a separate Minister – currently Anika Wells MP.

106 ITAA 1936 (n 34) s 23(g)(iii) (emphasis added).

107 Taxation Laws Amendment (No 2) Act 1990 (Cth).

108 ITAA 1997 (n 1) s 50-45.

not specify why the change was occurring, although this was presumably as a result of lobbying by those involved with sports that did not involve 'athletic sport', or games or sports involving animals rather than humans as the sole participants.

A significant number of non-charitable NFPs are sporting clubs or associations. Included in that category are the AFL, the NRL and the VRC. Although each of the sports represented has been played in Australia for a long time, they are very different from their forerunners in the 1950s. Perhaps the biggest change is that these entities now receive significant revenue from the sale of broadcast rights and gambling, and the playing and presentation of the sports occur in a very professional setting.

### 12.3.2 Professional Sporting Clubs – Examples

The revenue received by professional sporting clubs in Australia is very significant – each of the entities considered qualifies as a 'large business' according to the ATO definition, i.e., has combined turnover greater than AUD 250 million.[109] Moreover, much of the income comes from the sale of commercial broadcasting rights and from sponsorship from gambling companies – ticketing receipts now make up a very small proportion of revenue. In addition to the high salaries paid to administrators (discussed below), players in the various competitions also earn large amounts,[110] although this may reflect the fact that professional sportspersons have a limited period to earn such income, and the salaries are nowhere near what is paid in other jurisdictions.[111]

The AFL runs the competition for Australian Rules football comprising 18 teams across Australia. In 2019[112] the AFL reported revenue of AUD 793.9 million, including AUD 397 million from broadcasting and AUD 290 million from 'commercial operations' including memberships, ticketing and sponsorships.[113] It had an operating surplus of AUD 458.16 million,[114] suggesting that

---

109 ATO, 'Large Business' <https://www.ato.gov.au/business/large-business/>.

110 Australian Football League total player payment figures for 2021: Damian Barrett, 'Back in the Money: Who Are the AFL's Million-Dollar Men?' *AFL* (15 February 2022) <https://www.afl.com.au/news/704938/show-them-the-money-who-are-the-the-afls-million-dollar-men>.

111 Cristiano Ronaldo is reported to earn GBP 3.4 million per year playing for the Saudi team, Al-Nassr.

112 2019 figures have been used because of the impact of the pandemic on figures for 2020 and 2021.

113 Australian Football League, *2019 Annual Report* (2019).

114 Ibid.

it might have paid tax of approximately AUD 137 million if it were a taxable entity. In 2019, the AFL distributed AUD 314.7 million to the member clubs[115] and reported net assets of AUD 238.8 million.[116]

The NRL runs the competition for the Rugby League, comprising 17 teams. In 2019, the NRL had revenue of AUD 555.9 million, including AUD 324.6 million from broadcasting, game receipts of AUD 54.6 million, and sponsorship and wagering of AUD 84 million.[117] It had an operating surplus of AUD 257.1 million,[118] suggesting it might have paid tax of AUD 77 million if it were a taxable entity. In 2019, the NRL distributed AUD 228 million to member clubs and reported net assets of AUD 271.8 million.[119]

The VRC operates horse racing events at Flemington Racecourse, including the famous Melbourne Cup Carnival every November. In 2019 the VRC had revenue of AUD 204.8 million, including significant revenue from wagering, and a surplus of AUD 617,000.[120] It has net assets of AUD 366.7 million.[121] The VRC describes itself as 'recognised in Australia and around the world as a leader in racing and event entertainment'.[122] It should be noted that the VRC is the only professional sporting entity considered that does not pay its board of directors, except for the CEO.[123] The VRC has significant membership, and members are entitled to a number of benefits, with annual membership of the Chairman's Club costing AUD 45,900, entitling the holder to six seats at every race meeting.[124] The Melbourne Cup has been described as 'the race that stops the nation', although more recent commentary suggests that injuries to horses and the blight of problem gambling are eroding the popularity of the event.[125]

Two other features are worth noting. First, as noted, each of the entities mentioned receives significant income from gambling – each has an arrangement

---

115 Ibid.

116 Ibid.

117 National Rugby League, *Annual Report 2019* (2019).

118 Ibid.

119 Ibid.

120 Victoria Racing Club, *2019 Annual Report* (2019). The surplus in 2020 was AUD 5.7 million.

121 Ibid.

122 Victoria Racing Club, 'Our Vision and Values' <https://www.vrc.com.au/about-vrc/our-vision-and-values/>.

123 Victoria Racing Club, *2019 Annual Report* (n 120) 45.

124 Victoria Racing Club, 'The Chairman's Club Membership' <https://www.vrc.com.au/membership/become-a-member/the-chairman-s-club-membership/>.

125 Jonathan Horn, 'Melbourne Cup: The Race that … Warrants Some Uncomfortable Ethical Arithmetic' *The Guardian* (30 October 2021) <https://www.theguardian.com/sport/2021/oct/30/melbourne-cup-the-race-that-warrants-some-uncomfortable-ethical-arithmetic> accessed 26 June 2024.

with a particular betting company (Sportsbet and Tabcorp)[126] and gambling is promoted during the broadcasting of the games or activities. Much has been written about the social harm of gambling,[127] so it is surprising that it is readily accepted in these taxpayer-funded activities. Secondly, the executive officers of these entities receive significant salaries. In 2013 Andrew Demetriou was reported to have earned AUD 3.8 million.[128] The salary of his successor, Gillon McLachlan, was last disclosed in 2017 as AUD 1.73 million,[129] but is no longer disclosed in the AFL Annual Report.[130] The CEO of the NRL is reported as earning in excess of AUD 1.2 million per year.[131]

Most Australians would be appalled if the federal government made annual grants worth millions of dollars to these asset-rich entities every year, with no restrictions on how the money is spent, including on salaries and benefits for executives and the provision of lavish hubs for players and executives and their families during the pandemic. This can be contrasted with direct grants such as that announced by the Victorian government of AUD 225 million to upgrade Marvel Stadium, which is owned by the AFL, in 2018.[132] At least the Victorian government could claim that it secured the Grand Final to be played in Melbourne until 2047![133]

---

[126] AFL and NRL: Sportsbet; VRC: Tabcorp.

[127] See, for example, research by the Victorian Responsible Gambling Foundation: M Browne, N Greer, T Armstrong, C Doran, I Kinchin, E Langham and M Rockloff, *The Social Cost of Gambling to Victoria* (Research Report, November 2017) <https://responsiblegambling.vic.gov.au/resources/publications/the-social-cost-of-gambling-to-victoria-121/>.

[128] See Nathan Schmook, 'AFL CEO Andrew Demetriou Paid $3.8 Million in 2013' *AFL* (4 March 2014) <https://www.afl.com.au/news/108965/afl-ceo-andrew-demetriou-paid-38-million-in-2013> accessed 26 June 2024.

[129] Jake Niall, 'McLachlan's 11 Take 20 Per Cent Pay Cut' *The Age* (20 March 2020) <https://www.theage.com.au/sport/afl/mclachlan-s-11-take-20-per-cent-pay-cut-20200320-p54cf2.html> accessed 26 June 2024.

[130] See Will Glasgow and Christine Lacy, 'AFL Shifts the Goalposts on Pay Disclosure' *The Australian* (27 March 2018) 19.

[131] It has been reported that the CEO of NRL has a salary in excess of AUD 1.2 million: Brent Reid, 'Spotlight on NRL Executives as Salaries Cost Game Millions' *The Australian* (17 April 2020) 22.

[132] Hon Tim Pallas (Treasurer), *Victorian Budget 18/19: Getting Things Done, Budget Paper No 1, Treasurer's Speech* (2018) 11 <https://www.dtf.vic.gov.au/sites/default/files/2024-10/Treasurer%27s-Speech-2018-19_0.pdf>. See also Marvel Stadium press release (7 September 2023) <https://www.marvelstadium.com.au/stadium-redevelopment-about>.

[133] Austadiums, 'Victorian Government's $500M Cash Spash' (20 April 2018) <https://www.austadiums.com/news/599/victorian-governments-500m-cash

### 12.3.3 Taxation Ruling TR 2022/2

In September 2022, the ATO released TR 2022/2[134] which replaces TR 97/22 relating to the section 50-45 exemption for sports and games. The tenor of the ruling suggests that its focus is on the smaller end of town, or at least on individual clubs rather than the AFL etc. It confirms the wide meaning of the terms 'game or sport' which, in addition to sports such as netball and football, also extends to:

(i) non-athletic activities, such as chess or bridge,
(ii) activities where people use machines to participate, such as motor racing, and
(iii) non-competitive activities, such as mountaineering.[135]

On the other hand, the Commissioner's opinion is that activities such as stamp and coin collecting, bodybuilding and train modelling, keeping guinea pigs or fish, or participating in car owner clubs do not involve games or sports.[136]

### 12.3.4 Some Issues

One of the most difficult issues with the exemption is whether the entity is 'established for the encouragement or promotion of sports or games', that is, what is the purpose of the entity? The issue has arisen in the context of clubs providing social, gaming and entertainment facilities for members and visitors.[137] The Taxation Ruling provides a number of examples, but like the

---

-spash> accessed 26 June 2024.

[134] Australian Taxation Office, 'Income Tax: The Games and Sports Exemption', Taxation Ruling TR 2022/2 (14 September 2022) (TR 2022/2).

[135] Ibid [18].

[136] Ibid [23].

[137] Cases include *'The Waratahs' Rugby Union Football Club v Federal Commissioner of Taxation* (1979) 79 ATC 4337; *Cronulla Sutherland Leagues Club Ltd v Federal Commissioner of Taxation* (1990) 23 FCR 82; *North Suburban Club Inc v Federal Commissioner of Taxation* (1999) 99 ATC 2254; and *South Sydney Junior Rugby League Club Ltd v Federal Commissioner of Taxation* 2006 ATC 2150 where the exemption did not apply, and *Terranora Lakes Country Club Ltd v Federal Commissioner of Taxation* (1993) 93 ATC 4078 and *St Marys Rugby League Club Ltd v Federal Commissioner of Taxation* (1997) 97 ATC 4528 where it did.

decided cases, the question of whether the club has crossed the line so that its purpose is not encouragement of sport will be very fact specific.[138]

One issue that is not addressed is whether clubs, such as the professional clubs referred to above, are really about the encouragement of sport or about providing entertainment.

### 12.3.5 Sport as a Charitable Purpose

So far, the discussion has been about the specific exemption in section 50-45 of the ITAA 1997. It is perhaps worth noting at this stage that some entities that encourage or promote sport are registered as charities with the ACNC, although this is not because the promotion of sport is a charitable purpose. At common law, the promotion or encouragement of 'mere sport', that is, sport for competitive reasons or amusement, is not charitable.[139] Some commentators have expressed surprise at this position. For example, Ford and Lee note that cases have held that providing public sporting or recreational facilities can be charitable, so it is difficult to justify why the activity conducted within those facilities is not charitable.[140] It has also been noted by Dal Pont that the promotion of culture, including the arts, has been held to be charitable, so he questions why sport is not treated in the same way, particularly as Australians place great value on sport.[141] Perhaps the reluctance to include promotion of sport as a charitable purpose stems from a feeling, noted by the Charities Definition Inquiry, that 'the use of the word "charity" to apply to a sporting club appears semantically misconceived'.[142]

The Charities Definition Inquiry recommended a compromise position, namely that the encouragement of sport and recreation for purposes of amusement or competition was not a charitable purpose, but that the advancement of health, education, social and community welfare, religion, culture or the natural environment through the encouragement of sport and recreation should be considered a charitable purpose.[143] The Charities Act 2013 did not include sport as a charitable purpose, although it was noted in the consultation paper at the time that the United Kingdom had included 'the encouragement of amateur

---

138 TR 2022/2 (n 134) [30]–[104].

139 *Royal National Agricultural and Industrial Association v Chester* (1974) 48 ALJR 304, relying on *Re Nottage* [1895] 2 Ch 649.

140 WA Lee, Michael Bryan and John Glover, *Ford and Lee: The Law of Trusts* (Thomson Reuters 2016) [19.8090].

141 Dal Pont (n 32) [12.5]. See also Jennifer Batrouney and Angela Lee, 'Sports: Why Are They Not Charitable?' (2018) 92(4) Law Institute Journal 41.

142 Charities Definition Inquiry Report (n 30) 197.

143 Ibid recommendation 15.

or community sport that assists health' as a charitable purpose as well as creating a separate exemption for such entities.[144]

As noted above, some entities that encourage or promote sport are registered as charities.[145] The instances where this occurs are fairly limited and are likely to be where sport is related to the achievement of some other purpose, e.g., education or health-related purposes.[146] The desire to be seen as promoting health has increased since 2003, when a new category of charity was included in the tax legislation, a 'health promotion charity',[147] which importantly gives access to DGR status[148] and the FBT exemption.[149]

It can be argued that entities such as the AFL etc. are not in need of the support that might have been justified in the mid 1950s. They are wealthy and have significant income streams that are not being taxed. Moreover, there are issues about private benefit as well as social harms associated with gambling, and in the case of the VRC and similar 'sports', ill-treatment of animals. However, sport is an important part of Australian culture, and a compromise may be to adopt the approach of the United Kingdom, i.e., include promotion of amateur sport as a charitable purpose,[150] or limit the specific exemption in section 50-45 to community amateur sports clubs.[151] There are quite detailed guidelines in the UK dealing with what constitutes a 'community amateur sports club'.[152] In addition, it should be noted that the UK Charities Act defines

---

144 Australian Treasury, *A Definition of Charity, Consultation Paper* (October 2011).

145 An example of an entity that is registered as a charity is the Australian Sports Foundation Charitable Fund: ACNC, 'Australian Sports Foundation Charitable Fund' <https://www.acnc.gov.au/charity/charities/f72d97a0-3aaf-e811-a963-000d3ad244fd/profile> accessed 26 June 2024.

146 See for example *Lloyd v Federal Commissioner of Taxation* (1955) 93 CLR 645 and *Bicycle Victoria Inc v Federal Commissioner of Taxation* [2011] AATA 444, where it was held that the entity was not a health promotion charity but was a charity.

147 The term 'registered health promotion charity' is defined in s 995-1 of the ITAA 1997 (n 1) and requires the entity to be registered under the Australian Charities and Not-for-Profits Commission Act 2012 (Cth) with the subtype in s 25-5(5) Item 5, of an 'institution whose principal activity is to promote the prevention or the control of diseases in human beings'.

148 ITAA 1997 (n 1) s 30-20(1), Item 1.1.6.

149 FBTAA 1986 (n 3) s 57A(5).

150 Charities Act 2011 (UK) s 3(1)(g).

151 Corporations Tax Act 2010 (UK) s 662 and Community Amateur Sports Clubs Regulations 2015 (UK) SI 2015/725.

152 HM Revenue and Customs, 'Read the Community Amateur Sports Clubs: Detailed Guidance Notes' (Guidance, updated 17 March 2023) <https://www.gov

'sport' to mean 'sports or games which promote health by involving physical or mental skill or exertion'.[153]

## 12.4 SCHOOL BUILDING FUNDS

### 12.4.1 Introduction

The measure providing a tax deduction for gifts to school building funds (SBFs) was enacted in 1954,[154] at a time when the Commonwealth government was limited in its ability to make grants to non-government schools. The postwar period in Australia saw a rapid expansion in school enrolments, an expansion that State governments found increasingly difficult to resource adequately.[155] The predominant non-government sector was the Catholic sector, and these schools were suffering from overcrowding, inadequate buildings and shortages of properly trained teachers. The Commonwealth government faced two issues with extending funding. One was opposition to 'State aid' for non-government schools, in particular Catholic schools, on the basis that Church and State should be completely separate and that general taxpayer support for church schools was inappropriate.[156] A second issue was uncertainty over the legality of the Commonwealth being directly involved in education – education was not listed under section 51 of the Constitution, which sets out the legislative powers of the Commonwealth. This led the government to propose amendments to the Constitution; this resulted in a national referendum that allowed the Constitution to be amended to give the Commonwealth power to make laws 'with respect to the provision of benefits to students' in all States of Australia.[157]

This suggests that the SBF gift deduction may have been a way of providing indirect support to non-government schools when direct support was problematic. At around the same time, the Menzies government allowed a deduction

---

.uk/government/publications/community-amateur-sports-clubs-detailed-guidance-notes/community-amateur-sports-clubs-detailed-guidance-notes>.

153 Charities Act 2011 (UK) s 3(2)(d).

154 Income Tax and Social Services Contribution Assessment Act 1954 (Cth) s 8 introduced s 78(1)(a)(xv) into the ITAA 1936 (n 34). It is currently in ITAA 1997 (n 1) s 30-20, Item 2.1.10.

155 See Centre for Policy Development, *Uneven Playing Field: The State of Australia's Schools* (2016) <https://cpd.org.au/wp-content/uploads/2016/05/The-State-of-Australias-Schools.pdf>.

156 Greg McIntosh, 'State Aid for Non-Government Schools: The Emerging Debate' (Parliamentary Library Current Issues Brief No 2, 1996–97).

157 Ibid. See s 51(xxiiiA) of the Constitution.

for private school fees[158] – a position that was maintained until 1975 when it was replaced by a rebate[159] (worth about one-third of the value of the deduction), which was ultimately repealed in 1985.[160]

In the 1960s, various pressures were building up that led the Commonwealth, and then the States, to become directly involved with the funding and support of non-government schools. In 1962, a Catholic primary school in Goulburn was instructed by the State education department to install three additional toilets, which the parish insisted it could not afford. In response, the local Catholic diocese called on the government to pay for the works and then closed all local Catholic primary and secondary schools and sent the 600 children to the government schools. The 'strike' lasted only a week but was seen as a catalyst for the establishment of government funding to Catholic schools in Australia.[161] In 1964 direct Commonwealth funding for government and non-government schools began – the passage through the Commonwealth Parliament of the States Grants (Science Laboratories and Technical Training) Act 1964 enabled funding for science laboratories and equipment for secondary schools. A major change in Commonwealth policy also occurred in 1969 when the Commonwealth government introduced direct annual subsidies to private schools in the form of a recurrent grant per student.[162] The Commonwealth and State governments[163] continue to provide capital grants and targeted assistance to private schools.

The position now is that 'private', i.e., non-government, schools get recurrent and capital funding from the Commonwealth and State governments, but 'public', i.e., government, schools only get recurrent funding. On a per-student basis, it has been estimated that private schools received between two and four times more funding each year than public schools, or AUD 12,450 more

---

158 Income Tax and Social Services Contribution Assessment Act (No 3) 1952 (Cth) s 14 (introducing s 82J into the ITAA 1936 (n 34)). The deduction was initially capped at £50 but increased to AUD 400 in 1971.

159 Income Tax Assessment Act (No 2) 1975 (Cth) ss 17 and 13 respectively inserted s 159T into the ITAA 1936 (n 34) and s 82A, which provided a deduction for self-education expenses.

160 Taxation Laws Amendment Act (No 2) 1985 (Cth).

161 National Catholic Education Commission, 'Our Story' <https://ncec.catholic.edu.au/about-catholic-education/our-story/> accessed 26 June 2024.

162 Chris Ryan and Louise Watson, 'The Drift to Private Schools in Australia: Understanding its Features' (Australian National University Centre for Economic Policy Research Discussion Paper No 479, September 2004).

163 See, for example, the Victorian government Capital Grants Program for non-government schools: Victorian School Building Authority, 'Building Fund for Non-Government Schools – Independent' <https://www.schoolbuildings.vic.gov.au/building-fund-non-government-schools-independent> accessed 1 July 2024.

per student, over a ten-year period.[164] Economist Adam Rorris, who analysed capital funding in his report in 2021, *Investing in Schools, Funding the Future*, said the data showed '[i]nvestment in Australian schools has favoured private schools to an astonishing degree'.[165] He argued government funds for capital works would be better directed at under-resourced schools, presumably whether private or public.

This suggests that we have gone from the position in the 1950s, when many non-government schools needed assistance, to the current position where there is significant direct support for these schools from the national and subnational governments, as well as indirect support via the SBF gift deduction. It can be argued that, like the deduction for private school fees, this position is no longer justified.

### 12.4.2 The Position in Other Countries

The position in Australia is not unique. In the UK, a not-for-profit school can register as a charity and receive donations from parents. Provided the payment is not for services, i.e., fees, the donation will qualify for gift aid. There have been challenges to private schools as charities, on the basis that they provide private rather than public benefit,[166] but these have not resulted in any change to the status of such schools. There has been some discussion of private schools losing some tax privileges if a Labour government is elected in 2024.[167] In the US, non-profit schools are 'qualified organizations'[168] and so can receive tax-deductible donations. The deduction is only available to taxpayers who itemize donations rather than claiming the standard deduction.[169] The schools must

---

164 Ryan and Watson (n 162).

165 Adam Rorris, *Investing in Schools, Funding the Future* (April 2021) 5 <https://www.aeufederal.org.au/application/files/5716/2278/1619/AEU197_Investing_in_Schools_Report_v5_REV.pdf>.

166 *Independent Schools Council v Charity Commission for England and Wales* [2011] UKUT 421 (TCC).

167 Sally Weale, 'What Are Labour's Plans for Ending Tax Breaks for Private Schools?' *The Guardian* (29 May 2024) <https://www.theguardian.com/politics/article/2024/may/29/what-are-labours-plans-for-ending-tax-breaks-for-private-schools> accessed 26 June 2024.

168 Internal Revenue Code, 26 USC s 170(c) (2006).

169 Taxpayers who choose to itemize deductions must complete IRS Form 1040: Internal Revenue Service, 'About Schedule A (Form 1040), Itemized Deductions' (last reviewed or updated 26 February 2024) <https://www.irs.gov/forms-pubs/about-schedule-a-form-1040> accessed 26 June 2024.

provide a receipt stating that no goods or services were provided in respect of the donation.[170]

### 12.4.3 Some Concerns with the Australian Position

According to the ATO, there are currently 4,741 total active SBFs,[171] making this the second most common DGR category, and 80% are operated by non-government, often faith-based entities.[172] There are two objections that can be raised against the deduction. First, there are numerous examples of private schools using the funds to build lavish facilities rather than the basic infrastructure that was a concern in the 1950s. For example, according to a report by the Australian Broadcasting Corporation in 2019, 'Australia's four richest schools spent more on new facilities and renovations than the poorest 1,800 schools combined.'[173] The report revealed that in the decade to 2018, private schools outspent public schools on capital works by AUD 29.6 billion, which included hundreds of millions in government grants every year in addition to tax-deductible contributions. The report identified luxurious facilities of elite private schools: ultramodern science centres, libraries, auditoriums, theatres with orchestra pits, multiple sporting ovals, indoor Olympic-size swimming and diving pools, gymnasiums, tennis courts, wellness centres, equestrian centres, rowing tanks and boat sheds, and underground car parks.[174]

Secondly, there have been suggestions that the requirements of Division 30 of the ITAA 1997 relating to tax deductibility for gifts are not being complied with. A study of SBFs by the Australia Institute in 2004[175] suggested

---

170 Internal Revenue Service, *Charitable Contributions: Substantiation and Disclosure Requirements* (Rev 11-2023) <https://www.irs.gov/pub/irs-pdf/p1771.pdf>.

171 Australian Taxation Office, Taxation Statistics 2021–22 as at 1 July 2024. The total number of DGRs is 32,147.

172 Australian Taxation Office, 'Not for Profit Centre Key Messages' (Presentation, October 2021) (Presentation).

173 Inga Ting, Alex Palmer and Nathanael Scott, 'Rich School, Poor School: Australia's Great Education Divide' *ABC News* (13 August 2019, updated 24 April 2023) <https://www.abc.net.au/news/2019-08-13/rich-school-poor-school-australias-great-education-divide/11383384> accessed 26 June 2024.

174 See also Lucy Carroll, 'Sydney Private Schools Spend Millions on Land for New Campuses' *The Sydney Morning Herald* (4 March 2023) <https://www.smh.com.au/national/nsw/sydney-private-schools-spend-millions-on-land-for-new-campuses-20230224-p5cnin.html> accessed 26 June 2024.

175 Deb Wilkinson and Richard Denniss, 'Tax Deductibility of Donations to School Building Funds' (May 2004) <https://australiainstitute.org.au/wp-content/uploads/2020/12/apo-nid8750.pdf>.

that payments into some private (and public) school building funds may not meet the conditions required by the ATO. The ATO set out its views on SBFs in a Taxation Ruling in 2013,[176] and has recently expressed concern that SBFs, especially those endorsed before 2013, may not comply with the ATO interpretation of eligibility for DGR status.[177] However, the ATO will need to reconsider this Ruling given the recent decision on the meaning of a school. The decision of McKerracher J of the Federal Court in *The Buddhist Society of Western Australia Inc v Federal Commissioner of Taxation (No 2)*[178] takes a very broad view of what constitutes a 'school' and in that case said it included a meditation and yoga centre that was open to the public and did not offer any formal instruction. An examination of the history of the provision would appear to justify a narrower approach that limits the provision to primary and secondary schools – although this is clearly something that can be argued either way. The ATO did not seek to appeal the decision.

Returning to the 2004 study, the authors state that 'there is evidence to suggest donations to some private schools are not being given freely either because parents are unaware that the payment is voluntary or because they are pressured by the school to give. These pressures may include perceptions that their child may be disadvantaged if they fail to make a 'donation'.[179] The authors state that '[i]n addition, there is anecdotal evidence that some donors to SBFs receive a benefit from the gift, namely the enrolment of their children ahead of others on the waiting list. In these cases, claiming a tax deduction for a donation to a school building fund may not be legitimate'.[180] These are clearly issues relating to compliance that extend beyond the SBF provisions.

However, perhaps the more pressing issue is whether in 2024 the deduction is still justified or at least should be limited, either in dollar terms, or to schools (more narrowly defined than in the *Buddhist Society of Western Australia (No 2)* case) which are objectively judged as needy or disadvantaged. The difficulty will, of course, be formulating how notions of need or disadvantage might be spelt out.

---

[176] Australian Taxation Office, 'Income Tax: School or College Building Funds', Taxation Ruling TR 2013/2 (13 February 2013).

[177] Australian Taxation Office, Presentation (n 172).

[178] (2021) 113 ATR 798.

[179] Wilkinson and Denniss (n 175) 2.

[180] Ibid.

## 12.5 CONCLUSION – MAKING THE TAX REGIME FIT FOR PURPOSE

This chapter has considered a range of situations where particular tax concessions were granted to entities to achieve a specific purpose. It has been argued that over time either the nature of the entities receiving concessions has changed, or the concessions themselves can no longer be justified. One of the problems with the system of tax concessions is that once a concession is in place, it is rarely reviewed, and even if circumstances have changed dramatically, there appears to be little appetite to revisit the concession or issues of eligibility.

This chapter has argued that there are anomalies within the tax regime for charities and not-for-profits that should be addressed. This includes:

(i) removing the tax concessions available to large agricultural companies such as CBH and QSL;
(ii) restricting the tax concessions available to sporting clubs to community-based clubs that encourage participation; and
(iii) removing, or restricting, the gift deduction for gifts to SBFs that predominantly favour elite private schools.

There is also a need for wider reform in the area of taxation of charities and not-for-profits. This includes:

1. A simplification of the tax regime for charities and NFPs. If nothing else, a rewrite of the provisions, with a focus on whether many of the entities that are currently income tax exempt might not be 'charities' and consideration of whether other non-charitable entities are in fact providing public benefit, would improve the integrity of the regime.
2. Greater transparency for the 145,000 non-charitable NFPs that access tax concessions. It is good news that the ATO is embarking on a programme for annual self-assessment by these entities of their continuing entitlement to the concessions.[181] The first returns are due to be lodged by 31 March 2025. The disclosure requirements appear to be less onerous than the Annual Information Statement, and as the information is in a tax return, it will not be publicly available.[182]

---

[181] See n 27.

[182] See <https://www.ato.gov.au/businesses-and-organisations/not-for-profit-organisations/statements-and-returns/in-detail/reporting-requirements-to-self-assess-income-tax-exemption>.

3. Finally, harmonization of the definition of charity for the purposes of federal and State and Territory taxes. The continued reliance by subnational governments on the common law, and dismissal of the fact that entities might be charities under the federal Charities Act, have already resulted in some real anomalies.[183] The federal government should endeavour to negotiate with State and Territory governments to facilitate this harmonization.

It is also important to note that there has only been one dedicated review of the tax concessions available to charities and NFPs to date. The Not-for-Profit Sector Tax Concession Working Group was established in February 2012 by the then Assistant Treasurer, Senator the Hon Mark Arbib, although for most of the time the relevant Minister was the Hon David Bradbury.[184] The Terms of Reference asked the Working Group to consider 'whether there are fairer, simpler and more effective ways of delivering the current envelope of support provided through tax concessions to the NFP sector'.[185] The Working Group received more than 225 submissions and heard further submissions from stakeholders.[186] The final Report, containing 21 recommendations, was delivered to the Minister in May 2013, but the election in September of that year meant that none of the recommendations proceeded.

In 2018, the ATO Not-for-Profit Stewardship Group agreed to review the recommendations of the Working Group, describing the Report as 'a good example of collaborative work'.[187] Some recommendations were identified as being 'low-hanging fruit' that could be progressed.[188] They included:

(i) recommendation 2 — raise the AUD 416 tax-free threshold for NFP companies;
(ii) recommendation 9 — remove the AUD 2 minimum donation;

---

[183] See, for example, *Law Institute of Victoria v Commissioner of State Revenue* [2015] VSC 604 and other cases discussed in O'Connell, 'Is It Really a Charity?' (n 89); O'Connell, 'Stretching the Concept of Charity in the Tax Context' (n 89).

[184] The Hon David Bradbury was Assistant Treasurer from 5 March 2012 to 18 September 2013.

[185] Not-for-Profit Sector Tax Concession Working Group (n 9) ii.

[186] Ibid 3.

[187] Australian Taxation Office, 'Not-for-Profit Stewardship Group Minutes 25 July 2018' (18 December 2018): webpage no longer available, 16 March 2025.

[188] Australian Taxation Office, 'Not-for-Profit Stewardship Group Minutes 28 November 2018' (6 March 2019): webpage no longer available, 16 March 2025.

(iii) recommendation 14 — remove multiple caps for the FBT exemption and rebate (noting that medical professionals can be employed by several different employers and access multiple caps);
(iv) recommendation 18 — in relation to GST and fundraising — conflicting rulings need to be addressed.[189]

But several other recommendations of the Working Group are worth noting. One recommendation was to review and consolidate existing categories of entities for income tax-exempt status, with a view to limiting eligibility to entities that have purposes that are of *significant* public benefit.[190] A second recommendation was to raise and simplify the threshold for NFP entities that are taxable to AUD 10,000 (from the current bizarre AUD 416).[191] In fact, a move to allow a tax-free threshold (even at a much higher level) may be a good alternative to the ever-expanding number of income tax-exempt entities. A third recommendation was that DGR status should be extended to all registered charities, with some exceptions such as purely religious entities and schools.[192] It was also suggested that there should be a review of entities that are DGRs to determine whether they still merit DGR status, including those that are specifically listed as DGRs in Division 30 of the ITAA 1997.[193] It seems strange as a matter of principle that entities approved up to 50 years ago never have to satisfy anyone that the concession is still appropriate.[194] The Working Group also recommended replacing the FBT concessions for NFP entities (in relation to salary packaging arrangements) with an alternative support payment to eligible NFP employers.[195] Unfortunately, the consideration of the recommendations appears to have fallen off the agenda of the NFP Stewardship Group.

It is hoped that future governments will reconsider the recommendations of the Not-for-Profit Sector Tax Concession Working Group to ensure that the tax regime for charities and NFPs is fit for purpose, i.e., meeting its original objectives, and appropriate for the twenty-first century.

---

189 Ibid.

190 Not-for-Profit Sector Tax Concession Working Group (n 9) recommendation 1.

191 Ibid recommendation 2.

192 Ibid recommendation 6.

193 Ibid 26.

194 Although non-government DGRs, other than specifically named DGRs, are now required to register and report to the ACNC: Treasury Laws Amendment (2021 Measures No 2) Act 2021 (Cth).

195 Not-for-Profit Sector Tax Concession Working Group (n 9) recommendation 12.

## ACKNOWLEDGEMENTS

A version of this chapter was delivered as the John Emerson Oration 2021, 30 November 2021, on behalf of the Legal Practice Section's Charities and Not-for-Profit Committee of the Law Council of Australia. The author would also like to thank Professor Rick Krever for piquing her interest in the taxation of charities with his seminal chapter, 'Tax Deductions for Charitable Donations: A Tax Expenditure Analysis' in Richard Krever and Gretchen Kewley (eds), *Charities and Philanthropic Institutions: Reforming the Tax Subsidy and Regulatory Regimes* (Australian Tax Research Foundation 1991).

# 13. Energy and taxation

**Marco Greggi**

## 13.1 INTRODUCTION

Climate change and the present war in Ukraine are unrelated events, but they bring energy consumption, production and pricing under the spotlight in Europe and worldwide.

The necessity to tackle pollution and climate change and rethink lifestyles and production systems in developed countries has been apparent since the 1970s.[1] However, only a decade ago, it became a top priority in the policy agendas of several states, as some developing countries (most notably the BRICS members) increased the size of their industrial sectors, and consequently, the emission of polluting greenhouse gases.[2]

At the present time, economists are describing a 'perfect storm' scenario, where the scarcity of natural resources is coupled with an unprecedented level of greenhouse gas emissions and an increase in the global temperature never recorded before.[3]

The situation had already reached a tipping point and then the war in Ukraine erupted, leading to a struggle to replace the gas imported (to Europe) from Russia with something else.

---

1 The most important step in this direction was arguably the United Nations Conference on the Human Environment (Stockholm Conference) of 1972 where the United Nations Environment Programme (UNEP) was launched. Maria Ivanova, 'Designing the United Nations Environment Programme: A Story of Compromise and Confrontation' (2007) 7(4) International Environmental Agreements: Politics, Law and Economics 337.

2 Rafael Leal-Arcas, 'The BRICS and Climate Change' (2013) 4(1) International Affairs Forum 22.

3 Shaikh MSU Eskander and Sam Fankhauser, 'Reduction in Greenhouse Gas Emissions from National Climate Legislation' (2020) 10 Nature Climate Change 750.

The conflict brought about a surge of inflation that hit households, industries and eventually the financial sector, making the green transition more expensive, as was observed by the European Union (EU), which in 2022 tabled a set of proposals for a sustainable phasing-out of gas in favour of electricity.[4] The European strategy was to stop using polluting energy production facilities to minimize carbon emissions in the long run. This is the so-called 'Fit for 55' project,[5] whose ambitious goal is to reduce EU emissions by at least 55% by 2030 and to make the EU climate-neutral by 2050.

Then the war in the east erupted, and the EU had to redesign a policy conceived years ago and supposedly meant to be enacted in a medium- and long-term scenario. The model was revised, changes were accelerated, and new strategic decisions were adopted to strike a balance between the need to stimulate the green revolution while also preserving household purchasing power.

To achieve this result, several options were suggested, and the EU acted consistently with the guidelines provided by international stakeholders in the matter and with the steps taken by supranational organizations, such as during the Kyoto negotiations and the subsequent treaty.[6]

Taxation is pivotal among the various tools and means deployed to address the crisis. It may grant incentives to the companies that 'go green' and can make production more expensive using the traditional (depletable and not climate-neutral) energy sources.[7] However, while the second goal could be achieved via traditional tools such as increasing excise duties or value-added tax (VAT) where necessary, the first demands a more innovative approach. The

---

[4] See the REPowerEU Plan of the European Commission: Communication from the Commission to the European Parliament, the European Council, the Council, the European Economic and Social Committee and the Committee of the Regions, 'REPowerEU Plan', COM(2022) 230 final, 18 May 2022.

[5] European Commission, Communication to the European Parliament, the Council, the European Economic and Social Committee and the Committee of the Regions, 'Fit for 55': delivering the EU's 2030 Climate Target on the way to climate neutrality, COM/2021/550 final, 14 July 2021.

[6] Christoph Böhringer, 'The Kyoto Protocol: A Review and Perspectives' (2003) 19(3) Oxford Review of Economic Policy 451.

[7] Carsten Daugbjerg and Gert Tinggaard Svendsen, *Green Taxation in Question: Politics and Economic Efficiency in Environmental Regulation* (Springer 2001); Ana Carrera Poncela, 'Environmental Taxes in OECD Countries: Recent Developments' (2008) 36(12) Intertax 554; Cristina E Ciocirlan and Bruce Yandle, 'The Political Economy of Green Taxation in OECD Countries' (2003) 15(3) European Journal of Law and Economics 203; Giuseppe Melis and Federica Pitrone, 'Coordinating Tax Strategies at the EU Level as a Solution to the Economic and Financial Crisis' (2011) 39(8/9) Intertax 374.

urgent need for such an unprecedented and original strategy led the Union to introduce emission certificates.

The creation of emission certificates and a platform on which to negotiate them (Emissions Trading System, ETS from now on) is arguably one of the most original ideas ever conceived in the matter, both from a juridical and conceptual point of view, in the European continent at least.[8]

The European ETS system was launched in 2005, and it comprises four different phases for its full implementation (at the time of writing, phase 4 has been rolled out). Directive 2003/87/EC is the juridical basis for its implementation; it was passed on 13 October 2003, and it has been amended and updated over the years.[9] The ETS system is also relevant to European Economic Area (EEA) countries (such as Iceland, Liechtenstein and Norway).

According to this legal framework, certificates are attributed to businesses engaged in environmentally friendly production systems. The intensive use of renewable resources allows them to trade (sell) excess certificates to other companies which cannot (or do not wish to) abide by such green conditions. With the purchase of a certificate, the latter businesses are entitled to use traditional energy sources: the higher the carbon emissions by the undertaking, the higher the number of certificates that need to be owned to compensate for

---

[8] Before this, Ronald Coase (RH Coase, 'The Problem of Social Cost' (1960) 3 Journal of Law and Economics 1) suggested implementing the ETS system to address negative externalities. Coase's studies on the possibility of using (in the US) the ETS to compensate for the social costs of acid rain were the basis of the 1990 amendments to the Clean Air Act (42 USC ch 85 (ss 7401–7671q)). Timothy Laing, Misato Sato, Michael Grubb and Claudia Comberti, 'The Effects and Side-Effects of the EU Emissions Trading Scheme' (2014) 5(4) Wiley Interdisciplinary Reviews: Climate Change 509; Denny Ellerman, 'The EU Emission Trading Scheme: A Prototype Global System?' in Joseph E Aldy and Robert N Stavins (eds), *Post-Kyoto International Climate Policy: Implementing Architectures for Agreement, Research from the Harvard Project on International Climate Agreements* (Cambridge University Press 2010).

[9] European Parliament and Council of the European Union, Directive 2003/87/EC of 13 October 2003 establishing a scheme for greenhouse gas emission allowance trading within the Community and amending Council Directive 96/61/EC [2003] OJ L 275/32 (Directive 2003/87/EC). The latest update has been introduced via European Parliament and Council of the European Union, Directive (EU) 2023/959 of 10 May 2023 amending Directive 2003/87/EC establishing a system for greenhouse gas emission allowance trading within the Union and Decision (EU) 2015/1814 concerning the establishment and operation of a market stability reserve for the Union greenhouse gas emission trading system [2023] OJ L 130/134.

it. The price paid to the environmentally friendly business would be viewed as consideration for the extra costs such a business incurred.

In other words, the more a business invests in a sustainable production system, the more certificates it has (or saves) that can be sold to other, less-efficient companies, thus allowing them to operate traditionally. Earnings from the sale (or trade) of certificates would help compensate for the costs of the green transition by the companies that decided to take a step in that direction.

The (green allowance) certificates, as such, do not represent a 'right to pollute', as this would be against the spirit of the Directives regulating them. Instead, they are an assessment of a common good, the environment, and the impacts of the economic activity in each case: they are an attempt to price (under market conditions) the use of it.[10] With them, the idea of 'scarcity' has been introduced in a scenario where the unlimited tolerability of pollution was taken for granted for decades.

The certificates create a sort of *itemization* of the environment and securitization of the outdoors, intended as a common good, the usage of which is quantified and, therefore, priced.

Introducing such new legal instruments poses several fiscal issues never addressed before, as they can be created, assigned and circulated (sold, bought and traded). They are *fictio iuris*, but they virtually give rise to actual revenue

---

[10] The difference between common goods and public goods is clear in the literature. It has been addressed by supranational organizations such as UNESCO, as Tian and Liu note:

> UNESCO states that 'irrespective of any public or private origin', common goods 'are characterised by a binding destination and necessary for the realisation of the fundamental rights of all people'. It notes that 'goods of this kind are therefore inherently common in their "production" as well as in their benefits' and 'inherent to the relationships that exist among the members of a society tied together in a collective endeavor'. … This approach to common goods steps away from the long-disputed topic of public or private. Further, the notion of common goods may complement that of public goods. A public good is open to free-riding, whereas a common good highlights the collective endeavour of all participants.

Lin Tian and Nian Cai Liu, 'Higher Education in China: Rethinking It as a Public Good' in Claire Callender, William Locke and Simon Marginson (eds), *Changing Higher Education for a Changing World* (Bloomsbury Academic 2020) 239, citing UNESCO, *Rethinking Education: Towards a Global Common Good?* (UNESCO 2015) 77–8 (footnotes omitted).

for the seller, and with that, the necessity to understand whether their trade falls within the scope of VAT.[11]

Another significant point is the possibility for a business to create certificates beyond the thresholds set by the legislation and international agreements. Although, as a matter of principle, the number of certificates is limited and decided in advance by the states[12] according to their goal (namely to quantify and assess the use of a common good), another scenario might be considered.

In other words, what if a business positively impacts the environment, as the production system is intended to decrease the amount of gas emissions that can be tolerated? Logic would say that, in this case, the incorporation of certificates would be a necessity for pure symmetry. Recently, some countries have explored this possibility.[13]

This chapter is divided into three parts in an attempt to provide answers to these questions.

Section 13.2 will address the function of pollution certificates under the Kyoto agreement and the relevant policy guidelines developed by the international community. It will adopt the theory of common goods as a sort of *tertium genus* (third type) in the otherwise binary distinction between 'public' and 'private' goods, following in this pattern prominent academics, such as Stefano Rodotà.[14]

In sections 13.3 to 13.6, specific emphasis will be given to taxation of the certificates and their trade, with a particular focus on VAT, as this is the tax for which EU competence is stronger in regulation and policymaking than for income tax.

In section 13.7, the chapter will move back to policy aspects, taking into account the legal framework that emerged in the previous analysis, and considering the possibility of conceiving a business whose goal is to create certificates generating a positive impact on the environment (for instance, developing

---

11 Claudia Dias Soares, 'Energy Tax Treatment of Undertakings Covered by Emissions Trading' (2007) 16(4) EC Tax Review 184.

12 The European Union has its own certificate system, which is arguably the largest and most efficient in the world currently. Yet the certificates are so far non-negotiable outside the respective national (or regional, in the case of Europe) jurisdictions. In other words, it is not possible for a European business to purchase a Chinese certificate to compensate for its greenhouse gas emissions. As the emission occurs in Europe, the certificate must be European.

13 'Carbon Capture and Storage: Revenue Transparency Required' *Financial Times* (31 July 2023) <https://www.ft.com/content/dac34f85-0422-4d94-b35b-01582949c8f8> accessed 31 July 2023.

14 Stefano Rodotà, *Il terribile diritto. Studi sulla proprietà privata e i beni comuni* (Il Mulino 2013).

a technology capable of capturing greenhouse gases). Such a possibility would affect the certificate pricing and the traditional way of doing business, eventually allowing the persistence of the old production model to be coupled with technologies with a positive impact.

In section 13.8, the conclusion is set out that where having a (close to) zero-emission scenario would be too expensive, offsetting positive emissions with negative might prove cheaper and, if assisted with a proper tax regime, would make the green transition softer and more financially sustainable.

## 13.2 ENVIRONMENT AS A COMMON GOOD: THE THEORETICAL FOUNDATIONS OF ENERGY USE (AND POLLUTION)

For years, the environment was not legally recognized as a separate, independent good from those components forming it, either in Europe or third countries, from a legal point of view.[15] However, economists were already aware of the issue.[16]

Different legal systems provided for the protection of natural water, air quality and regulated waste disposal, yet without a comprehensive understanding of the environment. More to the point, the environment was not deemed a permanent asset, even in a philosophical or theoretical way, different from the components forming it (water, air, land, etc.). The need to preserve it or curb polluting technologies has, in recent times, found a way to achieve this objective in various legislative enactments. However, this always occurred according to specific situations and on a case-by-case basis.

It is evident that, in this respect, tax-related comprehensive policies were rarely enacted as they would lack one essential element: the asset intended to be protected (or assessed in the calculation of the tax due). In other words, it is difficult to have a common approach to green transition (or green taxation) if countries have a different idea of what the 'environment' is and how strong or broad its protection should be. Without a clear understanding of the extent and the meaning of the 'environment', it is hard to conceive a policy on the matter.

---

[15] David R Boyd, 'The Implicit Constitutional Right to Live in a Healthy Environment' (2011) 20(2) Review of European Community and International Environmental Law 171; Tim Hayward, 'Constitutional Environmental Rights: A Case for Political Analysis' (2000) 48(3) Political Studies 558; Lynda Collins, *The Ecological Constitution: Reframing Environmental Law* (Routledge 2021); Daniel Bodansky, 'Is There an International Environmental Constitution?' (2009) 16(2) Indiana Journal of Global Legal Studies 565.

[16] Coase (n 8) 19.

The environment cannot be owned or produced;[17] it is only possible for individuals to own or possess items that are part of it or to carry on activities that impact part of it. The same applies to energy, if we intend the meaning of this concept in scientific terms.

*Sensu stricto*, energy is a feature every entity has or might have. More precisely, there is a formulary equivalence between mass and energy that Albert Einstein discovered several decades ago;[18] consequently, 'taxation of energy', just like 'environmental taxation', is a concept deprived of any actual meaning unless more details are given to clarify what kind of energy would be considered.

The everyday scenario presents a different understanding of the situation.

We cannot tax energy as such, but we may consider sources of energy used for the production of it and we can assess how such activity might have an external impact on the environment and eventually calculate it in some way.

In the past, steps were taken to stimulate the use of more environmentally friendly energy sources, such as natural gas, and possibly incentivize renewables. However, this occurred without a proper and coherent agenda, as one element of the equation was missing: scarcity.

The environment was not considered scarce (or a scarce resource), and conversely, it was harder to qualify it as a good under the law.

The consideration of the environment as a good deserving protection is a recent achievement of most of the constitutions around the world. For instance, the Italian Charter introduced the environment as an asset deserving protection

---

[17] The environment/nature can be considered, just as the *Kosmos* (World Order) was by the ancient philosopher Heraclitus, 'the same of all, no God nor man did create, but it ever was and is and will be' (DK22B30 in the *Diels–Kranz List* of pre-Socratic sources: Hermann Diels and Walther Kranz, *Die Fragmente der Vorsokratiker* (Weidmann 1985), translated in Kathleen Freeman, *Ancilla to the Pre-Socratic Philosophers: A Complete Translation of the Fragments in Diels, Fragmente der Vorsokratiker* (Harvard University Press 1983)). See, however, Coase (n 8) on negative externalities and the impact on general well-being.

[18] Albert Einstein, 'Elementary Derivation of the Equivalence of Mass and Energy' (1935) 41(4) Bulletin of the American Mathematical Society 223.

only in 2023.[19] Until that year, it was safeguarded only via a purposive jurisprudence of the Italian Constitutional Court.[20]

From a logical standpoint, the possibility of considering the environment as an independent *good* anticipates and precedes any tax reasoning on that issue. This is also true for energy originating from it, either as fossil fuel or from renewable sources.

Only in recent years has the idea of scarcity (as applied to the capacity of the environment to absorb pollution) emerged, and with that, the necessity to hold accountable those who have been making the most of the natural resources by either extracting raw materials or introducing waste.

Philosophers and civil lawyers[21] found it difficult to configure the environment as an individual good different from those things composing it (air, seas, rivers, etc.). Moreover, even if it is possible to understand the environment as a 'new property', it is hard to decide to whom it belongs: a forest may belong to an individual (or a group of persons), but the environment as a whole may not.

In several legal systems, goods can be either privately owned or belong to the public: they are the state's asset or that of another public body. In either case, the notion of property is used in some way, as a *ius excludendi alios* (the possibility under the law to enjoy an asset exclusively).

The environment is not a private good (although privately owned goods may form part of it), and for the same reasons, it is not public in the proper sense of the word, as it does not belong to the state; it is impossible to exclude anybody from it. It is not owned by an entity representing the collectivity of individuals residing in a place or being part of it (such as the state).

---

[19] Article 9 of the Italian Constitution reads as follows: 'The Republic promotes the development of culture and scientific/technical research, protects the environment, biodiversity and ecosystems, in the interest of future generations also; the laws of the State will regulate the forms of protection of animals.' See also Prisco Piscitelli and others, 'Italian Constitution Amended to Include Environmental and Health Protection: A Model for Europe' (2022) 16 The Lancet Regional Health – Europe 100367.

[20] See for instance the judgment of the Italian Constitutional Court (Corte Costituzionale) 23 May 2019, no 179 ECLI:IT:COST:2019:179.

[21] Philippe Sands and Jacqueline Peel with Adriana Fabra and Ruth MacKenzie, *Principles of International Environmental Law* (3rd edn, Cambridge University Press 2012); Christopher L Bell and others, *Environmental Law Handbook* (21st edn, Government Institutes 2011); Dinah Shelton, *International Environmental Law* (3rd edn, Brill 2021); Mark Sagoff, *The Economy of the Earth: Philosophy, Law, and the Environment* (2nd edn, Cambridge University Press 2007); Bruce V Foltz and Robert Frodeman (eds), *Rethinking Nature: Essays in Environmental Philosophy* (Indiana University Press 2004).

Prominent theorists and academics introduced the notion of 'collective goods'[22] to address this loophole in various legal systems. A good is deemed to be 'collective' when it does not belong to anyone (not even to the state) but to the collectivity as such, which is entitled, under the law, to its management and protection.

The same collectivity deserves compensation in case of damage to the good as such (but the actual entitlement to associations and stakeholders to be eligible for reimbursement is in practice decided on a case-by-case basis).

The idea of 'collective goods' is a paradox in most continental systems, as it severs the traditional connection between ownership of a good and exclusive (or limited, *ius excludendi alios*) usage. Once we accept that a good is collectively owned, we implicitly admit that such an asset exists and can be quantified. Consequently, the idea of scarcity represented by the certificates traded under the ETS mechanism can find its place in the legal system.

Taxation aspects are not yet considered, as the collective nature of the goods renders it impossible to identify the taxpayer obliged to make the payment. No taxpayer is held accountable for the ownership of a collective good.

This situation should not be confused with *royalties* due to the state or taxes to be paid for using natural resources, which are typically charged to companies exploiting them. In such a scenario, collective goods are not considered; public goods are instead. These latter are legally owned by the state, which has the power to license them and derive the revenue in return either as consideration in a contract framework or via a tax introduced by law.[23]

The ETS mechanism and all the certificates negotiated therein can apportion the use of the common good (the environment) and itemize its usage in the interest of the collectivity.[24]

---

[22] See the bibliography in Edwin Amenta and Michael P Young, 'Making an Impact: Conceptual and Methodological Implications of the Collective Goods Criterion' in Marco Giugni, Doug McAdam and Charles Tilly (eds), *How Social Movements Matter* (University of Minnesota Press 1999).

[23] Robin Boadway and Frank Flatters, 'The Taxation of Natural Resources: Principles and Policy Issues' in Anwar Shah (ed), *Taxing Choices for Managing Natural Resources, the Environment, and Global Climate Change: Fiscal Systems Reform Perspectives* (Palgrave Macmillan 2023); Terry Heaps and John F Helliwell, 'The Taxation of Natural Resources' in Alan J Auerbach and Martin Feldstein (eds), *Handbook of Public Economics, Vol 1* (North-Holland 1985).

[24] Finn Roar Aune, Hanne Marit Dalen and Cathrine Hagem, 'Implementing the EU Renewable Target through Green Certificate Markets' (2012) 34(4) Energy Economics 992; Aviel Verbruggen and Erik Laes, 'Early European Experience with Tradable Green Certificates Neglected by EU ETS Architects' (2021) 119 Environmental Science and Policy 66.

Green certificates are not a fee to be paid to the state (this issue will be addressed further below) but are rather a way to apportion and calculate the usage of scarce resources. From an academic point of view, they are compulsory payments made by polluting businesses to carry out their activity. More precisely, businesses must obtain certificates if their pollution exceeds specific amounts. On the contrary, virtuous behaviour (that is, a level of pollution below the expected level) might become a source of profits for undertakings meeting these conditions. The latter might sell to others (those not so virtuous) the difference between the pollution expected and the level that occurred in practice, eventually monetizing their virtuous business model.

To summarize, the certificates introduce the scarcity of common goods or, more precisely, a way to calculate such scarcity. Once a common good becomes scarce, it is logically (and legally) possible to trade in and negotiate for it: as an ultimate consequence, tax issues arise, too.

## 13.3 CERTIFICATION OF SCARCITY AND THE TAX CONUNDRUM

As they are currently understood, green certificates were born with the Kyoto Protocol. The European scenario is perhaps the most successful example in which this environmental protection strategy has been implemented.

The Protocol was adopted on 11 December 1997, at the third session of the Conference of the Parties (COP 3) to the United Nations Framework Convention on Climate Change (UNFCCC)[25] in Kyoto, Japan.

Its primary objective[26] is to reduce greenhouse gas emissions that contribute to climate change, and it tries to achieve this goal by setting legally binding emission reduction targets for developed countries.

Under the Protocol, developed countries agreed to reduce their greenhouse gas emissions by an average of 5.2% below 1990 levels by 2012. The

---

[25] United Nations Framework Convention on Climate Change, concluded 9 May 1992, 1771 UNTS 107 (entered into force 21 March 1994) (UNFCCC); Kyoto Protocol to the United Nations Framework Convention on Climate Change, signed 11 December 1997, 2303 UNTS 162 (entered into force 16 February 2005) (Kyoto Protocol).

[26] Jonathan Kuyper, Heike Schroeder and Björn-Ola Linnér, 'The Evolution of the UNFCCC' (2018) 43 Annual Review of Environment and Resources 343; E Lisa F Schipper, 'Conceptual History of Adaptation in the UNFCCC Process' (2006) 15(1) Review of European Community and International Environmental Law 82; Lukas Hermwille, Wolfgang Obergassel, Hermann E Ott and Christiane Beuermann, 'UNFCCC Before and After Paris – What's Necessary for an Effective Climate Regime?' (2017) 17(2) Climate Policy 150.

Protocol also established flexible mechanisms such as the Clean Development Mechanism (CDM),[27] Joint Implementation (JI), and International Emissions Trading (IET),[28] which allow countries to meet their targets cost-effectively.

The Protocol is legally binding on the countries that have ratified it, meaning they must take the necessary steps to meet their emission reduction targets. As of September 2021, 192 countries have ratified the Protocol, including the European Union, Japan and Canada. The United States signed the Protocol but did not ratify it and formally withdrew from it in 2020.

The legal basis for emission certificates under the Kyoto Protocol can be found in Articles 5, 6, 12 and 17.

Article 5 establishes the flexibility mechanisms of the Protocol, which include the Clean Development Mechanism (CDM), Joint Implementation (JI), and International Emissions Trading (IET). These procedures allow countries with emission reduction targets to achieve their targets cost-effectively by investing in emission reduction projects in other countries or trading emissions credits. Article 6 outlines the rules for the Clean Development Mechanism, which is a project-based mechanism that allows developed countries to invest in emission reduction projects in developing countries and receive certified emission reductions (CERs) for the emissions reductions achieved.

Article 12 sets out the rules for Joint Implementation, which is a mechanism that allows developed countries to invest in emission reduction projects in other developed countries and receive emission reduction units (ERUs) for the emissions reductions achieved. Article 17 then establishes the rules for International Emissions Trading, which allows countries to trade emissions allowances among themselves to meet their emission reduction targets.

Other legal instruments, including the Paris Agreement and the EU ETS, regulate emission certificates in addition to the Kyoto Protocol, upon which this analysis is based.

The Paris Agreement, adopted in 2015, is a follow-up to the Kyoto Protocol and sets out a more ambitious target of limiting global warming to well below

27 Martin Cames and others, *How Additional Is the Clean Development Mechanism? Analysis of the Application of Current Tools and Proposed Alternatives* (Study prepared for DG Clima, CLIMA.B.3/SER12013/0026r, Öko-Institut, 2016).

28 Edwin Woerdman, 'Implementing the Kyoto Protocol: Why JI and CDM Show More Promise than International Emissions Trading' (2000) 28(1) Energy Policy 29.

2°C above pre-industrial levels.[29] The EU ETS is the world's largest ETS and operates within the framework of the EU's climate and energy policy.[30]

From a legal standpoint, a certificate might represent the possibility of introducing a specific amount of greenhouse gases into the environment or, more appropriately, using a part of the common good. The certificate is a licence: permission to produce greenhouse gases and, consequently, to contribute to an increase in the global temperature.

It could be argued that, via the certificates, the international community is trying to measure the use of the common good, implicitly admitting its limited nature, as was observed above.

The decision to limit such a possibility creates value (from a legally induced scarcity) and wealth. Each certificate has a value that can be issued, traded and used.

Value creation is not derived from the free decisions of individuals or from an existing underlying asset that is privately owned, such as in the case of cryptocurrencies or other financial instruments. In the latter case, value creation is purely fictitious as it comes from fluctuations of the speculative market once an investor has poured real, fiat currency into the cryptocurrency system. More to the point, cryptocurrencies have a negative value, as their mining and maintenance demand calculation power and hence waste energy.

In the case of certificates, the value derives from the apportionment of a common good, which is measurable in terms of well-being and health; consequently, their value is effective as long as the underlying asset, although a common good, exists and has an economic value per se.

To some extent, creating a certificate would show similar aspects to copyright or industrial properties. They did not exist in traditional Roman law; they were invented later via a state decision limiting the possibility of replicating writing, attributing it only to the author and the publisher. When this occurred, the law of the state created an asset that did not exist before.[31]

However, a difference exists: while in the case of intellectual property, value is created from zero (as it derives from human genius) and is then made scarce (prohibition of replicating it without permission), in the case of certificates, the scarcity is intrinsic (as unsustainable growth would eventually lead to the

---

29 Paris Agreement to the United Nations Framework Convention on Climate Change, adopted 12 December 2015, 3156 UNTS 79 (entered into force 4 November 2016).

30 Frank J Convery, 'Origins and Development of the EU ETS' (2009) 43(3) Environmental and Resource Economics 391.

31 See for instance, Marco Greggi, 'European Taxation of Dividends, Interests and Royalties: The Impact on Third Countries Investors' (2009) 3 Verslo ir Teisės Aktualijos 118.

extinction of human beings and animals) while the authority's intervention is limited to its apportionment.

The creation of wealth entails consequences from a fiscal standpoint, as certificates may be negotiated and traded before they are used to allow greenhouse gas emissions.

Eventually, from a logical perspective, it should also be possible to create wealth by individuals or businesses if the activity they carry on has a positive aspect on the environment (absorption of greenhouse gases); should the possibility be allowed by the legislator, any activity with a positive externality on the environment would become an enterprise as it would create (taxable) wealth.[32]

## 13.4 MAKING SENSE OF (TAXING) GREEN CERTIFICATES

The law-induced scarcity of a good is not born with the certificates.

The European Union and many Organisation for Economic Co-operation and Development (OECD) countries have followed this pattern in several sectors, including the right to develop[33] land (the dimension of new buildings must be negotiated with the relevant local authority in many legal systems to limit urban development to a sustainable level). Another example is the milk quotas that were used once in the EU to limit the production of dairy products by farmers, thus keeping prices higher.[34] A similar conclusion could also be reached regarding planting authorizations, which have been used in the EU to limit the development of vineyards.

All these limitations brought about two consequences: the creation of value, which reverberates in a higher price of products that would otherwise be lower if the quota system were not in force (the cost of milk per litre was much higher than it would have been without such limitations), and the creation of an asset (the permission to milk, to build, to plant) that circulates independently from the business it is connected to.

As a matter of fact (and under law), certificates can be traded and sold with an intrinsic value. For example, in the case of the right to build, which relates to the land that will be developed, such a right can be sold independently from

---

[32] See n 11 above.

[33] Marianna Rinaldo, 'Gli strumenti di micropianificazione urbanistica negoziale e la loro natura. Il genus eterogeneo dei diritti edificatori e la species primigenia della cessione di cubatura' (2021) 6 Rivista del Notariato 1113.

[34] Vincent Réquillart, Zohra Bouamra-Mechemache and Roel Jongeneel, 'Economic Analysis of the Effects of the Expiry of the EU Milk Quota System' (Institut d'Economie Industrielle, 2008).

the land suitable for cultivation. In the case of milk quotas, they could have been pooled by producers or sold by those going out of business in favour of other, more profitable investments or business activities.

The independent circulation of the certificates raises questions concerning the possible taxes to be applied, both in Europe and beyond (the green certificates negotiated under the ETS will be addressed in this discussion, but the same reasoning might be applied in all the other similar scenarios depicted above).

The first question is whether the trade of certificates, and possibly their production, might be considered a business activity, and if yes, what would be the tax to be applied. An affirmative answer seems plausible as the law-induced scarcity of an asset determines its value (it is a value creation phenomenon), and henceforth, certificates are valuable assets under European law whose trade might generate (taxable) profits under the rules applicable generally to any other kind of business.

The place of taxation is also relevant, considering that different legal systems might introduce different sorts of certificates that may not be entirely exchangeable with one another as their regulation depends on domestic – or European – law adopted in the Kyoto Protocol framework and the Paris Agreement.

The second question concerns VAT: where and if applicable. Even in this case, the affirmative answer seems the most appropriate, and the case law of the Court of Justice of the European Union (CJEU) has confirmed it.[35]

In this respect, the trade of a certificate is considered a service under European VAT law. Therefore, it should be taxed in the country where the purchaser is resident, if it is a business, as in all other current cases.

Another interesting point to be considered under VAT is the connection between the certificate and the underlying asset (the greenhouse gas emission *quotas*). Gases (if they produce energy[36]) are qualified goods under VAT, but this is not the case for greenhouse gases which, with the current level of scientific research, do not produce energy. However, the trade of a certificate is not necessarily a trade of the underlying asset: more specifically, the certificate is not necessarily a financial instrument representing the underlying asset, as it usually occurs in the stock market, where shares or bonds represent part of the equity capital or the loan granted to a company.

---

[35] See n 43 below.

[36] Council of the European Union, Directive 2006/112/EC of 28 November 2006 on the common system of value added tax [2006] OJ L 347/1, Art 14 (Directive 2006/112/EC). The reference to the 'production of energy' is not clearly stated in the letter of the law in that Article, though.

Nevertheless, the qualification of the certificate as a quasi-financial instrument would determine the consequences of the possible application of the exemption regime introduced by the EU Directive on VAT for equivalent certificates.

In other words, it is the VAT-related aspects of the greenhouse gas certificates and the ETS scheme that sound more complicated from a tax perspective.

## 13.5 GREENHOUSE CERTIFICATE AS A FINANCIAL INSTRUMENT? APPROACHING THE COMPLEXITY OF THE SCENARIO AND THE TAX CONSEQUENCES

The financial nature (or lack thereof) of the greenhouse gas certificates significantly influences the definition of their tax regime. It might impact the calculation of the capital gain (or revenue) generated from their trade according to the applicable domestic legislation as, in EU law, there is no harmonization in this matter. It might also have a decisive influence on VAT as a financial instrument, and its trade is exempt from VAT without the right of deduction.[37]

Although EU law regulates greenhouse gas emission certificates through Directive 2003/87/EC,[38] their legal definition is unclear under the law, and it is still debated in the literature as several specific disciplines are involved.

Under the Markets in Financial Instruments Directive (MiFID II) (2014/65/EU), the certificates might be qualified as financial instruments (or similar assets) according to their trade and legal regime. Such a consideration has been mirrored by domestic systems, including the Italian system, which implemented the Directive consistently. Under Italy's domestic legal system, greenhouse gas emission certificates are considered a financial instrument, as the domestic law refers to Annex I, section C, item 11 of the Directive.[39]

---

[37] Tina Ehrke-Rabel and Lily Zechner, 'VAT Treatment of Cryptocurrency Intermediation Services' (2020) 48(5) Intertax 498; Jan Weissbrodt, 'Disaggregation of Financial Instruments in International Tax Law' (2023) 51(5) Intertax 414; Howell H Zee, 'VAT Treatment of Financial Services: A Primer on Conceptual Issues and Country Practices' (2006) 34(10) Intertax 458.

[38] Directive 2003/87/EC (n 9).

[39] Annex I, section C, item 11 to Directive 2014/65/EU refers to 'Emission allowances consisting of any units recognised for compliance with the requirements of Directive 2003/87/EC (Emissions Trading Scheme)': European Parliament and Council of the European Union, Directive 2014/65/EU of 15 May 2014 on markets in financial instruments and amending Directive 2002/92/EC and Directive 2011/61/EU [2014] OJ L 173/349.

However, the point is that the qualification given by commercial law cannot be automatically transplanted into taxation. Different solutions might be considered when applying VAT and income taxation.

This is probably why the CJEU has rejected the assimilation of the certificates to financial instruments,[40] as they do not represent an underlying financial value but rather (in the view of the Court) the right to pollute up to a certain level.

Although this last consideration could be questioned (it was pointed out earlier that the certificate is a representation of a legally induced scarcity), the position of the Court is not in contrast with the MiFID framework. The latter aimed to grant a robust and secure legal environment for circulation of the certificates and the development of the market. At the same time, the CJEU addressed a different perspective: they do not collide but operate on different layers.

The judges' reasoning is based on the fact that the underlying asset is not financial. Consequently, it is not reasonable, nor legally possible, to qualify the ETS-traded certificate as an instrument equivalent to a share or a derivative contract traded on the market.

The CJEU, in a leading case on the matter for VAT purposes,[41] considered the certificate to be an intangible asset and treated it accordingly.[42] Such a definition entails the necessity to use the territoriality rules introduced for services rather than for goods, and the delivery of a certificate is liable to tax for VAT purposes in the country where the purchaser is resident.

This conclusion has given rise more recently to interesting consequences in the case of VAT-related fraud involving certificates.

In a decision taken two years ago,[43] the CJEU was asked to rule on the application of VAT on the sale of a certificate in the framework of a VAT carousel fraud. To be precise, a set of certificates was sold in a 'business-to-business' transaction and in a cross-border scenario (involving German and Austrian undertakings). When the fraud was discovered, the Austrian tax administration (as the seller was a resident there) demanded the application of VAT to claw back the tax, which had been waived due to the intra-EU nature of the transaction.

---

[40] Case C-453/15 *A and B* ECLI:EU:C:2016:933 (8 December 2016).

[41] Ibid.

[42] The Court refers to Article 56, section 1(a) of Directive 2006/112/EC (n 36).

[43] Case C-641/21 *Climate Corporation Emissions Trading* ECLI:EU:C:2022:842 (27 October 2022). Anna Miotto, 'La territorialità IVA e le deroghe fraudis causa: il caso degli Emission Trading Certificates' (2023) 2 Diritto e pratica tributaria internazionale 731.

The CJEU denied such a possibility, although it was a fraud case beyond any reasonable doubt. The legal point was that the certificate, as an intangible, is deemed to be a service for VAT purposes. According to the ordinary VAT territoriality rules, such a service is taxed in the state where the purchaser is resident (in this specific case, Germany). The fraudulent nature of the transaction cannot be used as a sound legal argument to thwart the regulations deciding which state should be granted the power to tax.

Such a conclusion is coherent and consistent with the understanding of the ETS-negotiated certificate as an intangible and, therefore, with the necessity to treat its circulation according to the rules ordinarily applicable to services.

More to the point, the Court for the second time excluded the possibility of considering the certificate a financial instrument (which would have allowed the exception) and demanded the full application of the tax.

## 13.6 CERTIFICATES, ENERGY AND THE ANCILLARITY RULE IN VAT

ETS-negotiated certificates are frequently sold with the energy resources they are connected to. For instance, gas is sold to the business to be used in the production processes together with the certificates authorizing the introduction into the atmosphere of other gases derived from the combustion of the gas sold. These certificates are sold for an amount that varies depending on the nature of the energy used and the pollution issuing from its usage.

As these transactions might sometimes occur together, another interesting point in practice and theory is whether the VAT regime applicable to the underlying asset could be extended to the attached certificate.

European VAT has both positive and judge-made rules[44] to define the conditions under which a service or a good can be considered ancillary or relevant to another service or good. Should this connection occur, it would entail relevant consequences for applying the tax. More precisely, the minor transaction (that is, the one which is ancillary – or pertinent – to the other) would lose its autonomous VAT treatment and would fall into the scope of the principal one. The tax base of the principal transaction would consequently increase by an amount equal to the price of the ancillary goods or services, and the tax regime of the former would be extended.

In practical terms, such a conclusion is crucial as it would change the applicable territoriality rules, the rate (should the principal transaction fall under a different VAT rate), and possibly the moment the transaction is considered to take place for VAT. Ancillarity is, consequently, treated carefully by the

---

[44] Case C-581/19 *Frenetikexito* ECLI:EU:C:2021:167 (4 March 2021).

interpreter and the judiciary, as it might entail possible abusive strategies by the taxpayer or misapplication of the tax.

Despite several attempts, there is no clear rule addressing ancillarity and, in the more doubtful cases, a guide allowing interpreters to identify the secondary (ancillary) action and the principal one is needed.

In the particular case of the certificates, it is evident that the sale of energy would be the principal action (sale of goods), and the sale of certificates (delivery of services) would be the ancillary one. The question is whether this relationship would be relevant for VAT purposes or not.

In other words, is it possible to consider the certificate as ancillary to a delivery of goods and, therefore, extend the VAT regime of the energy resources to the certificate? This would be significant in practice, as most energy resources (gases) enjoy a reduced VAT rate that would be extended to the value of the certificates.

The case was raised in Italy and decided by the Supreme Court, which denied the connection between the certificate and the underlying energy resource that would be traded with the former.[45] More to the point, the Supreme Court pointed out that a 'strategic relevance of the certificates exists', and such a characteristic makes them fully independent from a commercial standpoint, and thus entitled to a separate, specific VAT regime.

This interpretation was suggested earlier by the Italian tax authority[46] and by a relevant series of cases of the CJEU[47] that the Italian Supreme Court mentioned in the final decision.[48]

Irrespective of the reduced VAT rate charged on natural gas (equivalent to 10%), the sale of certificates falls under the (domestic) 22% rate when it occurs in a business-to-business scenario within the territory of the state. It falls outside the scope of VAT purposes in Italy when the sale occurs between an Italian seller and a foreign purchaser in another state.

## 13.7 THE FUTURE OF THE ETS: THE (STRANGE) CASE OF CERTIFICATE PRODUCTION BY COMPANIES

Certificates are issued by states worldwide; in Europe, this is done within the framework of EU law. They are, consequently, calculated according to quotas

---

[45] Italian Supreme Court (Corte di Cassazione) case no 3872 decided on 16 February 2018.

[46] Italian Tax Office Resolution (Ruling) no 6/E of 11 February 1998.

[47] Case C-111/05 *Aktiebolaget* [2007] ECR I-02697 and Case C-349/96 *Card Protection Plan* [1999] ECR I-00973.

[48] Italian Supreme Court (Corte di Cassazione) case no 3872 (n 45).

under the policy programme decided by the relevant authorities.[49] As the goal of all green policies enacted around the world is the reduction of greenhouse gas emissions, it is evident that the usage of certificates and the implementation of the 'cap and trade' policy are assumed to be among the most efficient tools.

The 'cap and trade' policy is unilateral in its application: essentially, if the goal is to reduce the emission of greenhouse gases, the most efficient tool is to reduce the quantitative emission of gases: the lower the emissions, the better the environment. In this respect, the implementation of certificates should lead, in the long run, to a system where emissions are zero (or close to zero), and certificates would disappear, as a Pigouvian tax would do once the policy goal had been achieved.

This is not the only policy that can be pursued should a state wish to reach that goal, and perhaps not the most efficient one. An alternative would be to allow the emission of greenhouse gases, as in the past, but to impose the implementation of policies aimed at capturing and cleaning the gases already produced via proactive behaviours by individuals and companies.

In other words, either a company reduces the production of gases or keeps the production at the same level but introduces proactive actions aimed at clawing them back, such as planting trees and introducing capture mechanics, as the United Kingdom is apparently planning to do,[50] or an equivalent. More to the point, if the difference between emissions released and captured is positive (with more emissions captured than released), a company should be entitled to issue certificates: a new kind of business would be born.

The Italian experience casts some light in this direction, as a ruling has been requested in the recent past[51] from the tax authority by a company that claimed to be in a position to capture greenhouse gas emissions, quantify them, calculate the equivalent certificate, and then trade it. The business was claimed to be connected to agriculture, as farming businesses in Italy benefit from a special tax status.

---

[49] Ion Plumb and Andreea-Ileana Zamfir, 'A Comparative Analysis of Green Certificates Markets in the European Union' (2009) 20(6) Management of Environmental Quality 684; Sandra Schusser and Jūratė Jaraitė, 'Explaining the Interplay of Three Markets: Green Certificates, Carbon Emissions and Electricity' (2018) 71 Energy Economics 1; Patrik Söderholm, 'The Political Economy of International Green Certificate Markets' (2008) 36(6) Energy Policy 2051; Lene Nielsen and Tim Jeppesen, 'Tradable Green Certificates in Selected European Countries: Overview and Assessment' (2003) 31(1) Energy Policy 3.

[50] See n 13 above.

[51] Italian Tax Office Resolution (Ruling) no 365/E issued on 16 September 2020.

The answer from the tax authority was negative, arguing that such an activity would be a commercial business and disconnected from agriculture, which implies a direct connection of the proceedings with the soil. The sale of certificates would not be possible using the reverse charge mechanism as it is for other renewables (such as solar energy) produced similarly, due to the lack of precise legal regulation allowing the trade and circulation of certificates produced by private companies.[52]

The consequence is that ETS trading is considered a business activity both for income and VAT purposes and is taxed accordingly.

## 13.8 CONCLUDING REMARKS: TOWARDS PROTECTION OF THE ENVIRONMENT AND ENERGY USAGE VIA A DYNAMIC OFFSET OF THE EMISSIONS

The ETS mechanism has dramatically changed how energy is used in the production system, and it will arguably be extended to other scenarios, such as households and residential buildings, in the medium term.[53] There is a common understanding now that greenhouse gas emissions do not derive solely from factories but also from homes and, more generally, from the lifestyle of people in the most developed countries.

The common acceptance of the instruments and the complexity of the applicable VAT rules should not lead to underestimation of the potential for development and wealth creation once the legislator, European or otherwise, has introduced scarcity.

Limitation creates value and, with that, a proper pricing policy. However, for the environment, scarcity is derived from the global scenario and determined

[52] The legal basis would be in the Italian VAT Article 17, section 6, letter (d-ter), Decree no 633, passed on 26 October 1972.

[53] On 15 December 2021, the European Commission adopted a major revision (recast) of the Energy Performance of Buildings Directive (EPBD), as part of the 'Fit for 55' package (Directive 2018/844/EU): the Directive was eventually approved by the European Parliament on 12 March 2024: European Parliament, Legislative resolution of 12 March 2024 on the proposal for a directive of the European Parliament and of the Council on the energy performance of buildings (recast) (COM(2021)0802 – C9-0469/2021 – 2021/0426(COD)). See also Alan Abela, Mike Hoxley, Paddy McGrath and Steve Goodhew, 'A Comparative Analysis of Implementation of the Energy Performance of Buildings Directive in the Mediterranean' (2013) 5(3) International Journal of Law in the Built Environment 222.

by the planet's capacity to absorb a determined amount of gas before adjusting (in terms of temperature) accordingly.

In the case of cryptocurrencies, for instance, or non-fungible tokens (NFTs), the scarcity is intrinsically built into the instrument. But in the case of the environment, intended as a common good, it is possible to imagine and implement policies aimed at expanding it, virtually eroding the scarcity of the underlying asset (nature).

A good environmental policy is not only based on greenhouse gas limitation but also on implementing favourable policies aimed at capturing excess greenhouse gases to offset emissions from businesses where limitation would be expensive or counterproductive. With a proper VAT regime applicable to this business activity and its necessary assimilation into the farming industries, European policymakers would have another option to advance the green agenda more sustainably for households and businesses.

# PART V

# Tax reform: lessons for the future

# 14. The New Zealand general anti-avoidance rule: sharpening an old blade on the jurisprudential whetstone

**Craig Elliffe**

## 14.1 RE-ENGINEERING THE RUSTY INSTRUMENT: INTERPRETATION PROBLEMS

New Zealand's experience using a general anti-avoidance rule (GAAR) to combat tax avoidance extends over 140 years. Over this lengthy period, the original and persistent inadequacies in the statute have enabled judge-made changes in the law and provided significant opportunities to reflect on the structure, role and application of general anti-avoidance laws.

The New Zealand GAAR is older and blunter than most, if not all, of its international counterparts. It formed a part of the introductory income tax in New Zealand in 1891.[1] This GAAR was based on a provision introduced in 1878 designed to prevent arrangements that had the purpose or effect of defeating or evading land taxes and, in particular, preventing a landlord from passing the incidence of the land tax to the tenant.[2] The original design had, therefore, a different purpose in mind from the avoidance of income taxes.[3]

The New Zealand GAAR is well known for its textual breadth and overreach. The current GAAR is found in section BG 1 of the Income Tax Act

---

[1] Land and Income Assessment Act 1891 (NZ) s 40.

[2] Land Tax Act 1878 (NZ) s 62.

[3] *Mangin v Inland Revenue Commissioner* [1971] AC 739, 754 (PC) (*Mangin*). Lord Wilberforce, in his strongly worded dissent in the Privy Council, in the context of this dubious history of different purposes (*inter partes* effects and fiscal effects, or both) and the unclear language, felt it was unsurprising that 'a section should emerge which indubitably lacks clarity of purpose and may indeed largely fail of effect'.

2007 (NZ), but it relies on the definitions in section YA 1 for its substance.[4] The central concept is to strike at tax avoidance arrangements that directly, or indirectly, have the purpose or effect of 'tax avoidance'. 'Tax avoidance' is defined to include:

- directly or indirectly altering the incidence of any income tax;
- directly or indirectly relieving a person from liability to pay income tax or from a potential or prospective liability to future income tax;
- directly or indirectly avoiding, postponing, or reducing any liability to income tax or any potential or prospective liability to future income tax.

The breathtaking width of the language and scope of this anti-avoidance provision can immediately be noted. When read on a literal basis, an *arrangement* that *in any way alters* the *incidence* of tax or *relieves* a taxpayer from paying tax would include a sole trader whose business had grown to the point where, commercially, it was desirable to incorporate.[5] The provision would catch many other ordinary events that might occur[6] and lead to its application to cases it would be hardly conceivable the legislature had in mind when formulating the provision,[7] resulting in the 'avoidance of transactions which were obviously not aimed at by the section'.[8]

Although it is an old-fashioned word now, the process of sharpening used to be called 'whetting'.[9] One sharpens a blade by running or rubbing it across a stone with special qualities called a 'whetstone'. The story of the New Zealand GAAR is a story of unusual statutory interpretation and of a blunt instrument being sharpened by the jurisprudential whetstone. Dealing with a provision

---

[4] Income Tax Act 2007 (NZ), particularly the definitions of 'tax avoidance' and 'tax avoidance arrangement'.

[5] For context, the current New Zealand corporate income tax rate is 28%, whereas the current highest marginal personal income tax rate is 39%.

[6] For example, technical tax avoidance includes a tax lawyer deciding to leave their partnership and become a tax academic, who would experience a significant reduction in (or relief of) their tax liability because of the lower income, and also someone who decides to leave New Zealand and go to work in another country.

[7] Per Fullagar J, when considering a similar provision (Australia's Income Tax Assessment Act 1936 (Cth) s 260, which was in turn based upon the New Zealand provision found in the Land and Income Assessment Act 1900 (NZ) s 82) in the High Court of Australia decision of *Federal Commissioner of Taxation v Newton* (1957) 96 CLR 577, 646.

[8] Per McCarthy P, in the New Zealand Court of Appeal decision *Commissioner of Inland Revenue v Gerard* [1974] 2 NZLR 279, 280.

[9] The word 'whet' means 'sharpen'. In another context, when one talks about 'whetting your appetite', it is about sharpening the need or desire for food.

which Lord Wilberforce once famously declared as inoperable: 'I think that we have here a rusty instrument which breaks in our hands and is no longer capable of repair',[10] the New Zealand courts have confronted the challenges of the section by developing jurisprudence which is quite remarkable in its approach and effectiveness.

### 14.1.1 Reconciling the GAAR to Other Operative Provisions in the Tax Legislation

At the heart of the operation of any anti-avoidance provision is the extent to which it applies when the rest of the tax rules prescribe a clear tax outcome, such as allowing a deduction, permitting offsets of company group losses, or respecting the legal form of a transaction (a share sale rather than a dividend). This application of taxation to a transaction where the law expressly provides that tax ought not to be applied is the most challenging paradox in applying GAARs to transactions that are otherwise fully compliant with income tax law. Legislation, or judicial guidance, has to focus on the relationship between express provisions, which provide for specific tax outcomes, and the GAAR, which, in certain circumstances, prevents these tax outcomes.

This universal issue of statutory interpretation remained unresolved in New Zealand for many decades while the courts batted it about.

### 14.1.2 The New Zealand Supreme Court and the Tandem Approach to Interpretation

The *Ben Nevis* decision in 2008 involved the application of the GAAR to a transaction involving a forestry investment scheme.[11] All the judges in the Supreme Court held that it was tax avoidance, but with different reasoning between the majority[12] and the minority.[13]

---

10 *Mangin* (n 3) 757.

11 *Ben Nevis Forestry Ventures Limited v Commissioner of Inland Revenue* [2009] 2 NZLR 289 (*Ben Nevis*).

12 Tipping, McGrath and Gault JJ, whose approach is discussed in this chapter.

13 Elias CJ and Anderson J, who took the view that the use of a specific provision outside its scope in the scheme of the Act was an unauthorized use of the provision and therefore, on a purposively construed interpretation, the Commissioner could disallow the claim for the deduction without recourse to the GAAR (*Ben Nevis* (n 11) [2]). Such an approach, their Honours felt, was consistent with the UK decisions in *W T Ramsay Ltd v Inland Revenue Commissioners* [1982] AC 300 (HL) and *Furniss (Inspector of Taxes) v Dawson* [1984] AC 474 (HL).

Tipping, McGrath and Gault JJ, giving the majority judgment, acknowledged the difficulty of their task, given 'little explicit guidance on the legislation' and the 'complex' case law 'encumbered by considerations and tests that the legislation does not specify'.[14] Their Honours, therefore, outlined that they 'must identify a means for determining where permissible use of specific provisions ends and tax avoidance begins'.[15]

Their Honours described the means they chose as the *tandem approach* to interpretation,[16] which they reconciled to the previously articulated scheme and purpose approach of Richardson J in the New Zealand Court of Appeal,[17] but highlighted that the Court should focus on specific provisions in a much broader context.[18] This approach focuses on Parliament's purpose for the specific tax provisions and the general anti-avoidance provision. Their Honours stated:

> The presence in the New Zealand legislation of a general anti-avoidance provision suggests that our Parliament meant it to be the principal vehicle by means of which tax avoidance is addressed. The general anti-avoidance regime is designed for that purpose, whereas individual specific provisions have a focus which is determined primarily by their ordinary meaning, as established through their text in the light of their specific purpose.[19]

---

[14] *Ben Nevis* (n 11) [13].

[15] Ibid.

[16] Ibid [103].

[17] Richardson J, in the New Zealand Court of Appeal, in cases such as *Challenge Corporation Ltd v Commissioner of Inland Revenue* [1986] 2 NZLR 513, 549, had formulated an approach to the interpretation of the GAAR, which relied on the

> respective roles of the particular provision and s 99 [the relevant GAAR provision under the 1976 Income Tax Act] under the statute and of the relation between them. That is a matter of statutory construction and the twin pillars … are the scheme of the legislation and the relevant objectives of the legislation.

[18] *Ben Nevis* (n 11) [99]. This point is noted by Justice Susan Glazebrook, 'Statutory Interpretation, Tax Avoidance and the Supreme Court: Reconciling the Specific and the General' (Paper prepared for the New Zealand Institute of Chartered Accountants 2013 Tax Conference, Auckland, 7–9 November 2013) 43 <https://www.courtsofnz.govt.nz/assets/speechpapers/1hjg1t.pdf> ('Statutory Interpretation, Tax Avoidance and the Supreme Court'), where Her Honour observes: 'Therefore, while the tandem approach is not necessarily new, it has been emphatically re-asserted by the Supreme Court.'

[19] *Ben Nevis* (n 11) [103] (footnote omitted).

The consequences arising from the tandem approach to interpretation were to dismiss the argument that once the ordinary meaning of the specific provision was satisfied, the tax avoidance provision could not be applied; and to make clear that the GAAR was not subservient to the purpose of the specific provision or some backstop (as it was described in *Auckland Harbour Board*).[20]

The majority in *Ben Nevis* noted that the GAAR's function is to prevent the use of specific provisions that fall outside the intended scope of Parliament in the overall scheme of the Act and give rise to an impermissible tax advantage.[21] The role of the courts is to determine whether such an impermissible tax advantage has arisen from the use of the specific provision and to assess whether the taxpayer has used that provision in a way within the *contemplation and purpose of Parliament* when it enacted the provision.[22]

### 14.1.3 Questions of Statutory Interpretation

The history of the New Zealand GAAR is probably not unique among other countries, with GAARs having a sustained focus on statutory interpretation. One can immediately see that the problem created by an open-textured anti-avoidance provision such as the New Zealand GAAR was not only how to reconcile the literal textual application of the general anti-avoidance provision to the otherwise satisfied requirements of the specific provisions (or black letter law) of the tax legislation, but also how to make sense of the actual text of the New Zealand GAAR. Therefore, the New Zealand GAAR story is the story of ingenious statutory interpretation.

Dealing with the GAAR has required the New Zealand courts to exercise purposive interpretation, possibly developing the law in this area of tax law in a way ahead of, or at least different from, statutory interpretation in other areas of the law. The GAAR is thus very much a provision that, when considering the development of the tests for tax avoidance, might be regarded as evolving

---

20 Ibid [104]. The New Zealand Supreme Court felt it needed to address prior case law and in particular the concept that the GAAR was a 'long stop'. The Privy Council decision in *Commissioner of Inland Revenue v Auckland Harbour Board* [2001] 3 NZLR 289 [11] (PC) (*Auckland Harbour Board*) is expressly referred to by the majority in *Ben Nevis* (at [100]) as a decision creating 'continuing uncertainty about the interrelationship of the general anti-avoidance provision with specific provisions. That makes it desirable for this Court to settle the approach which should be applied in New Zealand.'

21 *Ben Nevis* (n 11) [106].

22 This is why the New Zealand test is known as the parliamentary contemplation test, because of the reference in para 107 of the *Ben Nevis* judgment; *Ben Nevis* (n 11) [107].

judge-made law. This point is somewhat ironic given the early historical statutory nature of the New Zealand GAAR.

The width of various definitions and language in the GAAR, such as the definition of tax avoidance,[23] has required judges to consider the purpose of the provisions significantly more than interpreting the actual text. The New Zealand courts certainly consider the purpose of the GAAR provision, but they arguably do more than purposively interpret the statute. Concentration on the words of the statute might otherwise lead a judge to the same conclusion as that made by Lord Wilberforce in *Mangin*, namely, that the statute had surpassed the limits of liberal or commonsense judicial interpretation and consequently desperately needed reform.[24]

Senior New Zealand judges, while recognizing the deficiencies of the statute, have successfully worked with the GAAR. Recently retired New Zealand Supreme Court judge, Sir William Young (author of the majority judgment in *Frucor*, the most recent Supreme Court tax avoidance decision)[25] is uncertain that orthodox interpretive analysis (such as purposive interpretation) illuminates the problem of deciding whether it is the GAAR or the other tax provision relied upon by the taxpayer that should prevail. His Honour describes the operation of the GAAR as 'a twilight zone'.[26] By this, his Honour means that the GAAR-impugned arrangement is effective without the operation of the GAAR, yet voidable for tax purposes because of the operation of the anti-avoidance provision. Therefore, the application of the GAAR 'sits extremely awkwardly in the highly prescriptive legislative context provided by the Income Tax Act. Orthodox statutory interpretation principles provide, at best, only limited assistance'.[27]

---

[23] Income Tax Act 2007 s YA 1 defines that *tax avoidance* includes: (a) directly or indirectly altering the incidence of any income tax; (b) directly or indirectly relieving a person from liability to pay income tax or from a potential or prospective liability to future income tax; (c) directly or indirectly avoiding, postponing, or reducing any liability to income tax or any potential or prospective liability to future income tax.

[24] *Mangin* (n 3) 756–7.

[25] *Frucor Suntory New Zealand Ltd v Commissioner of Inland Revenue* [2022] 1 NZLR 603 (*Frucor*).

[26] Hon Justice William Young, 'The Evolution of the Approach of the New Zealand Courts to Tax Avoidance' (2016) 11(1) Journal of the Australasian Tax Teachers Association 1, 3 ('The Evolution of the Approach of the New Zealand Courts').

[27] Hon Justice William Young, 'Looking Back on the Approaches of the Courts to Tax, After More Than 24 Years on the Bench' (2022) 17(1) Journal of the Australasian Tax Teachers Association 8, 19.

His Honour observed that the application of the GAAR is always 'particular to the facts of the case at hand' and 'thus involves application as much as interpretation'.[28] Despite these reservations, clearly some form of purposive interpretation is being advocated in the tandem approach to interpretation. Despite using the word 'tandem' in the *Ben Nevis* case (suggesting interpretation of both the specific provision and the GAAR), it seems clear that the GAAR is the overriding provision in circumstances where the facts of the case demand that it is tax avoidance.[29]

More conventionally, Dame Susan Glazebrook, a current New Zealand Supreme Court judge, when writing about the statutory interpretation of tax avoidance provisions, was expecting to trace the interpretation of tax avoidance provisions and reconcile them to the journey from literal interpretation to purposive interpretation found in other areas of the law.[30] Her Honour notes that, whereas close textual interpretation was very much the order of the day for different areas of the law, the tax avoidance cases had led the way in the early adoption of purposive interpretation:

> I started on my analysis of tax avoidance cases expecting to be able to make learned observations about the evolution of statutory interpretation only to find that a purposive approach had found favour, at least in relation to tax avoidance jurisprudence, in the early cases in the Court of Appeal and long before the purposive approach had taken general hold in New Zealand. Of course, when I thought about it, I realised that it is not surprising that courts did not take a totally literal approach to the interpretation of tax avoidance provisions.[31]

Having established that purposive interpretation gives little traction to the purpose of the specific provisions in the presence of a powerful GAAR and factual circumstances that warrant its exercise, this chapter now turns to the key 'engine' of the New Zealand GAAR, the 'parliamentary contemplation test', as developed by the majority in *Ben Nevis.*

---

28 Young, 'The Evolution of the Approach of the New Zealand Courts' (n 26) 2.

29 John Prebble, *Fundamentals of Income Taxation* (Thomson Reuters 2018) para 78.18.

30 Justice Susan Glazebrook, 'Statutory Interpretation and Tax Avoidance' (Paper prepared for the Tax Avoidance in the 21st Century Conference, University of Melbourne, 17 May 2013) <https://www.courtsofnz.govt.nz/assets/speechpapers/sihg.pdf> accessed 31 October 2023.

31 Ibid 2, referring to the article by DAS Ward, 'Trends in the Interpretation of Statutes' (1956–1958) 2(3) Victoria University of Wellington Law Review 155, 160 and 168–71, in support of this proposition.

The decision in *Ben Nevis* made two profound contributions to New Zealand GAAR jurisprudence. First, the Supreme Court settled the law after over 130 years of inconsistency by clarifying the relationship between the general and specific provisions. Secondly, it articulated the new parliamentary contemplation test.

The next part of this chapter discusses the parliamentary contemplation test to analyse its effectiveness and, on a more general basis, the possible implications for other countries' general anti-avoidance provisions.

## 14.2 THE PARLIAMENTARY CONTEMPLATION TEST

In 2008, the New Zealand Supreme Court, as the final court of appeal in the New Zealand legal system,[32] was called upon for the first time to decide when the 'use of specific provisions will amount to proscribed tax avoidance'.[33]

### 14.2.1 The Key Test(s)

The Supreme Court thought the taxpayers had engaged in a tax avoidance arrangement involving investment in a forestry plantation. The majority's *Ben Nevis* judgment sets out a two-step analysis.[34] If the taxpayer has used any specific provision, it must satisfy the Court that its use was within the scope of the provision. Such an analysis is preliminary to 'any question of avoidance', with the Court 'concerned primarily with the legal structures and obligations the parties have created and not with conducting an analysis in terms of their economic substance and consequences, or of alternative means that were available for achieving the substantive result'.[35]

The Supreme Court in *Frucor* subsequently has made clear that this 'first inquiry can be dealt with on a largely textual basis',[36] without the type of scheme and purpose interpretation consideration typically applied to the construction of a statutory provision. So: 'If, on the wording of the provisions relied on, an arrangement appears to warrant the tax position adopted, the court can move to the second enquiry. When tax avoidance is in issue, it is the second inquiry that is of paramount importance.'[37]

---

[32] Replacing the Privy Council in 2004: Supreme Court Act 2003 (NZ).

[33] *Ben Nevis* (n 11) [13] (footnote omitted).

[34] Ibid [107].

[35] Ibid [47].

[36] *Frucor* (n 25) [58].

[37] Ibid, per William Young J for the majority (Winkelmann CJ, William Young, O'Regan and Ellen France JJ).

In the second step, the crucial question that must be answered when determining whether an arrangement has a tax avoidance purpose or effect under the parliamentary contemplation test was set out as follows: 'The ultimate question is whether the impugned arrangement, viewed in a commercially and economically realistic way, makes use of the specific provision in a manner that is consistent with Parliament's purpose.'[38]

A central theme of this chapter is that the parliamentary contemplation test encapsulates the two competing components of the GAAR analysis: (1) the purpose of Parliament in enacting the legislation (legal analysis), and (2) the taxpayer's use of the provision viewed in a commercially and economically realistic way (factual analysis).[39]

If the use of the specific provision is in a manner consistent with Parliament's purpose, it will be on the side of the line that denotes acceptable tax planning (not subject to the anti-avoidance rule). On the other side of the line is tax avoidance – because using the specific provision is beyond Parliament's contemplation. The parliamentary contemplation test is an aid to the court, formulated to examine the taxpayer's use of the tax rules against a parliamentary purpose or intent, which it has been noted 'will always, to a degree, be a hypothetical exercise'.[40]

Before *Ben Nevis,* it was observed that factors such as '[a]rtificiality, contrivance, pretence, circularity of funds, timing mismatches, unnecessary insertion of steps into a transaction, lack of a business purpose, a divergence between the economic and legal effects of a transaction and dealings between non-arm's length parties have often been cited as hallmarks of tax avoidance arrangements'.[41]

These recognizable features of tax avoidance continue to be important in determining whether the use of the provision is outside parliamentary contemplation because the Supreme Court says that consideration must be given as to

---

38 *Ben Nevis* (n 11) [109], quoted in *Frucor* (n 25) [53].

39 The writer is grateful to Howard Davis (Group Leader, Customer Advice, Tax Counsel Office Inland Revenue) for his observations on this matter in the paper 'Differential Tax Rates – Practical and Emerging Issues' published by the New Zealand Law Society at a conference (March 2023). This 'two competing factors' discussion is expanded upon in section 14.4.

40 Glazebrook, 'Statutory Interpretation, Tax Avoidance and the Supreme Court' (n 18) 31.

41 Craig Elliffe and Jess Cameron, 'The Test for Tax Avoidance in New Zealand: A Judicial Sea Change' (2010) 16 New Zealand Business Law Quarterly 440, 451.

whether the taxpayer gains the benefit of the specific provision 'in an artificial or contrived way'.[42]

The *Ben Nevis* majority made it clear that a court must consider *all* relevant factors under the parliamentary contemplation test, including how the arrangement was carried out, the role of all relevant parties and the relationship they may have with the taxpayer, the economic and commercial effect of documents and transactions, the duration of the arrangement, and the nature and extent of the financial consequences for the taxpayer.[43] In considering these matters, the courts are not limited to purely legal considerations but should consider the use of the specific provisions 'in the light of the commercial reality and the economic effect of that use'.[44] When the majority in *Ben Nevis* directed that the court must examine the underlying economic substance of, and commercial purposes for, the transaction, they were inviting a factual analysis on top of, or in addition to, consideration of the specific provisions purposively interpreted.

In circumstances where a particular provision permits a deduction, for example, the inquiry focuses on whether the taxpayer's economic burden is actually borne, irrespective of the legal form. In *Ben Nevis,* the taxpayer claimed deductions for licences and insurance premiums paid by the assumption of liability through a promissory note, which would be repaid out of the proceeds of the plantation harvest in 50 years. The Supreme Court looked through or beyond this purely legal form and contractual analysis. Accordingly, the Supreme Court in *Ben Nevis* concluded that neither the licence[45] nor the insurance premium[46] led to tangible economic consequences, since the taxpayer did not bear the expenditure burden (because the expenditure was never incurred commercially).

The taxpayers argued that the *Ben Nevis* Court should not deprive them of tax-beneficial choices,[47] nor should the tax avoidance legislation be interpreted

---

[42] *Ben Nevis* (n 11) [108]. See also, confirming the focus on the elements of artificiality and contrivance in the most recent New Zealand Supreme Court case, *Frucor* (n 25) [81]–[85].

[43] *Ben Nevis* (n 11) [108].

[44] Ibid [109].

[45] Ibid [128], where the majority stated that 'the court is permitted, when considering the question of tax avoidance, to examine the commercial nature of the incurred cost and any factors that might indicate that the expenditure will never be truly incurred'.

[46] Ibid [147], where the majority stated: 'The simple fact is that the second premium was not paid in any real sense by means of the promissory note. … The purported payment did not give rise to any economic consequences on either side.'

[47] Ibid [111].

to deny them reasonable certainty in tax planning.[48] These are common taxpayer concerns in the utilization of the GAAR provisions. The New Zealand Supreme Court made it clear that taxpayers can structure transactions to their best tax advantage.[49] Tax incentives can be utilized if the applicable legislative text provides for that outcome when the law is interpreted in its context and purpose. However, they cannot utilize tax incentives when the specific provisions are used in a way 'proscribed by the general anti-avoidance provision'.[50] On the question of certainty, the Supreme Court was equally unsympathetic, noting that Parliament had left the general anti-avoidance provision deliberately general. Accordingly, 'the courts should not strive to create greater certainty than Parliament has chosen to provide'.[51]

## 14.3 THE APPLICATION OF THE PARLIAMENTARY CONTEMPLATION TEST: ECONOMIC SUBSTANCE

The decision in *Ben Nevis* makes it clear that this parliamentary contemplation of the legal provision's use is conducted in a commercially and economically realistic way, going beyond the legal form.

It is insightful, and not overly simplistic, to regard this as essentially a *legal* analysis of the purpose of the provision and a *factual* analysis of what has occurred through the lens of commercial and economic reality. When viewed this way, it can be said that the superior New Zealand courts (including the Privy Council) have developed this emphasis on the factual commercial and economic features to develop a test of *economic substance* in determining the presence (or absence) of tax avoidance.[52]

The Privy Council decision in *Challenge* was described as '[t]he first of the modern cases'[53] concerning the utilization of group loss offset rules (the requirements of which were technically met) in circumstances where it was obvious that the taxpayers had obtained a tax advantage without suffering any

---

48 Ibid [112].

49 Ibid [111].

50 Ibid.

51 Ibid [112].

52 In this respect, the decision in *Ben Nevis* (n 11) [100] distinguished the approach of the Privy Council in *Challenge Corporation Ltd v Commissioner of Inland Revenue* (PC) [1986] 2 NZLR 513 (*Challenge* (PC)) from that in *Auckland Harbour Board* (n 20), making it clear (as discussed at n 20, above) that it was 'desirable for this Court to settle the approach which should be applied in New Zealand'.

53 In the majority judgment of Winkelmann CJ, William Young, O'Regan and Ellen France JJ, while Glazebrook J dissented, in *Frucor* (n 25) [52].

of the loss or expenditure which Parliament would intend (or anticipate) would be suffered or incurred to qualify for loss grouping.[54] Instead, the loss was 'artificially generated by purchase'.[55] In substance, the Challenge Corporation had not sustained the economic burden of incurring the losses sufficiently to offset the loss. Glazebrook has noted extrajudicially that[56] the Privy Council in *Challenge*[57] and the Court of Appeal in *Mills v Dowdall*[58] had both considered economic substance in considering what constitutes tax avoidance in those cases.

Similarly, in *Penny v Commissioner of Inland Revenue*,[59] the New Zealand Supreme Court saw a commercial and economic mismatch between a structure's tax advantages and the taxpayer suffering the reduction in income. Blanchard J in the Supreme Court observed: 'In reality, the taxpayers suffered no actual loss of income but obtained a reduction in liability to tax as if they had, to adapt Lord Templeman's dictum in *Challenge*.'[60]

These two cases, *Challenge* and *Penny and Hooper*, were discussed in the 2022 New Zealand Supreme Court decision *Frucor*, which confirms this factual *economic substance* approach to tax avoidance.

The *Frucor* case was a genuine commercial transaction involving a French company, Group Danone SA (Danone), acquiring all the shares in a New Zealand beverage company (Frucor) for approximately NZ $300 million. An investment bank (Deutsche Bank) approached Danone with the proposed funding structure for their acquisition of Frucor. It was a complicated arrangement whereby the bank lent Frucor $204 million under an optional convertible note (note). The notes were repayable in cash unless the bank elected to take non-voting shares. Simultaneously with the issuance of the note, Frucor's parent company (through its Singapore-based subsidiary) entered into a forward purchase agreement regarding these non-voting shares to acquire the shares for no further payment upon maturity. The Singapore Danone entity paid $149 million immediately in return for the obligation to transfer the shares on the note's maturity in five years. This meant that of the $204 million lent under the convertible note to Frucor, only $55 million was actually financed by the bank (the Singapore-based company owned by the parent having immediately

[54] *Challenge* (PC) (n 52) 560–61.

[55] Glazebrook, 'Statutory Interpretation, Tax Avoidance and the Supreme Court' (n 18) 18.

[56] Ibid 43–4.

[57] *Challenge* (PC) (n 52).

[58] *Mills v Dowdall* [1983] NZLR 154 (CA).

[59] *Penny v Commissioner of Inland Revenue* [2012] 1 NZLR 433 (*Penny and Hooper*).

[60] Ibid [47] (footnote omitted).

returned to the bank $149 million through the forward purchase agreement). During the five years of the note's existence, Frucor paid interest amounting to $66 million on the face value of the note ($204 million). The New Zealand Commissioner asserted that, in reality, Frucor had borrowed only $55 million from Deutsche Bank and sought to limit the interest deduction to just $11 million (the surplus above the principal amount). Frucor had claimed the $66 million interest deduction in full because it had borrowed $204 million as a separate entity and argued that the amount paid by a non-resident associated company for the forward purchase of the shares was irrelevant.

The High Court (the court of first instance) held that the note's face value ($204 million) was treated as the amount lent following the legal form. Delivering the majority judgment of the Supreme Court, William Young J rejected the finding of fact in the High Court, advising: 'In company with the Court of Appeal, we see the facts very differently.'[61] His Honour then went on to describe the funding arrangement as a matter of economic substance and commercial reality as follows: 'Despite the apparent complexity of the funding arrangement as a whole, *its economic substance* was straightforward.'[62]

Deutsche Bank advanced the $55 million '[i]n economic substance',[63] and in examining this from a GAAR perspective, there could be 'no sensible objection' to looking at the transaction from an overall perspective.[64] The expenses claimed by the taxpayer were purportedly interest but, in substance, they were repayments of principal. Under the relevant deduction provisions of the Act, it was 'outside of parliamentary contemplation' to allow the provision to be used in this way.[65]

Glazebrook J dissented from the majority view. Her Honour held that consideration of the economic substance of the transaction was appropriate but differed from the majority in the analysis of whether the provisions were being used in a way not contemplated by Parliament.[66] Her Honour accepted that Deutsche provided debt funding amounting to $55 million in economic substance.[67] Where Her Honour differed from the majority was that, in Her Honour's economic substance view of the facts, the loan to Frucor was the total face value amount of $204 million under the convertible note, with the balance beyond the Deutsche funding ($55 million) being indirectly provided by Danone Asia (as to $149 million). In Glazebrook J's view, the legal form of

61 *Frucor* (n 25) [74].
62 Ibid [75] (emphasis added).
63 Ibid [76].
64 Ibid [79].
65 Ibid [86].
66 Ibid [163].
67 Ibid [171].

the transaction was effective provided that the debt and equity structure was within parliamentary contemplation. This was the case in Her Honour's view because Parliament gave taxpayers the choice of using debt and equity, and *Frucor* had availed itself of these choices.[68]

## 14.4 REFLECTIONS ON THE NEW ZEALAND GAAR EXPERIENCE

What are the crucial lessons of the last 140 years of New Zealand's GAAR experience?

The first is that the courts in New Zealand have usually, sometimes eventually, applied common sense and liberal purposive interpretation to make the anti-avoidance rule work. Undoubtedly, applying the GAAR is an unusual exercise in statutory interpretation.[69] As this chapter has attempted to explain, the New Zealand GAAR has required a special kind of purposive interpretation, particularly in reconciling specific provisions (and specific anti-avoidance provisions) to the expansive GAAR. The New Zealand Supreme Court in *Ben Nevis*[70] recognized that specific provisions would not read down the GAAR. The *Ben Nevis* decision confirmed the approach of the Privy Council decision in *Challenge* and dispensed with the indeterminacy and inconsistency of New Zealand tax jurisprudence after that decision. This 'awkward'[71] relationship between the GAAR and specific provisions is a common feature of other jurisdictions' GAAR decisions.[72] The New Zealand statute suggests that the statutory rule does not need to be overly prescriptive nor texturally accurate if the anti-avoidance purpose of the legislation is clear.

Secondly, there are two components to be considered in applying the New Zealand, and indeed any, GAAR. The judge-formulated parliamentary contemplation test requires an assessment of the arrangement from both legal and factual perspectives.[73] The legal examination focuses on the use of the

---

[68] Ibid [171]–[182].

[69] As Rothstein J observed in the Canadian Supreme Court decision *Copthorne Holdings Ltd v Canada* [2011] 3 SCR 721 [66], the difficulty in applying the GAAR arises because it confers upon courts the 'unusual duty of going behind the words of the legislation'.

[70] *Ben Nevis* (n 11).

[71] 'Awkwardness' is the term used by the majority in the New Zealand Supreme Court decision of *Frucor* (n 25) [51]–[52].

[72] See, for example, the Canadian Supreme Court in *Deans Knight Income Corp v Canada*, 2023 SCC 16 (*Deans Knight*).

[73] Parallels can be drawn with the Canadian GAAR jurisprudence analysis, which includes: first, interpreting the provisions relied upon for the tax benefit to

provisions the taxpayer relies on to ensure that it is being complied with in a way Parliament would have contemplated. The factual perspective arises because, in formulating that assessment, the court must view the arrangement in a commercially and economically realistic way. This factual perspective is essential because courts in New Zealand[74] and elsewhere[75] establish that consideration of purely legal concerns is insufficient in an avoidance analysis.

Thirdly, the New Zealand courts have dynamically developed and applied new tests and doctrines. Examining the factual situation in a 'commercially and economically realistic way' has led the New Zealand Supreme Court to review the *economic substance* of the transaction. This approach can be traced to the Privy Council in *Challenge*,[76] so there are consistent concepts through time. Economic substance was an essential consideration in *Ben Nevis*[77] and *Penny and Hooper*.[78] It was repeatedly referred to in *Frucor* by both the

---

determine their object, spirit and purpose, and secondly, undertaking a factual analysis to determine whether the avoidance transaction is consistent with or frustrates the object, spirit and purpose of the provisions. See the majority judgment of the Canadian Supreme Court per Côté J in *Canada v Alta Energy Luxembourg SARL*, 2021 SCC 49.

74 *Ben Nevis* (n 11) [109], per Tipping and McGrath JJ: 'In considering these matters, the courts are not limited to purely legal considerations.'

75 See, for example, *Deans Knight* (n 72) [69] per Rowe J: 'Courts must go beyond the legal form and technical compliance of the transactions; they must compare the result of the transactions to the underlying rationale of the provision and determine whether that rationale has been frustrated.'

76 *Challenge* (PC) (n 52) 562, per Lord Templeman, who stated:

> In an arrangement of tax avoidance the financial position of the taxpayer is unaffected (save for the costs of devising and implementing the arrangement) and by the arrangement the taxpayer seeks to obtain a tax advantage without suffering that reduction in income, loss or expenditure which other taxpayers suffer and which Parliament intended to be suffered by any taxpayer qualifying for a reduction in his liability to tax.

77 *Ben Nevis* (n 11) [128], where the majority (per Tipping and McGrath JJ) noted the timing mismatch between legal and economic payment, stating (as noted at n 45, above) that 'the court is permitted, when considering the question of tax avoidance, to examine the commercial nature of the incurred cost and any factors that might indicate that the expenditure will never be truly incurred'.

78 *Penny and Hooper* (n 59) [47], per Blanchard J, when discussing the reduced taxpayers' taxable earnings (due to the low salary levels) in contrast to the company's earnings available to him through the family trusts (as noted previously (see text at n 60 above)). 'In reality, the taxpayer suffered no actual loss of income but obtained a reduction in liability to tax as if they had, to adapt Lord Templeman's dictum in *Challenge*.'

majority and minority decisions as an appropriate consideration in considering the relevant facts of the case.[79] Economic substance is not 'economic equivalence', a doctrine that does not respect the legal form and which earlier case law has rejected. However, even in the 1970s, the courts preserved its application in circumstances involving the GAAR.[80]

There is nothing in the New Zealand provision concerning economic substance, so examining this feature of the arrangements is an entirely judicial test. The New Zealand courts' approach, with an increasing focus on economic substance in determining tax avoidance, is consistent with other countries. Considering and comparing the economic position with the tax result is a common feature of international general anti-abuse[81] and anti-avoidance rules in Australia.[82] In the United States, the doctrine of economic substance,

---

[79] Although the majority and minority might have agreed on considering the aspect of economic substance, they disagreed on how that should be applied in respect of the funding under the convertible note.

[80] *Inland Revenue Commissioner v Europa Oil (NZ) Ltd* [1971] AC 760, 771–2 (PC) where Lord Wilberforce stated that taxation by end result or economic equivalence is not acceptable, unless it was in the circumstances of applying the GAAR.

[81] For example, consider the UK's General Anti-Abuse Rule Advisory Panel Opinions (APOs), <https://gov.uk/government/groups/general-anti-abuse-rule-advisory-panel> accessed 31 October 2023. It is common for the reasonableness of the taxpayer's conduct to be considered against a matrix of features, one of which is where the tax result does not match the economic position. In HM Revenue and Customs, 'GAAR Advisory Panel opinion of 11 April 2019: employee rewards using a second hand bond, gilt options, additional contributions and "cooling off rights" (individual)' (Guidance, 20 May 2019) 11, the scheme involved rewarding employees with various assets, despite there being no individual income tax obligations: 'Thus the £1.5 million of cash received (or receivable) by the Individual represents income of the Individual for economic purposes. However it is argued that the amount is not income of the Individual for the purposes of income tax or national insurance contributions.'

[82] In Australia, the Income Tax Assessment Act 1936 (Cth) s 177D(2)(b) requires the form and substance of the scheme to be considered. In a recent decision of the Full Federal Court, *Federal Commissioner of Taxation v Guardian AIT Pty Ltd* (2023) 115 ATR 316 [201], Hespe J (Perry and Derrington JJ agreeing) applied a comparison of form and substance to establish the presence of tax avoidance, as follows: 'A comparison of the form and substance of the scheme supports a conclusion that a party carrying out the scheme did so for the dominant purpose of enabling Mr Springer to obtain a tax benefit.'

originally a common law doctrine,[83] was codified in the Tax Code in 2010.[84] Canada proposes incorporating an economic substance rule in its amendments to the Canadian GAAR.[85]

Reflecting on the New Zealand GAAR experience suggests that because of common-sense purposive interpretation, broad assessment of the law and facts, and the flexible, dynamic development of principles, the courts are better than the legislature at applying and implementing effective GAARs to emerging and difficult cases. Despite the criticism of the New Zealand GAAR, this means that there is no need for legislative amendments because judge-made law will continue to evolve, meeting any taxpayer ingenuity in aggressive tax planning head-on.

## ACKNOWLEDGEMENTS

This chapter is a summarized and restructured version of an article that appeared in the British Tax Review, 'Designing a Powerful General Anti-Avoidance Rule: Reflections on the New Zealand Experience' (2023) (5) British Tax Review 704.

83 *ACM Partnership v Commissioner*, 157 F3d 231 (3rd Cir 1998), affirming 73 TCM (CCH) 2189 (1997), cert denied, 526 US 1017 (1999).

84 Defined in subsection (o) of the US Code, Title 26, s 7701 as amended by the Health Care and Education Reconciliation Act of 2010.

85 See Government of Canada, *Budget 2023, Tax Measures: Supplementary Information* (2023) 37 <https://www.budget.canada.ca/2023/report-rapport/tm-mf-en.html#a82> accessed 31 October 2023, and subsequent post-Budget announcements.

# 15. History informing the future: can we improve tax policy and legislation with respect to taxing capital gains? A New Zealand perspective

**Adrian Sawyer**

## 15.1 INTRODUCTION AND OVERVIEW

One could be forgiven for thinking, why have another contribution to the debate over a capital gains tax (CGT) for New Zealand? Contributions to the debate can be traced back to the 1960s with the Ross Report,[1] along with subsequent tax reviews.[2] Academic contributions to the debate continue to be made. Politically, the topic of a CGT is somewhat of a 'hot potato', with a CGT forming part of the manifesto of several political parties. To date, all of this remarkable effort has come to naught, at least in terms of having as much as a government consultative document seeking public submissions. Even the most recent contribution from the Tax Working Group,[3] which provided a comprehensive blueprint for a CGT in 2019, was rejected by the government.

All of this 'failure' comes against a backdrop of growing support for a CGT, or at least that a formal proposal be developed and be open to public consultation (illustrated by the discussion in section 15.2 of this chapter). Perceptions of unfairness in the current tax system in New Zealand abound, especially

---

[1] Taxation Review Committee (Lewis Ross, chair), *Taxation in New Zealand: Report of the Taxation Review Committee* (1967) (Ross Report).

[2] For example, Task Force on Tax Reform (Peter McCaw, chair), *Report of the Task Force on Tax Reform* (1982); Tax Review 2001 (Robert McLeod, chair), *Tax Review 2001: Final Report* (2001) (McLeod Review); Tax Working Group (Hon Michael Cullen, chair), *Future of Tax: Final Report* (*Volume I: Recommendations* and *Volume II: Design Details of the Proposed Extension of Capital Gains Taxation*) (2019) (TWG).

[3] TWG (n 2).

when it comes to the growing burden of taxation on wage and salary earners, and final consumers. Rather than acknowledge these issues, the most recent efforts to tax some 'capital gains' have been through extending the income tax to residential property sales and denial of interest deductions. This ad hoc approach has created numerous unintended consequences, and goes against international best practice for taxing capital gains, where a separate tax should be put in place that provides mechanisms to accommodate most of the major concerns in taxing capital gains (e.g., lumpiness, taxing nominal gains (instead of 'real gains'), discount factors, lower rates compared to income tax rates, the tax base, etc.).

Why has New Zealand got itself into such a mess? It surely cannot be for want of academic analysis, as the literature is substantial. Overseas experience abounds with potential blueprints for what works well and what not so well when taxing capital gains. This overwhelming evidence, along with New Zealand's standalone approach in the Organisation for Economic Co-operation and Development (OECD), creates what might be seen as a mystery. Has the overwhelming majority of the developed world got it wrong and New Zealand got it right in not having a CGT (or for that matter, any form of direct taxation of wealth)? To almost all, the present author expects, the answer is that New Zealand is somewhat stuck in a never-ending loop (like a mouse in a treadmill), with no apparent way to free itself and progress the calls for a CGT. The root of the problem is politics, or for that matter, politicians, who are too timid to admit that a CGT is needed, and that this may engender some political heat.

As has been acknowledged, New Zealand has failed for some time to seriously review its tax system and revisit whether it is appropriate. The last major rebalancing occurred in the 1980s under a Labour government. This led to the broad-base, low-rate (BBLR) model emerging whereby New Zealand should operate with a broadly defined tax base (that is, to tax a number of forms of activity), which allows tax rates to be lower, thereby reducing the costs associated with taxation. The BBLR model has been endorsed by the McLeod Review[4] and the Victoria University of Wellington Tax Working Group (VUWTWG).[5] Significant changes occurred in 2010 following the VUWTWG, although a CGT was not pursued. Thus, the current version of the BBLR lacks a broad base in that there are no forms of wealth tax (including a CGT).

---

4 McLeod Review (n 2).

5 Victoria University of Wellington Tax Working Group (Professor Bob Buckle, chair), *A Tax System for New Zealand's Future: Report of the Victoria University of Wellington Tax Working Group* (Centre for Accounting, Governance and Taxation Research, Victoria University of Wellington, January 2010) (VUWTWG).

The perfect opportunity to remedy this defect was provided by the Tax Working Group's report,[6] but a timid major coalition party let its minor coalition partner have sway, 'forcing' the government of the time to reject pursuing the TWG's CGT proposal. Furthermore, the then Prime Minister, Jacinda Ardern, painted herself (and her party) into a corner by stating that there would be no work on a CGT during her time as prime minister. Since then, New Zealand has had another prime minister, from late January 2023 until the General Election held in October 2023, when a new coalition government was formed under Prime Minister Christopher Luxon. At the time of writing, a CGT is not on the agenda of the new government.

The theme of this chapter is whether history can inform the future through improving tax policy and legislation. The prior literature, which will not be discussed comprehensively in this chapter, suggests that history continues to repeat itself and we appear to be learning nothing from it, making the same suboptimal decisions, predominantly due to political timidity. Alongside this literature are calls from international bodies, such as the International Monetary Fund and OECD, recommending that New Zealand implement a capital gains tax.[7] In this regard, New Zealand's largest professional accounting body, Chartered Accountants Australia and New Zealand, is calling for an informed debate over a CGT, with its taxation lead John Cuthbertson stating that 'a CGT was the missing piece of the tax puzzle and that it had to be part of a discussion around the appropriate mix of taxes in this country'.[8]

Why should we be concerned about, or have an interest in, tax history, and in the context of this chapter, CGT? As Avi-Yonah notes of the conclusion by the authors of a recent tax history volume: 'We do not necessarily understand taxation better than our predecessors, and in fact we can learn from their experience.'[9]

---

6 TWG (n 2).

7 See, for example, Thomas Dalsgaard, 'The Tax System in New Zealand: An Appraisal and Options for Change' (2001) OECD Economics Department Working Paper No 281; International Monetary Fund (IMF), 'New Zealand: Staff Concluding Statement of the 2024 Article IV Mission' (19 March 2024) <https://www.imf.org/en/News/Articles/2024/03/19/mcs-new-zealand-staff-concluding-statement-of-the-2024-article-iv-mission#:~:text=IMF%20staff%20expect%20a%20gradual,the%20output%20gap%20turns%20negative> accessed 10 June 2024.

8 Reported in Brent Edwards, 'Lighter Version of Capital Gains Tax Preferred by CA ANZ' *National Business Review* (11 April 2024) <https://www.nbr.co.nz/politics/john-cuthbertson-story/> accessed 11 April 2024.

9 Reuven S Avi-Yonah, '*Rebellion, Rascals, and Revenue*: Pleasingly Gaudy and Preposterous, Book Review of *Rebellion, Rascals, and Revenue: Tax Follies*

This chapter takes a historical perspective and as such will look to the past and the context in which events and proposals were made, and use this to assist in informing what should occur in the future. Stanford states that 'an objective knowledge of the past can only be obtained through the subjective experience of the scholar'.[10] Furthermore, it has also been stated by Fleishman and co-authors that: 'It has been said that historians study the past, whilst social scientists use the past to understand the present. Many historians today would reject this dichotomy and ascribe to their own work critical contemporary importance.'[11]

Frecknall-Hughes reviews research methods in taxation history, and concludes:

> While on the surface, approaches may appear very different, once a detailed analysis is done of what is actually going on, there is an underlying similarity between the different academic areas. The great difference is that law, history and legal history generally do not seek to analyse or justify their approaches with as much formality as the social sciences.[12]

This chapter sets out to take the approach of a social scientist who accepts that their analysis of the past will be more subjective than objective in that interpretations will be made of the past with the benefit of hindsight. The chapter also builds upon the observations of others who have interpreted past events. In terms of research on New Zealand tax history, this is relatively limited, as Vosslamber observes:

> Prior to the publication of Goldsmith's recent work, Marriott and Fowler noted that, 'Historical research on taxation in New Zealand is limited'. Goldsmith provides a detailed and well-documented grand tour through the history of New Zealand taxation. … This research makes a contribution to our understanding of an aspect of taxation history.[13]

---

*and Wisdom Through the Ages*, by Michael Keen and Joel Slemrod' (2021) 170 Tax Notes Federal 1885, 1885.

[10] Michael Stanford, *The Nature of Historical Knowledge* (Blackwell Publishing 1986) 27.

[11] Richard K Fleischman, Patti A Mills and Thomas N Tyson, 'A Theoretical Primer for Evaluating and Conducting Historical Research in Accounting' (1996) 1(1) Accounting History 55, 63.

[12] Jane Frecknall-Hughes, 'Research Methods in Taxation History' (2016) 3(1) Review of Behavioral Economics 5, 18.

[13] Rob Vosslamber, 'How Much? Taxation on New Zealanders' Employment Income 1893–1984' (2009) 15(4) New Zealand Journal of Taxation Law and Policy 299, 302, citing Paul Goldsmith, *We Won, You Lost, Eat That! A Political History of Tax in New Zealand since 1840* (David Ling Publishing 2008); Lisa

Hobbs, in his doctoral dissertation, provides an excellent review of undertaking historical research in a New Zealand context (land taxation) through the theoretical framework of historical institutionalism.[14]

This chapter does not seek to apply a theoretical lens as prior research has comprehensively critiqued the unsuccessful journey of CGT proposals and the accompanying debate. It does, however, seek to summarize that prior debate, extract some of the more noteworthy features, and draw some potential lessons for the future. The current author acknowledges his inherent bias in favour of developing a CGT for New Zealand, including advocating a proposal through the generic tax policy process (GTPP).[15] Essentially the GTPP is a process that incorporates transparency and consultation in a structured manner (including feedback loops) that links high-level fiscal policy with annual revenue programmes through policy development and legislative enactment via Parliament.[16] Specifically, this chapter adds to the debate over a CGT that forms part of New Zealand tax history, but it also sets out to draw from this history to inform the future. Informing the CGT debate in New Zealand are some major contributions involving Professor Rick Krever as an author. This includes his early work with Professor Neil Brooks and more recently with Professor Chris Evans. More on these contributions will be discussed later in the chapter.

This chapter takes an exploratory case study approach, focusing on one jurisdiction, New Zealand, with which the author is familiar. In adopting a sole case study approach, the design and analysis considerations are of significant importance, along with the description of events or scenarios under review.[17] The need for a case study frequently arises out of the desire to understand complex social phenomena. It enables the researcher to investigate and review

---

Marriott and Carolyn Fowler, 'From Social Policy to Economic Policy: Taxation Incentives for Retirement Income Savings in New Zealand (1910–2005)' (2007) 12(1) Accounting History 87, 88.

[14] Dillon Hobbs, 'The Use of Land Value Taxation in New Zealand (1891–1991)' (PhD thesis, Victoria University of Wellington 2019).

[15] See, in particular, Adrian Sawyer, 'Reviewing Tax Policy Development in New Zealand: Lessons from a Delicate Balancing of "Law and Politics"' (2013) 28(2) Australian Tax Forum 401; Adrian Sawyer, 'Tax Policy without Consultation: Is New Zealand on a "Slippery Slope"?' (2022) 37(4) Australian Tax Forum 481.

[16] The GTPP was proposed by the Organisational Review Committee (Sir Ivor Richardson, chair), *Organisational Review of the Inland Revenue Department: Report to the Minister of Revenue (and on Tax Policy, Also to the Minister of Finance)* (1994).

[17] Robert K Yin, *Case Study Research and Applications: Design and Methods* (6th edn, Sage Publications 2017).

in a holistic and meaningful way the various characteristics of real-life events. While focusing on New Zealand's experience, the analysis offers insights for other jurisdictions that may be contemplating taxing capital gains with respect to what to avoid and how to overcome the challenges. It also serves as a reminder to those jurisdictions with a CGT of the challenges that may arise should they wish to review their particular regime.

The remainder of this chapter is set out as follows. Section 15.2 provides a 'brief history' of taxing capital gains in New Zealand, including the failed attempts to formally adopt or implement a CGT. From this discussion, section 15.3 seeks to set out what we can learn from this historical review, and in the current context, how we might take these learnings to improve the future in terms of developing CGT policy and, later on, legislation. Section 15.4 provides some concluding comments.

## 15.2 A BRIEF HISTORY OF THE TAXING OF CAPITAL GAINS IN NEW ZEALAND

Much has been written concerning efforts to develop a CGT for New Zealand. Indeed, the current author has contributed to this debate through a co-authored paper with Professor Kerrie Sadiq in 2019.[18] That article reviews the history up until the introduction of the bright-line test on residential property in New Zealand (discussed further below), but does not include the most recent extension to the bright-line test in 2021 (and its restoration to the original two-year test in 2024), and the final recommendations of the TWG on a CGT in 2019. Sadiq and Sawyer also set out some tentative suggestions for how a CGT could be advanced in New Zealand.[19]

The following discussion largely takes a chronological approach as this serves to underline a repeated pattern of a review, academic comment and analysis, a further review, followed by more academic analysis, even to the point of detailed proposals. In every instance a CGT is rejected by the incumbent government, with the closest point to a genuine political CGT proposal being in the late 1980s. Section 15.3 of this chapter draws this analysis together to highlight themes and issues.

It is important to go back to the earliest opportunity when New Zealand might have contemplated a CGT, or at least some form of taxation of capital gains, namely when it introduced its income tax in 1891. Krever and Brooks observe that when income tax legislation was first introduced in 1891, it was

---

[18] Kerrie Sadiq and Adrian Sawyer, 'New Zealand's "Experience" with Capital Gains Taxation and Policy Choice Lessons from Australia' (2019) 16(2) eJournal of Tax Research 362.

[19] Ibid.

drafted sufficiently broadly to incorporate a tax on capital but, like other Commonwealth jurisdictions, New Zealand decided to limit this to the concept of income under trust law (as this was understood at the time).[20] Furthermore, the earliest reports on taxation in New Zealand did not deal extensively with the taxation of capital gains.[21]

The taxation of capital gains was considered by the Ross Committee in its 1967 Report[22] and again by the McCaw Committee in its 1982 Report.[23] Furthermore, the sizeable report of the Royal Commission on Social Policy in 1988[24] considered tax issues, including the taxation of capital gains. When Australia introduced its CGT in the mid 1980s, a significant debate commenced in New Zealand, although this debate resulted in a vastly different outcome for New Zealand than Australia, with the 'deferral' and eventual abandonment of the proposals at that time. Indeed, during the latter years of the Lange–Douglas Labour government in the late 1980s, there were genuine expectations that a CGT proposal would emerge. Interestingly, CCH published a book in anticipation of a CGT![25] This is the closest New Zealand has come to a CGT.

Alston offers an early perspective on taxing capital gains in New Zealand, examining the arguments for and against, plus the challenges of implementing a CGT.[26] He draws upon the Australian and Canadian experiences and highlights the arbitrary nature of whether capital gains are taxed or not taxed in New Zealand.

Arnold and Edgar provide an early comparative analysis of capital gains taxation between Australia, New Zealand, the United Kingdom and the United States.[27] An early contribution to the New Zealand debate is made by Oliver,

[20] Richard Krever and Neil Brooks, *A Capital Gains Tax for New Zealand* (Victoria University Press for the Institute of Policy Studies 1990).

[21] For a review of these reports see Adrian Sawyer, *The Effectiveness of Tax Reviews in New Zealand: An Evaluation and Proposal for Improvement* (University of Canterbury Centre for Commercial and Corporate Law 2020) (*The Effectiveness of Tax Reviews in New Zealand*).

[22] Ross Report (n 1).

[23] McLeod Review (n 2).

[24] Royal Commission on Social Policy (Sir Ivor Richardson, chair), *The April Report* (1988).

[25] CCH New Zealand, *Looking Ahead to a Capital Gains Tax in New Zealand* (1998).

[26] Andrew Alston, *The Taxation of Capital Gains in New Zealand: A Review of the Options and Problems of Introducing Such a Tax, An Occasional Paper* (rev edn, Victoria University Press for the Institute of Policy Studies 1986).

[27] Brian J Arnold and Tim Edgar, 'Selected Aspects of Capital Gains Taxation in Australia, New Zealand, the United Kingdom and the United States' (1995)

a senior Inland Revenue official, in his private capacity.[28] He concludes as follows, identifying the nub of the issues:

> The basic issue in practice is not whether or not, but the extent to which, capital gains should be taxed. The extent should be chosen after careful analysis of what optimizes fairness and efficiency, all within the context of each country's tax structure and system. There is probably no unique and perfect design for such a tax system.[29]

Cheng and co-authors provide an early proposal for designing a CGT for New Zealand, drawing upon other jurisdictions (especially Australia and the United Kingdom).[30] By 2001, the CGT issue returned to prominence with the consideration of the measure by the McLeod Committee,[31] when it proposed the rather controversial risk-free rate of return method (RFRRM). Numerous commentators, predominantly academics, point to the compelling evidence for a CGT in New Zealand. The following analysis includes a number of contributions, many drawing from publications in the New Zealand Journal of Taxation Law and Policy, which has been a major vehicle for making these contributions to the debate.[32] Other contributions include analysing how a CGT may affect the housing market.[33]

Kenny concludes his work as follows: 'Given the convergence of at least three of the tax policy criteria: efficiency, adequacy and equity, the case for the introduction of a comprehensive capital gains tax in New Zealand is compelling.'[34]

---

21(Supp) *Canadian Public Policy/Analyse de Politiques* S58.

[28] Robin Oliver, 'Capital Gains Tax: The New Zealand Case' in Herbert G Grubel (ed), *International Evidence on the Effects of Having No Capital Gains Taxes* (Fraser Institute 2001) 73 <https://www.fraserinstitute.org/studies/international-evidence-on-the-effects-of-having-no-capital-gains-taxes> accessed 1 March 2023.

[29] Ibid 86.

[30] Alvin Cheng, Keith Hooper and Howard Davey, 'A Capital Gains Tax for New Zealand: A Comparative Study of the UK and Australian Models' (2000) 8(2) Asian Review of Accounting 43.

[31] McLeod Review (n 2) para 3.14.

[32] The author acknowledges a potential or perceived conflict of interest in that he has served as the chair of the editors of the New Zealand Journal of Taxation Law and Policy since 2001.

[33] Andrew Coleman, 'The Long-Term Effects of Capital Gains Taxes in New Zealand' (2010) 44(2) New Zealand Economic Papers 159.

[34] Paul Kenny, 'Capital Gains Taxation for New Zealand: Fairer and More Efficient' (2001) 7(4) New Zealand Journal of Taxation Law and Policy 265, 290 (footnote omitted).

Burman and White, writing a couple of years later, observe: 'There is no perfect way to tax capital gains in a real-world income tax. Not taxing them, or taxing them in an *ad hoc* and inconsistent fashion as is done in New Zealand invites unproductive tax avoidance, creates uncertainty for taxpayers, and is inequitable.'[35]

Singleton,[36] in contrast to Kenny, and Burman and White, provides one of the more pessimistic views (from the perspective of advocates for a CGT), following the outcome of the McLeod Review.[37] Singleton also acknowledges the frequent efforts to broaden the scope of the income tax when he concludes: 'With the Government's acceptance of the recent New Zealand Tax Review 2001 finding that the concerns about a comprehensive CGT as sufficiently serious so as not to recommend introduction, I do not see the introduction of a realised CGT regime taking place in New Zealand.'[38]

Moving on several years, Elliffe concludes with respect to taxing capital gains in New Zealand:

> [T]he most compelling case for change arises from the inequity of having significant gains not subject to tax at all, whilst other forms of economic income (particularly earned income) are taxed at a disproportionately high rate. The question of equity and fairness is usually the first principle of good tax policy.[39]

Huang and Elliffe observe that New Zealand is 'unique' in not taxing capital gains comprehensively, concluding:

> The reason historically that New Zealand does not have a CGT is not because New Zealand policymakers fail to recognise the benefits of such a form of taxation, but because they have been overawed by the perceived problems and cost associated with it. ... One of the advantages of being the last to adopt something is that you can learn from others' mistakes. ... It seems logical to assume that New Zealand can learn something from other countries' mistakes, and, even in some cases, successes.[40]

[35] Leonard Burman and David White, 'Taxing Capital Gains in New Zealand' (2003) 9(3) New Zealand Journal of Taxation Law and Policy 355, 385.

[36] Paul Singleton, 'Should New Zealanders Be Burdened with an Even More Comprehensive Capital Gains Tax?' (2003) 9(1) New Zealand Journal of Taxation Law and Policy 42.

[37] McLeod Review (n 2).

[38] Singleton (n 36) 63.

[39] Craig Elliffe, 'Building a Better Bridge: The Case for Taxing Capital Gains in New Zealand' (2010) 16(2) New Zealand Business Law Quarterly 178, 202.

[40] Chye-Ching Huang and Craig Elliffe, 'Is New Zealand Smarter than Other Countries or Simply Special? Reconsidering a Realisation-Based Capital Gains

From this limited selection of early contributions to the CGT debate, it would seem that New Zealand has failed to learn from the successes (and mistakes) of other countries, notwithstanding the compelling evidence. Nevertheless, this is not the end of the debate.

Another major opportunity arose in 2009–10 to rekindle the debate, with the VUWTWG review, although the VUWTWG effectively sidelined the debate at that time, stating, 'most members of the TWG have significant concerns over the practical challenges arising from a comprehensive CGT and the potential distortions and other efficiency implications that may arise from a partial CGT.'[41]

The perceptions of academics concerning this latest review soon emerged, with Cheng and co-authors providing the results of their survey of tax teachers concerning the taxation of capital gains.[42] One particular aspect of their observations is pertinent to this chapter:

> Consequently, tax experts often present very different views on the taxation of capital gains. In exploring their attitudes towards the formulation of a CGT, we therefore need to investigate the reasons behind those attitudes. For tax teachers, equity and other non-taxation factors, such as social and political factors, played an important role in their decision-making process.[43]

Cheng and Yong provide a tax practitioners' perspective based on using a survey instrument concerning the taxing of capital gains in New Zealand.[44] From this survey it would appear that tax practitioners are generally opposed to a CGT, partly, the current author would argue, due to self-interest. The authors conclude: 'The results showed that most of them preferred the status quo and opposed a comprehensive CGT largely because of the added compliance costs and the complexity associated with such a regime.'[45]

---

Tax in the Light of South Africa's Experience' (2010) 16(3) New Zealand Journal of Taxation Law and Policy 269, 304–305.

[41] VUWTWG (n 5) 11.

[42] Alvin Cheng, Howard Davey and Keith Hooper, 'The Perceptions of Tax Teachers on Taxing Capital Gains in New Zealand' (2010) 16(3) New Zealand Journal of Taxation Law and Policy 217.

[43] Ibid 237.

[44] Alvin (MH) Cheng and Sue (SE) Yong, 'Explorations of Structure and Choice in Taxing Capital Gains in New Zealand: Tax Practitioners' Perspectives' (2011) 8(1) Social and Management Research Journal 51.

[45] Ibid 80.

Barrett and Veal examine media content on the CGT debate, including how arguments were framed.[46] They conclude:

> Specifically, we have identified why clusters of articles regarding a CGT emerged at different times in the period between 1993 and 2011. Before 2011, the articles tended to be technically specific and written by specialist financial journalists. ... After July 2011, the CGT became as much a political issue as a technical financial one.[47]

Moving on a few years, Maples analyses the Labour Party's 2011 proposal for a CGT, which he concludes was a 'fairly standard' CGT.[48] Maples concludes:

> The success of a CGT, or any tax, will depend on a clear policy rationale which informs the design, consultation and implementation phases. A failure to clearly articulate its purpose and adhere to it will potentially lead to a poorly designed and functioning CGT. Further, policymakers can expect to face heavy lobbying with any such future tax. Keeping a clear focus of the object(s) of the tax will ensure that pressure from lobby groups do[es] not derail the tax.[49]

Jacomb is optimistic that a CGT is a step closer, although subsequent events proved otherwise. She poignantly observes that '[t]he question of whether to introduce a CGT or not is now approaching 50 years of discussion'.[50] Maples and Karlinsky compare the taxation of capital gains in New Zealand and the United States, concluding: 'In the event that NZ does ultimately progress down the path of implementing a CGT it is therefore hoped that NZ maximises this opportunity to draw on overseas experiences.'[51]

Griffiths explores why New Zealand lacks a CGT, observing the preference by successive governments to include certain gains within an extended

---

[46] Jonathan Barrett and John Veal, 'Equity versus Political Suicide: Framing the Capital Gains Tax Debate in the New Zealand Print Media' (2013) 19(1) New Zealand Journal of Taxation Law and Policy 91.

[47] Ibid 101.

[48] Andrew J Maples, 'A Comprehensive Capital Gains Tax in New Zealand – No Longer Political Hari-Kari?: A Consideration of the Labour Party Proposal of 2011' (2014) 20(2) New Zealand Journal of Taxation Law and Policy 144.

[49] Ibid 167–8.

[50] Melinda Jacomb, 'A History of Taxing Capital Gains in New Zealand: Why Don't We?' (2014) 20 Auckland University Law Review 124, 147.

[51] Andrew Maples and Stewart Karlinsky, 'The United States Capital Gains Tax Regime and the Proposed New Zealand CGT: Through Adam Smith's Lens' (2014) 16(2) Journal of Australian Taxation 156, 204–5.

definition of income (a definition that has continued to grow since the original one in 1891!).[52] She concludes:

> The intertwining of these cultural and economic values made New Zealand a somewhat infertile environment for CGT in the second half of the 20th century. Nonetheless, for particular reasons and in response to particular issues the legislature has often chosen to include various capital gains within the definition of income.[53]

Quintal and co-authors 'sit on the fence' concerning whether New Zealand should develop a CGT, concluding that '[w]hether a CGT is the right move for New Zealand as a whole is unclear'.[54] White offers some personal reflections on taxing capital gains in New Zealand.[55] His analysis illustrates the tensions in the debate and approaches taken in prior reviews, along with the guiding principles that were used.

Looking at wealth taxes generally (including a CGT), Marriott concludes that a CGT should be a core aspect of New Zealand's BBLR approach: 'Moreover, a capital gains tax is more aligned with the broad-base, low-rate philosophy than is its absence. Nonetheless, New Zealand's approach to capital gains taxes appears entrenched, despite support for them from international agencies (such as the OECD) and the Treasury.'[56]

James and Maples discuss lessons for New Zealand from the United Kingdom's CGT regime, with the authors endorsing the New Zealand BBLR model.[57] The authors conclude that '[i]n an ideal world the design of a CGT should complement the BBLR approach'.[58]

---

52 Shelley Griffiths, '"The Game is Not Worth the Candle": Exploring the Lack of a Comprehensive Capital Gains Tax in New Zealand' (2015) 21(1) New Zealand Journal of Taxation Law and Policy 51.

53 Ibid 68.

54 Aaron Quintal, David Snell and Nicholas Chan, 'Key Issues in the Design of Capital Gains Tax Regimes: The Impact on Tax Practice' (2015) 21(2) New Zealand Journal of Taxation Law and Policy 137, 158.

55 David I White, 'Personal Capital Gains Taxation: Reflections on the Influence of Economic Theory on Tax Reform Proposals' (2015) 21(1) New Zealand Journal of Taxation Law and Policy 18.

56 Lisa Marriott, 'Advancing Better Tax Policy: The Role of Wealth Taxes in New Zealand' (2016) 12(3) Policy Quarterly 74, 80.

57 Simon James and Andrew Maples, 'The Relationship between Principles and Policy in Tax Administration: Lessons from the United Kingdom Capital Gains Tax Regime with Particular Reference to a Proposal for a Capital Gains Tax for New Zealand' (2016) 14(2) eJournal of Tax Research 455.

58 Ibid 483.

Reid and Tan[59] examine the original bright-line test on residential property,[60] concluding that (based on the initial two-year period) it is unlikely to raise much in terms of revenue and is a limited form of a capital gains tax. They conclude somewhat optimistically: 'One day, when the tax system reaches a point where there are too many pseudo capital gains taxing regimes in place, then perhaps the Government will concede that a comprehensive capital gains tax is indeed essential.'[61]

Evans and Krever reviewed the arguments that are often put forward in favour of introducing a CGT regime, along with those against, as well as how capital gains are taxed in other countries (most frequently within a specific CGT regime).[62] Evans and Krever also observe that New Zealand has a reputation for being proactive in taxation, as well as innovative (such as with the GTPP). However, this is not the case with CGT; in fact, it is the complete reverse! Writing after the TWG had been established but well before it released its final report in 2019, Evans and Krever observe:

> New Zealand enjoys an enviable reputation for the range and quality of many aspects of its tax policy process, legislative provisions and administrative systems. Much of the innovation is based upon its status as a 'first mover' in tax (and other) matters. Ironically, it is a 'last mover' so far as CGT is concerned, but that may not be such a bad thing.[63]

Griffiths, in a contribution subsequent to her 2015 article discussed above, provides a New Zealand chapter to a book edited by Professors Elliffe and Littlewood; the chapter navigates the history of attempts to develop a CGT in New Zealand, commencing with the work in the 1920s, through to the most

---

59 Ian Reid and Lin Mei Tan, 'The Bright-Line Test on Residential Property Sales: Another Pseudo Capital Gains Tax Regime?' (2016) 22(2) New Zealand Journal of Taxation Law and Policy 157. These partial additions to including the taxation of capital gains within the income tax net include components of the land taxation provisions in sections CB 6A to CB 23B, along with the bright-line test for residential land.

60 The original bright-line test required income tax to be paid on any gains from the disposal of residential land that is acquired and disposed of within two years, subject to some exceptions. This test supplemented the 'intention test' in the land sale rules that had proved extremely difficult for the Inland Revenue to establish.

61 Reid and Tan (n 59) 171.

62 Chris Evans and Richard Krever, 'Taxing Capital Gains: A Comparative Analysis and Lessons for New Zealand' (2017) 23(4) New Zealand Journal of Taxation Law and Policy 486.

63 Ibid 509.

recent efforts at the time of writing the chapter.[64] She then traverses the ways in which capital gains have in a piecemeal fashion been included in the definition of income, and some of the associated design problems. Griffiths concludes, in a manner comparable to her 2015 article, that the process has reflected New Zealand society's resistance and reluctance to develop a CGT proposal as far as draft legislation, and has instead taken an incremental approach.

Taking a different approach, Littlewood asks the question, 'What would a capital gains tax look like?'[65] Littlewood works through the key design principles, and how design issues could be resolved, concluding:

> The various issues that arise in designing the tax should therefore generally be resolved on the basis of the following principles: (a) doing whatever is simplest (or, at least, least complex); and (b) doing whatever will minimise the burden of compliance and the cost of administration; and (c) erring on the side of less liability to tax rather than more (because the tax will inevitably be inequitable; and inequity in a light tax is less problematic than in a heavy one).[66]

Sawyer and Sadiq, in reviewing the CGT debate up to the time of their study, observe the important role of academics, among others:

> As such, it is academics who have been significant contributors to the CGT debate in New Zealand. A review of their contributions since 2000 reveals a common theme of studying the experiences of overseas jurisdictions to learn from mistakes, as well as best practice. … The lack of any sort of 'political champion' has meant that the substantive contribution to the debate has been led by academics.[67]

Coleman[68] offers an economic analysis (using material from the TWG's interim report in 2018[69]) and a review of the ways that the taxation of capital income in New Zealand may be affecting the economy. He observes that the current system favours certain types of investments. Coleman emphasizes that part of the problem is a lack of a comprehensive capital gains tax, while another is relatively high taxes on business and capital income.

---

64 Shelley Griffiths, 'New Zealand' in Michael Littlewood and Craig Elliffe (eds), *Capital Gains Taxation: A Comparative Analysis of Key Issues* (Edward Elgar Publishing 2017).

65 Michael Littlewood, 'What Would a Capital Gains Tax Look Like?' (2018) (6) New Zealand Law Journal 179.

66 Ibid 181.

67 Sadiq and Sawyer (n 18) 372.

68 Andrew Coleman, 'Taxing Capital Income in New Zealand: An International Perspective' (2019) University of Otago Economics Discussion Paper No 1902.

69 Tax Working Group, *Future of Tax: Interim Report* (2018).

In terms of the latest proposal for a CGT in New Zealand, the TWG's[70] comprehensive analysis has engendered the most recent debate over a CGT. The first volume of their 2019 report provides the overall recommendations from their review (including a preferred form of CGT), with the second volume containing the details of their recommended CGT.

Essentially, all members of the TWG agreed that more income from capital gains should be taxed from the sale of residential rental properties. A majority (8–3) recommended going further and broadening that approach to include all land and buildings, business assets, intangible property and shares. While this would increase compliance and efficiency costs, it was expected to reduce the biases towards certain types of investments and improve the fairness, integrity and fiscal sustainability of the tax system. The TWG recommended that a tax on capital gains would commence when an asset is sold or changes hands (a realization basis), following an earlier valuation day for assets to be covered by the regime, and would be applied with no discounted tax rate and no allowance for inflation. Gains would be calculated from when any new law comes into force. These gains would become part of a person's ordinary income and be taxed at their marginal tax rate. Thus, in effect, it would not be a completely standalone CGT, but a more comprehensive addition to the taxation of income. In effect, if this proposal were adopted, it would be one of the most 'severe' CGTs in existence in terms of how the relevant tax rate would be applied (for many this would now be at 39%). The TWG estimated that broadly taxing more income from capital gains would raise roughly NZD 8 billion over the first five years. The Australian evidence also suggests that a CGT can raise a significant amount of tax revenue.[71]

The debate commenced very promptly following the TWG's proposal being released and the New Zealand government's rejection of a CGT in April 2019. Sutton and Pavlovich conclude their article by setting out how a CGT should be developed for New Zealand:

> There has been considerable discussion, arriving at considerably fewer firm proposals for the specification of a CGT in New Zealand. It is timely that these issues be raised, that proposals for CGT specification be raised and debated, be tested, empirically and theoretically, and that, cumulatively, New Zealand arrives at the best possible system of CGT.[72]

---

[70] TWG (n 2).

[71] See, for example, Evans and Krever (n 62).

[72] David Sutton and Alison Pavlovich, 'Implementing CGT in New Zealand: How Should We Do It?' (2019) 25(1) New Zealand Journal of Taxation Law and Policy 31, 50.

Evans, also writing after the release of the TWG's 2019 report, writes in favour of the proposal while acknowledging that compliance costs and compromise on the composition of the proposed CGT must be closely watched:

> The key message that emerges from this article is that CGT compliance costs, whilst significant, are nowhere near as onerous as suggested by anecdote, and can, to large extent, be mitigated by sensible design. … If it does re-emerge, it is to be hoped that any enacted CGT regime would retain its relative purity and not become compromised as special interests seek to argue for changes and expansion of concessions, inevitably leading to increased compliance costs.[73]

Maples and Yong suggest that New Zealand missed an important opportunity with the TWG's recommendations for a CGT.[74] They conclude: 'New Zealand is in a unique position as a potential late adopter of a CGT to look at, and learn from, the practices of other jurisdictions. However, in designing any tax, it is important that it has a clear policy rationale supported by evidence (including international experience).'[75]

Khaghaany and Sutton provide a capitalist argument in support of a CGT.[76] Accepting the argument generally made in the literature that a CGT improves equity, they find that there is no compelling evidence that CGT materially decreases economic efficiency and that, conceptually, it is likely to increase economic efficiency. Sutton and Khaghaany, in a further contribution, explore whether compliance costs may be hindering progress on a CGT for New Zealand, concluding that the 'focus should be on optimal system design, rather than the continued refusal to tax capital gains in New Zealand'.[77]

Wong and Wong provide a combined empirical and theoretical analysis of the amount of CGT revenue that could be raised from New Zealand's listed property companies.[78] While not a huge amount, their estimates are

---

[73] Chris Evans, 'The Compliance Costs of Taxing Capital Gains: Implications for New Zealand' (2019) 25(4) New Zealand Journal of Taxation Law and Policy 381, 408.

[74] Andrew Maples and Sue Yong, 'The Tax Working Group and Capital Gains Tax in New Zealand – A Missed Opportunity?' (2019) 21(2) Journal of Australian Taxation 66.

[75] Ibid 85.

[76] Maithm Khaghaany and David Sutton, 'A Capitalist Argument for Capital Gains Tax' (2019) 25(3) New Zealand Journal of Taxation Law and Policy 235.

[77] David Sutton and Maithm Khaghaany, 'Capital Gains Taxes and Compliance Costs: Are Capital Gains Too Expensive (for New Zealand)?' (2019) 25(3) New Zealand Journal of Taxation Law and Policy 261, 282.

[78] Jilnaught Wong and Norman Wong, 'Taxing Capital Gains: A Study of New Zealand Investment Property Companies' (2019) 25(3) New Zealand Journal of

non-trivial. Extrapolating this to estimate the level of CGT revenues from all sources (investment properties, farms, shares, etc.) based on other countries' experience with CGT, they come to a broad-brush estimate of between NZD 340 million and NZD 2.9 billion, estimates that are economically diverse yet significant.

Sutton considers whether a CGT is a poor source of revenue, an argument frequently raised against having a CGT.[79] He concludes:

> This article argues the case that CGT revenues are non-trivial in absolute terms where CGT is levied on a comprehensive basis. Secondly, and central to the key thesis of this article, existing regimes represent flawed designs that limit the revenue-raising potential of an effective, competent and coherent CGT regime. By minimising or eliminating defective tax system design elements it is likely that the implementation of a CGT regime in New Zealand can enhance tax system efficiency and equity, as well as raise more revenue than is otherwise the case under existing comprehensive CGT systems.[80]

In a subsequent contribution, Sutton asks the question as to why New Zealand is unique in not having a CGT.[81] His answer is blunt and to the point; in Sutton's view, it is a failure of political advocacy following a lack of political will, which is a view that the current author largely endorses. Sutton states: 'The synthesis of potential explanations for New Zealand's failure to implement a comprehensive CGT reduces to the failure of advocacy. This explanation combines the lack of political will with the ignorance of the general population about the issues at stake, combined with the strength of opposition to a CGT.'[82]

Sutton and co-authors subsequently ask the question of whether a comprehensive CGT would be preferable to the piecemeal and complex legislative developments to tax residential property through the now expanded complex bright-line test rules.[83] They conclude:

---

Taxation Law and Policy 213.

[79] David Sutton, 'Capital Gains Tax: A Poor Source of Revenue?' (2019) 25(1) New Zealand Journal of Taxation Law and Policy 53.

[80] Ibid 67.

[81] David Sutton, 'Why New Zealand Is Alone in the OECD in Resisting the Introduction of a Capital Gains Tax: Examining the Recent Debate' (2020) 26(1) New Zealand Journal of Taxation Law and Policy 31.

[82] Ibid 53.

[83] David Sutton, Jeremy Parker and Anthony Lake, 'The Taxation of Residential Property, Tax Complexity, and Economic Efficiency: How Do Current Legislative Developments Compare with CGT?' (2020) 26(4) New Zealand Journal of Taxation Law and Policy 407.

> In effect, the argument appears to be that a single, coherent, principle-driven comprehensive CGT regime is necessarily more complex than a plethora of rules, driven by no clear principles, which have arisen successively over long periods of time. At a structural level it is difficult to imagine how this could reasonably be the case.[84]

Minas and Maples conclude that in examining the political debate and economic conditions in the lead-up to the introduction of a CGT in each of Australia, Canada and the United Kingdom, a CGT would be a viable option for New Zealand.[85] The authors comment on the 'surprise' arising from the rejection of the TWG's CGT proposal, but suggest that a reconsideration of the New Zealand tax system may be needed. The authors conclude that a CGT for New Zealand is an important tax policy objective and that the political costs of enacting it have been greatly overstated.

Maples[86] comments further on the failure of the New Zealand government to progress the TWG's[87] CGT proposal and explores further by providing some insights into the views of individual submitters to one of the poll questions of the TWG, namely, 'Are we taxing the right things?'[88] Themes that emerge among those supporting changes to the taxation of property include issues of fairness, inequality and the tax burden. Addressing these issues saw support for a range of tax measures. Opposition to tax changes focused on the negative impact on saving and investment, fairness, avoidance and resistance behaviour.

Maples[89] compares the contributions of the Consultative Committee on the Reform of the Taxation of Income from Capital in December 1989[90] to that of the TWG in 2019.[91] Both contributions, Maples suggests, offer significant insights and the results of extensive research into how New Zealand could develop a CGT, yet both suffered the same result – political inaction.

---

[84] Ibid 430.

[85] John Minas and Andrew Maples, 'A Comprehensive CGT for New Zealand: "Political Suicide" or Tax Policy Saviour?' (2021) 36(1) Australian Tax Forum 71.

[86] Andrew Maples, 'The Taxation of Capital Income – Reflections on the 1989 Consultative Document on the Taxation of Income from Capital' (2022) 28(1) New Zealand Journal of Taxation Law and Policy 11.

[87] TWG (n 2).

[88] Andrew Maples, 'The Tax Working Group Question "Are We Taxing the Right Things?" – The People Speak' (2022) 28(3) New Zealand Journal of Taxation Law and Policy 255.

[89] Ibid.

[90] Consultative Committee on the Reform of the Taxation of Income from Capital, *Consultative Document on the Taxation of Income from Capital* (1989).

[91] TWG (n 2).

Most recently, Maples and Minas reviewed the first 50 years of capital gains taxation reviews in New Zealand (1951–2000).[92] The authors also include a brief postscript of major developments since 2000. Drawing on these reviews, and the observations of others, Maples and Minas suggest that the reasons why New Zealand does not have a CGT can be attributed to the resulting outcome of pressure, of sectional self-interest and of delicate political balancing. A further reason is that it is in the interests of certain classes of taxpayers, along with those who represent their interests, to not impose such a tax.

What can we take away from the discussion that focuses on the academic debate? This will be the subject of the next section of the chapter.

## 15.3 WHAT CAN WE LEARN?

There are many well-known sayings about history and the future, including those to the effect that history repeats itself, and that the main lesson from history is that we do not learn anything and therefore make the same mistakes. It has also been said that in trying to predict the future it can be helpful to look at the past and assess how today's trends and events reflect history. In turn, we can draw parallels from the present to past eras and then extrapolate to the future based on current trends. Thus, in some respects the past, or history more specifically, can inform the future. In the context of this chapter, what has been written about the past and trending issues at the time with respect to the taxation of capital gains (and CGTs) can be useful to inform tax policy, law and practice today, and very cautiously to make tentative predictions about the future.

Slocum states with respect to history repeating itself that it may occur 'simply because human experience recognizes the "necessity" of repeating actions and of using available resources'.[93] The discussion in section 15.2 of this chapter reflects some recurring themes. There is a flurry of predominantly academic debate over a CGT for New Zealand, usually following some significant development such as a tax review suggesting New Zealand needs a CGT (or does not need to have one). On occasion one or more political parties (usually the Labour Party or the Green Party) appear brave enough to propose a CGT, yet they have failed to win a general election when they have headed in with such a proposal, and (incorrectly in the present author's view) put the failure down to having a proposal for a CGT. Until this is disproved, there is really

---

[92] Andrew Maples and John Minas, 'Capital Gains Tax Reviews in New Zealand – The First 50 Years (1951–2000) (or the Wheel Turns Slowly)' (2023) 29(1) New Zealand Journal of Taxation Law and Policy 79.

[93] Elliot L Slocum, 'Necessity, a Lesson of History' (1995) 18(1) Accounting Historians Notebook 21, 22.

little hope for a CGT in New Zealand. Even when a single party has control of Parliament, as the Labour Party did from 2020–23, it did not advance a CGT proposal, largely due to comments made by the prime minister at the time, Jacinda Ardern, and more recently by her successor, Chris Hipkins.

Many of the contributions to the debate are historical, reflecting upon prior experiences with debating a CGT, while others focus on providing evidence in support of having a CGT, or at least formally debating a policy proposal. The outcome is almost always the same – the politicians cave in or argue (based on vested interests) that we do not need a CGT. History, it would seem, certainly repeats itself, and it would seem that we do not learn as the same arguments and outcomes repeat! Even contributions from those experts who come from jurisdictions that have extensive experience of a CGT, and who provide compelling arguments in favour of developing a proposal, fail to gain traction. Thus, if we fail to take heed of the advice provided, we run the risk of making the same mistakes or taking less-than-optimal decisions with respect to taxation choices.

In terms of where to find the overwhelming majority of academic contributions on CGT in New Zealand during the last 20 years or so, one needs to go no further on most occasions than the New Zealand Journal of Taxation Law and Policy (the Journal). That is not to say that there are no other important contributions in other high-quality publication outlets, most of which are based in Australia. While the Journal is an internationally peer-reviewed academic journal, it aims for its contributors to engage with a much wider readership, including policy officials, practitioners, the judiciary, and hopefully politicians (or political parties). Debate is also present in the news media, through (edited) books and various blogs. The strength of the evidence is very apparent, when reading these contributions, that the debate needs to move on from analysing the pros and cons to having a detailed policy proposal for public consultation. The TWG[94] provided such a 'straw man', but this straw man could not stand up to the 'political hot air' that followed.

The more extensive contributions (other than those from various tax reviews) have predominantly been from academics (in New Zealand and elsewhere) who are charged with undertaking research. New Zealand universities and their academic staff are collectively legally required to be the critic and conscience of society (pursuant to the Education Act 1989). This is both a huge responsibility and a privilege for academics. Other groups who have contributed include tax practitioners, who might be seen as advocating on behalf of their clients, many of whom might be worse off with a CGT. This comment

---

94 TWG (n 2).

should not be taken out of context as some practitioners will contribute to the debate for what they see as being for the greater good of 'New Zealand Inc'.

What are the prospects for the future? Back in 2019, it was expected by many that the government of the time would respond to the TWG's Final Report[95] positively, given that the Labour Party had established the TWG, installed a former Labour finance minister as the chair, and largely 'controlled' the legislature. Rather, the Labour-led government met concerted resistance from lobbyists as well as from its coalition partner, the New Zealand First Party. As noted earlier, this minority coalition partner would not accept the recommendation, and rather than possibly advance a majority view as the Labour Party, the government became nervous and repeated the old adage that a consensus was needed. Thus, when the New Zealand government subsequently renounced any intention to pursue a comprehensive CGT in its response in April 2019, it threw away the best opportunity in decades to advance a CGT by way of a formal policy proposal. It assigned the months of analysis by the TWG and the CGT debate contributors to, at best, long-term storage, but with the potential for future research analysis.

Many of those who argued against the introduction of a CGT were delighted and saw this as a permanent outcome, or at least until New Zealand had a new prime minister (but even with a change in prime minister in early 2023, nothing has effectively changed in this regard). Furthermore, following the October 2023 general election, a CGT remains off the political agenda of the coalition government. Notwithstanding the political reluctance to introduce a CGT, growing concerns about its absence remain. These include the growing share of capital in national income (much of which is not taxed), increasing wealth inequality, the ongoing 'cost of living crisis', repeated calls from the OECD to introduce a CGT, housing unaffordability, and an implicit over-taxation of other forms of income. In 2024 these conditions have not improved; indeed, one might say they have become worse. How can New Zealand politicians, in the face of the historical debate over a CGT and the overwhelming evidence on the need to seriously revisit the decision not to tax wealth in some form (such as with a CGT), not take action? Why do they struggle to think beyond the next general election (that is, in periods of no more than three years at a time)? If they believe in BBLR, then why do they not work to ensure we have a real and genuine BBLR in place with a broad base of taxes? In addition, without a 'political champion' for a CGT, it would appear that necessary political support will not eventuate.

Perhaps what is needed is some form of independent review body. The present author has previously developed an argument for creating the New

95 Ibid.

Zealand Taxation Review Commission (NZTRC), which is set out in Figure 15.1, and can be summarized as follows.

> Essentially the NZTRC would be established as a New Zealand Crown entity, with the NZTRC preferably developed as an 'independent Crown entity', meaning that it would be generally fully independent of government policy. That said, *it could be instructed to undertake specific reviews from the responsible minister but setting its own terms of reference and scope of the review following best practice.* Nevertheless, it would be naïve [not] to expect that a review that has been initiated by the NZTRC and is not in line with the political direction of the Government at the time (as has been the case with many of the tax committees), then its reviews will most probably be ignored. This may be less likely where [the] minister initiates the review (but still possible).[96]

Thus, it would appear that the only lesson to take away in the context of the taxation of capital gains in New Zealand is that we learn nothing from history. At best, an incremental expansion of the New Zealand income tax base will occur in an ad hoc and complex manner, without addressing the real issues of concern that plague New Zealand society with the absence of taxation of wealth, such as with a CGT. While we leave this in the hands of the politicians, we should expect more of the same. Perhaps the creation of the NZTRC and the development of a well-researched and balanced CGT proposal, with a political champion for a CGT, might see New Zealand avoid the constant circular trap of failing to learn from history and making the same 'mistakes'.

## 15.4 CONCLUDING THOUGHTS

In terms of what we can learn from past contributions to the literature on the taxation of capital gains, perhaps the most important takeaway, in the present author's view, is that we need to read it and think about it carefully, reflect upon its instructional guidance and use this to inform our thinking both now and in the future. However, even this approach is unlikely to be sufficient, as many in the past have followed it, and it has failed to reap rewards. It will take much more than academic papers, reviews by panels, and perspectives from overseas experts and organizations that are familiar with various CGT regimes. Even tax policy officials, who might be persuaded on the balance of the evidence that a CGT proposal needs to be developed, are unlikely to do so without a formal direction given to them by the government. In this regard, a CGT is more than a form of tax base protection or mechanism to improve the ability of the Inland Revenue to carry out its functions.

---

[96] Sawyer, *The Effectiveness of Tax Reviews in New Zealand* (n 21) 120 (emphasis added).

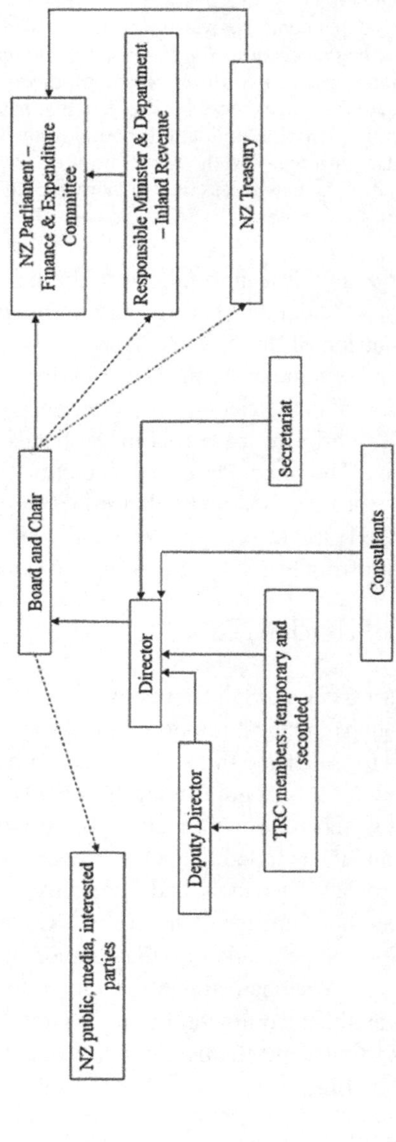


*Source:* Sawyer, *The Effectiveness of Tax Reviews in New Zealand* (n 21) 121.

*Figure 15.1 Proposed organizational structure of the New Zealand Taxation Review Commission*

How might we develop a CGT (proposal) in New Zealand? One important step is to evaluate the policy choices and key issues, based on the key principles to be achieved (these might be based on Adam Smith's principles of taxation or some other basis, such as those introduced by the Taxation Principles Reporting Act 2023, although the Act was subsequently repealed in late December 2023 prior to taking full effect[97]).

Given the preceding discussion, readers would be forgiven for thinking that this is suggesting the impossible, or at best, offering a theoretical solution for which there is no reasonable likelihood of success. This would be true for anyone who is a pessimist and probably for many who see themselves as realists. After all, this is the most likely assessment based on the prior evidence and New Zealand's history with respect to the taxation of capital gains. Only an optimist, and there are unlikely to be many of these left in New Zealand, could see a future when New Zealand has an effective CGT regime in place, informed by global best practice and the benefits of embracing contributions from the historical debate. That said, it would be rather foolish and potentially life threatening to hold one's breath for this to occur.

What is needed is politicians who have the foresight to develop a cross-party proposal for consultation, where the challenges faced by society and the economy can be remedied in part through reinforcing the BBLR model to ensure there is taxation of wealth in New Zealand (at least in one form such as a CGT). Ad hoc tax review bodies have failed to convince governments (and key politicians more specifically) to do this, although it is not from a lack of trying. Perhaps the approach suggested above by the present author might be a way forward, with a semi-independent continuing Commission being established to develop such a proposal. Even this, the author would suggest, is not sufficient. A CGT needs a political champion, such as a Minister of Finance or Minister of Revenue who is prepared to 'fight' for this, persuade their Cabinet colleagues, and work with other politicians on a cross-party proposal. Furthermore, this politician needs a politically salient reason for change and the ability to compromise to achieve what is possible now (with possible improvements that can come later). They also need a politically salient message in favour of the proposal and evidence that it would help and not hurt them at the polls in a general election. The last such person to hold this role, in the present author's view, was Roger Douglas in the mid to late 1980s. Who might be prepared to step up into this role today?

---

97 Adrian Sawyer, 'The Rise and Demise of the New Zealand's Taxation Principles Reporting Act – A Lost Opportunity?' (2024) (2) British Tax Review 261.

It is important to ask whether having a CGT would serve more than just underpinning that New Zealand's tax system reflects something closer to a BBLR approach. As noted earlier, New Zealand is facing tough fiscal conditions and has a heavy reliance on taxing the income and expenditure of individuals. While New Zealand has a relatively high per capita income that, judging from a Gini coefficient of 0.32 in 2022, would give the appearance that income is distributed in a reasonable fashion,[98] its taxation and other revenue-to-GDP ratio is around 30%, and as at 2022, its debt-to-GDP ratio was manageable, albeit growing to above 50%. While these may suggest that New Zealand is in an enviable fiscal position, the outlook significantly worsened in 2024, with calls from both the IMF and the OECD that New Zealand seriously needs to consider introducing a CGT to expand its revenue base.[99] One important question is, if a CGT were introduced, would it be set at a rate to allow for sufficient revenue to be raised to offset some reduction in income tax rates as part of a balancing exercise to further support the BBLR model?

The prior analysis is not constrained to New Zealand. Focusing on the earlier discussion in terms of guidance from other jurisdictions, a number of factors can assist in successful tax reform, including having a 'political champion' for a CGT, sound policy processes in operation (such as New Zealand's GTPP before 2019), and an independent review body, among others. Further guidance based on many years of experience is provided by Paul Tilley, who carefully lists and develops four factors (sound tax policy arguments, the right change processes, strong political leadership and good timing) that can lead to successful outcomes.[100] These and further factors (including the existence of a vision, sound economic principles, a package of reforms and an appetite for reform) have also been advanced.[101]

---

[98] See OECD, Income inequality (indicator) (2024), <https://data.oecd.org/inequality/income-inequality.htm>. The Gini Index is a measure of how equal a country's distribution of income is, scored between 0 (income equally shared between all persons) and 100 (complete inequality – income owned by a single person).

[99] IMF (n 7) ('reforms should combine comprehensive capital gains tax, land value tax, and changes to corporate income tax'); OECD, *OECD Economic Surveys: New Zealand* (OECD Publishing 2024) 37 ('To ensure the tax system is not overly distorting saving and supporting broader growth, capital gains taxation reform should be done as part of a wider review of tax settings for saving').

[100] Paul Tilley, *Mixed Fortunes: A History of Tax Reform in Australia* (Melbourne University Press 2024).

[101] Chris Evans, John Hasseldine, Andy Lymer, Robert Ricketts and Cedric Sandford, *Comparative Taxation: Why Tax Systems Differ* (Fiscal Publications 2017) ch 12.

This chapter has a number of limitations, several of which could be overcome by future research. The chapter is a single jurisdiction case study of a singular issue, namely the absence of, and associated debate concerning, the taxation of capital gains via a CGT. While this could in part be overcome by a multiple jurisdiction study, in terms of comparative jurisdictions, one would need to search high and low to find one that does not tax capital gains or wealth comprehensively. At best, it could be a comparison between New Zealand and a country that has a CGT that would be instructive for New Zealand. Australia is one such example.

A further limitation is that this chapter reflects a subjective view of the present author, albeit drawing upon the contributions of others. It does not add new data or any form of quantitative analysis to the debate. This could be overcome by a comprehensive analysis of the potential fiscal impact of different forms of taxing wealth, building upon earlier contributions of bodies such as the TWG.[102] This would require input from the Inland Revenue and the Treasury, among others. Related to this, it is acknowledged that there will be other contributions to the CGT debate that have not been captured in this analysis – this is in part due to space limitations as well as the oversight of the present author.

Future research could also seek to develop a CGT (or another form of wealth tax) proposal and open this up for debate. This would be a significant challenge, requiring a research team that has access to a wide range of technical skills, economic and tax data, and extensive financial resources. As was shown on previous occasions (such as following the adoption by the New Zealand government of many of the VUWTWG's proposals[103]), a CGT would need to come as part of an overall package that adjusts the income tax rates (and modifies the base to avoid double taxation), with measures to ensure that BBLR is enhanced, and to have a 'political champion' for it.

In summary, we owe it to ourselves and those to come to ensure we learn from history, especially that concerning a CGT and the taxation of capital gains generally, and that we do not repeat the mistakes of the past. Rather, we must draw upon the insights and experiences of history to improve the present and hopefully the future. The CGT debate in New Zealand needs to move on from just a debate to concrete action. However, we should not hold our breath.

102 TWG (n 2).
103 VUWTWG (n 5).

## ACKNOWLEDGEMENTS

The author would like to thank the two anonymous reviewers for their very helpful comments and suggestions which have improved this chapter. Any remaining errors are those of the author. The analysis in this chapter is current as at the end of May 2024.

# Index